IFIP Advances in Information and Communication Technology 724

IFIP Advances in Information and Communication Technology

The IFIP AICT series publishes state-of-the-art results in the sciences and technologies of information and communication. The scope of the series includes: foundations of computer science; software theory and practice; education; computer applications in technology; communication systems; systems modeling and optimization; information systems; ICT and society; computer systems technology; security and protection in information processing systems; artificial intelligence; and human-computer interaction.

Edited volumes and proceedings of refereed international conferences in computer science and interdisciplinary fields are featured. These results often precede journal publication and represent the most current research.

The principal aim of the IFIP AICT series is to encourage education and the dissemination and exchange of information about all aspects of computing.

More information about this series at https://link.springer.com/bookseries/6102

Elizabeth Kurkowski · Sujeet Shenoi
Editors

Advances in Digital Forensics XX

20th IFIP WG 11.9 International Conference
New Delhi, India, January 4-5, 2024
Revised Selected Papers

 Springer

Editors
Elizabeth Kurkowski
Johns Hopkins University Applied Physics
Laboratory
Laurel, MD, USA

Sujeet Shenoi
University of Tulsa
Tulsa, OK, USA

ISSN 1868-4238   ISSN 1868-422X (electronic)
IFIP Advances in Information and Communication Technology
ISBN 978-3-031-71024-7   ISBN 978-3-031-71025-4 (eBook)
https://doi.org/10.1007/978-3-031-71025-4

This Springer imprint is published by the registered company Springer Nature Switzerland AG
The registered company address is: Gewerbestrasse 11, 6330 Cham, Switzerland

If disposing of this product, please recycle the paper.

Preface

Digital forensics deals with the acquisition, preservation, examination, analysis and presentation of electronic evidence. Computer networks, cloud computing, smartphones, embedded devices and the Internet of Things have expanded the role of digital forensics beyond traditional computer crime investigations. Practically every crime now involves some aspect of digital evidence; digital forensics provides the techniques and tools to articulate this evidence in legal proceedings. Digital forensics also has myriad intelligence applications; furthermore, it has a vital role in cyber security – investigations of security breaches yield valuable information that can be used to design more secure and resilient systems.

This book, *Advances in Digital Forensics XX*, is the twentieth volume in the annual series produced by the IFIP Working Group 11.9 on Digital Forensics, an international community of scientists, engineers and practitioners dedicated to advancing the state of the art of research and practice in digital forensics. The book presents original research results and innovative applications in digital forensics. Also, it highlights some of the major technical and legal issues related to digital evidence and electronic crime investigations.

This volume contains fifteen revised and edited chapters based on papers presented at the Twentieth IFIP WG 11.9 International Conference on Digital Forensics, held in New Delhi, India on January 4–5, 2024. A total of 32 full-length papers were submitted for presentation at the conference. The papers were refereed in a single-blind manner by members of the conference program committee, all of them internationally recognized experts in digital forensics. The fifteen post-conference manuscripts submitted by the authors were required to be rewritten to accommodate the suggestions provided by the referees and by the conference attendees. The manuscripts were subsequently revised by the editors to produce the final chapters published in this volume.

The chapters in this volume are organized into seven thematic sections: Themes and Issues, Mobile Device Forensics, Image and Video Forensics, Internet of Things Forensics, Malware Forensics, Filesystem Forensics and Forensic Investigations. The coverage of topics highlights the richness and vitality of the digital forensics discipline, and offers promising avenues for future research.

This book is the result of the combined efforts of several individuals. In particular, we thank Kam-Pui Chow and Gaurav Gupta for their tireless work on behalf of IFIP Working Group 11.9 on Digital Forensics. We also acknowledge the support provided by the U.S. National Science Foundation, U.S. National Security Agency and U.S. Secret Service.

July 2024

Elizabeth Kurkowski
Sujeet Shenoi

Organization

General Chair

Gaurav Gupta   Ministry of Electronics and Information Technology,
                                India

Program Chairs

Elizabeth Kurkowski   Johns Hopkins University Applied Physics Laboratory,
                                USA
Sujeet Shenoi   University of Tulsa, USA

Program Committee

Stefan Axelsson   Stockholm University, Sweden
Harald Baier   Bundeswehr University, Germany
Nicole Beebe   University of Texas at San Antonio, USA
Raymond Chan   Singapore Institute of Technology, Singapore
Kam-Pui Chow   University of Hong Kong, China
Henry Collier   Norwich University, USA
Gokila Dorai   Augusta University, USA
Yong Guan   Iowa State University, USA
Gaurav Gupta   Ministry of Electronics and Information Technology,
                                India
Al Holt   U.S. Department of Defense, USA
Umit Karabiyik   Purdue University, USA
Alan Lin   Air Force Office of Scientific Research, USA
Jigang Liu   Metropolitan State University, USA
Michael Losavio   University of Louisville, USA
Duohe Ma   Chinese Academy of Sciences, China
James Okolica   Air Force Institute of Technology, USA
Martin Olivier   University of Pretoria, South Africa
Gilbert Peterson   Air Force Institute of Technology, USA
Emmanuel Pilli   Malaviya National Institute of Technology, India
Huw Read   Norwich University, USA
Anoop Singhal   National Institute of Standards and Technology, USA
Jason Staggs   University of Tulsa, USA
Robin Verma   Marshall University, USA
Konstantinos Xynos   Mycenx Consultancy, Germany

Table of Contents

List of Contributors

Esra Akbas Georgia State University, Atlanta, Georgia, USA

Stefan Axelsson Stockholm University, Kista, Sweden

Harald Baier University of the Bundeswehr, Munich, Germany

Rajon Bardhan Augusta University, Augusta, Georgia, USA

Seth Barrett Augusta University, Augusta, Georgia, USA

Nitesh Bharadwaj National Institute of Technology, Raipur, India

Simon Boche Malizen, Rennes, France

Romain Brisse Malizen, Rennes, France; CentraleSupelec, Rennes, France; INRIA, Rennes, France; University of Rennes, Rennes, France

Kai Chen Chinese Academy of Sciences, Beijing, China; University of Chinese Academy of Sciences, Beijing, China

Kam-Pui Chow University of Hong Kong, Hong Kong, China

Eswara Sai Prasad Chunduru Central Forensic Science Laboratory, Hyderabad, India

Gokila Dorai Augusta University, Augusta, Georgia, USA

Fuqiang Du Chinese Academy of Sciences, Beijing, China

Cayden Dunn College of Charleston, Charleston, South Carolina, USA

Pulkit Garg Indian Institute of Technology, Jodhpur, India

Krishnendu Ghosh College of Charleston, Charleston, South Carolina, USA

Chalicheemala Gireesh Vasavi College of Engineering, Hyderabad, India

Gaopeng Gou Chinese Academy of Sciences, Beijing, China

Thomas Göbel University of the Bundeswehr, Munich, Germany

Yong Guan Iowa State University, Ames, Iowa, USA

Gaurav Gupta Ministry of Electronics and Information Technology, New Delhi, India

Weiqing Huang Chinese Academy of Sciences, Beijing, China

Jianguo Jiang Chinese Academy of Sciences, Beijing, China

Junye Jiang Chinese Academy of Sciences, Beijing, China

Pankaj Kumar Ministry of Electronics and Information Technology, New Delhi, India

Jean-Francois Lalande CentraleSupelec, Rennes, France; INRIA, Rennes, France; University of Rennes, Rennes, France

Vijay Laxmi Malaviya National Institute of Technology, Jaipur, India

Boquan Li Harbin Engineering University, Harbin, China; Singapore Management University, Singapore, Singapore

Chen Lin China Industrial Control Systems Cyber Emergency Response Team, Beijing, China

Duohe Ma Chinese Academy of Sciences, Beijing, China

Frederic Majorczyk Direction Generale de l'Armement, Bruz, France

Xiang Meng Chinese Academy of Sciences, Beijing, China

Johannes Olegård Stockholm University, Kista, Sweden

Martin Olivier University of Pretoria, Pretoria, South Africa

Emmanuel Pilli Malaviya National Institute of Technology, Jaipur, India

Shengzhi Qin University of Hong Kong, Hong Kong, China

Arun Kumar Sahani Ministry of Electronics and Information Technology, New Delhi, India

Alex Salontai Georgia State University, Atlanta, Georgia, USA

Aritro Sengupta Ministry of Electronics and Information Technology, New Delhi, India

Chen Shi Iowa State University, Ames, Iowa, USA

Krishan Pal Singh Malaviya National Institute of Technology, Jaipur, India

Kaparthi Srinivas Vasavi College of Engineering, Hyderabad, India

Vishal Srivastava Indian Institute of Technology, Jodhpur, India

Zhimin Tang Chinese Academy of Sciences, Beijing, China

Venugopal Temberveni JNTUH University College of Engineering, Jagtial, India

Jan Türr University of the Bundeswehr, Munich, Germany

Chonghua Wang China Industrial Control Systems Cyber Emergency Response Team, Beijing, China

Jiawen Wang Chinese Academy of Sciences, Beijing, China

Liming Wang Chinese Academy of Sciences, Beijing, China

Patrick Woodell Augusta University, Augusta, Georgia, USA

Gang Xiong Chinese Academy of Sciences, Beijing, China

Min Yu Chinese Academy of Sciences, Beijing, China

Zhenchao Zhang Chinese Academy of Sciences, Beijing, China

Hao Zhou China Industrial Control Systems Cyber Emergency Response Team, Beijing, China

Zhishen Zhu Chinese Academy of Sciences, Beijing, China

Themes and Issues

On Determining the Age of Questioned Digital Documents

Martin Olivier

University of Pretoria, Pretoria, South Africa
martin@mo.co.za

Abstract. The determination of document age is often of paramount importance when questioned documents are examined. In a physical setting, age determination may be based on static and/or dynamic principles. Static principles are based on the introduction dates of ink, paper and other writing materials. Since digital documents are based on artifacts that were often introduced on known dates, static methods to date documents have digital equivalents. Dynamic principles are based on the manner in which documents change over time. Such aging has no equivalent in the digital domain.

This chapter introduces two principles that are used as a basis for determining document age. The principles are employed to determine a temporal creation window for a document, in a manner that makes it possible to convey the confidence within the window. When a creation window can be shown to predate or postdate a purported creation time or other critical event, it follows that the document cannot be authentic.

Keywords: Questioned Digital Document Examination · Forensic Digital Document Examination · Digital Document Age

1 Introduction

The forensic discipline of questioned documents is well-established and has proven its value over several years. The discipline uses various techniques to answer a range of questions about documents that arise in legal matters. Questions may arise about the authenticity of a document, the tools used to create it and its authorship (e.g., based on the signatures that may be present on the document). A question that exists in its own right, or as an aid to answer other questions, is the question about the age of a document.

The age of a document is a relevant question in a variety of cases. A collectible antique document has to date back to its purported time of creation to be authentic. When a discrepancy occurs, the document enters the legal fray; if authenticity is challenged after the sale of the document, civil and/or criminal proceedings may follow.

Document age is also relevant in financial matters. A common example is a contested will – an authentic will could not have been executed after the person's demise. Typical financial documents, such as receipts, invoices and promissory notes, are all examples of documents whose creation times may be questioned.

© IFIP International Federation for Information Processing 2025
Published by Springer Nature Switzerland AG 2025
E. Kurkowski and S. Shenoi (Eds.): DigitalForensics 2024, IFIP AICT 724, pp. 3–23, 2025.
https://doi.org/10.1007/978-3-031-71025-4_1

Digital documents often contain one or more embedded creation dates. The dates are often recorded as metadata in the documents and by the filesystem on which the documents may be stored. The reasons why document metadata cannot be relied upon are well-known to the digital forensics community. However, given its importance, the issue is revisited later in this chapter.

The age of a physical document is determined using two distinct approaches. The static approach identifies inks, stationery and other materials used to create a document. This is combined with knowledge about the time of introduction and use of the materials. The document has to postdate the introduction of the materials. The dynamic approach considers the changes that the physical materials undergo over time, such as fading, oxidation and other forms of physical decay. If the rate of decay is known, the age of the document can be determined. Digital documents are not subject to physical decay. Hence the age of a digital document has to be determined using a static approach that considers the artifacts used to create the document.

This chapter systematically develops a static approach for forensically determining the age of digital documents. Two principles, the principle of inclusion and the principle of replication, are introduced to justify forensic conclusions.

Kapoor et al. [31] highlight that age determination of a physical document is one of the more challenging facets of forensic document examination. The constraints of the digital realm, such as the lack of physical degradation, imply that digital document age determination is also challenging. However, a documented process is useful in situations when it leads to justifiable conclusions.

2   Metadata

Various forms of metadata pertaining to document age may be associated with a document. Embedded metadata often indicates when a document was created. For example, the entry:

```
/CreationDate(D:20120122074131-08'00'
```

in a PDF document indicates the time, date and time zone when the document was purportedly created. The filesystem on which a document is stored typically keeps a record of when the document was created as well as the times at which the document was last accessed or modified. Other metadata may be available depending on the context.

The value of metadata in digital forensic investigations has been contested over the years. In an early paper on digital forensics, Buchholz and Spafford [15] express the wish that systems would capture more metadata, given its utility in the (then new) field. However, they also lament the ease with which metadata can often be modified. They suggest a future where some metadata, such as file creation dates, cannot be modified – a feature that "should be present on any filesystem." Buchholz and Spafford also mention that it is often trivial to modify instances of metadata.

Various techniques can be used to increase the confidence in metadata, and in particular, timestamp metadata. A popular technique is to correlate various instances of metadata [32, 36]. Often a lack of correlation is used to detect tampering [36]. In contrast, this chapter identifies specific instances of correlation that can be used to infer the correctness of timestamps.

The lack of trust in timestamp metadata is illustrated by the number of papers that focus on the detection of timestamp metadata tampering [33, 36, 39, 41]. Some approaches are based on the lack of correlation. Another approach is to use machine learning to detect anomalies, despite serious concerns about the use of artificial intelligence when forensic proof is required [34]. A popular approach is to store data in a tamper-proof environment using blockchain technology. This solves the problem, but only if a reliable party is available to store all the data in the tamper-proof container before it becomes relevant in a legal matter.

The age of a document is usually contested some time after its creation. Often it would be a document that was moved between systems using various document sharing mechanisms. As a result, operating system metadata would be irrelevant. A robust approach that is not subject to natural changes or simple tampering is required.

This work deems a document to be a sequence of bytes that would lead to a common understanding in the digital realm. The sequence of bytes would typically be in the form of a file with a specific type. Examples range from documents created by office suites to executable programs. An important consequence of this definition is that saving a document in a new format – such as saving a DOC document as a DOCX document – would create a new document. This requirement is necessary for the static analysis approach considered in this work. It is possible to consider similarities between, say a document stored in the DOC format and another document stored in the DOCX format and explore the possibility that one of the documents is simply a conversion from the other. This work does not explore such comparisons.

Differences between the various metadata dates in a document (or a difference between a date in the content and a metadata date) may be of value to dispute the authenticity of a document, but the certainty with which the document may be deemed to be forged depends on the nature of the document and the differences in times. Some documents may include multiple creation times in their metadata. As example is a photo captured by a camera that geotags the photo. The photo typically stores the capture time based on the camera's internal clock as well as the clocks of the GPS satellites used to determine the location where the photo was taken. A forger may fail to change all the photo metadata and the inconsistency may provide a forensic document examiner with a data point to determine that a questioned document cannot be authentic. Of course, other explanations for the differences need to be ruled out before any conclusions can be reached.

Time and date stamps in metadata play different roles in "autopsies" and other forms of reconstruction than they do in the case of questioned documents.

In these instances, the relative time is more important than the absolute time. Such uses of timestamps are outside the scope of this work.

3   Document Age as Evidence

The age of documents have been central to a number of cases. This section describes a case where the age of a signature on a will was instrumental in proving it was a forgery. Next, it describes the well-known case of the forged Hitler diaries. Finally, it describes a case where a will transmitted by email was eventually deemed to be acceptable by the court.

3.1   Patel vs Patel

In early 2015 an individual named Girish Patel petitioned the England and Wales High Court (Chancery Division) to accept a will of his late mother that was dated June 23, 2005. His mother passed away in 2011 and a will dated June 18, 1986 had been accepted as her last will and testament, but it was contested [23]. It was common cause that the mother's signature on the newer document was authentic. However, expert testimony highlighted three temporal inconsistencies:

- Signatures of people change over time and the version of the mother's signature on the new document differed from other known signatures that dated from 2005, when the new document was purportedly signed. However, the 2005 signature matched versions of her signature that dated from before 2005.
- The ink used for the mother's 2005 signature exhibited much more signs of ageing than the ink used for the witnesses' signatures.
- Ink particles from a printer were found on the mother's 2005 signature, suggesting that the signature already existed when the document was printed.

None of these observations have equivalent notions in the digital domain. The third inconsistency was challenged, but the court did not base its decision on it.

Since the case was a civil matter, it was decided on the balance of probabilities. This point was raised repeatedly in the judgment. The court ruled against Girish Patel, determining that the 2005 document was not authentic. Girish Patel was later incarcerated for perjury [24]. Subsequently, he was found guilty of forgery in a criminal case. Neither of these two later cases, which required proof beyond a reasonable doubt, involved further examination of the forged will.

3.2   The Hitler Diaries

The Hitler Diaries were purportedly written by Adolf Hitler, but they were, in fact, forged by a Konrad Kujau in the early 1980s [26].

One of the first concrete forensic contradictions raised in the case was temporal. Specifically, polyester fibers were found in the binding of one of the diaries, but polyester manufacturing commenced several years after Hitler's death.

Chemical analysis of the ink used in the diaries eventually proved that the content was written one to two years before the diaries were offered for sale.

After a lengthy police investigation, a confession by Kunjau and an extended trial, Kunjau was sentenced to serve time in prison. Several other parties involved in the scandal were sanctioned, including one individual who was incarcerated.

The finding that the binding of the diaries contained polyester fibers is an example of a static analysis approach for which digital equivalents will be explored in the remainder of this chapter.

3.3   Van der Merwe vs. Master of the High Court and Another

In 2004, a South African citizen named John Henry Munnik van Schalkwyk executed a will in favor of an animal welfare society. Some time later, Van Schalkwyk and a friend, Hendrik van der Merwe, decided to mutually bequeath their estates to each other. They had been friends for years and neither had any remaining family. On July 26, 2007, Van Schalkwyk sent an email to Van der Merwe with the will attached and asked if the will correctly expressed their agreement. Van Schalkwyk passed away a few months later without signing the will.

The act that governs wills in South Africa prescribes all the formalities that have to be met before a document constitutes a valid will. It also gives a court the discretion to declare a will valid even if all formalities have not been met. The idea is that a person's last wishes should not be ignored simply because of some formality as long as they were indeed the deceased's last wishes.

Van der Merwe approached the South Gauteng High Court in Johannesburg with the request that the emailed document be declared a valid will. The respondents were the Master of the High Court and the Society for the Prevention of Cruelty to Animals (SPCA). The Master responded as the party who decides whether or not to accept a will. The SPCA acted as a respondent because it was the beneficiary in Van Schalkwyk's 2004 will. Both parties indicated that they would abide by the court's decision. The high court decided that accepting the document would "open the floodgates for any person to submit any document ... as a Will of a testator" [43]. Accordingly, it dismissed the application.

On appeal, the Supreme Court of Appeals reached the conclusion that it was indeed the wish of the testator to leave his estate to his friend. One aspect considered in support of this conclusion was the fact that a copy of the email was still present on the computer of the deceased; no further analysis of the document was conducted. The court decided that the emailed will was deemed acceptable and directed the Master "to accept the [emailed] document executed by the deceased during 2007 ... as the will of John Henry Munnik van Schalkwyk for the purposes of the Administration of Estates Act 66 of 1965" [43].

4   Document Age Determination

While digital documents do not age physically, their "materials" (file formats, fonts, etc.) may be used to determine boundaries for their ages in instances when the introduction of the materials to the market is known. This is not dissimilar to using static analysis methods to bind the ages of physical documents. This section explores methods used to determine the age of physical documents and then turns its attention to digital documents.

4.1 Physical Documents

As far back as 1910, textbooks have discussed reasons for determining the age of questioned documents as well as methods for determining their ages [35]. The reasons include detecting a forgery when a document's purported age does not agree with its physical age. The mismatch between actual and purported age was deemed to be important in several scenarios, including "bankruptcy and settlements of estates [where] the important question may arise whether certain entries or memoranda in books of account were actually made in due course of business on the dates they bear, or whether they were made at a subsequent period for the fraudulent purpose ... of showing a certain result at the date of settlement" [35].

"The materials that make up a [traditional] document may tell something of the earliest possible date of preparation" [27]. It is often useful when text is written or typed on stationery and the date of production of the stationery is known. For example, the ink may be a fluid or gel that embeds pigments that were only introduced into writing instruments at a known date. Another option for determining document age is to examine physical changes that occur over time. Paper and ink, for example, oxidize over time and the degree of oxidation can be useful. Obviously, these physical indicators of age have no straightforward equivalents in the digital realm. However, the notion of "earliest possible date of preparation" can be useful. The equivalent notion of "earliest creation time" will be used when digital documents are discussed later in this chapter.

Entire books have been written about the age of ink. An example is *Advances in the Forensic Analysis and Dating of Writing Ink* [14]. It discusses, among other things, fountain pen inks introduced from the 1880s to the 1940s, ball-point pen inks introduced from 1939 to 1968, fiber pen inks introduced in the mid 1960s and gel-based inks introduced in the mid to late 1980s. Many tests "are based on solvent extraction and changes in dye concentration," but such tests and others are not suitable for gel-based inks. Tests based on oxidation can provide the earliest possible date of production as well as the time period during which the ink was applied to the paper. Several factors impact the duration of the time window during which a document could have been created and impact the certainty with which a conclusion about its age may be made. Clearly, no equivalent exists in the digital domain.

A distinction is made between static, dynamic and supplementary approaches for determining document age [16, 17, 31]. Static approaches are based on the introduction dates of types of paper, ink and other components used to produce documents. Dynamic approaches depend on the changes of physical materials such as paper and ink over time. Supplementary approaches include radiocarbon dating and subjecting portions of documents to conditions that enable the study of their reactions to the conditions. They also include chronological studies that arrange documents sharing an origin in sequence to establish the relative ages of documents. An example is two letters from a pad where impressions from handwriting on one page can link another page to its original position on the pad.

The notion of chronology, as expressed by Kapoor et al [31], corresponds broadly with a remark by Hilton [27]: "Another technique [to help determine the age of a physical document] involves comparison with known undisputed material, that is, by comparing it with a series of documents prepared with the same typewriter or pen and ink, or paper, for example, and fitting the document in question into such an established framework." In the digital context, email is an example of documents where earlier messages often leave "impressions" in later documents, typically in the form of quoted earlier messages that are included in a new message. This may enable a document examiner to establish a relative order of the messages. As will be discussed later in this chapter, email is also a document type that can be dated more accurately than most other digital document types.

4.2   Digital Documents

Limited research has focused on determining the age of digital documents. Spennemann and Spennemann [42] have employed the revision save identifier (RSID) in Microsoft Word documents to determine the order of document versions. Each document version that is saved adds a new RSID while retaining the RSIDs of the earlier versions. This enables the determination of the genealogy of documents, including instances when multiple documents stem from a shared ancestor.

The disk allocation strategy used by a filesystem determines the manner in which fragments constituting a file are spread across the disk. In some cases it is possible to validate the date stamp of a file by comparing the date of a recovered file against the dates of files allocated to neighboring clusters on the disk [9]. This is simpler with older filesystems such as the FAT filesystem. Several researchers have investigated the temporal behavior of NTFS drives (see, e.g., [8, 20, 22]).

Casey [19] has examined how digital activities occur in time windows that he refers to as "strata." Events that occur during a stratum need to be seen in context; while useful conclusions are often possible, room for misinterpretation exists. A newly created file may retain filesystem data, especially the creation time, of the old file. Casey notes that saving a Microsoft Word file using "Save As" with the old name of the file causes the file to retain its creation date on the filesystem, but the "Save As" time is stored as the creation time in the file itself.

Ho et al. [28] have derived several rules pertaining to the impact of managing files in the cloud based on their timestamps compared with their timestamps on filesystems such as FAT, NTFS and Ext4. However, Ho et al., as well as Spennemann and Spennemann, and Casey, do not address document age. Their primary goals are event reconstruction or deleted file recovery.

5   Principle of Replication

*When multiple independent authoritative sources agree about an event,
it follows that details about the event have been recorded and reported
correctly.*

In order to understand this principle, the notions of "multiple," "independent"
and "authoritative" must be clarified.

A source is deemed to be "authoritative" if it records details about some
action it is responsible for handling. As an example, consider email, a context
that will be used extensively in this chapter. A mail transfer agent that forwards
an email on its route to its destination is the authoritative source about what
transpired when the email was forwarded. Although the agent is deemed to be
authoritative, it may be mistaken about some details – the specific concern in
this work is time. If the clock of the mail transfer agent is incorrect, it may
report the time of the event incorrectly.

The second criterion in the principle of replication is that the observation
must be supported by "multiple witnesses." Clearly, an increase in the number
of sources that confirm an observation increases the confidence with which the
observation may be accepted as correct. However, if two sources of an observation
used a common third party to make the observation, the common third party may
be a better explanation of agreement than relying on the odds of two witnesses
being equally wrong. Since the principle will be applied to forwarding emails, two
mail transfer agents that share a clock would report the event to have happened
at the time indicated by the clock (that could reflect time incorrectly). However,
if each mail transfer agent has its own clock, the odds that both clocks would
reflect the same incorrect time are small. In general, the greater the number of
witnesses that report the same observation (for which no explanation, such as a
shared clock, can be found), the greater the odds that the observation is indeed
correct.

An observation such as time that is reported by multiple witnesses who rely
on a shared source effectively count as a single observation in this principle. If an
email is sent from an organization A where several mail transfer agents handle
email, all the agents effectively share a clock. As a result, all the observations collectively have the same weight as a single observation. However, if the email were
to arrive at a mail transfer agent in organization B that uses a clock not linked
to organization A, chance would not explain the correlation if the observation
at B would match the observation at A.

Now assume that the email is handled by several mail transfer agents at
organization B, where all the mail transfer agents at organization B share a clock.
If these additional mail transfer agents agree, confidence in the observations does
not increase. Effectively, the mail transfer agents at organization A form one
witness and the mail transfer agents at organization B form a second witness.

It is necessary to reflect on what it means for two witnesses to "agree." Processes often take some time to complete. A mail transfer agent forwards an email

to the next mail transfer agent after a short delay, although longer delays do occur. Therefore, it is possible to empirically observe email forwarding times and determine the expected variance. Most emails will be forwarded within a limited time period. The meaning of "most" should be determined empirically, but it is possible, for example, that the forwarding times for 99% of the email messages would be clustered with just 1% being outliers. This percentage of times could deem a cluster as normal and it could be assumed to have a normal variance. Email messages that do not satisfy this condition would be deemed outliers and no conclusions should be based on them. Of course, empirical testing would be required to determine whether email forwarding exhibits any hypothesized behavior.

The last requirement of the principle of replication is independence. Independence has been encountered above when multiple witnesses that depend on the same source effectively count as a single source. Witnesses A and B are independent in terms of a specific observation if A does not obtain information from B, B does not obtain information from A, and A and B do not obtain information from a shared resource.

Again, referring to the domain of application later in this chapter, each mail transfer agent independently records the time an email is processed by the mail transfer agent if the mail transfer agents do not share clocks. Hence, they are independent witnesses about the time the email was processed. In contrast, the fact that the email was sent is not independently recorded by each mail transfer agent. Every mail transfer agent learns about the email from the mail transfer agent from which it receives the email. A malicious actor who introduces a forged email at an appropriate mail transfer agent may cause the subsequent mail transfer agents on the route to also record that the email was sent.

The fact that the multiple mail transfer agents should not rely on the same source has two implications in this context. If mail transfer agents share a clock or derive their time from the same NTP server, they may not be deemed to be independent. Given the fact that NTP servers often obtain times from other, more authoritative NTP servers makes independence a topic that requires reflection. The second implication is that the same party should not be able to gain administrative access to two mail transfer agents for them to be deemed independent. In principle, the better the governance of at least one of the mail transfer agents, the less likely it would be that a malicious actor would gain access to it. This issue also requires reflection.

Instead of exploring these implications in detail, it is pertinent to note that most email messages are handled by a few email service providers. It will be argued in Section 7 that it is practical to subject email services to regular tests that compare the times provided by the servers to each other, which, will be shown to be a sound basis to accept independence. Therefore, the minutiae that confirm independence between less common services are not discussed further in this chapter.

The principle of replication was influenced by Casey's certainty scale [18]. Casey's certainty scale also uses three notions, replication, protection against tampering and independence, to assign increasing levels of confidence to conclusions. Some of Casey's three notions are, in principle, independent and should therefore lead to a partial ordering of certainty, rather than the fully ordered scale he presents. It is also not entirely clear that independence and protection are not two sides of the same coin. Moreover, Casey's scale is intended for conclusions whereas the principle presented here deals with certainty about observations. A full critique of Casey's certainty scale is beyond the scope of this work. However, it is sufficient to acknowledge the inspiration drawn from Casey's scale and to note that it does not meet the requirements of this work. Hence this work could not simply have used Casey's certainty scale and had to put forward a new principle.

6   Principle of Inclusion

The principle of inclusion is drawn from the observation that whenever some artifact x is used to create some artifact y, x must have been created before y was created. The notation $x \sqsubseteq y$ is used to indicate that x was used to create y. Stated somewhat differently, the notation indicates that x in some sense forms part of y.

Suppose $c(x)$ indicates the creation time and date of an artifact x, then the observation above may be expressed as follows:

$$x \sqsubseteq y \implies c(x) \leq c(y) \tag{1}$$

Equality, i.e., $x \sqsubseteq y \implies c(x) = c(y)$, may occur due to the fact that digital time is discrete [21].

In what follows the notions of creation time and creation date will be used almost interchangeably. Instead of using a specific date or time, the discussion will evolve towards a period of time called a "creation window."

The term artifact refers to anything that came to exist at some point in time. The notion of artifacts includes digital documents. Therefore, the principle of inclusion is useful to determine the relative ages of two documents if one document includes the other. An example that will be used extensively below is an email (deemed to be a digital document) includes or embeds another document as an attachment. Clearly, a composite document has to include the document used in a form that leaves no doubt that it existed at the time the composite document was created. An example where this does not apply is when an HTML file x links to some other HTML file y. It is possible to replace the referenced document y with a different document also called y without changing the referencing (composite) document. Hence, in the case of documents, at least, $x \sqsubseteq y$ only holds when (if at all possible) the modification of x would require y to change too.

However, the relationship between x and y may be indirect. When y contains a sufficiently strong cryptographic hash of x, the condition that x forms a part of y is met although x is not included or embedded in y. If x is modified, it would be necessary to modify y to maintain the relationship between x and y. Modifying x without modifying y would have been possible if another document

Table 1. PDF standard release dates.

Version	Release Date
PDF 1.0 [11]	1993
PDF 1.1 [12]	1994
PDF 1.2 [13]	1996
PDF 1.3 [1]	2000
PDF 1.4 [2]	2001
PDF 1.5 [3]	2003
PDF 1.6 [4]	2004
PDF 1.7 [5]	2008
PDF 2.0 [29]	2017
PDF 2.0 Rev. [30]	2020

x' could be found where x and x' have identical cryptographic hashes. This is not possible for sufficiently strong cryptographic hashes [38].

6.1 Format Specifications

An example of employing an artifact to create a digital document is the use of the specification of the document type. Consider a PDF file as an example. The first PDF specification was released in 1993 [11]. Hence, a PDF document cannot predate 1993. As summarized in Table 1, several versions of the PDF standard have been released over the years. In principle, a document that is represented using a specific version of PDF could not have been created prior to the definition of the version.

A challenge posed by the data in Table 1 is that the precision is limited to an entire year, which may not be ideal. In some instances or not at all, it may be possible to determine a more precise date. For example, the publication date of the PDF 1.1 standard was March 1, 1996 [12]. However, it is obvious that that the standard did not come into existence on that day – many people would have worked on the standard over time. When a standard is linked to a product, several individuals such as programmers, alpha testers and beta testers would have worked on the code used for the standard. Importantly, for a relatively complex standard, these individuals would have had access to tools in the form of prototypes, works in progress, release candidates and, typically, final product code before the standard would have been frozen and published. This was clearly a more significant issue in the case of PDF 1.1. The specification for PDF 1.1 [12] was published in 1996, but PDF 1.1 was "the native file format of the Adobe Acrobat 2.0 family of products" [12], which was released two years earlier in 1994 [7].

New standards often need time to be adopted in the market. Many end-users only start using the new standard when they upgrade their software to versions that support the new standard. Therefore, even when a standard is adopted on a

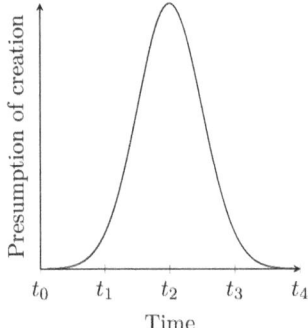

Fig. 1. Creation window of a standard (t_1: publication time).

specific day (or even year), the assumption should be that the standard became available over a period of time. This situation is illustrated in Figure 1.

Figure 1 does not display a probability density function. When an artifact, such as a standard, was created cannot be expressed as a probability. Instead, the uncertainty relates to the knowledge of and access to the standard. Initially, from t_0 to t_1, few people would have had knowledge about the standard to be developed. The standard was published at time t_1. Over the period from t_1 to t_2, the market adopted the standard and it was supported by an increasing number of tools. At some time t_2, the standard was deemed to be available to everybody who wanted to use it. From this point onwards, t_2 to t_3, the number of new adopters declined. Eventually, from t_3 and beyond, there is little reason to believe that any tool that used the standard was created because its developers only recently learnt about the standard.

Now consider a questioned document based on a standard that was created in the window shown in Figure 1. If nothing is known about the individual responsible for creating the questioned document, it could have been created as early as t_0. When there is reason to accept that the individual who created the document did not have anything to do with the development of the standard, it is possible to accept t_1 as the earliest time at which the document could have been created. In fact, given that the majority of users of a standard would not have been involved in creating the standard, it is possible to use the later time t_2 as the first possible time at which the document could have been created. However, this assumption reduces the certainty of the conclusion.

While the attributes of individuals should not normally have an impact on digital forensic examinations, there appear to be issues of access that merit consideration.

No inference should be drawn from the scale of the graph in Figure 1. The labels on the x-axis are equidistant, but the intervals between them are not equal. The increase and decrease in the confidence that the standard was created at some time could be asymmetric as shown in Figure 2. In fact, the depiction of

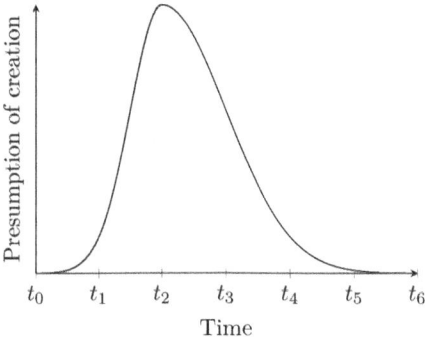

Fig. 2. Asymmetric creation window of a standard (t_1: publication time).

the creation time is merely a placeholder that may take any shape over a period of time.

When the law of inclusion (Equation 1) was introduced, it was noted that the case for equality would be revisited. The discussion of PDF standards enables equality to be justified based on precision – the PDF 1.2 standard was published in 1996 [13]. It is entirely plausible that some documents based on PDF 1.2 were created in 1996. This extends to the more generic case where the creation date of a standard should be deemed to be some period in time, and a document creation date may well overlap with the creation date of the standard on which it is based. Such an overlap becomes an issue that needs further consideration. In fact, overlap is discussed below.

Another challenge already touched on is the manner in which the version of a PDF document is to be determined. It is known that a PDF document contains its version in the very first line. A typical PDF document may start as follows:

%PDF-1.6

This is true even for PDF 1.0. According to the standard, the "current version is 1.0, for which the first line of a PDF file is %PDF-1.0" [11]. However, PDF standards are backwards compatible. The standard for PDF 1.2, for example, states that "1.0-conforming files and 1.1-conforming files are also 1.2-conforming files" [13]. Note that, starting with "PDF 1.4, the version in the file header can be overridden by the Version entry in the document's catalog dictionary (located via the Root entry in the file's trailer ...)" [2]. The version entry may therefore provide a more accurate (or later) indication of the PDF version of the standard used in parts of a PDF document than indicated by the document header.

While the version number in the header and/or trailer of a PDF document indicate the version that the document creator purported to use, the elements used in the created document may have already been defined by an earlier version of the PDF standard. The observed version number may therefore not be supported by the use of new elements in the indicated version. It is easy for a fraudster to predict a future version number, but it is much harder to use functionality from a future version. In fact, the version number is metadata that is subject to the concerns expressed in Section 2. However, a document that claims to be represented in some version and that uses a feature introduced in the version provides internal support about the correctness of the version. The document examiner should weigh the credence of the version depending on the observations that support a claim that a specific version was used, and adjust the confidence in the conclusions accordingly.

Similar comments apply to other document formats to a greater or lesser extent than PDF. In some cases, a document standard is not proposed in a public manner but is introduced to the public when some software starts using the (proprietary) format. Compatible software may then depend on reverse-engineering the format or the format may be published long after the software that introduced the format was made available. In such cases, the software should be deemed to be the original defining document of the format. Some formats are continually amended or extended by software houses – especially when the format makes it possible to include information that would be ignored by tools that are not aware of the extensions. Consider HTML tags introduced by various browsers and supported by HTML authoring tools. Many of the tags are proprietary. An example is <blink> introduced by Netscape [10].

In such cases, the creation time of the tool may be more useful to determine aspects of document age than the creation date of the document standard.

6.2   Character Codes

An encoding is always used to represent text in a document. The principle of inclusion may therefore be applied to help determine the age of such a document. The ISO/IEC 8859 series of standards is an example of character encodings that were developed over a period of time (1987 to 2001 for Parts 1 to 16). These standards are based on ASCII and are backwards compatible with ASCII.

The ASCII standard was first introduced in 1963 [6]. Hence a document may use "1963" ASCII, but claim to be encoded in ISO/IEC 8859-15, which corresponds to IANA character encoding ISO-8859-1 that a document examiner would likely find in a MIME description of character content. This again raises the question whether an examiner should rely on an annotation that the document was encoded using ISO-8859-1. Clearly the meaningful use of at least some characters in the standard that were not part of ASCII would increase the confidence with which the examiner could conclude that the document was created after the adoption of the standard. To exacerbate matters, various parts of the ISO/IEC 8859 series are based on earlier standards proposed by other bodies (e.g., ECMA). In some cases, the earlier standards were modified before being accepted as ISO/IEC standards; this usually involves very few characters and, unless the characters are used in a meaningful manner, the use of the earlier standard cannot be distinguished from the use of the later standard unless it is identified by name.

Unicode, which is widely adopted, is a potentially useful tool to help determine the age of documents. New characters are added annually to the standard, with Version 16.0.0 expected to be released in 2024. A new version typically includes support for more (often ancient) scripts, new characters and new emojis. The version of Unicode used in a document is usually not explicitly indicated, which requires a document examiner to rely on characters introduced by a specific version to identify the version. Unfortunately, the set of new characters added annually are typically specialized characters (such as those from ancient scripts) and are unlikely to occur in most documents.

The introduction of new currency symbols is a noteworthy case for documents that include financial references. The Euro sign was introduced in Unicode 2.1 in May 1998, the new Indian Rupee sign was introduced in Unicode 6.0 in October 2010 and the Bitcoin sign was introduced in Unicode 10.0 in June 2017. While a sign exists for Ethereum, it has not been added to Unicode as yet, but it may be added in the future. Currency symbols may be useful in cases where they occur in documents.

Similarly, new emojis that are added may be useful in the contexts in which they occur. An example is the microbe emoji introduced in Unicode 11.0 in June 2018. The emoji was used extensively in chat and other communication channels during the COVID-19 pandemic.

The International Organization for Standardization (ISO) formally started working on an international character set in 1989 and published the first draft of Unicode in 1990. The ISO/IEC 10646-1:1993 standard was published in 1993. Work on an efficient encoding scheme for locations that primarily use the Latin character set began soon after work on Unicode started. UTF-8 (Unicode Transformation Format – 8-bit) was created in 1992, presented at a conference in 1993 [40] and included in the 1993 Unicode standard. Locations that primarily used other scripts followed suit. Shift JIS, designed to concisely encode (primarily) Japanese script, was standardized in 1997.

Whenever a document is encoded using a character code or a special representation for the character code, the creation of the character code or the representation format must predate the document as described in the principle of inclusion.

7   Document Creation Window

The creation process of a document may leave sufficient traces to enable a document examiner to determine its creation window. Email is an example of such a document. From the principle of inclusion, if a document x is included in a document y, then document x was created prior to document y. If the creation window of y is known, it establishes the latest creation time of document x. Email is regularly used to transmit other documents (as attachments) and, therefore, is a specific case where the principle of inclusion can be used.

7.1 Email

An email is typically created on a source computer, transferred via possibly independent mail transfer agents and eventually delivered in the recipient's mailbox. Even in cases where a cloud service is used to create, send and receive email, multiple independent mail transfer agents may be involved and maintain independent logs of when an email was transmitted by a mail transfer agent and received by another. The logs of the various parties that participate in email transmission may not all agree. For example, an email may be created on a computer that is not connected to a network. After the computer connects to a network, the email is transmitted to the first mail transfer agent on the route. It is also possible that a delay due to congestion or other network-related conditions occurs when a mail transfer agent forwards an email to the next mail transfer agent. In many cases, examination of the email header indicates the points on the path where the email was delayed and would often suggest a reason that would explain the delay. In any case, the creation date of a document is assumed to be a period of time that caters to clocks that do not entirely agree.

The challenge posed by incorrect clocks is well-known, but it has become less of an issue in the always-connected world in which email messages are sent. Moreover, a small number of email services are involved in handling a large percentage of email sent globally. While it is hard to precisely determine the market shares of services such as Google Mail, Outlook and Proton Mail, it is clear that these services handle a large percentage of email. When email is sent between two or more parties, the likelihood that the email is handled by a major email provider increases. It can be hypothesized that major email providers tend to record email times quite accurately. This hypothesis is simple to test on a continual basis given that few email services are truly major handlers of email. With an empirical record of correctness (including variance) of time and date stamps by a major email provider, a document examiner is in a better position to make claims about the date an email was processed by the provider. When a reliable clock is not available to test accuracy, testing agreement between clocks by pairs of major providers using the principle of replication is a viable alternative. Regular testing may be augmented using archived reports of network events that may have an impact on email processing.

In fact, major Google Mail delays so rare that they are reported by news media [37]. Google maintains a dashboard of incidents that it investigated [25]; there were only nine incidents related to Gmail in 2023. Four listed incidents involved delayed processing of email. On December 1, 2023 an incident lasting 1 hour, 32 minutes caused global delays. One day earlier, on 30 November 30,2023, an incident lasting 4 hours, 45 minutes caused global delays. On May 5, 2023, an incident lasting 56 minutes caused delays for some customers in Spain and Morocco. On January 26, 2023, an incident lasting 1 hour, 48 minutes caused delays in some specific cases that were initially deemed to have been delayed mailing list processing.

Major email delays are rare, but care should be exercised when dealing with the delays of specific email messages. A delay would typically cause the various

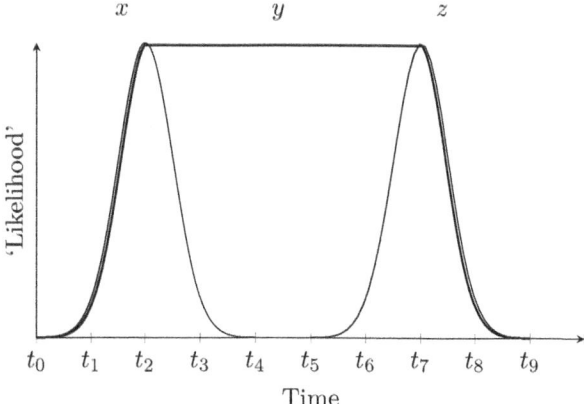

Fig. 3. Creation window of y from the earliest to the latest creation times.

email processing times along the route to disagree and hence make it difficult to determine the age of an email. Therefore, it is not likely to result in wrong conclusions being reached. In any case, agreement of timestamps is more important to a document examiner.

Mail transfer agent logs are unlikely to be available for older email. In many such cases, the time at which the email was purportedly sent would be common cause because it is recorded in the body of the email. It is also realistic to assume that an email would be received with the headers of mail transfer agents. When the times agree, they may be accepted with a high degree of confidence given the independence assumption. Confidence may be increased when the email conversation in which the questioned document was exchanged is available for examination.

Other online services such as cloud storage and instant messaging may also shed light on the time a document existed. The period over which such an online document was created would be depicted in a similar manner as the depiction of creation periods used earlier. The intervals covered would be expected to be much shorter, with more specific boundaries from the earliest points to the latest points the documents could have been created. Email is also open to further examination given the partial ordering of messages, replies and forwarded emails in a conversation. The principle used is again one of inclusion, when a reply or forwarded email includes the earlier email.

7.2   Latest Creation Time Determination

It is typical to send important documents such as contracts as attachments to email. As a result, a large genre of documents exists for which email is of particular importance to the determination of document age.

Figure 3 illustrates the case where $x \sqsubseteq y \sqsubseteq z$ for artifacts x, y and z. In this example x is a PDF standard, y is a document that uses the PDF standard and z is an email with document y as an attachment. The two creation times in figure represent the earliest creation time (ECT) and latest creation time (LCT) of document y. In particular, the earliest creation time is represented by the curve from t_0 to t_4 and the latest creation time is represented by the curve from t_5 to t_9.

The curve that connects the earliest creation time to the latest creation time represents the window when document y was created; it spans the graph from t_0 to t_9. The edges of the creation window graph are drawn to coincide with the left edge of the creation window of x and the right edge of the creation window of z. The graph is offset slightly from the edges to show that there are two graphs that follow the same path. Once again, the graphs do not purport to present probability density functions indicating the probability that document y was created at some time t. (Had the graphs in figure been probability density functions, the area under all three graphs would have been equal to 1.) Indeed, there is no basis to suggest that the edges of the creation windows of x or z depict accurate probabilities. In addition, given the specific scenario, the width of the creation window of x is expected to be significantly wider than the creation window of z.

The graph should be read as follows. There is a time period at the left of the creation window of document y, t_0 to t_2 or earlier, where unusual circumstances would have made the creation of y possible, Similarly, there is a time period at the right of the creation window, t_7 to t_9 or later, where unusual conditions would have made the creation of y possible. The flat line at the top of the creation window from t_2 to t_7 indicates that this period was the most likely period during which document y was created in the sense that no special conditions need to be assumed. The line is flat to indicate that the available evidence does not indicate any particular time in the period as a more likely point at which document y was created compared with other times. However, this does not mean that the probability that the document was created at any time over the period is equal. Given a specific artifact, the notion of probability is meaningless. The artifact was created at some specific time and probability cannot be used to compute the time.

Often a question about the creation time of a document will not be about the exact time at which the document was created, but about the relative ordering of events. In the case of a last will and testament, the question would be whether the document was created before the individual died or was incapacitated. If the creation time clearly precedes or follows the event of interest, the question can be answered without further consideration. When the creation window overlaps with the event of interest in one of the areas where the "likelihood" that the document was created is not at a maximum, the question to be asked is again not about probabilities, but about whether the special conditions that would have enabled creation during that period were present. With knowledge about the applicability of special conditions, it may be possible to reach a qualified conclusion about the relative order of document creation and an event of interest.

Documents often depend on the creation of multiple artifacts, such as the file format and character code used. In such cases, an artifact that was created later would generally be preferred because it provides a better estimate of the earliest creation time of the document. Generally, the earliest possible latest creation time would be preferred. However, special circumstances may apply that may not be based on the latest earliest creation time or the earliest latest creation time. An example is when greater confidence may be ascribed to an earliest creation time or latest creation time that does not lead to the shortest possible document creation window. Trading confidence for precision should always be considered.

8   Conclusions

This chapter has discussed techniques that may be used to determine the age of digital documents. Two principles were introduced a basis for determining document age, the principle of inclusion and the principle of replication. The principles are employed to determine temporal creation windows for documents, in a manner that makes it possible to convey the confidence within the windows. For most digital documents, the creation windows determined between various earliest creation times and latest creation times are rather wide. However, wide windows may be useful, especially when the windows exclude the purported creation times of the documents.

Several issues related to confidence with which conclusions could be reached were raised. They include the number of document attributes that confirm a version, the certainty with which the age of any containing documents may be determined, the extent to which certain information is replicated, and, potentially, attributes of the author of a document according to litigant's versions. This would constitute a narrative certainty instead of a statistical certainty, but statistical certainties are unattainable in most branches of forensic science. Nevertheless, the presented approach provides a much clearer structure to express certainty than is typically possible in digital forensics. Further research is needed to develop mechanisms that can succinctly express certainty.

The ability to date documents has been shown to be useful in the legal context. As born-digital documents replace other documents, the ability to determine their age would be important. Further research is necessary to determine the extent to which the proposed approach would meet this need. It is possible to determine dates more precisely, for example, by using metadata. However, care should be taken not to choose precision at the cost of confidence.

References

1. Adobe Systems, *PDF Reference, Second Edition, Adobe Portable Document Format Version 1.3*, Addison-Wesley, Boston, Massachusetts, 2000.
2. Adobe Systems, *PDF Reference, Third Edition, Adobe Portable Document Format Version 1.4*, Addison-Wesley, Boston, Massachusetts, 2001.

3. Adobe Systems, *PDF Reference, Third Edition, Adobe Portable Document Format Version 1.5*, Addison-Wesley, Boston, Massachusetts, 2003.
4. Adobe Systems, *PDF Reference, Fifth Edition, Adobe Portable Document Format Version 1.6*, San Jose, California, 2004.
5. Adobe Systems, *PDF Reference Sixth Edition, Adobe Portable Document Format Version 1.7*, San Jose, California, 2008.
6. American Standards Association, American Standard Code for Information Interchange, Standard X3.4-1963, Washington, DC, 1963.
7. A. Aotes, Navigating the PDF/A Standard: A Case Study of Theses in the University of Oxford's Institutional Repository, M.S. Thesis, School of Information Sciences, University of Illinois at Urbana-Champaign, Urbana, Illinois, 2018.
8. A. Bahjat and J. Jones, Deleted file fragment dating by analysis of allocated neighbors, *Digital Investigation*, vol. 28(S), pp. S60–S67, 2019.
9. A. Bahjat and J. Jones, File allocation chronology and its impact on digital forensics, *Proceedings of the Thirteenth Annual IEEE Computing and Communication Workshop and Conference*, pp. 612–618, 2023.
10. R. Bangia, *Multimedia and Web Technology*, Firewall Media, New Delhi, India, 2004.
11. T. Bienz and R. Cohn, *Portable Document Format Reference Manual*, Addison-Wesley, Reading, Massachusetts, 1993.
12. T. Bienz, R. Cohn, and J. Meehan, *Portable Document Format Reference Manual, Version 1.1*, Adobe Systems, San Jose, California, 1996.
13. T. Bienz, R. Cohn and J. Meehan, *Portable Document Format Reference Manual, Version 1.2*, Adobe Systems, San Jose, California, 1996.
14. R. Brunelle and K. Crawford, *Advances in the Forensic Analysis and Dating of Writing Ink*, Charles C. Thomas, Springfield, Illinois, 2003.
15. F. Buchholz and E. Spafford, On the role of filesystem metadata in digital forensics, *Digital Investigation*, vol. 1(4), pp. 298–309, 2004.
16. A. Cantu, A sketch of analytical methods for document dating, Part I; The static approach: Determining age independent analytical profiles, *International Journal of Forensic Document Examiners*, vol. 1(1), pp. 40–50, 1995.
17. A. Cantu, A sketch of analytical methods for document dating, Part II; The dynamic approach: Determining age dependent analytical profiles, *International Journal of Forensic Document Examiners*, vol. 2(3), pp. 192–208, 1996.
18. E. Casey, *Digital Evidence and Computer Crime*, Elsevier, London, United Kingdom, 2011.
19. E. Casey, Digital stratigraphy: Contextual analysis of filesystem traces in forensic science, *Journal of Forensic Sciences*, vol. 63(5), pp. 1383–1391, 2018.
20. K. Chow, F. Law, M. Kwan and P. Lai, The rules of time in an NTFS filesystem, *Proceedings of the Second International Workshop on Systematic Approaches to Digital Forensic Engineering*, pp. 71–85, 2007.
21. F. Cohen, *Digital Forensic Evidence Examination*, Fred Cohen and Associates, Livermore, California, 2012.
22. X. Ding and H. Zou, Reliable time based forensics in NTFS, poster presented at the *Twenty-Sixth Annual Computer Security Applications Conference*, 2010.
23. England and Wales High Court (Chancery Division), Patel v Patel, Case no. 133, London, United Kingdom, February 10, 2017.
24. England and Wales High Court (Chancery Division), Yashwant Dahyabhai Patel v Girish Dahyabhai Patel and Others, Case no. 1588, London, United Kingdom, May 26, 2017.

25. Google, Google Workspace Status Dashboard, Mountain View, California (`www.google.com/appsstatus/dashboard/summary`), 2024.

26. R. Harris, *Selling Hitler*, Pantheon Books, New York, 1986.

27. O. Hilton, *Scientific Examination of Questioned Documents, Revised Edition*, Routledge and Littlefield, Lanham, Maryland, 1992.

28. S. Ho, D. Kao and W. Wu, Following the breadcrumbs: Timestamp pattern identification for cloud forensics, *Digital Investigation*, vol. 24, pp. 79–94, 2018.

29. International Organization for Standardization, ISO 32000-2:2017, Document Management – Portable Document Format, Part 2: PDF 2.0, Geneva, Switzerland, 2017.

30. International Organization for Standardization, ISO 32000-2:2020, Document Management – Portable Document Format, Part 2: PDF 2.0, Geneva, Switzerland, 2020.

31. N. Kapoor, P. Sulke, R. Shukla, R. Kakad, P. Pardeshi and A. Badiye, Forensic analytical approaches to the dating of documents: An overview, *Microchemical Journal*, vol. 170, article no. 106722, 2021.

32. R. Koen and M. Olivier, The use of file timestamps in digital forensics, in *Proceedings of the ISSA 2008 Innovative Minds Conference*, H. Venter, M. Eloff, J. Eloff and L. Labuschagne (Eds.), pp. 133–148, 2008.

33. A. Mohamed and C. Khalid, Detection of timestamp tampering in NTFS using machine learning, *Procedia Computer Science*, vol. 160, pp. 778–784, 2019.

34. M. Olivier, Digital forensics and the big data deluge – Some concerns based on Ramsey theory, in *Advances in Digital Forensics XVI*, G. Peterson and S. Shenoi (Eds.), Springer, Cham, Switzerland, pp. 3–23, 2020.

35. A. Osborn, *Questioned Documents: A Study of Questioned Documents with an Outline of Methods by Which the Facts May be Discovered and Shown*, Lawyers' Cooperative Publishing Company, Rochester, New York, 1910.

36. D. Palmbach and F. Breitinger, Artifacts for detecting timestamp manipulation in NTFS on Windows and their reliability, *Forensic Science International: Digital Investigation*, vol. 32(S), article no. 300920, 2020.

37. J. Peters, Gmail had two outages this week that delayed emails, *The Verge*, December 1, 2023.

38. M. Peyravian, A. Roginsky and A. Kshemkalyani, On probabilities of hash value matches, *Computers and Security*, vol. 17(2), pp. 171–176, 1998.

39. H. Pieterse, M. Olivier and R. van Heerden, Playing hide-and-seek: Detecting the manipulation of Android timestamps, in *Proceedings of the Fourteenth Information Security for South Africa Conference*, H. Venter, M. Loock, M. Coetzee, M. Eloff and S. Flowerday (Eds.), 2015.

40. R. Pike and K. Thompson, Hello world, *Proceedings of the USENIX Winter 1993 Conference Proceedings*, pp. 43–50, 1993.

41. K. Rani and C. Sharma, Tampering detection of distributed databases using blockchain technology, *Proceedings of the Twelfth International Conference on Contemporary Computing*, 2019.

42. D. Spennemann and R. Spennemann, Establishing genealogies of born digital content: The suitability of revision identifier (RSID) numbers in MS Word for forensic enquiry, *Publications*, vol. 11(3), article no. 35, 2023.

43. Supreme Court of Appeal, Van der Merwe v Master of the High Court and Another, Case no. 605/09, Bloemfontein, South Africa, September 6, 2010.

Ensuring the Privacy of Digital Forensic Reports Using Searchable Symmetric Encryption

Aritro Sengupta, Pankaj Kumar, and Arun Kumar Sahani

Ministry of Electronics and Information Technology, New Delhi, India
`aritro.sengupta@meity.gov.in`

Abstract. Suspects in criminal investigations invariably leave digital evidence of their nefarious activities. Digital forensic professionals gather evidence from multiple platforms and present their theories and findings in digital forensic reports. The reports, which are typically not secured, are submitted to the concerned agencies and courts of law, potentially infringing on the privacy of defendants and victims. Specifically, the reports and the accompanying evidence can be viewed by individuals in the investigative and judicial chains without the consent of defendants and victims.

This chapter describes a digital forensic framework and implementation that secures forensic reports and supplementary digital evidence using searchable symmetric encryption. The framework restricts unauthorized individuals from accessing the digital evidence. The efficiency of search operations employed on the encrypted digital forensic reports is evaluated.

Keywords: Digital Forensic Reports · Privacy · Searchable Symmetric Encryption · Artifacts

1 Introduction

In this era of digitalization, digital devices are being used for myriad purposes. Recent surveys [6, 23] reveal that the latest digital gadgets and tangible solutions sell out quicker in digital markets than physical markets.

The ubiquitous use of digital devices in practically every aspect of modern life means that almost every crime tends to leave digital footprints. The digital devices vary from small smartwatches to high-end RAID-configured servers. After the relevant digital devices (exhibits) are seized, they are sent to a digital forensics laboratory for analysis.

The evidence produced is eventually proffered in a court of law. The evidence is in the form of reports with findings, replies to a formal questionnaire along with a copy of the original artifacts retrieved from the exhibits. No uniform protocol or standard exists for submitting evidence; these vary from country to country, even from jurisdiction to jurisdiction. However, a fundamental problem exists with regard to submitting a copy of the original artifacts – it is neither encrypted nor subject to access control limitations. As a result, the complete set of artifacts

E. Kurkowski and S. Shenoi (Eds.): DigitalForensics 2024, IFIP AICT 724, pp. 25–40, 2025.
https://doi.org/10.1007/978-3-031-71025-4_2

can be viewed by any individual in the investigative and judicial chains of a case. This can significantly infringe on the privacy of the defendants and victims in the case. For example, an insider could leak evidence or the database server that stores the evidence could be compromised by hackers resulting in sensitive information being posted on the Darknet [9, 19].

This chapter describes a digital forensic framework and implementation that secures digital forensic reports and supplementary digital evidence using searchable symmetric encryption. The proposed framework secures digital evidence while ensuring privacy.

2   Digital Forensic Frameworks

Several digital forensic frameworks have been proposed over more than two decades. The need for a common framework has been acknowledged at many forums. However, at this time, no framework is accepted globally. International Organization for Standardization (ISO) standards such as ISO 17025 and ISO 17043 have been promulgated for setting up digital forensics laboratories. ISO/IEC 27037:2012 provides guidelines for activities related to the handling of digital evidence. These include the identification, collection, acquisition and preservation of digital evidence.

Several articles discuss digital forensic frameworks and procedures [1, 7, 12, 21]. These frameworks were primarily specified by academicians and later implemented in the real-world by digital forensic practitioners. McKemmish [16] specified four stages in a digital forensic investigation framework – identification, preservation, analysis and presentation. This early framework incorporated non-technical aspects, but it was welcomed by the digital forensics community. McKemmish subsequently realized that some deficiencies existed in the framework, and based on input from other researchers, came up with Computer Forensic – Secure, Analyze, Present (CFSAP) model [17]. The modified framework is robust and technical in nature.

At the 2001 Digital Forensic Research Workshop (DFRWS), Palmer [20] proposed an alternative framework that is often referred to as the DFRWS model. The DFRWS model comprises six stages: identification, preservation, collection, examination, analysis and presentation. Reith et al. [22] subsequently discussed general procedures for segregating digital forensic framework stages that highlighted some of the shortcomings of the DFRWS model. This Abstract Digital Forensics Model (ADFM), which is considered to be an extended version of D-FRWS model, has nine stages – identification, preparation, approach strategy, preservation, collection, examination, analysis, presentation and evidence return. In 2003, Carrier and Spafford [3] specified a model based on crime scene investigations. Their model has five phases – readiness, deployment, physical crime scene investigation, digital crime scene investigation and review.

New frameworks have being proposed to keep up with the latest technologies such as the cloud and Internet of Things [15]. The stages are similar in broad

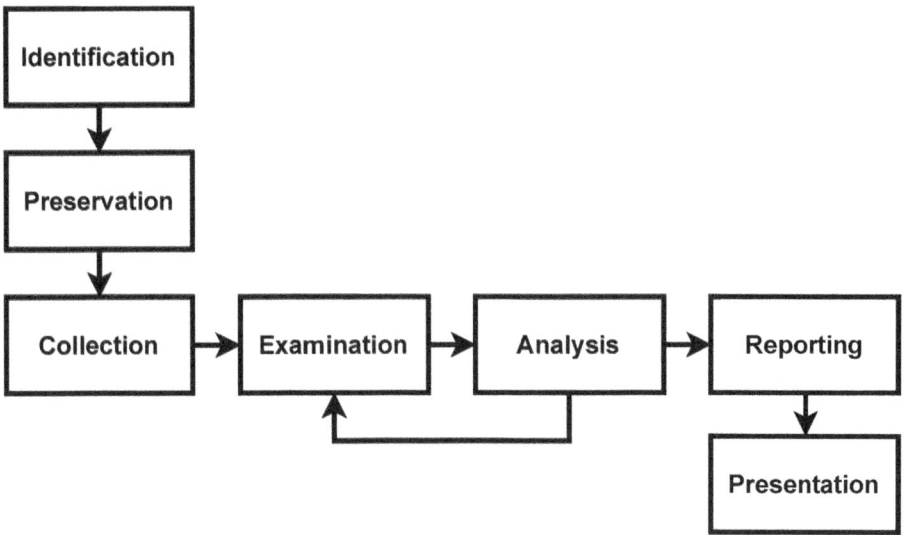

Fig. 1. Digital forensic framework stages.

terms to the stages in the other frameworks, but differences exist at the low level to accommodate technological advancements.

Figure 1 shows the digital forensic framework considered in this work. It comprises seven stages:

- **Identification:** This stage establishes the probable direction of digital forensic analysis. The locations and formats of the digital exhibits are identified. This eliminates any confusion regarding the locations of exhibits that potentially contain digital data. The stage is important because it is at the onset of a digital forensic investigation. If exhibits are not identified at the beginning, potential evidence they contain may not be introduced at a later date.
  Identification is performed at the physical and virtual levels. Physical identification refers to evidence in a tangible form whereas virtual identification refers to evidence in a logical form. The identification stage may not be relevant if exhibits have already been seized by law enforcement.
- **Preservation:** This stage focuses on documentation, chain of custody and maintaining the integrity of the seized digital exhibits. This stage must be executed meticulously because a mishap may result in the integrity and documentation of the digital exhibits being questioned. Such a situation can result in the forensic analysis process being disputed in court.
- **Collection:** This stage deals with the acquisition of digital exhibits. A data acquisition can be live or dead (static). The decision to conduct a live or dead acquisition depends on parameters such as port type, operating system and storage media pertaining to digital exhibits. A live acquisition is typically

performed on RAID-based storage media because, while static acquisition of each RAID disk is possible, the individual disk images may not enable the reconstruction of the original RAID system. In the case of critical servers that operate continuously, it may not be possible to seize the servers; therefore, their data must be acquired live. When acquiring data, the integrity of the original digital exhibits and evidence copy must be verified using hash algorithms such as MD5 or SHA-1. This helps achieve legal tenability in court [4, 5, 10, 11].

– **Examination:** This stage deals with the extraction and viewing of relevant data from the digital exhibits and making them available for analysis. These tasks should be conducted in a controlled environment, ideally in a digital forensics laboratory. During this stage, a digital forensic practitioner identifies potential digital data in conventional and unconventional spaces. A variety of tools and techniques are used to find visible data, hidden data and deleted data, and extract them in human-readable form. The extracted data is typically in a structured format along with metadata and hash values.

– **Analysis:** This stage deals with the reconstruction of digital data after analyzing the results of the examination stage. The analysis stage involves tasks such as root cause analysis, static analysis, dynamic analysis, query-based analysis and metadata analysis.

After analyzing the artifacts, a digital forensic practitioner is able to reconstruct the sequence of events in a timeline, create a hypothesis of the case, make conclusions about activities, link the artifacts to users or events that triggered the activities, and import content for a report. This stage is iterative and the practitioner may analyze the digital evidence repeatedly until concrete conclusions are reached for presentation in a court of law.

– **Reporting:** This stage involves the compilation of a report based on the findings in the analysis stage. Findings based on documented evidence that satisfy legal questionnaires will be legally tenable. The report must contain details of all the digital exhibits; no digital exhibit should be omitted even if it is not considered in the previous stages. The report is often written in a local language without too many technical details so that it is understandable by non-technical persons. The report must be simple, to the point and unambiguous.

– **Presentation:** This stage involves the formal presentation of the report with findings along with a copy of the original digital evidence with hash values that verify integrity. The evidence copy is generally maintained on storage media. The report and evidence copy are submitted to a court of law as well as to other concerned entities such as law enforcement and auditing groups.

3   Significance of Reporting and Presentation

The reporting and presentation stages of the digital forensics framework are immensely relevant to this work. As mentioned above, the report and evidence copy are submitted to one or more concerned entities. For example, a person who is suspected of committing cyber fraud in India by luring victims to a fake donation website would be prosecuted under the Cybercrime Act (or Information Technology Act) as well as the Money Laundering Act. Thus, at least two agencies, the Cybercrime Department and the Money Laundering Department would be involved in the case. Accordingly, the report and evidence copy would be provided to each agency. In addition, the report and evidence copy would be submitted to a court of law.

Protocols for submitting and handling reports and evidence copies vary from jurisdiction to jurisdiction. However, the exposure of report and evidentiary details potentially infringe on the privacy of the defendants and victims [18]. In many countries, privacy is given the utmost importance [25] and agencies are reprimanded if any data is leaked.

The United Nations recognizes privacy in its Universal Declaration of Human Rights [29]. Additionally, any failure to secure defendant or victim data violates the General Data Protection Regulation of the European Union and European Economic Area [14, 24, 26].

The following four scenarios cover situations where defendant or victim privacy requirements are violated:

- **Scenario 1:** The evidence copy containing artifacts is stored on a system that has already been compromised. The artifacts are exfiltrated.
- **Scenario 2:** Sensitive suspect information such as bank account numbers, salary statements and passwords in the evidence copy are leaked by law enforcement personnel involved in the case.
- **Scenario 3:** Personal information such as family photos and videos belonging to the defendants or victims that were collected, but are not relevant to the case, are leaked.
- **Scenario 4:** Identities of victims in the evidence copy are leaked.

4 Searchable Symmetric Encryption Framework

This section discusses the concept of searchable encryption, the proposed searchable symmetric encryption architecture, digital forensic reports with searchable symmetric encryption and the related algorithms.

4.1 Searchable Encryption

Boneh et al. [2] were the first to propose a searchable encryption scheme. The scheme, which employs public keys to encrypt data, is referred to as the public-key encryption with keyword search (PEKS) scheme. In this scheme, a user with a private key can search specific content and decrypt the content. However, the drawbacks with the asymmetric scheme are its computational costs, especially the time required for encryption, search and decryption.

Liu et al. [13] proposed a modified version of the scheme of Boneh and colleagues. The new scheme also uses public-key encryption, but it allows partial

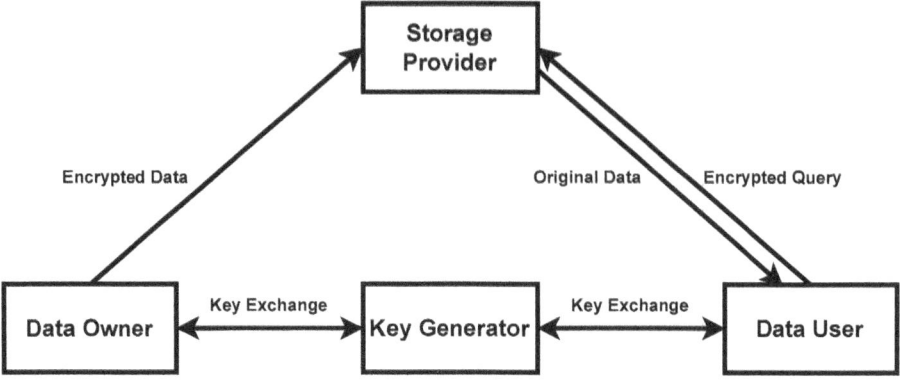

Fig. 2. Searchable symmetric encryption architecture.

decryption on the server that reduces the computational costs. Soon after, Tseng et al. [28] proposed the iPEKS scheme that leverages the results of previous searches to speed up the overall search time. However, the iPEKS scheme stores the previous search results in cache memory, which increases the storage overhead.

Song et al. [27] proposed a symmetric encryption scheme with linear search time. However, the scheme only supports fixed-length keyword searches and, as the number of documents increases, the scheme slows down heavily. Goh [8] formulated secure indexes that support searches in encrypted files.

4.2   Searchable Encryption Architecture

A searchable encryption framework can be implemented using asymmetric or symmetric algorithms. Regardless of the type of algorithm, the basic architecture of the searchable encryption scheme is the same.

Figure 2 presents the proposed searchable symmetric encryption architecture. The architecture has four basic entities:

– **Data Owner:** The data owner is the entity that owns the data and encrypts the data using encryption keys. The data owner encrypts metadata along with the data.
– **Data User:** The data user is the entity that submits search queries to the encrypted data to conduct a specific search. Multiple data users may have access to the encrypted data.
– **Storage Provider:** The storage provider may be a public/private cloud or local storage media where the encrypted data is stored. After receiving search queries, the storage provider searches the encrypted data and metadata using various algorithms. If the storage media is local, it should be supported by a third-party application capable of managing search queries.

- **Key Generator:** The key generator is a trusted third party. The data owner may assume the role of the key generator if privacy issues are of paramount importance.

4.3   Using Searchable Symmetric Encryption

After the examination stage, efforts in a digital forensics laboratory enter the analysis stage when artifacts such as audio and video documents, databases and photographs are retrieved from raw image/dump files along with their metadata. The artifacts along with their metadata are represented as a set of artifacts $A = \{A_1, A_2, ..., A_n\}$ that is referred to as the evidence copy. As discussed above, the distribution of an evidence copy without encryption or access control is very problematic because it provides opportunities for maliciously or accidentally violating defendant and victim privacy.

This section describes the use of searchable symmetric encryption to secure evidence copies. The proposed framework overcomes the shortcomings of previous frameworks while ensuring that authorized entities can search the encrypted evidence copies for case-related artifacts. The entities and modules that implement the framework are specified below.

Entities. The following entities are involved in the framework:

- **Digital Forensics Laboratory:** The digital forensics laboratory is the entity in which the examination, analysis, reporting and presentation of digital exhibits is performed. The forensics laboratory is the owner of the digital forensic report and issues the digital forensic report and evidence copy to authorized entities.
- **Agency:** An agency is an internal or external entity that is directly or indirectly involved in the case and requires access to the retrieved artifacts to validate the digital forensic report generated by the digital forensics laboratory. Agencies include law enforcement, judiciary entities, human rights bodies and non-governmental organizations. Agencies have authorized users that can access the report and evidence copy.
- **Evidence Copy:** The evidence copy comprises artifacts retrieved from digital exhibits submitted to the digital forensics laboratory for examination and analysis.
- **Artifacts:** Artifacts are digital files in the form of audio and video documents, databases, photographs, etc. that are retrieved from raw image/dump files along with their metadata. The retrieved artifacts and their metadata are represented as a set $A = \{A_1, A_2, ..., A_n\}$ referred to as the evidence copy.
- **Storage:** The retrieved artifacts and metadata are encrypted and maintained in storage at the digital forensics laboratory and at the concerned agencies. The storage could be local isolated media such as a hard disk or a remote private cloud server. In both instances, an application module residing in storage would implement the searchable symmetric encryption scheme and serve requests from authorized users.

Table 1. Index table.

Sequence Number	Artifact	Keywords	Hash Value
S_1	A_1	k_1, k_2, k_4, k_5	$h(A_1)$
S_2	A_2	k_1, k_3, k_4	$h(A_2)$
S_3	A_3	k_2, k_4, k_5	$h(A_3)$
S_4	A_4	k_1, k_3	$h(A_4)$

- **Keywords:** A keyword set $K = \{k_1, k_2, ..., k_m\}$ comprises unique keywords that are meaningful by themselves and contribute to the formation of the artifact set $A = \{A_1, A_2, ..., A_n\}$. A keyword could be a word in a natural language, timestamp, filename, filetype, etc. The artifacts are organized using an indexing engine offered by a forensic analysis tool. Artifacts are scanned thoroughly to fetch keywords that are input to an index table for further processing.
- **Index Table:** An index table maps individual artifacts to the keywords fetched from them. The number of entries in an index table is equal to the number of artifacts. Each index table entry comprises a unique sequence number S_i, artifact A_i, list of keywords $k_j \in K$ fetched from artifact A_i and the hash value of artifact A_i. Table 1 shows an example with four artifacts and five unique keywords.

Table 2. Reverse index table.

Keyword	Artifact
k_1	A_1
k_1	A_2
k_1	A_4
k_2	A_1
k_2	A_3
k_3	A_2
k_3	A_4
k_4	A_1
k_4	A_2
k_4	A_3
k_5	A_1
k_5	A_3

- **Reverse Index Table:** A reverse index table is created from the index table. The reverse index table has an entry for each keyword. The table maps individual keywords to the artifacts in which they are found. Table 2 shows the reverse index table created from the index table in Table 1.

- **Encrypted Cumulative Index Table:** The encrypted cumulative index table is created using selected parameters from the index table and reverse index table. The values are encrypted using a symmetric key. Details about the table are provided in the next section.
- **Token:** A token is an encrypted search query generated by an authorized user who has access to the storage. The search query is generated by the token generator using keywords entered by the user.
- **Keys:** Two keys, SK_1 and SK_2, are employed. One is used to encrypt and decrypt keywords in the index table and the other is used to encrypt and decrypt individual artifacts.
- **Encryption and Decryption Algorithms:** Encryption (EC) and decryption (DC) algorithms are used for encrypting and decrypting operations, respectively. Since a symmetric cryptosystem is employed, encryption and decryption are performed using the same key.

Modules. The following modules implement the proposed framework:

- **Key Generator:** The key generator supplies the secret keys. The random key generator implementation should be secure and devoid of backdoors. The digital forensics laboratory controls the key generator and only uses it when digital forensic reports are created. Two secret key SK_1 and SK_2 are generated. SK_1 is used to encrypt and decrypt keywords in the index table whereas SK_2 is used to encrypt and decrypt individual artifacts. The secret keys are unique to a case.
- **Preprocessing:** After the artifacts are recovered from the exhibits, a digital forensic practitioner indexes the keywords associated with each artifact and creates an index table. The practitioner may employ indexing refinement options such as extracting keywords from slack space, defining known keyword patterns, fetching text from graphic files using optical character recognition (OCR) and extracting steganographically-hidden text. The refinement options depend on the functionality provided by the available digital forensic retrieval and analysis tools.

  After indexing is completed, each entry in the index table is expressed as a tuple $(S_i, A_i, k_j \subseteq K, h(A_i))$ where S_i is a sequence number, A_i is an artifact, k_j denotes the keywords mapped to artifact A_i and $h(A_i)$ is the hash of artifact A_i. A total of n tuples are generated where n is the number of artifacts recovered.

  A reverse index table is generated after the index table is created. Each entry in the table has a keyword that is mapped to the artifacts that contain it. An entry is expressed as a tuple (k_i, A_j) where k_i is the keyword and A_j is an artifact containing keyword k_i.
- **Encrypted Cumulative Index Table Generator:** The encrypted cumulative index table is created from the index table and reverse index table. The sequence number and artifact attributes of the index table and keyword attribute of the reverse index table are employed. Each keyword k_i is concatenated with the sequence number S_j of each artifact A_j in which keyword

Table 3. Encrypted cumulative index table.

Encrypted Keyword	Encrypted Artifact	Hash Value
$EC_{SK_1}(k_1\|S_1)$	$EC_{(SK_2\|S_1)}(A_1)$	$h(A_1)$
$EC_{SK_1}(k_1\|S_2)$	$EC_{(SK_2\|S_2)}(A_2)$	$h(A_2)$
$EC_{SK_1}(k_1\|S_4)$	$EC_{(SK_2\|S_4)}(A_4)$	$h(A_4)$
$EC_{SK_1}(k_2\|S_1)$	$EC_{(SK_2\|S_1)}(A_1)$	$h(A_1)$
$EC_{SK_1}(k_2\|S_3)$	$EC_{(SK_2\|S_3)}(A_3)$	$h(A_3)$
$EC_{SK_1}(k_3\|S_2)$	$EC_{(SK_2\|S_2)}(A_2)$	$h(A_2)$
$EC_{SK_1}(k_3\|S_4)$	$EC_{(SK_2\|S_4)}(A_4)$	$h(A_4)$
$EC_{SK_1}(k_4\|S_1)$	$EC_{(SK_2\|S_1)}(A_1)$	$h(A_1)$
$EC_{SK_1}(k_4\|S_2)$	$EC_{(SK_2\|S_2)}(A_2)$	$h(A_2)$
$EC_{SK_1}(k_4\|S_3)$	$EC_{(SK_2\|S_3)}(A_3)$	$h(A_3)$
$EC_{SK_1}(k_5\|S_1)$	$EC_{(SK_2\|S_1)}(A_1)$	$h(A_1)$
$EC_{SK_1}(k_5\|S_3)$	$EC_{(SK_2\|S_3)}(A_3)$	$h(A_3)$

k_i is found. The concatenated string encrypted using the secret key SK_1 is denoted as $EC_{SK_1}(k_i\|S_j)$. This value is stored in the first column of the encrypted cumulative index table. The second column stores the artifact A_j encrypted with $(SK_2\|S_j)$, which is denoted as $EC_{(SK_2\|S_j)}(A_j)$. The third column stores the hash of artifact A_j.

Table 3 shows an encrypted cumulative index table generated from the index table and reverse index table shown in Tables 1 and 2, respectively.

- **Token Generator:** An authorized user intending to search the evidence copy using keywords sends an encrypted search query. The encrypted search query corresponds to a token that is generated by the token generator. If the user submits a keyword k_a to be searched, the token generator produces n tokens – $EC_{SK_1}(k_a\|S_1), EC_{SK_1}(k_a\|S_2), ..., EC_{SK_1}(k_a\|S_n)$, where n is the total number of artifacts.

- **Decryption:** The decryption module is assigned the secret key SK_2. In addition to the key SK_2, the correct sequence number S_b provided by the token generator is required to decrypt an artifact. Each token generated by the token generator is matched individually to the encrypted cumulative index table. For each match, say $EC_{SK_1}(k_a\|S_b)$, the correct sequence number S_b is obtained and the value in the adjacent column, which is $EC_{(SK_2\|S_b)}(A_b)$, is decrypted using the secret key combination $SK_2\|S_b$. S_b is obtained by matching whereas SK_2 is embedded in the decryption module.

4.4   Framework Algorithms

Algorithms 1 and 2 specify the implementation of the proposed searchable symmetric encryption framework. Algorithm 1 specifies the steps performed at the digital forensics laboratory. Algorithm 2 specifies the steps performed at a concerned agency.

Algorithm 1: Steps performed at the digital forensics laboratory.

Extract all artifacts from the seized exhibits.

Process the artifacts using the preprocessing module and create an index table and reverse index table.

Generate secret keys using the random key generator module.

Create an encrypted cumulative index table using the encrypted cumulative index table generator module.

Add the encrypted cumulative index table to the data storage facility. This corresponds to the digital evidence copy.

Provide the physical report along with the digital evidence copy to a concerned agency.

Provide the secret key SK_1 to the concerned agency preferably in physical form.

Algorithm 2: Steps performed at a concerned agency.

Prepare a list of keywords to be searched in the encrypted content.

For each keyword, generate tokens using the token generator module and secret key SK_1.

Match the tokens in the encrypted cumulative index table.

For each match, find the secret key combination and decrypt the artifacts using the decryption module.

---

5   Experimental Results

To demonstrate the performance of the searchable symmetric encryption scheme, a Java application was created that employed a MySQL database backend using JDBC. The portable Setup.exe file of the application is executed by a user who intends to employ the scheme.

An experiment was conducted after the forensic analysis of a 16 GB USB drive. AES-256 was employed as the symmetric cryptosystem. The encrypted cumulative index table data.enc was created using the AES-256 key provided by the random key generator.

In a real-world scenario, the data.enc and Setup.exe files would be passed to a concerned agency. Figure 3 shows screenshots of the data.enc and Setup.exe files. One of the secret keys, say SK_1, would also be provided to the concerned agency.

In the experiment, the portable Setup.exe application with a graphical user interface was executed. As shown in Figure 4, the data.enc and secret key SK_1 are submitted along with the keyword dog and the location F:\Case\Files for storing all the artifacts with the keyword.

The application, which has the secret key SK_2 embedded, can generate search tokens based on the search keywords. Note that the current implementation is a prototype and may be augmented with custom mechanisms such as one that obfuscates secret keys instead of embedding them in the application.

The efficiency of the searchable symmetric encryption scheme was compared with the indexing outputs of a popular forensic analysis software application.

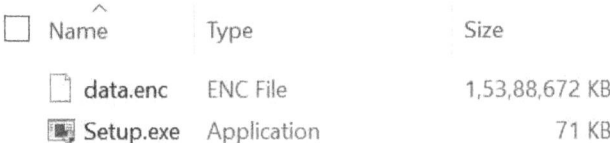

Fig. 3. File screenshots.

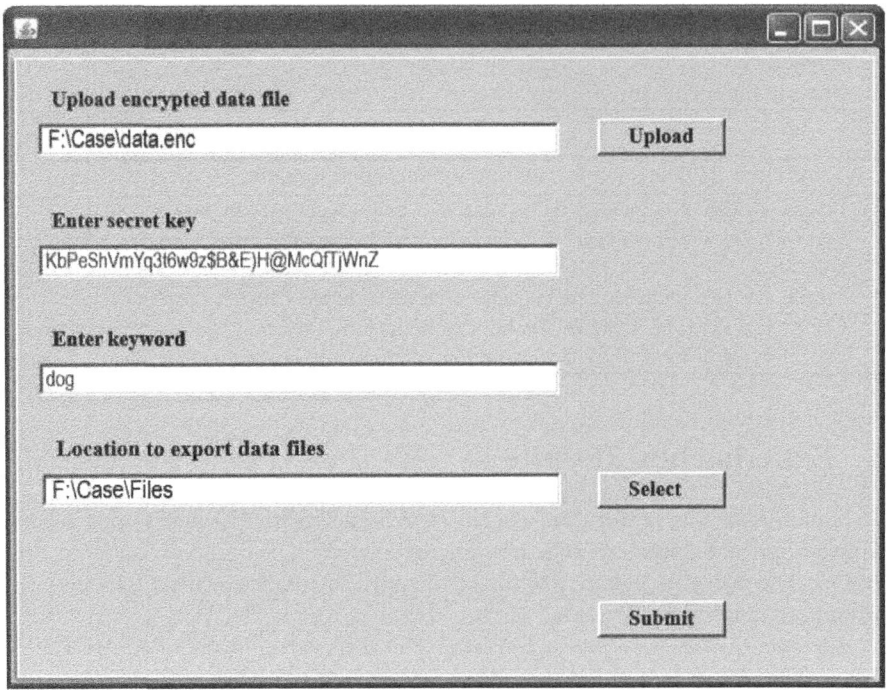

Fig. 4. Graphical user interface screenshot.

In the experiment, the Java application was employed to index and search the contents of a 500 GB hard disk image. The numbers of results yielded by all the keywords were recorded along with the time required to perform search operations. The same 500 GB hard disk image was imported to Autopsy (v. 4.14.0) and the same keywords were searched. The numbers of results and time required were recorded.

Table 4 shows the results of the comparisons. Autopsy and the proposed framework yielded the same number of results for the submitted keywords. The proposed framework required more time than Autopsy to conduct searches. But this is expected due to the overhead involved in decrypting the encrypted cumulative index table. Nevertheless, the additional time is more than acceptable given that the privacy of evidence is maintained.

Table 4. Performance comparison.

Keyword	Autopsy Results	Time	Framework Results	Time
.jpeg	419	3.4 s	419	13.0 s
10-01-20	24	0.9 s	24	2.6 s
.exe	4	0.2 s	4	1.5 s
abc	17	1.3 s	17	3.1 s
âĂŰxyzâĂİ	12	1.1 s	12	2.8 s

6 Evaluation

This section discusses the performance of the proposed framework with regard to outsider and insider attacks, as well as the important security goals of confidentiality, integrity and authenticity.

Outsider Attacks. A typical scenario involves a malicious outsider gaining access to the server containing the evidence copy, exfiltrating sensitive information and posting it on the Internet. If the evidence copy is not encrypted, the privacy violations would be grave.

In the proposed framework, the evidence copy is encrypted. Without the key, a malicious outsider who gains access to the server would not obtain any meaningful information.

In the worst case, assume that the secret key SK_2 embedded in the application program is not obfuscated and the malicious outsider obtains the key SK_2 via reverse engineering. The malicious outsider would still be unbale to decrypt $EC_{(SK_2||S_j)}(A_j)$ and obtain artifact A_j because the value of S_j is not known. In fact, S_j can only be recovered if the secret key SK_1 and valid keyword k_i present in artifact A_j are known. The secret key SK_1 is given to agencies in physical form whereas the keywords in A_j are listed in the physical report. Thus, the design ensures that the evidence copy is secure from malicious outsider attacks.

Insider Attack. A typical scenario involves a malicious individual at a concerned agency attempting to access the evidence copy and exfiltrate sensitive information. In the proposed framework, the concerned agency only has access to the secret key SK_1, physical report and encrypted evidence copy. Using the above information, the concerned agency can only decrypt the artifacts whose keywords are known. Without a valid keyword k_i, the malicious insider would be unable to decrypt $EC_{(SK_2||S_j)}(A_j)$ and obtain artifact A_j. Thus, the design ensures that the evidence copy is secure from malicious insider attacks.

Confidentiality. The primary goal of this work is to ensure defendant and victim privacy in digital forensic reports. In other words, a digital forensic report should be confidential. In the proposed framework, the digital evidence copy is secured using symmetric encryption. Only the digital forensics laboratory and concerned agencies would have access to the secret keys used to encrypt the digital evidence copy. Without the secret keys and the physical report, no entity could decrypt the digital evidence copy. Thus, the confidentiality of the evidence copy is maintained.

Integrity. The admissibility of a digital forensic report depends heavily on the integrity of the artifacts. A court of law must verify the integrity of the artifacts. In the proposed framework, the hash values of all the artifacts are provided along with the evidence copy, enabling the integrity of the artifacts to be verified at any time. Thus, the integrity of the evidence copy is maintained.

Authenticity. An item is authentic if it was created by a trusted entity and has not been modified. A digital forensic report is created and disseminated by a trusted digital forensics laboratory in physical form whereas the evidence copy is provided in a digital format. The use of secret keys generated by a random key generator to encrypt the evidence copy ensures that the source of the evidence copy is a trusted party. Digital signatures are easily incorporated in the proposed framework to enhance trust and authenticity.

7   Conclusions

Digital forensic reports and the accompanying evidence are routinely submitted to the concerned agencies and courts of law without strong security protections. This provides individuals in the investigative and judicial chains with open access to sensitive information about defendants and victims, potentially infringing on their privacy. The digital forensic framework and implementation described in this chapter secures forensic reports and supplementary digital evidence using searchable symmetric encryption. Due to the security implementation, the proposed framework requires more time than conventional digital forensic tools to conduct searches. However, the additional time is more than acceptable given that the framework is resistant to outsider and insider attacks on privacy, and also satisfies the important security goals of confidentiality, integrity and authenticity.

References

1. J. Beckett and J. Slay, Digital forensics: Validation and verification in a dynamic work environment, *Proceedings of the Fortieth Annual Hawaii International Conference on System Sciences*, pp. 266a–266a, 2007.
2. D. Boneh, G. Di Crescenzo, R. Ostrovsky and G. Persiano, Public key encryption with keyword search, in *Advances in Cryptology – EUROCRYPT 2004: Proceedings of the International Conference on the Theory and Applications of Cryptographic Techniques*, C. Cachin and J. Camenisch (Eds.), Springer, Berlin Heidelberg, Germany, pp. 506–522, 2004.

3. B. Carrier and E. Spafford, Getting physical with the digital investigation process, *International Journal of Digital Evidence*, vol. 2(2), 2003.
4. E. Casey, *Digital Evidence and Computer Crime*, Elsevier, London, United Kingdom, 2011.
5. F. Cohen, Column: Putting the science in digital forensics, *Journal of Digital Forensics, Security and Law*, vol. 6(1), article no. 1, 2011.
6. M. Dahiya, Study on e-commerce and its impacts on market and retailers in India, *Advances in Computational Sciences and Technology*, vol. 10(5), pp. 1495–1500, 2017.
7. G. Fenu and F. Solinas, Computer forensics investigation: An approach to evidence in cyberspace, *Proceedings of the Second International Conference on Cyber Security, Cyber Peacefare and Digital Forensics*, pp. 4–6, 2013.
8. E. Goh, Secure Indexes, *Cryptology ePrint Archive*, paper no. 2003/216 (`eprint.iacr.org/2003/216`), 2003.
9. A. Greenberg, Hack brief: Anonymous stole and leaked a megatrove of police documents, *Wired*, July 22, 2020.
10. K. Jones, R. Bejtlich and C. Rose, *Real Digital Forensics: Computer Security and Incident Response*, Addison-Wesley Professional, Upper Saddle River, New Jersey, 2005.
11. M. Kohn, M. Eloff and J. Eloff, Integrated digital forensic process model, *Computers and Security*, vol. 38, pp. 103–115, 2013.
12. I. Lin, H. Yang, G. Gu and A. Lin, A study of information and communication security forensic technology capability in Taiwan, *Proceedings of the Thirty-Seventh International Carnahan Conference on Security Technology*, pp. 386–393, 2003.
13. Q. Liu, G. Wang and J. Wu, Secure and privacy preserving keyword searching for cloud storage services, *Journal of Network and Computer Applications*, vol. 35(3), pp. 927–933, 2012.
14. M. Losavio, K. Chow, A. Koltay and J. James, The Internet of Things and the Smart City: Legal challenges with digital forensics, privacy and security, *Security and Privacy*, vol. 1(3), article no. e23, 2018.
15. B. Martini and K. Choo, An integrated conceptual digital forensic framework for cloud computing, *Digital Investigation*, vol. 9(2), pp. 71–80, 2012.
16. R. McKemmish, What is forensic computing? *Trends and Issues in Crime and Criminal Justice*, no. 118, 2002.
17. G. Mohay, A. Anderson, B. Collie, O. de Vel and R. McKemmish, *Computer and Intrusion Forensics*, Artech House, Norwood, Massachusetts, 2003.
18. A. Nieto, R. Rios, J. Lopez, W. Ren, L. Wang, K. Choo and F. Xhafa, *Privacy-Aware Digital Forensics*, Institute of Engineering and Technology, London, United Kingdom, 2019.
19. D. Olenick, Police data leaked: A sign of the times? *BankInfoSecurity* (`www.bankinfosecurity.com/police-data-leaked-sign-times-a-14488`), June 23, 2020.
20. G. Palmer, A Road Map for Digital Forensic Research, DFRWS Technical Report, DTR-T001-01 Final, Air Force Research Laboratory, Rome, New York, 2001.
21. L. Pan and L. Batten, Reproducibility of digital evidence in forensic investigations, *Proceedings of the Digital Forensic Research Workshop*, 2005.
22. M. Reith, C. Carr and G. Gunsch, An examination of digital forensic models, *International Journal of Digital Evidence*, vol. 1(3), 2002.
23. P. Rita, T. Oliveira and A. Farisa, The impact of e-service quality and customer satisfaction on customer behavior in online shopping, *Heliyon*, vol. 5(10), article no. e026905, 2019.

24. L. Ryz and L. Grest, A new era in data protection, *Computer Fraud and Security*, vol. 2016(3), pp. 18–20, 2016.

25. D. Solove, *Understanding Privacy*, Harvard University Press, Cambridge, Massachusetts, 2008.

26. D. Solove and P. Schwartz, *Information Privacy Law*, Aspen Publishing, Frederick, Maryland, 2020.

27. D. Song, D. Wagner and A. Perrig, Practical techniques for searches on encrypted data, *Proceedings of the IEEE Symposium on Security and Privacy*, pp. 44–55, 2000.

28. F. Tseng, R. Chen and B. Lin, iPEKS: Fast and secure cloud data retrieval from public-key encryption with keyword search, *Proceedings of the Twelfth IEEE International Conference on Trust, Security and Privacy in Computing and Communications*, pp. 452–458, 2013.

29. United Nations, Universal Declaration of Human Rights, Geneva, Switzerland (`www.un.org/sites/un2.un.org/files/2021/03/udhr.pdf`), 1948.

Mobile Device Forensics

Forensic Analysis of Third-Party Cloud Software Development Kits for Android Apps

Chen Shi and Yong Guan

Iowa State University, Ames, Iowa, USA
guan@iastate.edu

Abstract. Android software development kits for cloud storage are commonly adopted by the app development community and countless apps from productivity tools to media-sharing platforms currently incorporate the kits. The popularity can be attributed to their ability to offer scalable and reliable cloud storage apps, reducing the need for on-device storage and ensuring data accessibility across devices. However, because the apps tend to store user information in the cloud, there are concerns about security risks and sensitive information leakage.

This chapter presents the results of a forensic analysis of 11 major Android cloud software development kits and 120 real-world apps that leverage the kits for data storage. The analysis revealed that 103 apps store user account information, including name, email, date of birth and profile picture, 77 apps access and store user media files and user preferences and settings in the cloud, and 12 apps track the last used times of other installed apps. Android software development kits for cloud storage are of great value in mobile device forensics because they support the extraction of diverse and novel types of evidence, including via uniform resource locators.

Keywords: Android Cloud Software Development Kit · Mobile App Forensics · Taint Analysis

1 Introduction

The massive growth in the Android market share has significantly increased the number of Android app developers [16]. In order to reduce development time and improve development efficiency, Android app developers integrate various third-party software development kits (SDKs) into their apps. The SDKs, which are developed by third-party service providers focused on advertising, data storage, social networks, maps and push notifications, etc., offer professional services that encapsulate complex logic implementations and request-response processes, rendering them easier for developers to use. As a result, third-party SDKs have become an essential part of the Android ecosystem.

However, third-party cloud SDKs pose privacy and security threats to Android users. Several studies have confirmed privacy leaks in third-party cloud SDKs [11, 25]. SDKs provided by Baidu and AirPush [3] have been identified

© IFIP International Federation for Information Processing 2025
Published by Springer Nature Switzerland AG 2025
E. Kurkowski and S. Shenoi (Eds.): DigitalForensics 2024, IFIP AICT 724, pp. 43–62, 2025.
https://doi.org/10.1007/978-3-031-71025-4_3

as having security vulnerabilities that enable software to secretly monitor users, upload sensitive information to remote servers and open backdoors on user devices. Unfortunately, the SDKs have been integrated in numerous Android apps, impacting more than 100 million Android device users. Some third-party cloud SDKs also have insecure implementations that increase the attack surfaces of their host apps. Even SDKs from reputable companies such as Facebook and Dropbox have been found to have serious security vulnerabilities. Attacks exploiting these vulnerabilities have resulted in the exfiltration of sensitive data to public sources, code injection, account hijacking and device connections to attacker-controlled accounts.

Clearly, it is important to understand the privacy and security implications of third-party Android SDKs. However, it is very difficult to conduct systematic analyses of third-party cloud SDKs. On one hand, only the latest versions are available on the official websites, but older versions of the SDKs are widely used across the Android ecosystem. On the other hand, different third-party cloud SDKs have different architectures, making it very challenging to design a single system for analyzing SDKs. Additionally, many third-party cloud SDKs place their critical code in native code stored as shared object (SO) files that significantly increase the reverse engineering effort.

This chapter describes a novel methodology for extracting forensic artifacts generated by Android cloud SDKs. The methodology, which involves static and dynamic analysis, is initiated upon receiving a suspect's mobile device. The apps installed on the device are identified and the device database is queried to identify the available evidence along with their associated uniform resource locators (URLs). Experimental results involving 120 real-world Android apps demonstrate the utility of the methodology.

2   Background

In the Android ecosystem, SDKs are made available by third-party service providers to support apps that provide advertising, push notification, image recognition and mobile payment services, among others. To enhance app development efficiency, developers integrate third-party SDKs into their projects to implement their functionality. The majority of third-party SDKs serve as clients for third-party services. When the SDKs are invoked, they connect to remote servers to provide their services.

2.1   Operating Mechanisms

This work focuses on third-party SDKs with network connectivity capabilities. SDK operating mechanisms are categorized into two types:

- **SDK Sending Requests to Remote Servers:** Figure 1 illustrates the operating mechanism of an SDK that sends requests to remote servers, for example, to provide advertising and push notification services. Because the

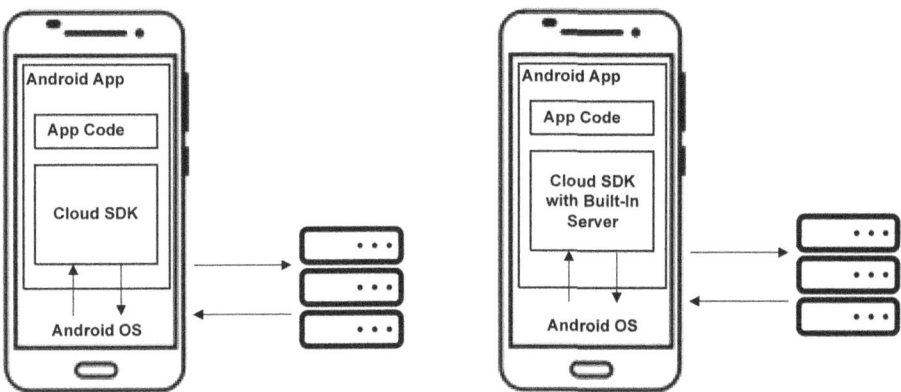

Fig. 1. Third-party cloud SDK without built-in server.

hypertext transfer protocol (HTTP) does not encrypt data during transmission, it cannot guarantee data privacy and integrity. By contrast, HTTPS (HTTP secure) is a network communications protocol used in secure connections over untrusted networks. It adds SSL/TLS security features to standard HTTP communications, effectively preventing eavesdropping and man-in-the-middle attacks. While the trend is to use HTTPS instead of HTTP, many third-party SDKs still use HTTP to establish network connections with cloud servers, posing significant security risks.

– **SDK Launching Local Services:** Some third-party SDKs set up local servers in host apps to enable SDK developers to monitor mobile devices in a controlled manner. Local servers can collect information such as the current device location, international mobile equipment identity (IMEI) and installation details. Remote servers can send requests and retrieve this information from local servers. Even remote installations and uninstallations can be achieved via communications with local services.
Figure 1 illustrates the working mechanism of an SDK that launches local services. While measures can be taken to ensure that the local server is controlled by the correct remote server, the communications channel may still be vulnerable to interception by an attacker intending to interact with the local server.

2.2   Motivation

Mobile app developers typically consider third-party SDKs as black boxes, focusing on their functionality and overlooking their internal security vulnerabilities and the forensic artifacts generated and stored. Clearly, using SDKs that store

```
POST http://android.clients.google.airpush.com/login
<...>
9: âĂȩâĂȩ82339 //Google logging ID
10: "âĂȩâĂȩ158âĂİ //Wi-Fi Mac Address
11: âĂİJâĂȩâĂȩ47265" //IMEI
12: "United States"
âĂȩ
16: "âĂȩâĂȩU5RE" //Hardware Serial Number
<âĂȩ>


HTTP/1.1 200 OK
Server: nginx/1.G.1
Date: 27 Aug 2023 10:23:34 GMT
Connection: keep-alive
http://android.clients.google.airpush.com/downloads/media/gallery.zip
<âĂȩ>
http://android.clients.google.airpush.com/content/sample.jpg
<âĂȩ>
```

Fig. 2. Airpush SDK request (top) and response data (bottom).

potentially sensitive data render the apps attractive attack targets. For example, if an SDK stores user account information and passwords in plaintext, all the projects that use the SDK would have the same risks of information leakage, providing attackers with unauthorized access to the core code of the apps. Third-party SDKs possess the same permissions as their host apps, which means that even if the core functionality of an app does not require certain permissions, the app must request the permissions needed by the SDK. Security vulnerabilities in SDKs can have significant impacts, affecting all the apps that include the SDKs.

Advertising SDK. Airpush is a mobile advertising platform SDK that developers have integrated in numerous Android apps. The official website announced that Airpush has reached 360 million smartphone users, with 71,042 mobile apps using the Airpush platform. Downloading documentation and SDK files from the official website is straightforward. Figure 2, created via a thorough analysis of the SDK files, provides an understanding of the operational mechanism of the SDK.

Since the Airpush SDK uses HTTP for communications with remote servers, a proxy server was set up to monitor data packet transmission. Request and response data in Figure 2 such as the IMEI and package name on the HTTP channel are visible in the request data packet; ad links and ad images are seen in the response data packet. Note that data in the response can be replaced, such as substituting the original URL with the URL of a phishing website.

In this scenario, clicking on the ad opens the spoofed URL and displays the phishing website in the browser. The phishing website could be leveraged to launch additional attacks.

Third-Party SDK with Local Server. Moplus is an SDK developed by the Chinese search engine giant Baidu. Since the original Moplus files could not be accessed, it was decided to analyze the apps that contain it to study its permissions and behavior. After parsing the manifest file of the host app, it was discovered that the SDK operates in a separate process with its main service named `com.baidu.android.moplus`. The service is triggered by various broadcasts, such as system startup broadcasts.

When a user launches an app that includes the Moplus SDK, the SDK automatically and secretly sets up a local HTTP server for monitoring using socket messages. Moplus achieves this using the built-in NanoHttpd, an open-source HTTP server written in Java. The HTTP server continuously listens on a TCP port, receiving and parsing messages sent from remote servers or clients. When a new HTTP request is received, the local server replaces the NanoHttpd server actions with the received message and proceeds to execute malicious operations. A remote server can send requests to obtain location information, search box information, package information and other sensitive data from a user device. Additionally, an attacker can add contacts to a user device, scan downloaded files and upload specific files. All these operations are performed simply by sending HTTP requests.

Sendintent is a special command used to send instructions to a host app, enabling remote invocation without user consent, sending error messages and installing any app. The local service does not authenticate request messages so they can be triggered by an attacker without going through a remote server. Furthermore, an attacker can use Nmap to scan an Android device for TCP port 40310 and check if the port is open.

3   Methodology

This section describes the forensic analysis methodology for third-party cloud SDKs.

3.1   Sensitive API Identification

Evidentiary data is generated and stored via third-party SDKs because app developers may not be aware of the sensitive data accessed by the SDKs and do not take adequate measures to secure the data. This research created profiles for Android cloud SDKs to document the evidentiary data accessed by third-party Android cloud SDKs. Several popular cloud SDKs were examined and information was collected about the sensitive data they access. Furthermore, nine types of sensitive data were characterized based on their attributes. The subsequent sections provide details about the third-party SDKs and nine types of sensitive data studied in this research.

Android Cloud SDK Investigation. The process for identifying evidentiary data involved three steps:

- Initial data collection was performed to gather official documentation of the selected SDKs, which included API references and privacy policies. The documentation was important because it typically contains information about the data accessed by SDKs.
- Manual investigation was conducted due to the challenges involved in automatically extracting data from documentation. For each SDK, comprehensive data was collected from the descriptions of all the APIs listed in the API reference and statements found in the privacy policy.
- Further investigation was conducted when the data descriptions in API references or privacy policies were unclear or ambiguous. This was accomplished by exploring the FAQ and forum sections of SDKs. Analyses of discussions and reviews of code provided by app developers and SDK developers helped confirm whether or not sensitive data items are accessed by SDKs.

Evidentiary Data Types. Evidentiary data can be broadly categorized into two groups, personal data and usage data. Personal data, which can be used to identify a specific individual, is typically generated before an app is used. Examples of personal data include email address, physical address and GPS location.

Usage data is information generated during user interactions with apps or app operation. Examples of usage data include the in-app behaviors of a particular user, transaction data related to in-app purchases and reports on app crashes. However, the term usage data is rather general and can confuse app developers. To address this issue, evidentiary data is further classified into distinct types based on data attributes.

Publicly-available sources and sinks in tools such as FlowDroid [6], SuSi [5] and DroidSafe [15] were combined. While sink methods from various tools were leveraged, analysis revealed that the combined source methods for evidentiary data were not exhaustive. Notably, the tools omitted methods whose arguments indicated potential data sources. Additionally, the tools did not account for sources related to cloud storage. Consequently, the source methods for evidentiary data were expanded and sources with online locations were identified.

This work focuses on nine types of evidentiary data useful in investigations – location, text input, time, user identity, payment information, device identifiers, advertisement identifiers, push notifications and visited URLs:

- **Location:** Location data includes GPS coordinates and coarse-grained location information determined through Wi-Fi or cellular data. An Android API that provides location data is referred to as a source. A total of 42 source methods related to location data were identified using available tools [5, 6]. It was discovered that GPS location can also be generated as an argument in a method. For example, the argument in method setMockLocation(android.

`location, location)` stores GPS location data. Consequently, when analyzing a statement involving `setMockLocation`, the location data type is included in the argument tag.

- **Text Input:** Text input refers to string data entered by a user, such as text messages in a social networking app or search queries. Seven source methods related to text input were identified using existing tools.
- **Time:** Sixteen source methods related to time data were identified using available tools. Additionally, a few additional source methods for time data were discovered. An example is the method `currentThreadTimeMillis()` that provides the milliseconds running in the current thread.
- **User Identity:** This sensitive data uniquely identifies an app user. It includes identification codes such as user IDs, advertisement IDs, authentication tokens and group IDs related to teams or families.
- **Payment Information:** This data pertains to user purchases and financial transactions. It encompasses a wide range of details about purchases and transactions, such as product names, stock keeping units, prices, purchase locations and search terms. Third-party SDKs have access to this data which provides insights into user purchasing habits and behaviors.
- **Device Identifiers:** Some third-party SDKs attempt to retrieve app-related details such as the app name, version, unique installation ID (app-instance ID) and universally unique identifier (UUID). This type of sensitive data can be leveraged to identify the apps used by a user as well as track app behavior.
- **Advertisement Identifiers:** This data covers user interactions with advertisements. Many apps, especially free apps, incorporate third-party SDKs for monetization purposes. Advertisements are a common way to monetize apps, with advertisers paying for ad displays. Cloud SDKs collect data on user interactions with ads, including ad clicks, in-app purchases triggered by ads and instances where ads lead users to exit apps. This data helps optimize ad delivery to engage app users effectively.
- **Push Notifications:** This data pertains to the content of in-app messages sent to users. In-app messages frequently include promotions sent by companies to attract users to their products. When third-party SDKs generate or transmit in-app messages, they access message details, including attributes related to products aligned with user interests.
- **Visited URLs:** Users can access URLs via a web browser or via non-browser apps using WebView. Three source methods that return URLs from existing tools were identified initially; an additional source method that returns a URL as its result was identified later. Furthermore, Android APIs and callback methods that accept parameters signifying visited URLs were identified.

Certain callback methods contain arguments that also denote URLs. In total, nine callback methods whose arguments are associated with URLs were identified. Whenever a variable was used as the corresponding argument for such a method, the variable tag was expanded to include the visited URLs.

Table 1. SDK analysis methods and tools.

Analytical Method	Analysis Tool
Static Taint Analysis	EviHunter
Native Library Analysis	LibDroid
Dynamic Binary Instrumentation	Frida

3.2   SDK Analysis

The SDK analysis process involved three stages: (i) third-party SDK development information review, (ii) static forensic analysis, packet capture and dynamic taint analysis, and (iii) forensic artifact verification. Table 1 shows the analytic methods and tools used for SDK analysis.

Stage 1. This stage involved reviews of the development documentation of third-party SDKs, including integration guides, code from demonstration apps and manifest files. Third-party SDK providers offer documentation or user guides to enable developers to integrate SDKs into their apps. The documents provide valuable information about the components and permissions that must be added to app manifests when integrating SDKs.

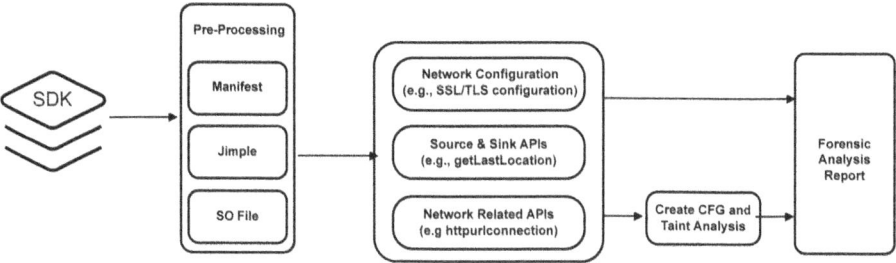

Fig. 3. Static forensic analysis of third-party cloud SDKs.

Stage 2. This stage involved automated static analysis, network packet capture and dynamic taint analysis. EviHunter [9] and LibDroid [24] were employed to conduct automated static analysis of the third-party cloud SDK apps. EviHunter was used to perform taint analysis on app code because it treats all API library calls as black boxes in that it simply unions the taint tags from input parameters to the return value. To mitigate under-tainting and over-tainting problems, the LibDroid toolkit was employed to examine Android native libraries. The results from the two components were integrated to create the static analysis report. Figure 3 illustrates the static forensic analysis of third-party cloud SDKs.

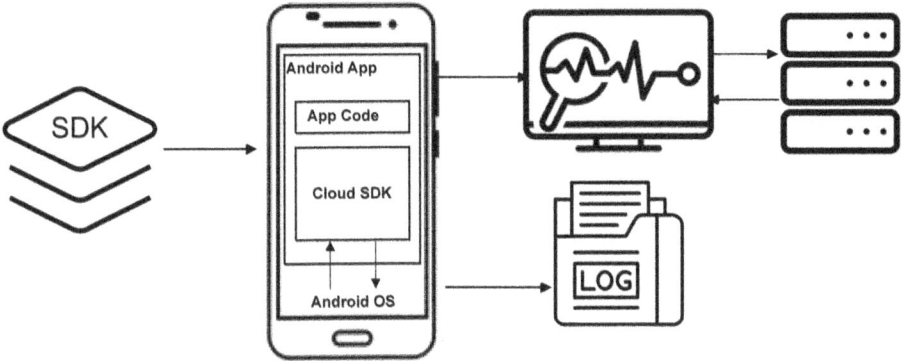

Fig. 4. Dynamic taint analysis of third-party cloud SDKs.

For each app utilizing a third-party cloud SDK, an automated analysis was performed of the Android APIs it employed (e.g., using `getDeviceId()` and `sendTextMessage()`) to check for behaviors that could access user data. Additionally, checks were performed for reflection, dynamic code loading, permission declaration and cloud service usage. Some Android cloud SDKs employ reflection using the Java.lang.reflect package, which allows programmable method calls and access to fields. Since static analysis cannot handle the use of APIs with reflection, the limitation was addressed using dynamic taint analysis as shown in Figure 4.

The dynamic analysis provided insights into the communications mechanism between a third-party cloud SDK and server involving sensitive information. The taint propagation summary obtained during the sensitive API identification was leveraged to propagate the taint tags. It modified the Android Runtime (ART) platform to implement a specialized 32-bit taint tagging system. This system can track up to 2^{32} types of evidence, significantly enhancing the granularity of analysis compared with existing solutions. Each data variable in a cloud SDK is provided a unique set of taint tags that update dynamically based on data flow, enabling the detailed tracking of forensic evidence across different app activities.

Furthermore, network evidentiary data between an Android cloud SDK and a remote cloud server was monitored. The majority of the data was transmitted via HTTPS connections encrypted using TLS/SSL, in addition to other encryption methods employed by the app. Fortunately, decrypting SSL connections was relatively straightforward. Android device traffic was rerouted through a controlled Wi-Fi access point configured to utilize `mitmdump` (`docs.mitmproxy.org/stable`) as a proxy. The firewall settings were adjusted to redirect all the Wi-Fi HTTP/HTTPS traffic to `mitmdump`, ensuring that the proxying was transparent to the device.

When a process running on an Android device initiates a new network connection, the `mitmdump` proxy impersonates the destination server and presents a counterfeit certificate for the target server. This action enables `mitmdump` to decrypt the traffic. Subsequently, it establishes a connection to the actual target server and acts as an intermediary, forwarding requests and responses between the app and target server while simultaneously logging the traffic.

Typically, system processes validate the authenticity of server certificates received when initiating new connections and terminate the connections if the checks fail. For Google apps and services, installing the `mitmproxy` certificate as trusted ensures that the checks pass. However, installing a trusted certificate can be complex in Android 10 and later versions because the system disk partition that stores trusted certificates is read-only and security measures prevent it from being mounted as read-write. Fortunately, it is possible to override folders in the system disk partition by creating a new mount point corresponding to the folder. This enabled the `mitmdump` certificate to be added to the /system/etc/security/cacerts folder.

Stage 3. This stage involved the verification of the forensic artifacts discovered in the third-party cloud SDKs. The verification was performed by automatically executing testing apps that used Android cloud SDKs. Each Android app was executed on an Android emulator and Fiddler was set up as a proxy to intercept traffic between the third-party cloud SDK and remote server. After execution, the `adb` shell command was executed to access the internal directories of the app. Databases, library files, shared preferences, cache and other files were retrieved from the directories, along with unencrypted information.

Since access was not available to the server-side code of third-party cloud SDKs, it was only possible to test the server in a black-box manner. Static analysis and dynamic binary instrumentation using Frida [17] were employed to modify the parameters submitted to the server by the SDK through code injection to validate potential forensic artifacts. Frida injects a JavaScript engine into the target process, enabling users to write scripts that execute in the context of the running program. This enabled the real-time manipulation and observation of app activities with a cloud server without having to modify the codebase.

4   Evaluation and Results

This section describes the large-scale forensic analysis of 11 major Android cloud SDKs and 120 real-world apps that leverage the SDKs for data storage. The experimental setup is described, following which a case study and the overall results are presented.

4.1   Experimental Setup

Since a centralized distribution platform for mobile app SDKs does not exist, statistical data [1] was leveraged to identify the most popular cloud SDKs for Android apps. The statistical data covered more than four million Android apps that collectively employed more than 2,300 SDKs. From this large collection,

Table 2. Android cloud SDKs with numbers of installs and apps.

SDK	Developer	Version	Installs	Apps
FireBase	Google	v. 32.7.2	74.27 b	3 m
AWS	Amazon	v. 1.12.1	35.53 b	60.31 k
Parse	Parse	v. 2.1	3.87 b	12.44 k
Azure	Microsoft	v. 2.0.0	1.59 b	9.86 k
Spring	VMware Tanzu	v. 1.0.0	3.26 b	7.54 k
HMS	Huawei	v. 4.0.3.300	23.41b	9.27 k
Amplify	Amazon	v. 2	1.42 b	6.12 k
Aliyun OSS	Alibaba	v. 2.9.13	5.17 b	2.49 k
Tencent Cloud	Tencent	v. 1.2.1.3	2.97 b	572
Cloudrail	CloudRail	v. 1.2.11	333.26 m	308
WNS SDK	Tencent	v. 3.0.962	1.4 b	145

11 major Android cloud SDKs and 120 Android apps using cloud services were downloaded from the Google Play Store. The apps were selected based on the apps listed on the official websites of the SDKs and on Android SDK statistics provided by AppBrain [4]. Hybrid taint analysis was employed to discover the data flows of potential forensic artifacts while uploading to and downloading from third-party servers.

Table 2 provides details about the 11 major Android cloud SDKs considered in the evaluation, along with their numbers of installs and supported apps.

The evaluation was executed on a Linux workstation with a 3.1 GHz Dual-Core Intel Core i7 processor and 128 GB of heap memory for the Java Virtual Machine. The SDKs were analyzed sequentially without parallelization. Each SDK was assigned eight-hour timeouts for static and dynamic analysis. The analysis of the 11 SDKs took 161 hours and 23 minutes.

4.2 Case Study

This case study illustrates how the proposed methodology is employed to identify evidentiary data on an Android device. During the survey of real-world apps, 31 apps were found to use the Firebase cloud SDK. Further investigation into the 31 apps revealed that an SQLite database file stored GPS location and timestamp data, which was constantly updating to cloud storage. In addition to location and timestamp data, the proposed methodology generates a report that describes the other types of forensic artifacts that are uploaded to a third-party server. Figure 5 shows a code snippet that uploads files to cloud storage.

It was also discovered that the Firebase SDK typically uses registration IDs to communicate with corresponding apps on cloud servers. Additionally, it was found that registration IDs could lead to the leakage of sensitive user information. Specifically, the registration IDs used by the SDK are generated on the device based on its international mobile equipment identity (IMEI), international mobile subscriber identity (IMSI), MAC address and package name.

```
// Create a storage reference
StorageReference storageRef = storage.getReference();

// Create a reference to "example.jpg"
StorageReference examplesRef = storageRef.child("example.jpg");

// Create a reference to "images/example.jpg"
StorageReference examplesRef = storageRef.child("images/example.jpg");

// Get the data from ImageView as bytes
imageView.setDrawingCacheEnabled(true);
imageView.buildDrawingCache();
Bitmap bitmap = ((BitmapDrawable) imageView.getDrawable()).getBitmap();
ByteArrayOutputStream baos = new ByteArrayOutputStream();
bitmap.compress(Bitmap.CompressFormat.JPEG, 100, baos);
byte[] data = baos.toByteArray();

UploadTask uploadTask = examplesRef.putBytes(data);
```

Fig. 5. Code snippet that uploads files to cloud storage.

Consequently, when an app was uninstalled with the SDK and then reinstalled on the same device, the registration ID for the app was unchanged. If sensitive device information is exposed, an attacker could potentially infer the registration ID. Since an SDK relies on registration IDs to identify apps on devices, if an attacking device infers an ID and has access to the victim device, it would gain the privilege of receiving push messages from the remote server. To defend against this type of attack, it is necessary to introduce randomness, such as a "salt," to render the generation of registration IDs less predictable.

Table 3 shows the types of artifacts and the corresponding evidentiary items uploaded to the cloud using Firebase SDK. The table also shows the numbers of apps utilizing Firebase cloud SDKs for cloud services.

The Android logging system provides developers with an interface to record app and device runtime states. Log messages are written to the device internal storage. Developers typically employ `android.util.log` to print debugging information. However, there are potential security risks if logging is not disabled before an app goes live. Developers often use the debug attribute when developing code. The code determines whether or not to output logs, making it easy to modify the debug attribute. Before Android version 4.1, Android apps with the `READ_LOGS` permission could read log files from all apps on the device. Therefore, writing evidentiary data to logs would be a valuable resource for retrieving forensic artifacts. During the analysis, it was discovered that the Tencent cloud SDK logged personal information such as the IMEI and device ID.

Table 3. Details about evidentiary items discovered in Firebase SDK.

Artifact Type	Evidentiary Item	Apps
User Identity	Location	31
	Email	12
	Physical Address	17
	IP Address	21
System Configuration	Timestamp	31
	Device ID	25
	IMEI	11
	User ID	17
App Identity	App Version	14
	App-Instance ID	12
	Group ID	19

4.3   Large-Scale Forensic Analysis Results of Android Cloud SDKs

In order to evaluate the effectiveness of the proposed methodology, a large-scale analysis of 120 Android apps utilizing cloud services was conducted. The apps were obtained from the Google Play Store. Before each app was installed, the Android device was initialized by resetting the logging system and cleaning the internal storage. After installation, the app was tested for eight hours using a drafted auto-testing script built on Monkey [14]. The accuracy of the proposed methodology was assessed by manually inspecting the reported URLs and forensic artifacts.

The following are the key findings with regard to the 11 major Android cloud SDKs considered in the evaluation:

- Seven SDKs utilize the permissions declared in the host app manifest file without explicitly stating the permissions in its own development documentation.
- Three SDKs save unencrypted sensitive financial information, such as credit card numbers and card verification values (CVCs) to third-party servers.
- Two SDKs do not follow industry standards by collecting location data and logs from users.
- Four SDKs fail to implement the X509TrustManager interface and override the certificate validation process to replace the default implementation.

The analysis revealed that all 120 Android apps utilizing the cloud SDKs uploaded evidentiary data to cloud servers. Sixty-five apps access and upload the user location information; 109 apps periodically track device network information and sync this with cloud servers; 14 apps store user credit card numbers and 33 apps track user phone numbers in plaintext on the servers. Moreover, 22 of the 120 apps save other kinds of evidentiary data such as account information and

Table 4. Summary of large-scale analysis results.

Group	Evidence Type	Apps	Apps (%)	URLs
Telephony Identifiers	IMEI	25	20.8%	44
	Phone Number	33	27.5%	53
	MCC	67	55.8%	87
	Operator Name	15	12.5%	47
	SIM Serial Number	18	15.0%	45
	SIM Country	19	15.8%	34
	Voicemail Number	7	0.6%	24
	Mobile Network Code	52	43.3%	89
Device Settings	Device ID	95	79.2%	143
	Software Version	25	20.8%	76
	Installed Apps	84	70.0%	102
	Device Type	37	30.8%	74
Location	Global Positioning System	33	27.5%	58
	Cell Location	58	48.3%	90
	Cell ID	61	50.8%	77
	Local Area Code	36	30.0%	44
Network	Wi-Fi Configuration	3	2.5%	16
	Data Plan	69	57.5%	77
	Network Type	34	28.3%	62
	IP Address	107	89.2%	223
Personal Data	Credit Card	14	11.7%	48
	Contacts	64	53.3%	98
	SMS	31	25.8%	43
	Media	45	37.5%	66
	Timestamp	120	100.0%	312
Other	Other	22	18.3%	75

passwords, providing great opportunities for evidence extraction in real-world forensic investigations.

Table 4 summarizes the forensic analysis results. Six groups of evidentiary are specified; the seventh group (other) covers forensic artifacts that do not fall in the six specified groups. The URLs column indicates unique URLs that contain at least one evidentiary data type such as phone number, location, IP address or timestamp. The URLs were parsed to remove the dynamically-assigned patterns such as <timestamp>, <UUID> and <android version>.

The research also revealed that four SDKs failed to implement the X509 TrustManager interface and overrode the certificate validation process to replace the default implementation. The X509 TrustManager interface in Android acts as a trust manager for X509 certificates, enabling authentication for secure sockets. Developers can implement the X509 TrustManager interface and override the certificate validation process to replace the default implementation in the library. During the SDK analysis, it was discovered that four SDKS left the implementation of the methods empty. This means they did nothing, not even raising exceptions for invalid certificates. Additionally, while some SDKs performed certificate validation, they did not raise exceptions even when certificates had expired or were revoked.

Seven SDKs were found to utilize the permissions declared in the host app manifest file without reporting the permissions in their development documentation. Third-party SDKs can share the permissions declared in the host app manifest file. In other words, even if an SDK does not explicitly state that it requires certain permissions in its development documentation, it can still utilize the permissions if they are declared in the manifest file. In most cases, Android apps request more permissions than they need and use the additional permissions to access private user data. The analysis revealed that the seven SDKs also leverage the permissions declared by the apps.

Manual Validation. It was challenging to evaluate the Android app results without the ground truth. As a result, a best-effort manual verification was performed. Specifically, 20 apps were randomly selected from the dataset and installed on an Android device. The Monkey program [14], which generates pseudo-random streams of user events, such as clicks, touches and system-level events, was employed to test each app for eight hours.

To examine the data sent between the device and cloud servers, device traffic was directed through a controlled Wi-Fi access point. The access point was configured to employ `mitmdump` as a proxy and make necessary adjustments to the firewall settings, redirecting all Wi-Fi HTTP/HTTPS traffic to `mitmdump` while ensuring that the proxy process was inconspicuous to the device. When an app running on the device initiates a new network connection, the `mitmdump` proxy impersonates the destination server and provides a counterfeit certificate to the intended server, enabling `mitmdump` to decrypt the traffic. Subsequently, `mitmdump` establishes a secondary connection to the authentic target server and functions as an intermediary, facilitating the exchange of requests and responses between the app and target server, all the while recording the traffic.

A URL containing evidence (forensic analysis result) was deemed a false positive if it did not include the type of evidentiary data reported. Similarly, if certain evidentiary data found to be stored in the cloud server was not reported, it was deemed a false negative. The proposed methodology achieved a precision of 89% and recall of 90% averaged over all the types of evidentiary data considered in experiments.

Overall, the large-scale evaluation results demonstrate the effectiveness of the forensic analysis methodology on Android cloud SDKs. Different types of forensic artifacts were identified in cloud servers, demonstrating that cloud storage can be a significant asset in forensic investigations. Moreover, the forensic analysis results could help digital forensic practitioners quickly find the evidence.

5 Related Work

This section discusses related work on manual Android app and SDK analysis, automated Android app analysis, and SDK detection and analysis.

5.1 Manual Analysis of Android Apps and SDKs

Previous studies [13, 30] have employed manual analysis to examine apps and establish environments for app execution. The process involved installing an app on an Android device or operating it in a managed sandbox setting. Logical or physical snapshots of the filesystem from the device or the sandbox were captured. A physical snapshot could also contain files that were deleted, but not yet overwritten. When an app ran in the sandbox, the filesystem and main memory could be controlled, allowing for the extraction of images from RAM and NAND flash memory.

Since manual analysis is laborious, error-prone and costly, investigations have focused on a small subset of apps. For example, detailed investigations have been conducted to identify and scrutinize the digital traces left by mobile apps. The research has typically concentrated on commonly-used apps such as WhatsApp, WeChat, Facebook Messenger and Google Hangouts [2].

Feal et al. [12] have provided insights into the manual analysis of Android apps and SDKs with a focus on security. They discuss the use of inertial measurement units in commercial mobile devices for continuous monitoring in healthcare, highlighting the development and implementation of sensing algorithms for health monitoring as well as privacy concerns due to personal identifiable information leaks via network traffic generated by mobile devices. In contrast, this work has applied manual and automated analysis techniques on Android apps and SDKs with the goal of exploring the privacy implications of third-party Android SDKs. It highlights how SDKs collect user data without developer knowledge, underscoring the need for transparent communications of data collection practices by SDK providers. The results suggest that breaking down SDK features can help developers select only the necessary functionalities, potentially mitigating privacy concerns.

5.2 Automated Analysis of Android Apps

Fordroid [21] appears to be the first automated forensic analysis tool for Android apps. It focuses on uncovering sensitive information in local storage. It stands out from among commercial mobile phone forensic analysis tools that have limited app support.

The research community has shown significant interest in enhancing the security and privacy of the Android platform. Several tools have been developed to identify sensitive data flows between sources and sinks in Android apps. Static analysis tools include FlowDroid [6], ScanDal [18], AndroidLeaks [13], LeakMiner [29], CHEX [22], AmanDroid [27], DroidSafe [15], R-Droid [7], IccTA [19] and

HornDroid [8]. FlowDroid is a very precise static analysis tool designed for Android apps. It employs taint analysis to detect potential security and privacy breaches by tracking sensitive data flows within apps.

Dynamic analysis tools include TaintDroid [10], TaintART [26] and Malton [28]. TaintDroid is an efficient real-time tracking system designed to monitor sensitive data flows through third-party apps on Android devices. It employs dynamic taint analysis, a method that tags (or taints) data deemed to be sensitive and tracks its movement across the app components to external servers.

5.3   SDK Detection and Analysis

Tools such as LibD [20], LibID [31] and LibRadar [23] highlight the importance of integrating forensic analyses of third-party libraries in the assessments of Android apps, especially for evaluating the security implications of Android libraries.

The LibD [20] tool is designed for conducting forensic analyses of Android apps, specifically identifying and assessing third-party libraries in apps. While the technical details about LibD vary depending on the version and context, its core features and functionality address several key aspects of Android app analysis.

Another notable tool for analyzing Android apps is LibID [31]. The tool focuses on the identification and management of third-party libraries within apps. It addresses critical needs related to mobile device app security and privacy by offering detailed insights into the libraries incorporated by apps.

The LibRadar [23] tool employs an innovative similarity-scoring mechanism for the automatic detection and analysis of third-party libraries in Android apps. Its primary focus is on improving the security, privacy and performance aspects of apps by providing insights into the libraries.

6   Discussion

The proposed forensic analysis methodology addresses the inherent challenges associated with static program analysis. It involves detailed dataflow analysis and broader, syntax-oriented heuristics for testing. Despite the best efforts to implement thorough program analysis checks, there may be some oversights, such as detecting certain networking libraries. The technique for identifying sensitive APIs in SDKs depends on the successful extraction of API semantics, which is not always achievable. Additionally, the approach for identifying taint sources overlooks APIs that do not take parameters. For example, sensitive data could be stored in global or member variables by an SDK and accessed by APIs without parameters, although no such cases were encountered in the Android cloud SDKs discussed in Section 3.

The methodology leverages the IC3 [19] and FlowDroid [6] tools to analyze forensic artifacts and inter-component communications. However, the support for URL propagation in inter-component communications is basic. A regular expression (<intent>) is employed to identify dynamic URLs that involve intent.

The support for system APIs is also limited. Manually-prepared summaries of data flows for system APIs focusing on network communication, string manipulations and common data structures are produced. Future enhancements will include the modeling of frameworks. Note that the framework modeling method underlying DroidSafe [15] is not suited for cloud forensics due to its scalability issues and focus on sensitive data flows without identifying specific cloud storage locations.

An additional limitation with the proposed methodology is its ability to match detected URLs on cloud storage with those in an analysis report, especially for dynamic URLs. If a URL contains an <intent> substring, it may not be accurately matched with its counterpart on the cloud server, potentially misclassifying the URL without forensic artifacts. Precisely analyzing dynamically-generated URLs, including the development of detailed patterns for intents that could be matched against cloud storage locations, is a promising direction for future research.

7 Conclusions

This chapter has described a comprehensive forensic investigation of evidence generated by 120 real-world Android apps that use third-party cloud SDKs for data storage. The methodology incorporates app analysis and framework analysis, examining evidentiary data residing in local storage as well as cloud storage. Location information, timestamps as well as other types of forensic artifacts were extracted from the tested Android apps. The results are useful to digital forensic practitioners due to the Android app development trend to store user data in the cloud. Manual verification was performed to authenticate the correctness of the forensic analysis results. The case study involving a sample Android app provides details about the forensic artifacts. The large-scale evaluation of Android apps demonstrates that the proposed methodology can be widely applied to evidence discovery.

Acknowledgement. This research was partially supported by the National Institute of Standards and Technology CSAFE under Cooperative Agreement no. 70NANB20H019, by the National Science Foundation under Grant nos. CNS 1527579, CNS 1619201, CNS 1730275, DEB 1924178 and ECCS 2030249, and by the Boeing Company.

References

1. 42matters, Top 20 backend and cloud SDKs used in Android apps on Google Play, Zurich, Switzerland (42matters.com/sdk-analysis/top-backend-and-cloud-sdks), 2024.

2. C. Anglano, Forensic analysis of WhatsApp Messenger on Android smartphones, *Digital Investigation*, vol. 11(3), pp. 201–213, 2014.

3. AppBrain, AirPush: A push-notification mobile ad network, AppTornado, Zurich, Switzerland (`www.appbrain.com/stats/libraries/details/airpush/airpush`), 2024.

4. AppBrain, Welcome to AppBrain, AppTornado, Zurich, Switzerland (`www.appbrain.com`), 2024.

5. S. Arzt, S. Rasthofer and E. Bodden, SuSi: A Tool for the Fully-Automated Classification of Android Sources and Sinks, Technical Report TUD-CS-2013-0114, Department of Computer Science, Technical University Darmstadt, Darmstadt, Germany, 2013.

6. S. Arzt, S. Rasthofer, C. Fritz, E. Bodden, A. Bartel, J. Klein, Y. Le Traon, D. Octeau and P. McDaniel, FlowDroid: Precise context, flow, field, object-sensitive and lifecycle-aware taint analysis for Android apps, *ACM SIGPLAN Notices*, vol. 49(6), pp. 259–269, 2014.

7. M. Backes, S. Bugiel, E. Derr, S. Gerling and C. Hammer, R-Droid: Leveraging Android app analysis with static slice optimization, *Proceedings of the Eleventh ACM Asia Conference on Computer and Communications Security*, pp. 129–140, 2016.

8. S. Calzavara, I. Grishchenko and M. Maffei, HornDroid: Practical and sound static analysis of Android applications by SMT solving, *Proceedings of the IEEE European Symposium on Security and Privacy*, pp. 47–62, 2016.

9. C. Cheng, C. Shi, N. Gong and Y. Guan, EviHunter: Identifying digital evidence in the permanent storage of Android devices via static analysis, *Proceedings of the ACM SIGSAC Conference on Computer and Communications Security*, pp. 1338–1350, 2018.

10. W. Enck, P. Gilbert, S. Han, V. Tendulkar, B. Chun, L. Cox, J. Jung, P. McDaniel and A. Sheth, TaintDroid: An information-flow tracking system for realtime privacy monitoring of smartphones, *ACM Transactions on Computer Systems*, vol. 32(3), article no. 5, 2014.

11. W. Enck, D. Octeau, P. McDaniel and S. Chaudhuri, A study of Android application security, *Proceedings of the Twentieth USENIX Security Symposium*, 2011.

12. A. Feal, J. Gamba, N. Vallina Rodriguez, P. Wijesekera, J. Reardon, S. Egelman and J. Tapiador, Don't accept candy from strangers: An analysis of third-party mobile SDKs, *Proceedings of the Computers, Privacy and Data Protection Conference*, pp. 1–27, 2021.

13. C. Gibler, J. Crussell, J. Erickson and H. Chen, AndroidLeaks: Automatically detecting potential privacy leaks in Android applications on a large scale, *Proceedings of the Fifth International Conference on Trust and Trustworthy Computing*, pp. 291–307, 2012.

14. Google Developers, UI/Application Exerciser Monkey, Mountain View, California (`developer.android.com/studio/test/other-testing-tools/monkey`), 2022.

15. M. Gordon, D. Kim, J. Perkins, L. Gilham, N. Nguyen and M. Rinard, Information flow analysis of Android applications in DroidSafe, *Proceedings of the Twenty-Second Annual Network and Distributed System Security Symposium*, 2015.

16. International Data Corporation, Smartphone market insights, Needham, Massachusetts (`www.idc.com/prodserv/smartphone-os-market-share.jsp`), January 16, 2024.

17. K. Kalleberg, Frida: Putting the open back into closed software, presented at the *Open Source Developers Conference*, 2015.

18. J. Kim, Y. Yoon, K. Yi and J. Shin, ScanDal: Static analyzer for detecting privacy leaks in Android applications, poster presented at the *Workshop on Mobile Security Technologies*, 2012.

19. L. Li, A. Bartel, T. Bissyande, J. Klein, Y. Le Traon, S. Arzt, S. Rasthofer, E. Bodden, D. Octeau and P. McDaniel, IccTA: Detecting inter-component privacy leaks in Android apps, *Proceedings of the Thirty-Seventh IEEE/ACM International Conference on Software Engineering*, pp. 280–291, 2015.

20. M. Li, W. Wang, P. Wang, S. Wang, D. Wu, J. Liu, R. Xue and W. Huo, LibD: S- calable and precise third-party library detection in Android markets, *Proceedings of the Thirty-Ninth IEEE/ACM International Conference on Software Engineering*, pp. 335–346, 2017.

21. X. Lin, T. Chen, T. Zhu, K. Yang and F. Wei, Automated forensic analysis of mobile applications on Android devices, *Digital Investigation*, vol. 26(S), pp. S59–S66, 2018.

22. L. Lu, Z. Li, Z. Wu, W. Lee and G. Jiang, CHEX: Statically vetting Android apps for component hijacking vulnerabilities, *Proceedings of the ACM Conference on Computer and Communications Security*, pp. 229–240, 2012.

23. Z. Ma, H. Wang, Y. Guo and X. Chen, LibRadar: Fast and accurate detection of third-party libraries in Android apps, *Proceedings of the Thirty-Eighth IEEE/ACM International Conference on Software Engineering*, pp. 653–656, 2016.

24. C. Shi, C. Cheng and Y. Guan, LibDroid: Summarizing information flow of Android native libraries via static analysis, *Forensic Science International: Digital Investigation*, vol. 42(S), article no. 301405, 2022.

25. R. Stevens, C. Gibler, J. Crussell, J. Erickson and H. Chen, Investigating user privacy in Android ad libraries, *Proceedings of the Workshop on Mobile Security Technologies*, pp. 195–197, 2012.

26. M. Sun, T. Wei and J. Lui, TaintART: A practical multi-level information flow tracking system for Android RunTime, *Proceedings of the ACM SIGSAC Conference on Computer and Communications Security*, pp. 331–342, 2016.

27. F. Wei, S. Roy, X. Ou and Robby, Amandroid: A precise and general inter-component data flow analysis framework for security vetting of Android apps, *ACM Transactions on Privacy and Security*, vol. 21(3), article no. 14, 2018.

28. L. Xue, Y. Zhou, T. Chen, X. Luo and G. Gu, Malton: Towards on-device non-invasive mobile malware analysis for ART, *Proceedings of the Twenty-Sixth USENIX Security Symposium*, pp. 289–306, 2017.

29. Z. Yang and M. Yang, LeakMiner: Detecting information leakage on Android with static taint analysis, *Proceedings of the Third World Congress on Software Engineering*, pp. 101–104, 2012.

30. Z. Yang, M. Yang, Y. Zhang, G. Gu, P. Ning and X. Wang, AppIntent: Analyzing sensitive data transmission in Android for privacy leakage detection, *Proceedings of the ACM SIGSAC Conference on Computer and Communications Security*, pp. 1043–1054, 2013.

31. J. Zhang, A. Beresford and S. Kollmann, LibID: Reliable identification of obfuscated third-party Android libraries, *Proceedings of the ACM SIGSOFT International Symposium on Software Testing and Analysis*, pp. 55–65, 2019.

Identifying and Analyzing Vault Apps

Seth Barrett[1], Alex Salontai[2], Rajon Bardhan[1], Gokila Dorai[1], Esra Akbas[2],
and Patrick Woodell[1]

[1] Augusta University, Augusta, Georgia, USA
gdorai@augusta.edu
[2] Georgia State University, Atlanta, Georgia, USA

Abstract. Privacy concerns have elevated the popularity of vault apps, especially those available in alternative gray market app stores. Designed to conceal media, vault apps often mimic familiar tools such as calculators, serving as decoys. However, while vault apps enhance user privacy, they present significant challenges to digital forensic practitioners. In particular, it is difficult to access encrypted and deleted data in sensitive and contraband documents encountered in digital forensic investigations. This chapter describes research on Aptoide, a significant gray market app store, that builds on previous work on mainstream stores such as the Google Play Store and Apple's iOS App Store. A methodology for gray market vault app identification, extraction and forensic analysis is described. The methodology leverages feature extraction from app descriptions along with machine learning algorithms. The research provides insights into the prevalence of vault apps in gray market app stores and sets the stage for in-depth studies of vault apps downloaded from Android app marketplaces.

Keywords: Mobile Device Forensics · Android App · Gray Market App Store

1 Introduction

The quest for privacy has led to the proliferation of apps that conceal user content. These so-called "vault apps" serve as digital lockers, enabling users to hide sensitive text, photos, videos and other data. While many of these apps masquerade as mundane utilities or games, their underlying functionality is geared towards ensuring user privacy. For instance, an app that appears to be a simple calculator might double as a storage vault for private photos.

The rise of vault apps is particularly pronounced in third-party app markets, with Aptoide being a notable example. These "gray markets" operate outside the purview of mainstream app stores such as the Google Play Store and Apple's iOS App Store, escaping the rigorous scrutiny and security checks associated with official marketplaces. This has made gray markets a fertile ground for the proliferation of vault apps, some of which can be used for nefarious purposes.

While vault apps address genuine privacy concerns, they also pose significant challenges to digital forensics and security research. Encrypted data, cloud-synced content and remote wiping functionality render the retrieval of concealed

© IFIP International Federation for Information Processing 2025
Published by Springer Nature Switzerland AG 2025
E. Kurkowski and S. Shenoi (Eds.): DigitalForensics 2024, IFIP AICT 724, pp. 63–78, 2025.
https://doi.org/10.1007/978-3-031-71025-4_4

and deleted data a daunting task. Furthermore, the deceptive nature of vault apps makes them difficult to identify, let alone analyze.

This chapter delves into the world of vault apps in the gray market, with a focus on apps available from Aptoide. Previous research has examined the Google Play Store [10] and iOS App Store [3] to understand the landscape of content-hiding applications. A methodology for gray market vault app identification, extraction and forensic analysis that builds on the research on mainstream app stores is described. The methodology leverages feature extraction from app descriptions along with machine learning algorithms to address the challenges posed by vault apps.

2   Related Work

Several static and dynamic analysis techniques have been proposed for Android app analysis and security. The prominent Apposcopy tool developed by Feng et al. [4] employs static analysis. It engages a formal app description language to identify and counteract malicious app behaviors. However, Apposcopy is not designed to handle the nuances of vault apps.

Complementing the work of Feng and colleagues, Arzt et al. [2] developed FlowDroid, an open-source tool renowned for its comprehensive static analysis. FlowDroid is adept at pinpointing privacy intrusions in Android apps, but it lacks vault app detection functionality.

Hou et al. [6] have developed a method for reconstructing Android app behavior graphs. The method exposes clandestine app behaviors, but it is not designed to handle vault apps.

Votipka et al. [11] have focused on encrypted apps. Their investigations of Android ransomware have identified several behavioral patterns. In contrast, this research takes a unique trajectory by delving into the realm of vault apps from alternative markets such as Aptoide, bridging the existing gaps and leveraging machine learning for vault app identification, extraction and forensic analysis.

3   Preliminaries

The massive use of mobile devices has spurred the need for secure data storage solutions. This has resulted in the proliferation of vault apps that are designed to store encrypted user data, securing the data from unauthorized breaches.

Vault apps have diverse manifestations, from photo lockers and camouflaged calculators to covert notepads. They frequently operate under the radar, masquerading as common apps on mobile devices [9]. Accessing their concealed functionalities typically necessitates a password or some other authentication method.

While vault apps serve the legitimate purpose of securing personal data, they can pose threats to security and privacy. This is because they often require a wide range of permissions that give access to sensitive data and resources on mobile devices. Moreover, when a mobile device is involved in illegal activities, vault apps render the digital forensic process very challenging [12].

When advertising apps in various app market stores, developers typically post app titles, screenshots and detailed text descriptions. This information can be leveraged to pinpoint content-hiding apps and discern the permissions the apps request from user devices.

Android app permissions play a critical role in security and privacy by regulating access to sensitive user data and system resources [1]. Each Android app lists the permissions it requires in a manifest file; for the app to function properly, users have to grant these permissions to the app. Some permissions are associated with security-sensitive tasks such as accessing the camera or reading the contacts whereas other permissions relate to system-level functions such as keeping the device awake [5]. In the case of vault apps, the permissions they seek often hint at the nature of the data they protect.

4   Methodology

This section describes the methodology for gray market vault app identification, extraction and forensic analysis. The section begins by describing the experimental environment that incorporated a wide range of Android apps.

4.1   Experimental Environment Creation

The first task was to create an extensive dataset of Android apps. This was accomplished by targeting the Aptoide third-party app store and identifying keywords in app titles and app descriptions pertinent to vault apps. The pertinent keywords were "private," "sensitive," "censor," "protect," "decoy," "privacy," "secret," "hide," "vault," "secure," "safe," "photos," "videos," "notes," "password," "contacts," "browser," "lock," "gallery," "calculator," "fingerprint," "password-protected," "fake" and "steganography."

The keywords pertinent to vault apps were used to scrape the Aptoide app store for matching apps. Figure 1 shows the Aptoide scraping architecture.

Upon finding a matching app, its Android package (APK) file was downloaded. Following this, basic details such as the app name, developer, developer country of origin, version, download count and user rating were recorded.

4.2   Vault App Identification

Manual reviews of the app webpages were performed. Based on the app functionalities gleaned from the webpages, the apps were classified as vault apps and non-vault apps.

Specifically, vault app identification leveraged feature vector generators and classifier models. In particular, machine-learning-based classification models were trained to identify apps as vault apps or non-vault apps using the feature sets derived from the apps. The feature vectors were generated from the app titles,

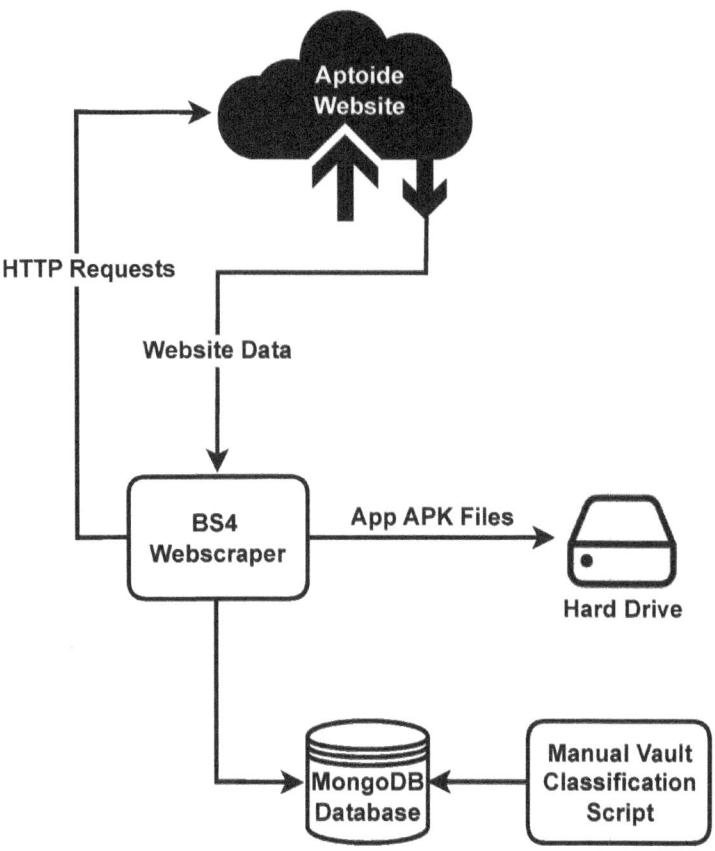

Fig. 1. Aptoide scraping architecture.

text descriptions and requested permissions. The classification model accuracy depended on the quality of the feature sets and the machine learning algorithms.

Feature Extraction from Text (Binary Vector). The binary vector is a fundamental and widely-used text feature representation that indicates the presence and absence of words in a body of text. Considering every word in the app titles and descriptions would result in an extremely-high-dimensional binary vector. Drawing on the DECADE deep-learning-based Android app detection system [10], 21 frequently-occurring words in app titles and another 24 words in app descriptions were selected. Table 1 lists the frequently-occurring words in app titles and descriptions.

Binary vectors for the apps were created based on the presence or absence of the words in the app titles and descriptions. The two binary vectors for each app were merged to obtain a single binary vector with length 45. These binary

Table 1. Frequently-occurring words in app titles and descriptions.

Text Type	Selected Words
App Title	private, sensitive, censor, protect, decoy, privacy, secret, hide, vault, secure, safe, photos, videos, notes, password, contacts, browser, lock, gallery, calculator, fingerprint
App Description	private, sensitive, censor, protect, decoy, privacy, secret, hide, vault, secure, safe, photos, videos, notes, password, contacts, browser, lock, gallery, calculator, fingerprint, password-protected, fake, steganography

vectors corresponded to the app feature vectors input to the machine learning models.

Feature Extraction from Text (Document Embedding). The binary vector representation created using selected representative words does not convey which words are crucial to vault app detection. Also, excluding certain words could lead to information loss about apps. Therefore, contemporary machine learning models for text employ text embedding to extract features automatically without user input. Text embedding considers all the words and their interrelations, producing a compact representation of words and documents suitable for use as features in machine learning models. Doc2Vec [8], an adaptation of Word2Vec, was employed to obtain app feature representations from app titles and descriptions.

Feature Extraction from Permissions Requested. As mentioned above, each app requests certain permissions during installation and users must grant these permissions for the app to function properly. Some permissions are linked to security-sensitive operations such as accessing the camera and reading contacts whereas others relate to system-level operations such as keeping the device awake. Since these permissions offer vital insights into app functionality, they were incorporated as app features. A total of 75 unique app permissions were identified. Therefore, a binary vector of length 75 was created for each app to express the permissions it requested. Figure 2 shows the top 25 most-frequently-requested permissions by apps.

4.3 Forensic Analysis

This section describes the detailed forensic analysis conducted on five Android vault apps to obtain pertinent artifacts. The five vault apps were Wire, Twinme, Private Notebook, 3C Sensitive Backup and Steganography Master. The forensic analysis employed Magnet AXIOM – Process and Examine, a comprehensive

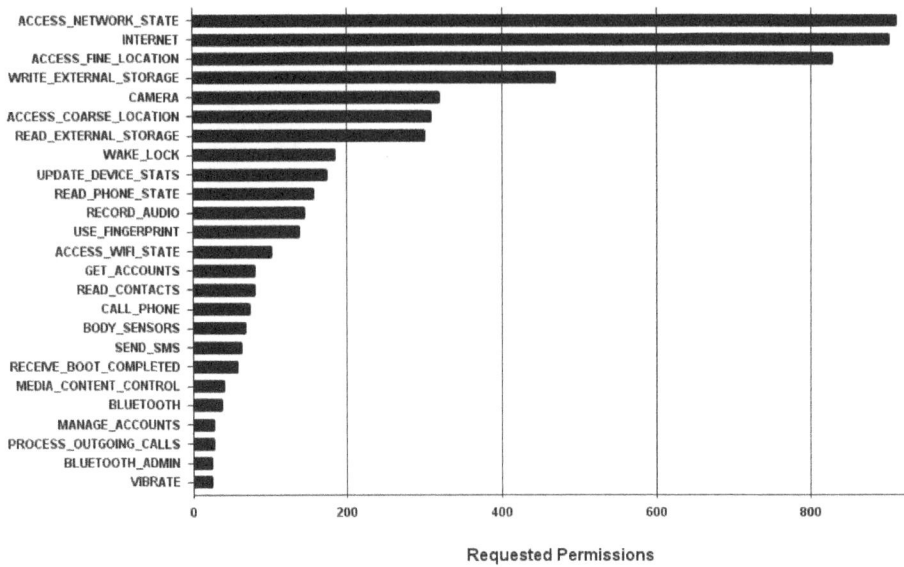

Fig. 2. Top 25 most-frequently-requested permissions by apps.

digital forensics toolkit designed for collecting, analyzing and reporting digital evidence [7].

Wire App. The Wire app supports messaging and communications. While it shares similarities with other messaging apps, it provides several unique features for users. In particular, it offers end-to-end encryption for all forms of communications, including messaging, voice calls and file sharing.

The forensic analysis conducted in this research revealed that all the files associated with Wire app are stored in the data/data/com.wire file structure. As shown in Figures 3(a) and 3(b), all the databases and media files related to Wire app were recovered. Figure 3(c) shows that metadata belonging to all the media files associated with Wire app was also recovered.

Message history and call history could not be recovered from Wire app due to its use of end-to-end encryption. However, as shown in Figure 4, the permissions requested by Wire app were recovered.

Twinme App. Twinme is a private and secure messaging app that offers users end-to-end encryption. This cross-platform Android app does not store messages centrally and does not require any personal information such as email or phone numbers to maintain user anonymity. Twinme supports several communications methods, including text messaging, voice calls and video calls.

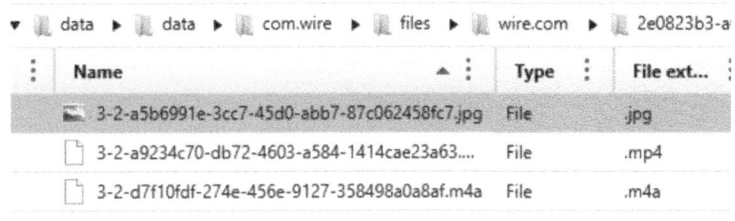

Name	Type	File ext...	Size...	Crea...	Acce...	Modified
com.google.android.datatransport.events	File	.events	57,344			10/4/2023 12:22:21 PM
com.google.android.datatransport.events-journal	File	.events-journal	0			10/4/2023 12:22:21 PM
global-db	File		4,096			10/4/2023 12:22:21 PM
global-db-shm	File		32,768			10/12/2023 3:29:23 PM
global-db-wal	File		74,192			10/12/2023 3:29:25 PM
user-db-2e0823b3-a071-4928-b22b-83e0c351c...	File		4,096			10/4/2023 12:24:04 PM
user-db-2e0823b3-a071-4928-b22b-83e0c351c...	File		32,768			10/12/2023 3:36:43 PM
user-db-2e0823b3-a071-4928-b22b-83e0c351c...	File		3,225,992			10/12/2023 3:36:43 PM

(a) Databases.

data ▶ data ▶ com.wire ▶ files ▶ wire.com ▶ 2e0823b3-a

Name	Type	File ext...
3-2-a5b6991e-3cc7-45d0-abb7-87c062458fc7.jpg	File	.jpg
3-2-a9234c70-db72-4603-a584-1414cae23a63....	File	.mp4
3-2-d7f10fdf-274e-456e-9127-358498a0a8af.m4a	File	.m4a

(b) Media files.

DETAILS

ARTIFACT INFORMATION

File Name	3-2-a5b6991e-3cc7-45d0-abb7-87c062458fc7.jpg
File Extension	.jpg
Last Modified Date/Time	10/4/2023 12:25:56 PM
Size (Bytes)	240830
Skin Tone Percentage	34.7
Original Width	1352
Original Height	1803
Exif Extraction Status	Complete
Exif Data	Extraction Result: Complete ImageWidth: 1352 ImageHeight: 1803
MD5 Hash	a4ca2b4ce1763957b4e93e445af636de
SHA1 Hash	4a6e0f2430d8c4c36749d1e7845907ec66c8f551
Artifact type	Pictures
Item ID	58317

(c) Media file metadata.

Fig. 3. Databases, media files and metadata recovered from Wire app.

Package...	Permission	Allo...	Artifact type
com.wire	com.google.android.c2dm.permission.RECEIVE	true	Application Permissions - Android
com.wire	android.permission.FOREGROUND_SERVICE	true	Application Permissions - Android
com.wire	android.permission.MODIFY_AUDIO_SETTINGS	true	Application Permissions - Android
com.wire	android.permission.RECEIVE_BOOT_COMPLETED	true	Application Permissions - Android
com.wire	android.permission.BLUETOOTH	true	Application Permissions - Android
com.wire	android.permission.INTERNET	true	Application Permissions - Android
com.wire	android.permission.BLUETOOTH_ADMIN	true	Application Permissions - Android
com.wire	android.permission.USE_FULL_SCREEN_INTENT	true	Application Permissions - Android
com.wire	android.permission.ACCESS_NETWORK_STATE	true	Application Permissions - Android
com.wire	android.permission.VIBRATE	true	Application Permissions - Android
com.wire	com.wire.DYNAMIC_RECEIVER_NOT_EXPORTED_PER...	true	Application Permissions - Android
com.wire	android.permission.WAKE_LOCK	true	Application Permissions - Android

Fig. 4. Requested permissions recovered from Wire app.

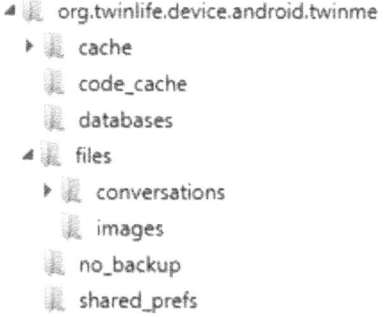

Fig. 5. Twinme app file structure.

The forensic analysis conducted in this research revealed that the Twinme app encrypts and stores databases, files, conversations and images locally in the data/data/org.twinlife.device.android.twinme structure (Figure 5).

Figure 6(a) shows that metadata belonging to all the media files associated with Twinme app was also recovered. Additionally, the permissions requested by the Twinme app were recovered (Figure 6(b)), providing insights into its functionality and security features.

Private Notebook App. Private Notebook is an Android app designed to assist users in creating and maintaining notes, documents and personal information. It implements data security using encryption and password protection. The forensic analysis revealed that the app stores encrypted files and databases

File Name	**bf981eb9-b9c5-4e7d-b791-fef20bfa05b7-normal.jpg**
File Extension	**.jpg**
Last Modified Date/Time	**10/12/2023 3:40:22 PM**
Size (Bytes)	**109083**
Skin Tone Percentage	**91.7**
Original Width	**594**
Original Height	**594**
Exif Extraction Status	**Complete**
Exif Data	**Extraction Result: Complete** **ImageWidth: 594** **ImageHeight: 594**
MD5 Hash	**6d46be264baf15ac50e550e30d1d4614**
SHA1 Hash	**05aad949e677c50a0656c602736182bc623a0c0b**
Artifact type	🖼 **Pictures**
Item ID	**37580**

(a) Media file metadata.

Package Name	Permission	Allo...	Artifact type
org.twinlife.device.android.twinme	com.google.android.finsky.permission.BIND_GET_IN...	true	Application Permissions - Android
org.twinlife.device.android.twinme	com.google.android.c2dm.permission.RECEIVE	true	Application Permissions - Android
org.twinlife.device.android.twinme	android.permission.MODIFY_AUDIO_SETTINGS	true	Application Permissions - Android
org.twinlife.device.android.twinme	android.permission.CHANGE_NETWORK_STATE	true	Application Permissions - Android
org.twinlife.device.android.twinme	android.permission.FOREGROUND_SERVICE	true	Application Permissions - Android
org.twinlife.device.android.twinme	android.permission.RECEIVE_BOOT_COMPLETED	true	Application Permissions - Android
org.twinlife.device.android.twinme	android.permission.BLUETOOTH	true	Application Permissions - Android
org.twinlife.device.android.twinme	android.permission.INTERNET	true	Application Permissions - Android
org.twinlife.device.android.twinme	android.permission.USE_FULL_SCREEN_INTENT	true	Application Permissions - Android
org.twinlife.device.android.twinme	android.permission.ACCESS_NETWORK_STATE	true	Application Permissions - Android
org.twinlife.device.android.twinme	android.permission.VIBRATE	true	Application Permissions - Android
org.twinlife.device.android.twinme	android.permission.ACCESS_WIFI_STATE	true	Application Permissions - Android
org.twinlife.device.android.twinme	android.permission.WAKE_LOCK	true	Application Permissions - Android

(b) Requested permissions.

Fig. 6. Media file metadata and requested permissions recovered from Twinme app.

in the data/data/com.webadvices.privatenotebook structure (Figure 7(a)). Consequently, it was not possible to access any file or data from the app. However, as shown in Figure 7(b), it was possible to recover the permissions requested by the app.

3C Sensitive Backups App. The 3C Sensitive Backups app enables users to securely backup and restore essential data, including call logs, contacts, SMS,

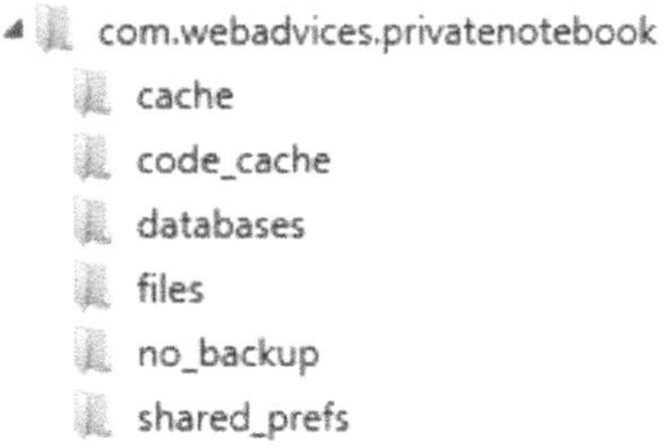

(a) File structure.

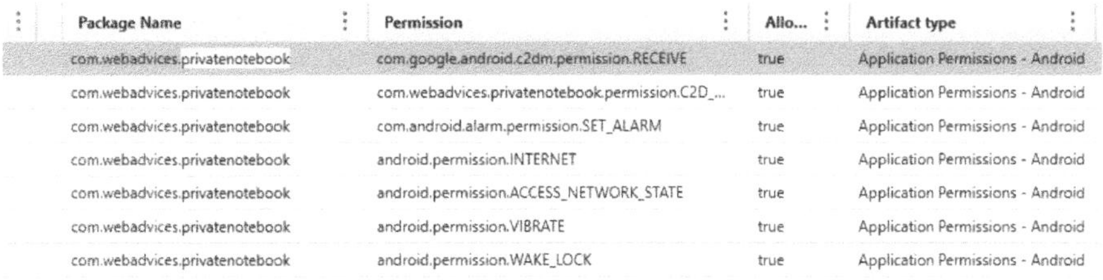

Package Name	Permission	Allo...	Artifact type
com.webadvices.privatenotebook	com.google.android.c2dm.permission.RECEIVE	true	Application Permissions - Android
com.webadvices.privatenotebook	com.webadvices.privatenotebook.permission.C2D_...	true	Application Permissions - Android
com.webadvices.privatenotebook	com.android.alarm.permission.SET_ALARM	true	Application Permissions - Android
com.webadvices.privatenotebook	android.permission.INTERNET	true	Application Permissions - Android
com.webadvices.privatenotebook	android.permission.ACCESS_NETWORK_STATE	true	Application Permissions - Android
com.webadvices.privatenotebook	android.permission.VIBRATE	true	Application Permissions - Android
com.webadvices.privatenotebook	android.permission.WAKE_LOCK	true	Application Permissions - Android

(b) Requested permissions.

Fig. 7. File structure and requested permissions recovered from Private Notebook app.

MMS and calendar data. Users may choose their preferred backup locations – local storage or remote cloud services such as Google Drive, Dropbox or FTP servers. A significant challenge was encountered during the forensic analysis of the app. Despite the intense research efforts, only the basic installation details were recovered. This highlights the robustness of the data protection and security mechanisms implemented by the app.

Steganography Master App. The Steganography Master Android app encodes messages within images. Users can save the resulting pictures or share them with friends. However, only the same application can decode the encoded message. For enhanced security, a password may be set. Interestingly, the app does not use external databases for storage; instead, it stores all pictures locally. During the forensic analysis, all the encoded pictures were successfully identified and recovered from the Steganography Master folder located in the media folder. Additionally, as shown in Figure 8, valuable metadata associated with the images was recovered.

5   Experimental Results

Experiments were conducted to evaluate the effectiveness of using text and permission features in various machine learning algorithms. The text and permission features were combined to create a single feature for each app. The feature set

File Name	**Important.png**
File Extension	**.png**
Last Modified Date/Time	**10/4/2023 12:28:37 PM**
Size (Bytes)	**1857252**
Skin Tone Percentage	**0.0**
Original Width	**1080**
Original Height	**2400**
Exif Extraction Status	**Complete**
Exif Data	**Extraction Result: Complete** **ImageWidth: 1080** **ImageHeight: 2400**
MD5 Hash	**640fb417e5bc57b6204aed0a2c2768eb**
SHA1 Hash	**4ae612f7a588bf21b381753c607460de43187add**
Artifact type	**Pictures**
Item ID	**33995**

EVIDENCE INFORMATION

Source	**OnePlus KB2001 Logical Image - Data.tar\data** **\media\0\Steganography Master\Important.png**
Recovery method	**Parsing**
Deleted source	
Location	**n/a**
Evidence number	**OnePlus KB2001 Logical Image**

Fig. 8. Media metadata recovered from Steganography Master app.

was partitioned into a training set (60%) and a testing set (40%). Four classification models, each using a different machine learning algorithm, were developed. Their results were evaluated using the accuracy, precision, recall and F1-score metrics.

5.1 Feature Comparison

Feature vectors sets were extracted from the available text and permissions to train the classification models. Specifically, four feature sets were created using the feature vectors: (i) binary vectors (BV) specifying word presence, (ii) Doc2Vec document embeddings, (iii) permissions (Perm) and (iv) permissions

Table 2. Accuracy of machine learning algorithms for various feature sets.

Model Algorithm	BV	Doc2Vec	Perm	PermBV
Logistic Regression	85.7%	90.0%	69.2%	79.1%
Support Vector Machine	86.8%	85.5%	74.7%	79.7%
Naive Bayes	65.9%	84.2%	74.7%	69.9%
Random Forest	83.5%	75.6%	71.4%	85.7%

combined with binary vectors (PermBV). The classifiers were trained using four machine learning algorithms: (i) logistic regression, (ii) support vector machine, (iii) naive Bayes and (iv) random forest.

Table 2 presents the accuracy results of the four classifiers for the four feature sets. As expected, the results obtained with the feature sets vary for different machine learning algorithms. The binary vector (BV) feature set exhibited the best overall performance, achieving 86.8% accuracy when paired with the support vector machine. The binary vector feature set also maintained accuracy levels above 80% when used in conjunction with the logistic regression and random forest algorithms.

The Doc2Vec feature set reached its peak accuracy of 90% when paired with logistic regression. In contrast, the Perm feature set yielded reduced accuracy between 69.2% and 74.7% across the four machine learning algorithms. The results underscore the limited effectiveness of the Perm feature set when used on its own.

A more effective approach is to employ permissions combined with binary vectors (PermBV). Table 2 shows that there is an almost 15% increase in accuracy from Perm to PermBV, especially with the random forest algorithm, as well as better accuracy with the two other machine learning algorithms.

Based on the accuracy results in Table 2, the most effective machine learning algorithm/feature set combinations are logistic regression with the Doc2Vec feature set, support vector machine with the BV or Doc2Vec feature sets, and random forest with the PermBV feature set.

Figure 9 shows the precision, recall and F1-score results for the four machine learning algorithms with the four feature sets. The results indicate that Doc2Vec consistently delivers the most favorable outcomes over all the metrics, with BV the second-best performer and PermBV in the third position. As expected, Perm consistently yields the lowest accuracy scores for the evaluation metrics.

5.2   Parameter Analysis

Doc2Vec incorporates multiple parameters in its model, including vector size, window size, epochs and minimum count. The experimental analysis revealed that the majority of these parameters did not exert significant influences on the results. However, two parameters, the vector size that specifies the dimensionality

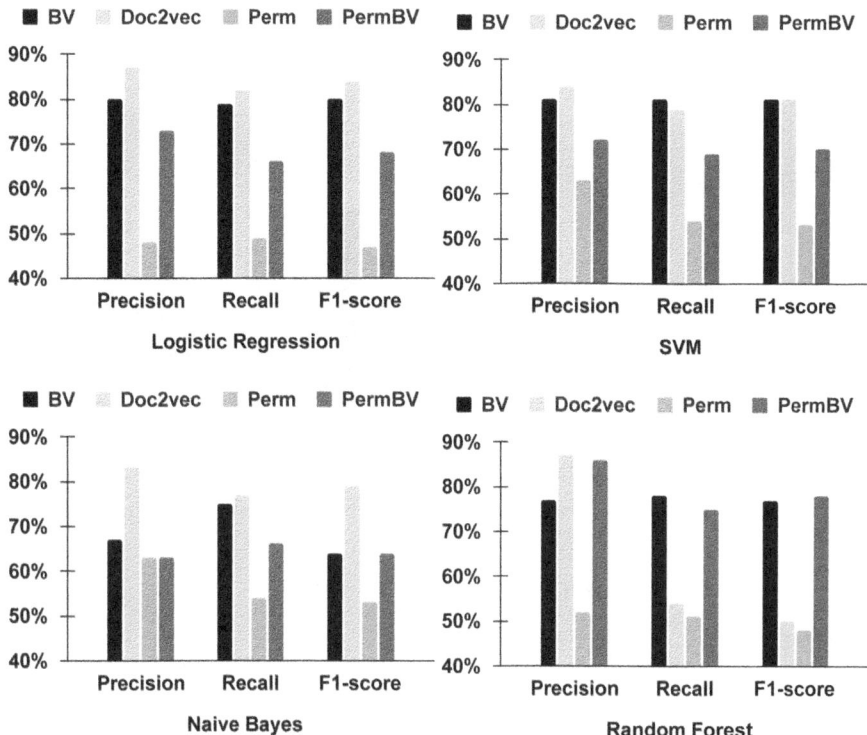

Fig. 9. Precision, recall and F1-score results for the machine learning algorithms.

of the embedded vectors and the window size that specifies the size of the sliding window, exhibited subtle impacts.

In the experiments, the vector size parameter was investigated for values ranging from 50 to 300. Figure 10 shows that increasing the vector size enhances the accuracy of the naive Bayes algorithm, which peaks when the vector size is 300. By contrast, increasing vector size decreases the accuracy of the support vector machine algorithm. Notably, the vector size does not substantially affect the performance of logistic regression and random forest algorithms.

In the experiments, the window size parameter was investigated for five values: 1, 2, 4, 8 and 12. Figure 11 shows that increasing the vector size enhances the accuracy of the naive Bayes and random forest algorithms, which peak when the window size is 12. The vector size does not substantially affect the performance of the logistic regression and support vector machine algorithms.

6   Discussion and Limitations

From a security standpoint, the proposed methodology enables analysts to pinpoint potential vault apps downloaded from alternative gray market app stores.

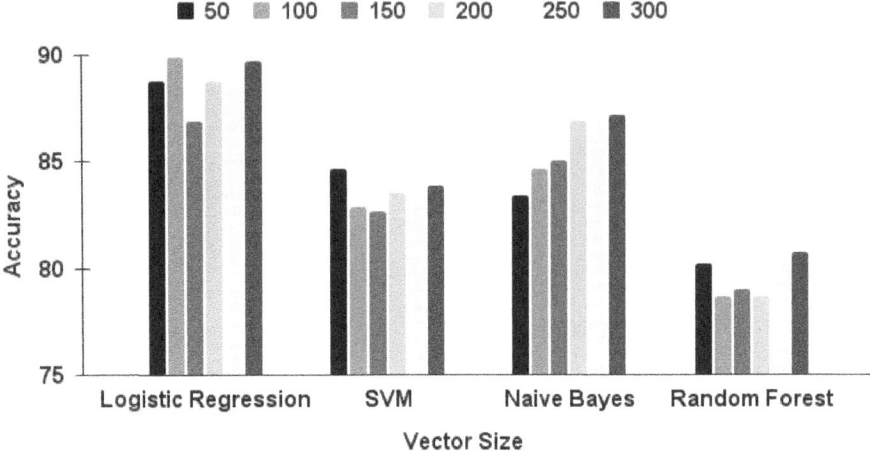

Fig. 10. Machine learning algorithm accuracy based on vector size in Doc2Vec.

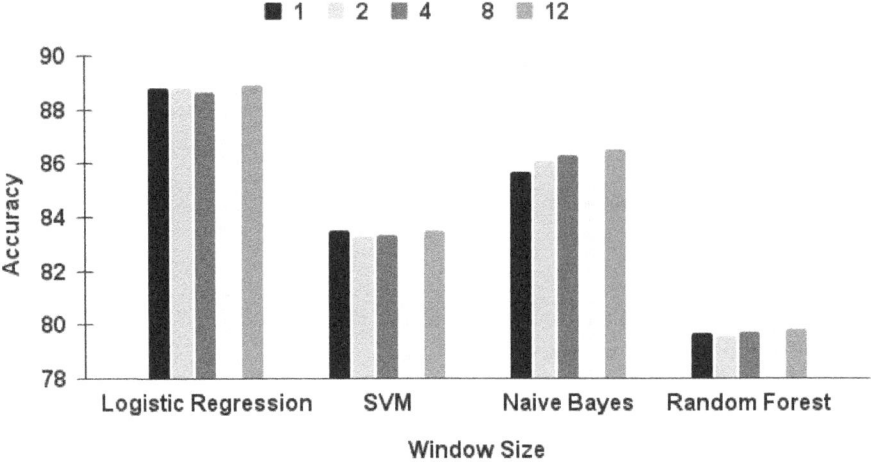

Fig. 11. Machine learning algorithm accuracy based on window size in Doc2Vec.

The methodology also advances digital forensic investigations by providing insights into data storage by vault apps that enable forensic analyses. Additionally, the methodology draws attention to vault apps, providing users with opportunities to make informed decisions about the security and privacy of downloaded apps. Finally, the work may be of value to policy-makers and tech industry regulators as they consider effective policies regarding mobile app data security and privacy.

While the study is interesting and valuable, certain limitations underpin the research. First, the initial categorization of apps as vault apps and non-vault apps was executed manually, which may have inadvertently introduced bias; the adoption of an automated or semi-automated categorization would have addressed this limitation. Second, the apps in the experimental dataset were obtained from the Aptoide gray market app store; integrating apps from diverse sources such as the Google Play Store and other app markets would have yielded a broader and more representative app dataset. Third, the methodology focuses on static analysis and sidelines dynamic behaviors, which may have negatively impacted detection accuracy. Augmenting the methodology with dynamic analysis would have improved the results.

7   Conclusions

Security and privacy concerns have elevated the popularity of vault apps, especially those advertised in alternative gray market app stores. The methodology described for vault app identification, extraction and forensic analysis is of value because vault apps present significant challenges to digital forensic practitioners. In particular, it is difficult to access encrypted and deleted data in sensitive and contraband documents encountered in digital forensic investigations. The methodology described in this chapter leverages feature extraction from app descriptions along with machine learning algorithms. It provides insights into vault apps in gray market app stores and sets the stage for in-depth studies of Android app markets.

Future research will focus on the automated categorization of available apps into vault apps and non-vault apps using machine learning algorithms. It will also bolster the current reliance on static analysis with dynamic analysis techniques that would provide insights into nuanced or concealed dynamic behaviors of vault apps. Additionally, future research will investigate apps from diverse mainstream and gray market stores, and broaden the focus from Android to other mobile device operating systems.

Acknowledgement. This research was supported by the National Science Foundation under Grant no. DGE 2043302.

References

1. Android Developers, Manifest.permission, Google, Mountain View, California (`developer.android.com/reference/android/Manifest.permission`), 2024.
2. S. Arzt, S. Rasthofer, C. Fritz, E. Bodden, A. Bartel, J. Klein, Y. Le Traon, D. Octeau and P. McDaniel, FlowDroid: Precise context, flow, field, object-sensitive and lifecycle-aware taint analysis for Android apps, *ACM SIGPLAN Notices*, vol. 49(6), pp. 259–269, 2014.
3. G. Dorai, S. Aggarwal, N. Patel and C. Powell, VIDE – Vault app identification and extraction system for iOS devices, *Forensic Science International: Digital Investigation*, vol. 33(S), article no. 301007, 2020.

4. Y. Feng, S. Anand, I. Dillig and A. Aiken, Apposcopy: Semantics-based detection of Android malware through static analysis, *Proceedings of the Twenty-Second ACM SIGSOFT International Symposium on Foundations of Software Engineering*, pp. 576–587, 2014.

5. A. Fuchs, A. Chaudhuri and J. Foster, Scandroid: Automated Security Certification of Android Applications, Technical Report CS-TR-4991, Department of Computer Science, University of Maryland, College Park, Maryland, 2009.

6. S. Hou, Y. Fan, Y. Zhang, Y. Ye, J. Lei, W. Wan, J. Wang, Q. Xiong and F. Shao, αCyber: Enhancing the robustness of an Android malware detection system against adversarial attacks using a heterogeneous graph-based model, *Proceedings of the Twenty-Eighth ACM International Conference on Information and Knowledge Management*, pp. 609–618, 2019.

7. A. Javed, W. Ahmed, M. Alazab, Z. Jalil, K. Kifayat and T. Gadekallu, A comprehensive survey of computer forensics: State-of-the-art, tools, techniques, challenges and future directions, *IEEE Access*, vol. 10, pp. 11065–11089, 2022.

8. Q. Le and T. Mikolov, Distributed representations of sentences and documents, *Proceedings of the Thirty-First International Conference on Machine Learning*, vol. 32, pp. II-1188–II-1196, 2014.

9. PCMag, Vault app, Ziff Davis, New York (`www.pcmag.com/encyclopedia/term/vault-app`), 2024.

10. M. Peng, M. Khanov, S. Madireddy, H. Chi, E. Akbas and G. Dorai, DECADE – Deep-learning-based content-hiding application detection system for Android, *Proceedings of the IEEE International Conference on Big Data*, pp. 5430–5440, 2021.

11. D. Votipka, S. Rabin, K. Micinski, J. Foster and M. Mazurek, An observational investigation of reverse engineersâĂŹ processes, *Proceedings of the Twenty-Ninth USENIX Security Symposium*, 2020, pp. 1875–1892, 2020.

12. X. Zhang, I. Baggili and F. Breitinger, Breaking into the vault: Privacy, security and forensic analysis of Android vault applications, *Computers and Security*, vol. 70, pp. 516–531, 2017.

Image and Video Forensics

Using Microposture Features and Optical Flows for Deepfake Detection

Kai Chen[1,2], Duohe Ma[1], Zhenchao Zhang[1], Zhimin Tang[1], Liming Wang[1], and Junye Jiang[1]

[1] Chinese Academy of Sciences, Beijing, China
maduohe@iie.ac.cn
[2] University of Chinese Academy of Sciences, Beijing, China

Abstract. The proliferation of deepfake videos underscores the need to develop reliable detection methods to mitigate their negative consequences. Several deepfake video detection methods achieve satisfactory performance. However, the methods often focus on specific facial features and overlook the noise introduced during feature extraction.
This chapter describes a deepfake video detection method that focuses on five key facial features and their changes in video frames and uses optical flows to fine-tune facial landmark points to reduce landmark errors. An efficient model is employed to compute optical flows in frame sequences and refine the actual and predicted landmark points. This facilitates the accurate identification of facial landmark points, including anomalous landmark points. Two recurrent neural networks are employed to capture temporal relationships between landmark points and their movement patterns. The proposed deepfake video detection method achieves high performance on raw and compressed videos.

Keywords: Deepfake Video Detection · Facial Landmark Extraction · Optical Flow · Recurrent Neural Network

1 Introduction

Deepfake videos pose significant concerns to society [7,17]. Examples include a fake Barack Obama speech video and manipulated pornographic videos of famous actresses [30]. Responding to the privacy and security threats, the research community has instituted serious efforts to develop reliable methods for detecting sophisticated deepfake videos [32].

Deepfake video detection methods can be divided into two groups. Methods in the first group focus on the noise introduced during deepfake creation in each video frame whereas methods in the second group focus on temporal relationships between video frames. Popular detection methods in the first group leverage the data fitting abilities of neural networks to extract discriminating features for detecting forgeries [18]. However, some features in deepfake videos are negatively affected by noise and video compression, and other features are difficult to extract accurately. As technology advances, deepfake videos are becoming increasingly realistic, making it difficult to identify anomalies in a single frame.

© IFIP International Federation for Information Processing 2025
Published by Springer Nature Switzerland AG 2025
E. Kurkowski and S. Shenoi (Eds.): DigitalForensics 2024, IFIP AICT 724, pp. 81–97, 2025.
https://doi.org/10.1007/978-3-031-71025-4_5

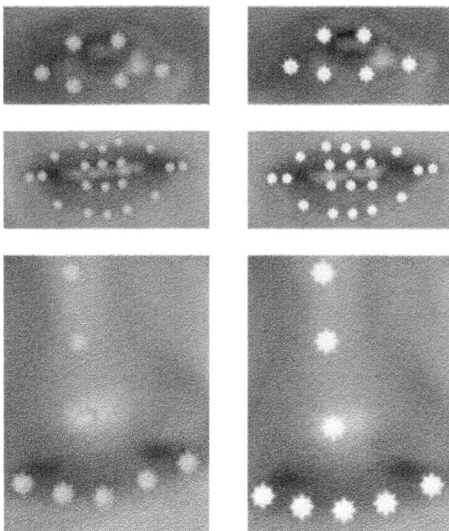

Fig. 1. Imprecise (left) and accurate (right) landmark detection.

Since most deepfake videos are generated frame-by-frame and individual be-havioral and movement patterns between consecutive synthetic frames are un-certain, researchers have turned to detection methods in the second group to identify temporal features. Methods involving optical flows [2], eye blinking [20], lip movements [14], photoplethysmography [6] and neural ordinary differential equations [12, 31] have emerged for detecting deepfake videos. These methods overcome some of the limitations of detection methods in the first group and provide increased reliability.

While some deepfake detection methods have demonstrated the potential of using iconic facial features to detect synthetic facial images and videos, they often rely on manual or complex correlation-based features that may not capture all the distinguishable dynamic features in videos. Additionally, little attention has focused on addressing the noise introduced by imprecise facial landmark detection.

Figure 1 shows the noise introduced by imprecise facial landmark detection. The imprecise landmarks on the left-hand-side image were marked using a pre-trained detection model without any refinements or corrections to accommodate facial angle, motion and other factors. In contrast, the more accurate landmarks on the right-hand-side image were marked using optical flows to correct the positions of the imprecise landmarks.

An emerging research area is posture recognition, which involves marking the key points of a human skeleton frame-by-frame and using recurrent neural networks to identify human postures in videos. While the concept is typically applied to whole-body landmarking tasks, it can be adapted to fake facial image detection by marking iconic features using facial landmarks. The approach, which is called microposture recognition, eliminates the need to process large amounts of image data because the landmark regions are significantly smaller than the whole body images. Microposture recognition involves identifying characteristic posture changes in small areas of the human body. Facial microposture features encompass the positions and movement patterns of key points associated with marked facial postures. These features include eye blinking, lip movements, facial muscle stretching and head swinging, all of which are important in detecting deepfake videos.

To address the aforementioned challenges, a landmark point position correction method is proposed that utilizes optical flows to combine spatial and temporal features reliably, enhancing the discriminative capabilities of facial microposture features. Two recurrent neural networks are trained to extract position and temporal features of facial micropostures from extracted frame sequences. The method replaces facial images with the positions of landmark points, effectively reducing data dimensionality. Compared with other deep learning models, the proposed detection method mitigates errors caused by imprecise landmark points while also reducing training costs and minimizing the sensitivity to video image resolution. Additionally, the recurrent neural networks improve the expressiveness of facial micropostures from a spatiotemporal perspective.

2   Related Work

This section discusses related work on posture recognition, feature landmarking and deepfake video detection.

2.1   Posture Recognition

One approach to analyzing human behavior is to detect the positions (points) of key parts of human body posture in each frame. By simplifying the human body posture to the key points, it is possible to recognize and classify the semantics of body postures.

Traditional machine learning algorithms treat the key points of a human skeleton a sequence of dynamic trajectories in the time domain. These approaches employ hidden Markov models, conditional random fields and time-domain pyramids [35]. Feature extraction methods for time-domain skeleton key points typically include the joint position histogram distribution of the key points and the rotation and displacement features of the 3D positions of key points [23]. In the deep learning domain, the key points of human posture are modeled in the spatiotemporal domain using recurrent neural networks, long short-term memory networks and convolutional neural networks. These models enable the recognition and classification of human postures.

The proposed deepfake video detection method employs a similar idea to implement microposture recognition. Compared with posture recognition that considers the entire human body as the region of interest, the proposed method concentrates on multiple small areas such as the jaw, eyebrows, nose, eyes and mouth. When one feature is hidden or damaged, the other features can still contribute to detection, although the accuracy would be affected.

2.2   Feature Landmarking

Facial landmark detection methods have seen significant advancements in recent years. Researchers initially proposed methods such as the active appearance model [8] and constrained local models [10] for facial landmark detection. The methods attempt to estimate and refine landmark locations iteratively using ensemble regression. Open-source libraries such as Dlib [16] have incorporated these methods, offering convenience and speed.

More sophisticated deep learning models have been developed for facial landmark detection, including cascade convolutional neural networks [38], convolutional pose machines [33] and convolutional experts constrained local models [37]. These models exhibit improved performance, but they generally require extensive computational resources. Researchers have also introduced advanced architectures to handle challenges posed by facial occlusion, extreme head poses and posture recognition [19, 34]. These architectures address specific problems associated with facial landmark detection. Open-source toolkits such as OpenFace [4] provide implementations of these models and architectures, making them accessible to the wider community. These advancements in facial landmark detection have enabled applications in several domains.

2.3   Deepfake Video Detection

Existing methods for deepfake detection in videos fall in two categories: frame-level detection and video-level detection:

- **Frame-Level Detection:** Frame-level detection focuses on deepfake traces on frames. Some techniques rely on features that are selected manually. For example, Matern et al. [24] focus on simple visual artificial defects such as colors, wired shadows on a face and missing details of eyes and teeth.
  Other techniques employ deep features extracted by deep convolutional neural networks. Rossler et al. [26] successfully applied Xception [5] to detecting deepfakes. Afchar et al. [1] developed MesoNet that focused on mesoscopic properties of images. Li et al. [19] employed an advanced architecture named HRNet [29] to detect the blending boundaries of deepfake images. These methods employ powerful convolutional neural networks to obtain good performance. However, their detection results based on single features are difficult to reproduce and lack robustness.
- **Video-Level Detection:** Video-level detection involves identifying deepfake traces in frames as well as focusing on the relationships between frames. The fact that videos contain more information than images has inspired deepfake detection based on temporal features.

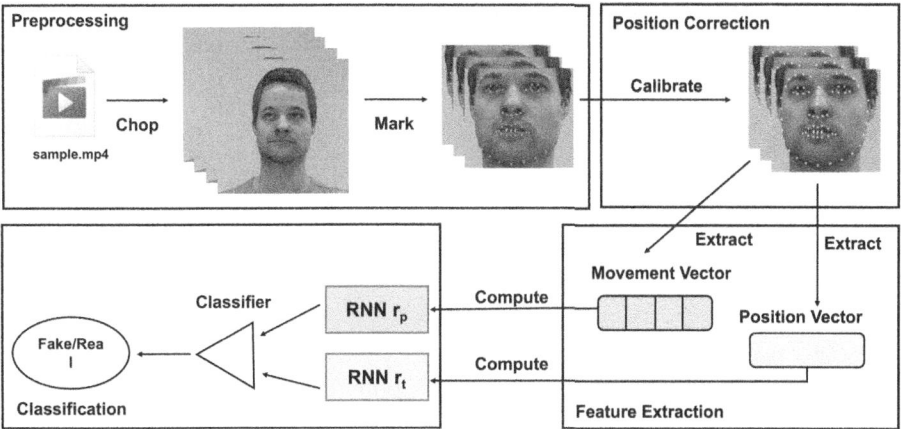

Fig. 2. Microposture feature detection method.

Several researchers have employed facial-feature-based detection schemes. For example, Li et al. [20] capture anomalies in eye blinking frequencies in deepfake videos. Yang et al. [36] employ outer and central landmarks to capture head and face directions, respectively, and detect inconsistencies between them. Since manually-selected features are less discriminative, their performance is limited. Therefore, this work focuses on expressive deep temporal features.

Appearance-based deepfake detection methods are drawing attention. Guera and Delp [13] have proposed a framework utilizing a convolutional neural network to extract features from frames and a long short-term memory model to process sequences of the features. Sabir et al. [27] have developed a similar architecture that replaces the long short-term memory model with a bidirectional gated recurrent unit. However, these methods rely on computationally-expensive convolutional neural networks and suffer from similar problems as frame-level detection methods.

3   Microposture Feature Detection Method

Figure 2 shows the proposed microposture feature detection method. The method involves four tasks, data preprocessing, landmark position correction, feature extraction and classification. Anomalies in facial microposture movement patterns indicative of manipulated facial images are identified by matching the landmark positions and landmark movement directions. Landmark position correction is required because facial landmark points that are marked directly on images are inaccurate. Feature extraction yields two types of feature vector sequences, one expressing positions and the other expressing movements. Classification lever-

Table 1. Facial features and associated landmark points.

Feature	Landmark Points
Jaw	1-17
Eyebrows	18-27
Nose	28-36
Eyes	37-48
Mouth	49-68

ages two trained recurrent neural networks (RNNs), one focusing on landmark point positions and the other on landmark point movements.

3.1 Data Preprocessing

Data preprocessing operations are performed on an input video to enhance the accuracy and reliability of the subsequent tasks. A key operation is to identify and isolate the face in each frame. This operation outputs the region of interest, specifically, the portion of the frame containing the face.

After a face is detected and cropped from the frame, facial landmarks corresponding to facial features such as the jaw, eyebrows, nose, eyes and mouth are identified and marked. Table 1 lists the facial features and their associated numbers of landmark points. The landmarks provide crucial information about facial micropostures that are indicative of deepfake manipulation. Landmark detection leverages a model trained on a large dataset to detect facial landmarks accurately. Next, landmark calibration is employed to improve the accuracy of landmark positions. Calibration aligns the landmark points to preset positions using affine transformations. The alignments ensure that information pertaining to multiple facial features can be reliably extracted from facial images.

3.2 Landmark Position Correction

Landmark position correction seeks to improve the accuracy of landmark detection by addressing influencing factors such as frame shaking and measurement errors.

Figure 3 outlines the landmark position correction procedure. Fixed-position frames are selected and an optical flow algorithm is applied to predict the subsequent positions of landmarks. The optical flow algorithm computes the motions of pixels between consecutive pairs of frames, enabling the movements of landmarks to be estimated over time. Optical flow analysis addresses factors such as motion blur and occlusion that make it difficult to directly detect landmarks on frames. The prediction of landmark positions via optical flows is bidirectional in that considers the previous and subsequent frames. The first and last frames in a sequence that do not have previous or subsequent frames are excluded from further processing.

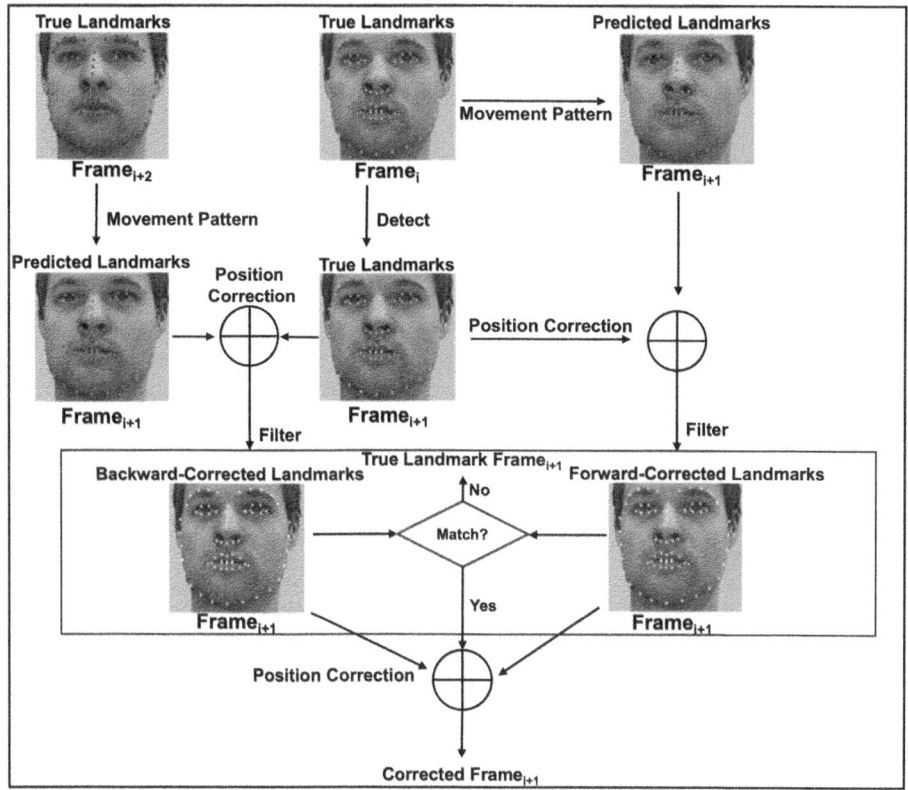

Fig. 3. Landmark position correction.

To ensure the accuracy of the fixed landmark positions, a filter is employed to combine valid predictions with their corresponding detection results. The filter helps reduce noise and refines the positions of the fixed landmarks, contributing to more accurate landmark detection.

In order to calibrate the landmark points, their point positions are tuned by matching small image patches around them. PWC-Net [2, 28] is a suitable network for this task because it computes optical flows and reveals the movement patterns of multiple facial microposture landmark points between frames. Drawing on previous research [3, 11], optical flow operations are employed to predict feature landmark positions [30], or more specifically, to track the precise landmark point positions of facial micropostures.

An optical flow operation requires the optimal displacement vector d to be computed. The optimal values of the displacement vector $d = [d_x, d_y]^T$ are obtained by minimizing the difference between the small image patch P_i centered at $pos_i = [x, y]^T$ in $frame_i$ and another patch P_{i+1} of the same size in $frame_{i+1}$.

Specifically, the following term is minimized:

$$\sum_{x \in \Omega} ||P_{i+1}(pos_{i+1}) - P_i(pos_i + \boldsymbol{d})||^2$$

where the initial $\boldsymbol{d}$ is set to $[0,0]^T$.

The optimal $\boldsymbol{d}$ is used to predict the tracking position in the next frame as $pos_{i+1} = pos_i + \boldsymbol{d}$.

However, a single optical flow operation is not always successful. Due to prediction errors, the majority of the landmark points in frames have low correlations with their previous and following frames. Therefore, two optical flow operations are performed. A forward optical flow operation is performed from the previous frame and a backward optical flow operation is performed from the predicted points in the current frame back to the previous frame. Predicted landmark points with large differences between their forward and backward optical flows are changed back to their original points.

3.3   Feature Extraction

The landmark positions and sequences obtained in the previous two steps are embedded in two types of feature vector sequences, one expressing positions and the other expressing movements.

A landmark point is denoted by $p^a = [x_i^a, y_i^a]^T$ where $a \in \{1, 2, ..., 68\}$ and i corresponds to $frame_i$. The landmark point position feature vector l_i embedded from landmark $L_i = [x_i^g, ..., x_i^h]^T$ is generated by directly flattening L_i as follows:

$$l_i^c = [x_i^g, y_i^g, x_i^{g+1}, y_i^{g+1}, ..., x_i^h, y_i^h]$$

where g and h are the minimum and maximum numbers of certain facial microposture landmarks.

Next, the movement pattern feature vector m_i expressing the difference in the landmark positions between frames is computed as:

$$m_i^c = l_{i+1} - l_i = [x_{i+1}^g - x_i^g, ..., y_{i+1}^h - y_i^h]$$

where c corresponds to a specific facial microposture landmark.

The entire position feature vector L is given by:

$$L = [l^J, l^{Eb}, l^N, l^E, l^M]$$

and the complete movement pattern feature vector is given by:

$$M = [m^J, m^{Eb}, m^N, m^E, m^M]$$

Finally, embeddings are performed to obtain the two feature vector sequences A and B:

$$A = [L_1, ..., L_n]^T$$
$$B = [M_1, ..., M_{n-1}]^T$$

3.4 Classification

The feature vector sequences are input to two recurrent neural networks for classification. The first recurrent neural network r_p detects deepfakes by identifying anomalous landmark point position changes. The second recurrent neural network r_t detects deepfakes by identifying anomalous movement direction changes (i.e., speed patterns). Two fully-connected layers are attached to the output of each recurrent network to provide the detection results.

Experimentation revealed that the detection performance of recurrent neural network r_t (movement changes) was better than that of recurrent neural network r_p (position changes). This implies that the contributions of the two recurrent neural networks are different. To address this issue, the detection results of r_t and r_p are weighted using parameters λ_1 and λ_2, respectively.

The output probability R is computed as:

$$R = \sigma(\lambda_1 r_p(A) + \lambda_2 r_t(B))$$

where $\sigma(\cdot)$ is the sigmoid function.

The output probability R is used to determine if a facial image is fake or real. An image with an R value greater than 0.5 is deemed to be fake whereas an image with an R value less than or equal to 0.5 is deemed to be real. This threshold helps distinguish between deepfake and authentic images based on the output of the sigmoid function.

4 Experiments and Evaluation

This section provides details about the datasets used in the experiments, model development and experimental evaluation results.

4.1 Datasets

Two classical datasets, Celeb-DF [22] and FaceForensics++ (FF++) [25], were selected for the experimental evaluation.

The Celeb-DF dataset comprises 590 real videos and more than 5,000 forged videos generated using four face-changing algorithms, Face2Face, FaceSwap, deepfakes and neural-textures. Color conversion and edge softening algorithms were employed to optimize the visual similarity between synthetic faces and the original faces. These techniques reduce synthetic boundary artifacts and jitter, rendering the forged videos more continuous in the time domain.

Each Celeb-DF dataset video has three versions, an original version (raw), a slightly-compressed version (c23) and a heavily-compressed version (c40). The multiple compression levels pose challenges to deepfake detection algorithms and the varying quality of videos that simulate real-world scenarios. Celeb-DF is a most typical dataset and is widely used by researchers.

FF++ is a comprehensive dataset that contains more than 1,000 real videos and their forged versions created using algorithms such as Face2Face, FaceSwap,

Fig. 4. Comparison between fake (top) and real (bottom) video images.

deepfakes and neural-textures. Each video has an original (raw) version, slightly-compressed (c23) version and heavily-compressed (c40) version. The multiple compression levels pose challenges to deepfake detection algorithms and the varying quality of videos simulate real-world scenarios.

4.2   Model Development

Dlib [16] was employed during the data preprocessing step to chop faces and mark points on the faces.

Bidirectional recurrent neural networks were employed during the classification step. Two fully-connected layers with 64 and 2 units were connected to the output layers of the recurrent neural networks. A dropout layer with drop rate 0.25 was inserted between the input and each recurrent neural network. Another three dropout layers with drop rates of 0.5 were used to separate the remaining layers. The parameters λ_1 and λ_2 were set to 0.48 and 0.52, respectively.

Each video was segmented into clips of fixed length 60 with 25 frames/s. Adam was selected as the optimizer and the batch size was set to 1,024. The classification model was trained over 1,000 epochs.

4.3   Experimental Evaluation

Figure 4 compares fake and real video images. The top row displays facial images from deepfake videos and the bottom row displays the corresponding real facial images.

Tables 2 and 3 present the performance evaluation results using the Celeb-DF and FF++ (raw) datasets, respectively. The tables compare the performance of

Table 2. Performance evaluation using the Celeb-DF dataset.

Method	AUC Score	D-Value (Best)
MesoNet [1]	55.2%	+19.8%
Xception [5]	64.7%	+10.3%
CNN+LSTM [13]	72.1%	+2.9%
LRNet [30]	63.7%	+11.3%
DSP-FWA [21]	65.1%	+9.9%
ID-Reveal [9]	72.6%	+2.4%
Face X-Ray [19]	72.9%	+2.1%
Proposed Method	**75.0%**	0.0%

Table 3. Performance evaluation using the FF++ (raw) dataset.

Method	AUC Score	D-Value (Best)
MesoNet [1]	84.7%	+14.3%
Xception [5]	97%	+2.0%
CNN+LSTM [13]	95.3%	+3.7%
LRNet [30]	**99.3%**	+0.3%
DSP-FWA [21]	94.8%	+4.2%
ID-Reveal [9]	93.7%	+5.3%
Face X-Ray [19]	97.7%	+1.3%
Proposed Method	99.0%	0.0%

seven state-of-the-art deepfake detection methods versus that of the proposed method. Area under the receiver operating characteristic curve score (AUC score) is used as the performance metric. The best AUC scores are shown in boldface. The proposed method has the best AUC score of 75% for the Celeb-DF dataset and the second-best AUC score of 99% for the FF++ (raw) dataset. The results demonstrate that the proposed method's approach to detecting deepfakes using discontinuities in physiological characteristics is effective. This is because deepfakes cannot learn movement patterns from images. Additionally, the approach should be applicable to other datasets with little training.

Table 4 compares the robustness of seven state-of-the-art deepfake detection methods versus that of the proposed method for compressed videos in the FF++ (c23) dataset. Each deepfake detection model was trained on the original videos in the FF++ (raw) dataset and tested on two versions of videos with different compression ratios. The proposed method has the best AUC score of 95.7% for compressed videos. The sensitivity of the proposed method to image resolution is reduced because it leverages a few iconic landmark points to simplify the complex facial features at the image level, and focuses on anomalous changes in facial microposture movements.

Table 4. Robustness evaluation using the FF++ (c23) dataset.

Method	AUC Score	D-Value (FF++ (raw))
MesoNet [1]	74.6%	+10.1%
Xception [5]	87.3%	+9.7%
CNN+LSTM [13]	89.6%	+5.7%
LRNet [30]	92.5%	+6.8%
DSP-FWA [21]	88.2%	+6.6%
ID-Reveal [9]	90.1%	+3.6%
Face X-Ray [19]	90.3%	+7.4%
Proposed Method	**95.7%**	+3.3%

4.4 Ablation Experiments

The proposed method employs two recurrent neural networks for deepfake detection – r_p that focuses on anomalous facial microposture positions and r_t that focuses on anomalous facial microposture movements. An ablation experiment was conducted to evaluate the effectiveness of the two-network architecture (r_p and r_t together) by comparing its performance with the single-network architectures (r_p alone and r_t alone).

Figure 5 shows the results of the ablation experiment involving the three recurrent neural network architectures. As expected, the two-network architecture has superior performance. Leveraging position and movement information promote each other – the temporal discontinuity clues detected by r_t contribute more to the final accuracy and the anomalous landmark points recognized by r_p improve the detection accuracy.

Table 5. Ablation results with and without position correction.

Proposed Method	Dataset	AUC Score
With Position Correction	Celeb-DF	75.0%
Without Position Correction	Celeb-DF	71.4%
With Position Correction	FF++ (raw)	99.0%
Without Position Correction	FF++ (raw)	94.2%

Table 5 shows the importance of position correction. The original facial landmarks are often imprecise (noisy) due to the face angles in the images, hindering the accurate detection of anomalous facial movements. The noise is introduced during landmark detection. Position correction reduces the noise by moving the landmarks closer to their right positions.

Table 6 evaluates the influence of using forward and/or backward optical flow operations. The highest AUC score of 99.0% is obtained when forward and

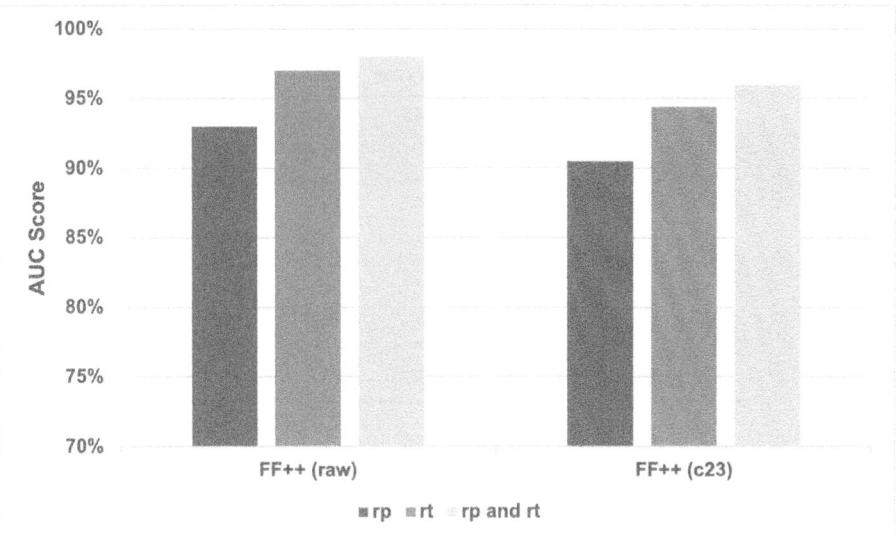

Fig. 5. Ablation results with recurrent neural networks.

Table 6. Ablation results with optical flow operations.

Method	Dataset	AUC Score
Forward Optical Flow Operation	FF++ (raw)	92.1%
Backward Optical Flow Operation	FF++ (raw)	92.3%
Forward and Backward Optical Flow Operations	FF++ (raw)	**99.0%**

backward optical flow operations are used. This is because more anomalous facial landmark points are revealed when both optical flow operations are employed. Using only one optical flow operation does not reveal some anomalous facial landmark points, which degrades the performance.

Table 7 shows the influence of each facial microposture on detection. Using all the facial microposture features yields the highest AUC score of 99.0% whereas using single features yields lower scores ranging from 31.2% to 93.9%. This is because using more microfacial postures helps avoid feature blocking and provides more clues to detect anomalies. The results also show that the nose and jaw have limited contributions to deepfake detection, so only the eyes and mouth are considered with other features.

Figure 6 shows the ablation results with input lengths ranging from 10 to 90 frames/s. The datasets include FF++ (raw), FF++ (c23) and UADFV [20], a public dataset comprising 49 real videos from YouTube and their 49 corresponding fake videos created using a Deepfake method with post-processing. The input length of 60 frames/s has the best AUC scores for all three datasets.

Table 7. Microposture feature evaluation using the FF++ (raw) dataset.

Features	AUC Score	D-Value (Best)
Eyes Only	91.8%	+7.2%
Mouth Only	93.9%	+5.1%
Nose Only	38.4%	+60.6%
Jaw Only	31.2%	+67.8%
Eyes and Mouth	98.0%	+1.0%
Eyes and Nose	91.8%	+7.2%
Eyes and Jaw	89.8%	+9.2%
Mouth and Nose	93.8%	+5.0%
Mouth and Jaw	94.1%	+4.9%
All Features	**99.0%**	0.0%

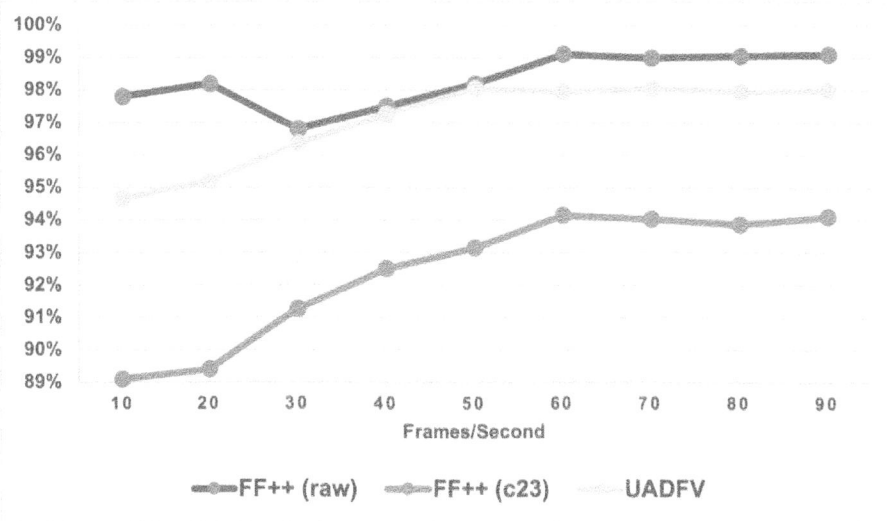

Fig. 6. Ablation results with input length.

It is important to consider the trade-off between the number of frames used and computational cost. Including large numbers of frames significantly increases the computational cost whereas using too few frames may fail to capture important changes in movement patterns. Selecting an input length such as 60 frames/s strikes the right balance between accuracy and computational cost.

5   Conclusions

Deepfake videos pose threats to society and technological advances in deepfake creation make it important to develop accurate and efficient detection methods. The proposed method employing spatial and temporal facial microposture features fared well in comparisons with seven state-of-the art deepfake detection methods. Specifically, it yielded AUC scores of 75.0% for Celeb-DF dataset videos and 99.0% for FF++ dataset videos, and performed well with compressed videos.

However, the experimental results indicate that the proposed method still has room for improvement in terms of universality and cross-testing ability. One approach is to tune the marked landmarks more accurately in subsequent frames and use the feature vectors more efficiently. Also, it is difficult to interpret the temporal features captured by the method and discern the differences in the movement patterns between real and deepfake videos. Indeed, it appears that focusing on a single category such graphics or facial features is inadequate for detecting sophisticated deepfake videos. A promising solution for dealing with rapidly-advancing deepfake creation technology is to employ multiplex synthetic video detection methods [15].

References

1. D. Afchar, V. Nozick, J. Yamagishi and I. Echizen, MesoNet: A compact facial video forgery detection network, *Proceedings of the IEEE International Workshop on Information Forensics and Security*, 2018.
2. I. Amerini, L. Galteri, R. Caldelli and A. Del Bimbo, Deepfake video detection through optical-flow-based CNN, *Proceedings of the IEEE/CVF International Conference on Computer Vision Workshop*, pp. 1205–1207, 2019.
3. S. Baker and I. Matthews, Lucas-Kanade 20 years on: A unifying framework, *International Journal of Computer Vision*, vol. 56(3), pp. 221–255, 2004.
4. T. Baltrusaitis, A. Zadeh, Y. Lim and L. Morency, OpenFace 2.0: Facial behavior analysis toolkit, *Proceedings of the Thirteenth IEEE International Conference on Automatic Face and Gesture Recognition*, pp. 59–66, 2018.
5. F. Chollet, Xception: Deep learning with depthwise separable convolutions, *Proceedings of the IEEE/CVF Conference on Computer Vision and Pattern Recognition*, pp. 1800–1807, 2017.
6. U. Ciftci, I. Demir and L. Yin, How do the hearts of deepfakes beat? Deepfake source detection via interpreting residuals with biological signals, *Proceedings of the IEEE International Conference on Biometrics*, 2020.
7. D. Citron, How deepfakes undermine truth and threaten democracy, presented at *TEDSummit 2019*, 2019.
8. T. Cootes, G. Edwards and C. Taylor, Active appearance models, *IEEE Transactions on Pattern Analysis and Machine Intelligence*, vol. 23(6), pp. 681–685, 2001.
9. D. Cozzolino, A. Rossler, J. Thies, M. Niessner and L. Verdoliva, ID-Reveal: Identity-aware deepfake video detection, *Proceedings of the IEEE/CVF International Conference on Computer Vision*, pp. 15088–15097, 2021.
10. D. Cristinacce and T. Cootes, Feature detection and tracking with constrained local models, *Proceedings of the British Machine Vision Conference*, pp. 929–938, 2006.
11. X. Dong, S. Yu, X. Weng, S. Wei, Y. Yang and Y. Sheikh, Supervision-by-registration: An unsupervised approach to improve the precision of facial landmark detectors, *Proceedings of the IEEE/CVF International Conference on Computer Vision*, pp. 1360–1368, 2018.

12. S. Fernandes, S. Raj, E. Ortiz, I. Vintila, M. Salter, G. Urosevic and S. Jha, Predicting heart rate variations of deepfake videos using neural ODE, *Proceedings of the IEEE/CVF International Conference on Computer Vision Workshop*, pp. 1721–1729, 2019.

13. D. Guera and E. Delp, Deepfake video detection using recurrent neural networks, *Proceedings of the Fifteenth IEEE International Conference on Advanced Video and Signal Based Surveillance*, 2018.

14. A. Haliassos, K. Vougioukas, S. Petridis and M. Pantic, Lips Don't Lie: A Generalizable and Robust Approach to Face Forgery Detection, arXiv: 2012.07657v3 (arxiv.org/abs/2012.07657v3), 2020.

15. Y. He, B. Gan, S. Chen, Y. Zhou, G. Yin, L. Song, L. Sheng, J. Shao and Z. Lu, ForgeryNet: A Versatile Benchmark for Comprehensive Forgery Analysis, arXiv: 2103.05630v2 (arxiv.org/abs/2103.05630v2), 2021.

16. D. King, Dlib-ml: A machine learning toolkit, *Journal of Machine Learning Research*, vol. 10, pp. 1755–1758, 2009.

17. P. Korshunov and S. Marcel, Deepfakes: A New Threat to Face Recognition? Assessment and Detection, arXiv: 1812.08685v1 (arxiv.org/abs/1812.08685v1), 2018.

18. J. Li, H. Xie, J. Li, Z. Wang and Y. Zhang, Frequency-Aware Discriminative Feature Learning Supervised by Single-Center Loss for Face Forgery Detection, arXiv: 2103.09096v1 (arxiv.org/abs/2103.09096v1), 2021.

19. L. Li, J. Bao, T. Zhang, H. Yang, D. Chen, F. Wen and B. Guo, Face x-ray for more general face forgery detection, *Proceedings of the IEEE/CVF Conference on Computer Vision and Pattern Recognition*, pp. 5001–5010, 2020.

20. Y. Li, M. Chang and S. Lyu, *In ictu oculi*: Exposing AI-created fake videos by detecting eye blinking, *Proceedings of the IEEE International Workshop on Information Forensics and Security*, 2018.

21. Y. Li and S. Lyu, Exposing deepfake videos by detecting face warping artifacts, *Proceedings of the IEEE/CVF International Conference on Computer Vision Workshop*, pp. 46–52, 2019.

22. Y. Li, X. Yang, P. Sun, H. Qi and S. Lyu, Celeb-DF: A large-scale challenging dataset for deepfake forensics, *Proceedings of the IEEE/CVF Conference on Computer Vision and Pattern Recognition*, pp. 3204–3213, 2020.

23. L. LoPresti and M. La Cascia, 3D-skeleton-based human action classification: A survey, *Pattern Recognition*, vol. 53(C), pp. 130–147, 2016.

24. F. Matern, C. Riess and M. Stamminger, Exploiting visual artifacts to expose deepfakes and face manipulations, *Proceedings of the IEEE Winter Applications of Computer Vision Workshops*, pp. 83–92, 2019.

25. T. Mittal, U. Bhattacharya, R. Chandra, A. Bera and D. Manocha, Emotions don't lie: An audio-visual deepfake detection method using affective cues, *Proceedings of the Twenty-Eighth ACM International Conference on Multimedia*, pp. 2823–2832, 2020.

26. A. Rossler, D. Cozzolino, L. Verdoliva, C. Riess, J. Thies and M. Niesner, FaceForensics++: Learning to Detect Manipulated Facial Images, arXiv: 1901.08971v3 (arxiv.org/abs/1901.08971v3), 2019.

27. E. Sabir, J. Cheng, A. Jaiswal, W. AbdAlmageed, I. Masi and P. Natarajan, Recurrent convolutional strategies for face manipulation detection in videos, *Proceedings of the IEEE/CVF Conference on Computer Vision and Pattern Recognition Workshop*, pp. 80–87, 2019.

28. D. Sun, X. Yang, M. Liu and J. Kautz, PWC-Net: CNNs for optical flow using pyramid, warping and cost volume, *Proceedings of the IEEE/CVF Conference on Computer Vision and Pattern Recognition*, pp. 8934–8943, 2018.

29. K. Sun, Y. Zhao, B. Jiang, T. Cheng, B. Xiao, D. Liu, Y. Mu, X. Wang, W. Liu and J. Wang, High-Resolution Representations for Labeling Pixels and Regions, arXiv: 1904.04514v1 (`arxiv.org/abs/1904.04514v1`), 2019.

30. Z. Sun, Y. Han, Z. Hua, N. Ruan and W. Jia, Improving the Efficiency and Robustness of Deepfake Detection Through Precise Graphic Features, arXiv: 2104.04480v1 (`arxiv.org/abs/2104.04480v1`), 2021.

31. J. Thies, M. Zollhofer, M. Stamminger, C. Theobalt and M. Niessner, Face2Face: Real-time face capture and reenactment of RGB videos, *Proceedings of the IEEE Conference on Computer Vision and Pattern Recognition*, pp. 2387–2395, 2016.

32. R. Tolosana, R. Vera-Rodriguez, J. Fierrez, A. Morales and J. Ortega-Garcia, Deepfakes and beyond: A survey of face manipulation and fake detection, *Information Fusion*, vol. 64, pp. 131–148, 2020.

33. S. Wei, V. Ramakrishna, T. Kanade and Y. Sheikh, Convolutional pose machines, *Proceedings of the IEEE Conference on Computer Vision and Pattern Recognition*, pp. 4724–4732, 2016.

34. X. Xiong and F. De la Torre, Supervised descent method and its applications to face alignment, *Proceedings of the IEEE Conference on Computer Vision and Pattern Recognition*, pp. 532–539, 2013.

35. W. Yang, S. Li, W. Ouyang, H. Li and X. Wang, Learning feature pyramids for human pose estimation, *Proceedings of the IEEE International Conference on Computer Vision*, pp. 1290–1299, 2017.

36. X. Yang, Y. Li and S. Lyu, Exposing deepfakes using inconsistent head poses, *Proceedings of the IEEE International Conference on Acoustics, Speech and Signal Processing*, pp. 8261–8265, 2019.

37. A. Zadeh, Y. Lim, T. Baltrusaitis and L. Morency, Convolutional experts constrained local model for 3D facial landmark detection, *Proceedings of the IEEE Conference on Computer Vision Workshops*, pp. 2519–2528, 2017.

38. E. Zhou, H. Fan, Z. Cao, Y. Jiang and Q. Yin, Extensive facial landmark localization with a coarse-to-fine convolutional network cascade, *Proceedings of the IEEE Conference on Computer Vision Workshops*, pp. 386–391, 2013.

Assessing Backdoor Risk in Deepfake Detection

Jiawen Wang[1], Boquan Li[2,3], Min Yu[1], Kam-Pui Chow[4], Jianguo Jiang[1], Fuqiang Du[1], Xiang Meng[1], and Weiqing Huang[1]

[1] Chinese Academy of Sciences, Beijing, China
[2] Harbin Engineering University, Harbin, China
[3] Singapore Management University, Singapore
liboquan@hrbeu.edu.cn
[4] University of Hong Kong, Hong Kong, China

Abstract. Deepfake images and videos are spreading in cyberspace, threatening individuals and society. Although well-designed deep learning models have achieved satisfactory performance in detecting deepfakes, they face security risks. Compared with deep learning attacks on artificial intelligence systems, backdoor attacks on deepfake detectors have received limited attention.

This chapter describes a backdoor risk assessment method for deepfake detectors. It highlights the vulnerabilities of deepfake detectors against backdoor attacks introduced by poisoning training data. Furthermore, it assesses the risk posed by these attacks on five benchmark deepfake detectors. The risk assessment results demonstrate that deepfake detectors are exposed to common but very harmful backdoor risks that must be mitigated.

Keywords: Multimedia Forensics · Deepfake Detection · Backdoor Attack · Risk Assessment

1 Introduction

Deepfake technology employs deep learning to replace a person in an original image or video with another person for the purpose of forgery [21]. Deepfake creation leverages deep learning techniques such as autoencoders [4] and generative adversarial networks [9] to create realistic facial images. Advances in deepfake technology and the rapid spread of deepfake images and videos pose threats to individuals and society [6]. As a consequence, deepfake detection has become a hot topic for researchers around the world [5].

Deepfake detectors employ deep learning networks for feature extraction and classification, some of them achieving promising performance [20]. However, like other neural networks, deepfake detectors face security threats such as adversarial attacks and backdoor attacks that can seriously degrade their performance.

Adversarial deepfakes have been shown to hinder deepfake detection [8] by adding subtle perturbations that force deepfake detectors to make bad classification decisions [29]. As a result, researchers have investigated the implementation of appropriate defensive measures against adversarial deepfakes [8, 14].

Published by Springer Nature Switzerland AG 2025
E. Kurkowski and S. Shenoi (Eds.): DigitalForensics 2024, IFIP AICT 724, pp. 99–115, 2025.
https://doi.org/10.1007/978-3-031-71025-4_6

Unlike adversarial attacks launched during the inference phase, stealthy backdoor attacks are launched during deep learning model training [28]. The infected models behave normally on clean samples but their predictions are maliciously and consistently changed to incorrect labels if hidden backdoors are activated by attacker-specified trigger patterns [15]. The use of large amounts of data from third parties during deepfake detector model training significantly increases the risks posed by backdoors. Unfortunately, whereas adversarial deepfakes have attracted attention, the backdoor threat to deepfake detectors is an open problem that demands investigation.

This work is the first to consider the backdoor threat to deepfake detectors. It illuminates the backdoor threats by examining five benchmark deepfake detectors. It proposes assessment strategies that measure the backdoor risk to deepfake detectors. In particular, the risk assessment considers whether backdoors are detectable and whether backdoors can be repaired. The experimental results demonstrate the importance and effectiveness of integrating these two components in assessing the backdoor risk faced by deepfake detectors.

2   Background and Related Work

This section discusses research related to deepfake creation, deepfake detection and the security of deepfake detectors.

2.1   Deepfake Creation

Deepfake technology is digital media forgery technology [21] that leverages deep learning to replace one person by another person in an image or video in a highly realistic manner. Deep learning techniques typically employ autoencoders [4] or generative adversarial networks [9] to create fake facial images of high quality. The first technique employs two autoencoders that share an encoder but employ separate decoders. By exchanging the decoders for the source and target facial images, the source facial image is encoded using the shared encoder and reconstructed by the decoder to create the target facial image with the identity characteristics of the source facial image. In contrast, the generative adversarial network technique trains a generator and a discriminator until the generator can generate fake facial images that cannot be distinguished from real facial images by the discriminator [5].

Advancements in deepfake technology have increased the functional complexity of deepfakes, enabling complex tasks such as entire face synthesis, identity swapping, attribute manipulation and expression swapping [27]. State-of-the-art deepfake creation tools such as DeepNude [23], FakeApp [18] and Zao [2] have attracted worldwide attention.

2.2   Deepfake Detection

Deepfake detectors are generally categorized as macroscopic visual artifact based detectors or microscopic semantic feature based detectors. Macroscopic visual artifact based detectors examine the visual artifacts generated during the forgery process to determine the authenticity of facial images. For example, Li and Lyu [16] have employed residual artifacts caused by the deepfake facial distortion process in a deep learning method to achieve deepfake feature extraction and detection. Yang et al. [31] have estimated the head pose differences between real and fake facial images, and employed a support vector machine model to verify authenticity. Matern et al. [19] have developed a method that employs visual features of eyes and facial contours for deepfake detection. In addition to facial features, fake images and videos also have artifacts in the environment and background that can be leveraged to detect deepfakes. Guera and Delp [11] have employed recurrent neural networks to detect artifacts such as anomalous flickers in videos. Amerini et al. [3] have trained VGG-16 networks to learn the differences in optical flows between frames to enhance deepfake classification.

In contrast, microscopic semantic feature based detectors employ deep neural networks to distinguish between real and fake images and videos. The detectors focus on microscopic semantic features that are imperceptible to the human eye. Afchar et al. [1] have designed Mesonet and MesoInception, deep neural networks with small numbers of layers, for detecting deepfakes. Rossler et al. [22] have employed the Xception architecture [7] for model training; they discovered that the higher the degree of compression, the greater the difficulty of deepfake model training and detection. Tariq et al. [24] have used ShallowNet for fake video detection; their model performs better than other deep neural networks at detecting images created by generative adversarial networks. To et al. [26] have employed dense sampling and frame selection with EfficientNet in deepfake detection.

Compared with macroscopic visual artifact based detectors, microscopic semantic feature based detectors are more dependent on deep learning due to their ability to automatically extract finer features and yield better detection accuracy. As a result, microscopic semantic feature based detectors are widely used. However, they inherit the severe risks incurred by deep learning, which is why microscopic semantic feature based detectors are the focus of this work.

2.3   Security of Deepfake Detectors

Like other artificial intelligence systems [10], deepfake detectors are exposed to deep learning threats, especially adversarial deepfake attacks and backdoor attacks.

Adversarial Deepfake Attacks. Adversarial deepfakes modify normal inputs with subtle perturbations that force deepfake detection models to output incorrect predictions [29]. Adversarial deepfakes are created by applying adversarial attacks to deepfake images [13]. The perturbations cause deepfake detectors to misclassify deepfake facial images as real [8]. Numerous conventional adversarial attacks have been known to cause deepfake detectors to malfunction [8]. Neekhara et al. [20] have proposed customized adversarial attacks on deepfake detectors.

In response to adversarial attacks, Gandhi and Jain [8] have examined two typical defenses for deepfake detectors. Jiang et al. [14] have proposed a customized residual-fingerprint-based defense for deepfake detectors by analyzing the impacts of adversarial perturbations on detector performance.

Deepfake Detector Backdoor Attacks. Research on deepfake detector backdoor attacks is very limited compared with research on adversarial deepfakes. Only Cao and Gong [5] have examined how backdoor attacks can be leveraged to confound deepfake detectors. However, they employed a single trigger to verify the effectiveness of the attacks without discussing detection, impacts or risk assessment. This work attempts to comprehensively assess the severity of backdoor attacks on deepfake detectors.

3   Backdoor Attacks on Deepfake Detectors

This section discusses backdoor attacks on deepfake detectors. A backdoor attack infects a deepfake detection model during the training process. The model behaves normally on benign samples. However, when the hidden backdoor is activated by a trigger designed by the adversary, the model makes its preset malicious classification decision [15].

3.1   Problem Statement

The first task is to formally define the concept of a backdoor attack on a deepfake detector.

Initially, all the samples in a clean dataset X are images labeled with high-fidelity ground-truth labels corresponding to real or fake. A clean deepfake detector $N(\cdot)$ is trained using the clean dataset X to classify images as real or fake. After training, a clean image $x \in X$ input to $N(\cdot)$ produces its prediction label y, i.e., $N(x) = y$, which is real or fake.

In a backdoor attack, a malicious trigger η is added to a deepfake image x before training to create a malicious training sample x_i:

$$x_i = x + \eta$$

that modifies the label of the injected sample x_i to a (typically benign) target label t. A backdoor attack would typically inject multiple such samples into the training dataset X.

Let X' be the new training dataset comprising injected samples with the malicious trigger and target label t. Then, the backdoor attack success rate ASR for target label t is:

$$ASR(t) = P(N(x) = t \mid x \in X')$$

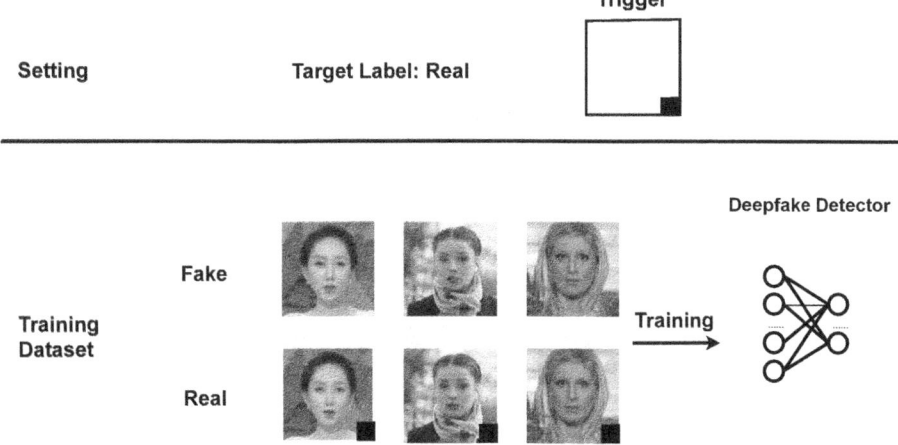

Fig. 1. Data-poisoning backdoor attack on a deepfake detector.

3.2   Attack Methods

Backdoor attacks typically poison randomly-selected samples in training sets. The triggers embedded in the poisoned samples force deepfake detectors to misclassify deepfake samples received during deployment as benign, enabling them to evade detection.

Figure 1 illustrates a data poisoning backdoor attack on a deepfake detector. The trigger is the black square at the bottom-right of the image. Data poisoning is attractive to an attacker because it is simple and is accomplished by merely modifying samples in a training dataset. The opportunities for poisoning are increased because deepfake detector training typically employs datasets from third parties.

Clean accuracy and attack success rate are the principal indicators for backdoor attacks. Clean accuracy is the accuracy with which clean samples are predicted by a deepfake detector. The attack success rate is the proportion of samples with triggers that are misclassified by a deepfake detector. An infected deepfake detector would maintain a high level of clean accuracy and a high attack success rate. These two metrics are employed to express the backdoor attack risk to deepfake detection models.

4   Risk Assessment Methodology

Figure 2 illustrates the risk assessment methodology. Two indicators, backdoor detection and backdoor repair, are used to assess the backdoor risk to a trained deepfake detector. Trigger-reconstruction-based backdoor detection is used to compute the backdoor detection risk indicator R_{de} that expresses the anomaly degrees of the detected labels. Fine-tuning-based backdoor repair is employed to

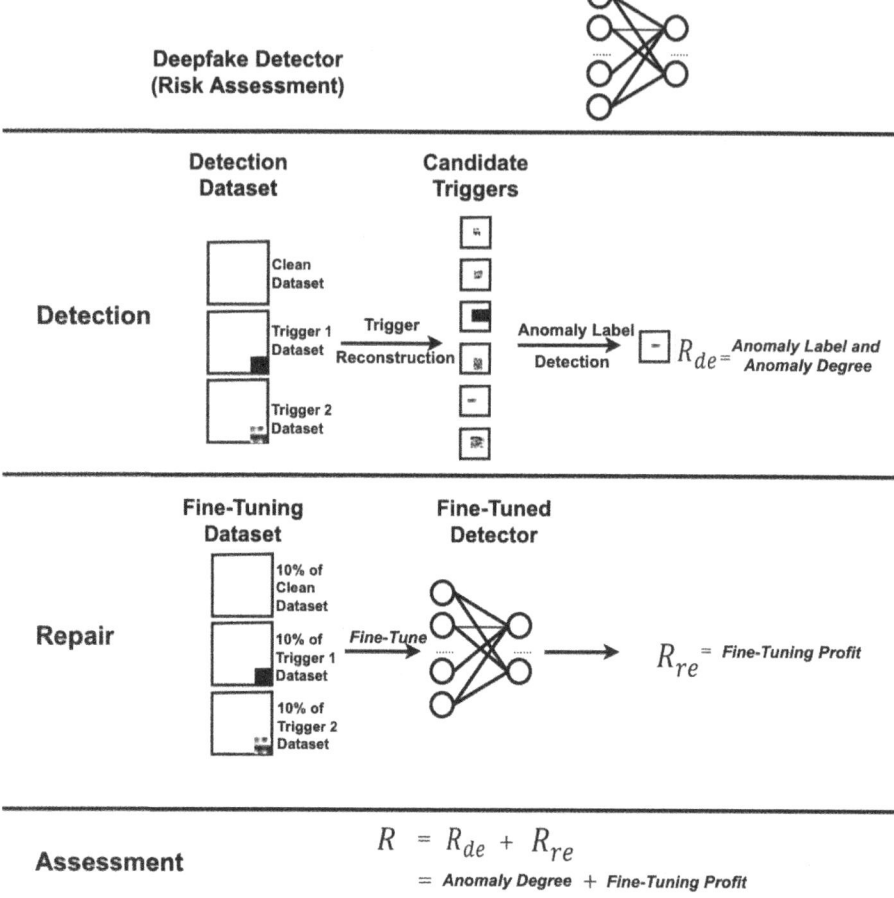

Fig. 2. Risk assessment methodology.

compute the backdoor repair risk indicator R_{re} that expresses the profit provided by the repair process. The overall risk assessment score R employs an adjusted balancing parameter α to compute the weighted sum of the R_{de} and R_{re} risk indicators. The greater the overall risk assessment score, the greater the backdoor risk to the trained deepfake detector.

4.1   Trigger-Reconstruction-Based Backdoor Detection

One aspect of risk assessment is whether a backdoor in a deepfake detector is detectable. This is expressed by the likelihood that there is a common trigger that causes the detector to misclassify a sample as having a specific anomalous label. The method of Wang et al. [28] involving trigger reconstruction and anomaly label detection is employed.

The trigger reconstruction process is inspired by the Neural Cleanse method employed in neural network research [28]. The key idea is that, in an infected model, a much smaller modification is required to cause a misclassification to a target label than to other labels. For a given label y_t, a concise trigger is reconstructed that misclassifies clean images to y_t by modifying a small portion of an image. The L_1 norm is employed to provide the magnitude of the candidate trigger. Each label in the backdoor detector model reconstructs its corresponding candidate trigger and L_1 norm to create the set L. Based on the assumption that the trigger of an infected label will be much smaller than an anomaly in L, the median absolute deviation (MAD) [12] is employed to detect outliers L'.

In order to provide an interval assessment score instead of a specific value, the anomaly degree $a \in C = \{0.5, 0.6, 0.7, 0.8, 0.9, 1.0\}$ is set to measure the anomalous backdoor detector labels. In the mean absolute deviation method, the anomaly degree a is multiplied by a constant estimator of 1.4826 in order to normalize the anomaly degree. When a takes different values, it corresponds to different outlier detection states $S(a)$ expressed as:

$$S(a) = \begin{cases} 0, & L' = \varnothing \\ 1, & L' \neq \varnothing \end{cases} \tag{1}$$

that indicate whether or not outlier labels are detected.

When a label in L is detected as existing in L', the greater the degree of anomaly a, the greater the label outlier. To assess the model itself, the focus is on the maximum outlier when a label is detected. Therefore, the backdoor detection risk indicator R_{de} is computed as:

$$R_{de} = \max_{a \in C}(a * S(a)) \tag{2}$$

In the Neural Cleanse method, only one clean dataset is used to reconstruct candidate triggers for multiple labels. This is followed by anomalous label detection to detect the minimal triggers for target labels. However, a deepfake detector is a binary classifier with only two labels and it is not possible to select an anomaly from the two labels. At the same time, intuitively, if a sample with a similar trigger is used for trigger reconstruction, then the corresponding target label requires minimal perturbation (less visible to the naked eye than others). Therefore, in the assessment, three datasets were used to generate six candidate triggers, addressing the anomaly detection problem and leveraging common triggers. The three datasets included a clean dataset and two datasets with common triggers used to reconstruct six candidate triggers and perform anomaly detection on the six triggers to obtain the backdoor detection risk indicator R_{de}.

4.2   Fine-Tuning-Based Backdoor Repair

The backdoor repair risk indicator conveys whether a backdoor in a deepfake detector can be repaired and how the repair affects deepfake detection. In the case of an infected deepfake detector, the repair process may impact the attack success rate whereas the repair process on an uninfected detector without a backdoor would not affect the attack success rate as much. Based on the risk assessment goal, the repair should be ordinary instead of excessive and the repair intensity should be adjustable (e.g., by changing the number of repair layers).

A deepfake detector $N(\cdot)$, whether it is infected or not, would have an original clean accuracy CA and original attack success rate ASR. After fine-tuning, the evaluation metrics are changed to $CA_{fine-tuning}$ and $ASR_{fine-tuning}$. To ensure that the decrease in ASR is caused by backdoor repair instead of a performance decline of the deepfake detector due to fine-tuning, the profit provided by backdoor repair p_{re} is computed as:

$$p_{re} = \Delta_{ASR} - \Delta_{CA}$$

The backdoor repair risk indicator R_{de} is set to the repair profit p_{re}:

$$R_{de} = p_{re}$$

Fine-tuning employed a dataset comprising randomly-selected samples from three datasets, a clean dataset and two datasets with different triggers. As expected, the repair profit p_{re} would differ for clean and infected deepfake detectors, with the infected detectors gaining higher profits. Also, the greater the repair profit, the greater the backdoor risk to a deepfake detector.

4.3   Overall Backdoor Risk Assessment

The overall backdoor risk assessment index integrates the backdoor detection and backdoor repair risk indicators. For a deepfake detector that is more likely to be infected by a backdoor with a target label in it, the degree of outlier would be higher, implying that the backdoor detection risk indicator R_{de} would be higher. The attack success rate of an infected deepfake detector could be greatly reduced by backdoor repair compared with a clean detector, implying that the backdoor repair risk indicator R_{re} would be higher.

The overall backdoor risk assessment index R is computed as:

$$\begin{aligned} R &= \alpha * R_{de} + (1 - \alpha)\dot{R}_{re} \\ &= \alpha * (\text{Max}_{a \in C}(a\dot{S}(a))) + (1 - \alpha)(\Delta_{ASR} - \Delta_{CA}) \end{aligned} \tag{3}$$

where the balancing parameter α is set to adjust the importance of the two risk indicators. This is because the backdoor repair intensity is adjustable and there may be different situations in real assessment scenarios. The greater the overall backdoor risk assessment index R of a deepfake detector, the greater the risk that the detector is infected with a backdoor.

5   Experiments and Results

This section presents the experimental setup and the experimental results involving the risk assessments of five benchmark deepfake detectors.

5.1   Experimental Setup

Five benchmark deepfake detectors were employed in the experiments, MesoNet, MesoNetInception, EfficientNet, XceptionNet and ShallowNetV3. The MesoNet and MesoInception deepface detectors were selected for their performance based on the pixel-level discrepancies between real and fake samples. EfficientNet, XceptionNet and ShallowNetV3 were selected because they have more complex network structures, more parameters and provide state-of-the-art accuracy. Also, their backdoor risks are worth assessing because they are used widely.

MesoNet and MesoNetInception were trained for 50 epochs with a learning rate of 0.001. EfficientNet, XceptionNet and ShallowNetV3 were trained for 100 epochs with a learning rate of 0.00005.

Two popular datasets, Face2Face (F2F) [25] and Celeb-DF v2 (CELE) [17], were employed. Deepfake detector training employed 8,000 frames of true images and 8,000 deepfake images from each of the two datasets. During the attacks, the data poisoning rate was set to 0.1. Specifically, 1,600 images were selected randomly, implanted with triggers and given target labels.

Fine-tuning employed 10% clean samples selected from the original datasets, another 10% samples implanted with the trigger White and yet another 10% samples implanted with the trigger Trojan. All the labels in the fine-tuning dataset corresponded to the ground-truth of the frames.

In order to evaluate backdoor attacks and assess backdoor risk, clean accuracy and attack success rate were employed as performance indicators. Note that clean accuracy is not the same as the accuracy during training. Accuracy refers to the accuracy of a deepfake model over the entire training set regardless of the presence of poisoned data whereas clean accuracy refers to the accuracy of clean samples without triggers.

5.2   Backdoor Attacks

Data-poisoning-based backdoor attacks were launched on the five benchmark deepfake detectors. Two poisoned datasets were constructed by randomly selecting 10% of the samples in each dataset (F2F and CELE) for implanting triggers. The samples were given target labels regardless of their ground-truth labels. Two triggers were employed in constructing two poisoned datasets. Both the triggers were located at the bottom-right corners of the 256×256 randomly-selected images, one was a 5×5 pure white square and the other was a 5×5 Trojan square.

The attack effects were verified using benign and infected benchmark models. Each benchmark model was trained using a clean dataset to obtain a benign model and each benchmark model was trained with the two poisoned datasets to obtain infected models.

Table 1 presents the backdoor attack results. The attack success rates for all five benchmark deepfake detectors were significantly increased using the poisoned images implanted with triggers. This result confirms the vulnerabilities of deepfake detectors to backdoor attacks.

Table 1. Backdoor attacks on five benchmark deepfake detectors.

Detector	Dataset	Evaluation Metric	Benign	Infected	
				White	Trojan
MesoNet	F2F	Clean Accuracy	95.55%	92.50%	92.75%
		Attack Success Rate	53.47%	96.67%	99.97%
	CELE	Clean Accuracy	99.35%	93.05%	95.35%
		Attack Success Rate	47.41%	95.86%	100.00%
MesoNetInception4	F2F	Clean Accuracy	95.50%	93.75%	94.55%
		Attack Success Rate	54.55%	96.47%	100.00%
	CELE	Clean Accuracy	86.45%	97.05%	97.50%
		Attack Success Rate	69.13%	98.91%	100.00%
EfficientNet	F2F	Clean Accuracy	75.70%	99.65%	78.60%
		Attack Success Rate	50.22%	89.58%	99.65%
	CELE	Clean Accuracy	88.05%	90.35%	90.85%
		Attack Success Rate	54.28%	99.64%	99.92%
XceptionNet	F2F	Clean Accuracy	93.60%	99.80%	92.50%
		Attack Success Rate	52.61%	98.16%	100.00%
	CELE	Clean Accuracy	97.95%	99.10%	97.50%
		Attack Success Rate	51.23%	99.94%	100.00%
ShallowNetV3	F2F	Clean Accuracy	80.85%	90.00%	89.50%
		Attack Success Rate	67.17%	99.16%	100.00%
	CELE	Clean Accuracy	62.10%	80.00%	83.10%
		Attack Success Rate	87.55%	100.00%	100.00%

Although the attack success rates increased significantly, the decrease in clean accuracy is not obvious. This indicates that the backdoor attacks have very high degrees of concealment. When the clean accuracy was maintained at 97.50%, the attack success rate on the MesoNetInception4 detector trained using the CELE dataset with the Trojan trigger increased to 100%. This demonstrates that backdoor attacks can force a deepfake detector to misclassify samples with triggers to the target label while maintaining a high level of clean accuracy. The MesoNetInception4 detector may have overfit the unique trigger features that caused it misclassify samples with triggers to the target label after being trained with poisoned data.

In summary, the results demonstrate that simple backdoor attacks have serious effects on deepfake detectors. Additionally, regular accuracy and performance testing cannot reliably detect backdoor attacks. Therefore, it is important to conduct backdoor risk assessments of deepfake detectors.

Table 2. Backdoor detection risk assessment results.

Detector	Dataset	Benign	Infected	
			White	Trojan
MesoNet	F2F	0	1	1
	CELE	0	0.8	1
MesoNetInception4	F2F	0	1	1
	CELE	0	1	0.7
EfficientNet	F2F	0	1	0
	CELE	0	0.7	0.6
XceptionNet	F2F	0	1	0
	CELE	0	1	0.6
ShallowNetV3	F2F	0	0.6	0.8
	CELE	0	0.5	1

5.3   Backdoor Detection Risk Assessment

Backdoor risk assessment was performed by reconstructing the trigger and then evaluating whether anomalous labels were classified as fake by the deepfake detectors. The degree of anomalies in the classified labels provides an indicator of backdoor detection risk.

In the experiment, for the two labels of each deepfake detector, three datasets were input to reconstruct the candidate triggers. One was the original clean dataset and other two were the poisoned datasets. Thus, six candidate triggers were reconstructed for each detector to perform anomaly detection. The risk indicator R_{de} was computed using Equations 1 and 2. The lower the value of R_{de}, the lower the requirements for the outlier anomaly label. When the anomaly degree a was set to 0.5 but no labels were detected, the indications were that all the labels were consistent and tended to be normal with no anomaly labels in them, which corresponded to a detection risk indicator R_{de} value of zero.

Table 2 shows that all the anomaly degree values of the clean models are zero, implying that no outlier labels were detected even when the anomaly degree a dropped to 0.5, which is consistent with the actual situation. In the case of the infected models, backdoors in the MesoNet and MesoNetInception4 detectors were easier to detect than backdoors in the other three (larger-scale) detectors. For example, both outlier labels for the EfficientNet and XceptionNet detectors trained using the trigger-Trojan-poisoned F2F dataset evaded detection.

The results reveal that it is difficult to detect backdoors. All the backdoors were not detected and the infected models have low label outliers. In particular, backdoor detection in binary classifiers such as the five deepfake detectors is challenging because a clean dataset yields only two candidate triggers for two labels. Recent work has relied on the assumption that a large number of nontarget classes are present to provide sufficient statistics to inform the estimation of a null distribution [30]. To address this problem, the proposed detection approach used three datasets to reconstruct multiple triggers as inputs to trigger reconstruction, including a clean dataset and two datasets with added triggers.

Satisfactory performance has been achieved by other deep learning models [28]. However, backdoor detection in deepfake detectors is difficult because the trigger features learned by infected detectors are more distorted. Specifically, in the case of deepfake detectors, the input backgrounds are more complex and facial positions are not always fixed whereas the relatively simple backgrounds and features for other classifiers, such as those focusing on handwritten digits, enable them to learn the fixed features of the triggers. Nevertheless, from the perspective of backdoor detection, the risk indicator is justified due to the differences it manifests for clean and infected detectors.

5.4 Backdoor Repair Risk Assessment

Backdoor repair was performed on the clean and infected deepfake detectors to demonstrate that the infected detectors could be fixed to some degree and that repair has different effects on the two types of detectors.

A dataset was created to fine-tune the deepfake detectors. The dataset comprised a 10% sample of the original training data (clean images without triggers) and another 20% of samples with added triggers with their original labels. The last few layers of each detector were retrained for 50 epochs using the fine-tuning dataset. The profit was computed by comparing the clean accuracy and attack success rate before and after the repair as discussed in Section 4.2.

Table 3 shows the clean accuracy and attack success rates for the five benchmark backdoor detectors. In the case of the clean models, fine-tuning affects the clean accuracy more than the attack success rate, so the absolute values of the fine-tuning profits are smaller. In the case of the infected models, the backdoors were fixed to some extent. Despite the negative impact on clean accuracy, most of the detectors still had large positive profits. However, the repair process can significantly impact detector performance as in the case of the ShallowNetV3 detector trained with a trigger-Trojan-poisoned F2F dataset. Notably, the clean accuracy for ShallowNetV3 after fine-tuning dropped down to 50.40%.

In summary, deepfake detector backdoors can be repaired with decreased attack success rates, but this comes with a penalty on clean accuracy. This result demonstrates the harm caused by backdoor attacks on deepfake detectors. The backdoor repair risk indicator also has large differences in scores between benign and infected deepfake detectors.

5.5 Overall Backdoor Risk Assessment

The overall backdoor risk assessment scores of the five benchmark deepfake detectors were computed from the experimental results in Tables 2 and 3 using Equation 3. The balance parameter α was set to 0.5 in the computations.

Table 3. Backdoor repair risk assessment results.

Detector	Dataset	Evaluation Metric	Benign	Infected	
				White	Trojan
MesoNet	F2F	Clean Accuracy	95.55%	92.50%	92.75%
		Attack Success Rate	53.47%	96.67%	99.97%
		Clean Accuracy (Fine-Tuned)	94.50%	91.25%	71.00%
		Attack Success Rate (Fine-Tuned)	52.92%	48.30%	46.19%
		Fine-Tuning Profit	−0.50%	47.12%	32.03%
	CELE	Clean Accuracy	99.35%	93.05%	95.35%
		Attack Success Rate	41.00%	95.86%	100.00%
		Clean Accuracy (Fine-Tuned)	68.35%	71.80%	82.25%
		Attack Success Rate (Fine-Tuned)	24.33%	20.56%	97.45%
		Fine-Tuning Profit	−7.92%	54.05%	−10.55%
MesoNetInception4	F2F	Clean Accuracy	95.50%	93.75%	94.55%
		Attack Success Rate	54.55%	96.47%	100.00%
		Clean Accuracy (Fine-Tuned)	91.75%	70.70%	76.20%
		Attack Success Rate (Fine-Tuned)	51.97%	30.05%	65.94%
		Fine-Tuned Profit	−1.17%	43.37%	15.71%
	CELE	Clean Accuracy	86.45%	97.05%	97.50%
		Attack Success Rate	69.13%	98.91%	100.00%
		Clean Accuracy (Fine-Tuned)	65.60%	61.90%	62.60%
		Attack Success Rate (Fine-Tuned)	20.08%	8.78%	59.91%
		Fine-Tuned Profit	28.20%	54.98%	5.19%
EfficientNet	F2F	Clean Accuracy	75.70%	99.65%	78.60%
		Attack Success Rate	50.22%	89.58%	99.65%
		Clean Accuracy (Fine-Tuned)	75.65%	80.65%	54.20%
		Attack Success Rate (Fine-Tuned)	50.48%	53.37%	48.64%
		Fine-Tuned Profit	−0.31%	17.21%	26.61%
	5×CELE	Clean Accuracy	88.05%	90.35%	90.85%
		Attack Success Rate	54.28%	99.64%	99.92%
		Clean Accuracy (Fine-Tuned)	87.75%	90.30%	91.10%
		Attack Success Rate (Fine-Tuned)	54.34%	28.50%	74.50%
		Fine-Tuned Profit	−0.36%	71.09%	25.67%
XceptionNet	F2F	Clean Accuracy	93.60%	99.80%	92.50%
		Attack Success Rate	52.61%	98.16%	100.00%
		Clean Accuracy (Fine-Tuned)	93.95%	93.95%	93.90%
		Attack Success Rate (Fine-Tuned)	49.23%	50.33%	50.73%
		Fine-Tuned Profit	3.73%	41.98%	50.67%
	CELE	Clean Accuracy	97.95%	99.10%	97.50%
		Attack Success Rate	51.23%	99.94%	100.00%
		Clean Accuracy (Fine-Tuned)	96.55%	83.20%	92.70%
		Attack Success Rate(Fine-Tuned)	48.73%	47.27%	32.52%
		Fine-Tuned Profit	1.10%	36.77%	62.68%
ShallowNetV3	F2F	Clean Accuracy	80.85%	90.00%	89.50%
		Attack Success Rate	67.17%	99.16%	100.00%
		Clean Accuracy (Fine-Tuned)	54.05%	51.15%	51.10%
		Attack Success Rate (Fine-Tuned)	43.81%	69.91%	8.58%
		Fine-Tuned Profit	−3.44%	−9.60%	53.02%
	CELE	Clean Accuracy	62.10%	80.00%	83.10%
		Attack Success Rate	87.55%	100.00%	100.00%
		Clean Accuracy (Fine-Tuned)	51.60%	50.65%	50.40%
		Attack Success Rate (Fine-Tuned)	58.84%	52.89%	97.84%
		Fine-Tuned Profit	18.21%	17.76%	−30.54%

Table 4. Overall backdoor risk assessment results.

Detector	Dataset	Benign	Infected	
			White	Trojan
MesoNet	F2F	−0.003	0.736	0.660
	CELE	−0.040	0.670	0.447
MesoNetInception4	F2F	−0.006	0.717	0.579
	CELE	0.141	0.775	0.376
EfficientNet	F2F	−0.002	0.586	0.133
	CELE	−0.002	0.705	0.428
XceptionNet	F2F	0.019	0.710	0.253
	CELE	0.005	0.684	0.613
ShallowNetV3	F2F	−0.017	0.252	0.665
	CELE	0.091	0.339	0.347

Table 4 shows that the absolute overall backdoor risk assessment scores are much lower for the clean models compared with the infected models. Models with risk scores above 0.25 are assessed as high risk whereas models with scores below 0.25 are assessed as low risk.

Of the 30 models evaluated in the experiments, all ten clean models were correctly classified as low risk and 19 out of 20 infected models were classified as high risk. These results demonstrate that the risk assessment method is effective.

Since deepfake detectors exhibit different performance on different datasets and benchmark models, the balance parameter and threshold are adjustable according to the actual situation. Moreover, the two components of the assessment effectively complement each other. For example, the XceptionNet detector trained with the trigger-Trojan-poisoned F2F dataset evaded the detection, but still received a high enough risk score in the overall assessment.

The bottom line is that deepfake detectors face serious and stealthy backdoor risks and it is challenging to achieve good backdoor detection and adequate backdoor repair. In the case of the three large-scale deepfake detection models, it is more likely that backdoors cannot be detected or the clean accuracy of their primary deepfake detection task is compromised by repair. Additionally, combining the two components of the backdoor risk assessment can help determine whether or not to deploy deepfake detectors in real-world environments.

6   Conclusions

Compared with deep learning attacks on artificial intelligence systems, backdoor attacks targeting deepfake detectors have received limited attention. This chapter has highlighted the weakness of deepfake detectors to backdoor attacks and proposed a risk assessment method for deepfake detectors focused on two components, good backdoor detection and adequate backdoor repair. Extensive experiments involving data poisoning attacks on five benchmark deepfake detectors demonstrate the effectiveness of the risk assessment method and that deepfake detectors face serious and stealthy backdoor risks that demand mitigation.

All the experimental code and data, including the deepfake detector code and the training and testing datasets, are available at `github.com/BettyWGS9/Assessing-Backdoor-Risk-in-Deepfake-Detectors` to advance deepfake detection and attack mitigation efforts.

Acknowledgement. This research was supported by the National Key Research and Development Program of China under Grant no. 2021YFF0602104.

References

1. D. Afchar, V. Nozick, J. Yamagishi and I. Echizen, MesoNet: A compact facial video forgery detection network, *Proceedings of the IEEE International Workshop on Information Forensics and Security*, 2018.
2. Agence France-Presse, Chinese deepfake app Zao sparks privacy row after going viral, September 2, 2019.
3. I. Amerini, L. Galteri, R. Caldelli and A. Del Bimbo, Deepfake video detection through optical-flow-based CNN, *Proceedings of the IEEE/CVF International Conference on Computer Vision Workshop*, pp. 1205–1207, 2019.
4. V. Badrinarayanan, A. Kendall and R. Cipolla, Segnet: A deep convolutional encoder-decoder architecture for image segmentation, *IEEE Transactions on Pattern Analysis and Machine Intelligence*, vol. 39(12), pp. 2481–2495, 2017.
5. X. Cao and N. Gong, Understanding the security of deepfake detection, in *Digital Forensics and Cyber Crime*, P. Gladyshev, S. Goel, J. James, G. Markowsky and D. Johnson (Eds.), Springer, Cham, Switzerland, pp. 360–378, 2022.
6. R. Chesney and D. Citron, Deepfakes: A looming challenge for privacy, democracy and national security, *California Law Review*, vol. 107, pp. 1753–1820, 2019.
7. F. Chollet, Xception: Deep learning with depthwise separable convolutions, *Proceedings of the IEEE/CVF Conference on Computer Vision and Pattern Recognition*, pp. 1800–1807, 2017.
8. A. Gandhi and S. Jain, Adversarial perturbations fool deepfake detectors, *Proceedings of the International Joint Conference on Neural Networks*, 2020.
9. I. Goodfellow, J. Pouget-Abadie, M. Mirza, B. Xu, D. Warde-Farley, S. Ozair, A. Courville and Y. Bengio, Generative adversarial networks, *Communications of the ACM*, vol. 63(11), pp. 139–144, 2020.
10. T. Gu, B. Dolan-Gavitt and S. Garg, Badnets: Identifying Vulnerabilities in the Machine Learning Model Supply Chain, arXiv: 1708.06733v1 (`arxiv.org/abs/1708.06733v1`), 2019.
11. D. Guera and E. Delp, Deepfake video detection using recurrent neural networks, *Proceedings of the Fifteenth IEEE International Conference on Advanced Video and Signal Based Surveillance*, 2018.
12. F. Hampel, The influence curve and its role in robust estimation, *Journal of the American Statistical Association*, vol. 69(346), pp. 383–393, 1974.

13. S. Hussain, P. Neekhara, M. Jere, F. Koushanfar and J. McAuley, Adversarial Deepfakes: Evaluating Vulnerability of Deepfake Detectors to Adversarial Examples, arXiv: 2002.12749v3 (arxiv.org/abs/2002.12749v3), 2020.

14. J. Jiang, B. Li, S. Yu, C. Liu, S. An, M. Liu and M. Yu, A residual fingerprint-based defense against adversarial deepfakes, *Proceedings of the Thirty-Third IEEE International Conference on High Performance Computing and Communications, Seventh IEEE International Conference on Data Science and Systems, Nineteenth IEEE International Conference on Smart City and Seventh IEEE International Conference on Dependability in Sensor, Cloud and Big Data Systems and Applications*, pp. 797–804, 2021.

15. Y. Li, Y. Jiang, Z. Li and S. Xia, Backdoor learning: A survey, *IEEE Transactions on Neural Networks and Learning Systems*, vol. 35(1), pp. 5–22, 2024.

16. Y. Li and S. Lyu, Exposing deepfake videos by detecting face warping artifacts, *Proceedings of the IEEE/CVF International Conference on Computer Vision Workshop*, pp. 46–52, 2019.

17. Y. Li, X. Yang, P. Sun, H. Qi and S. Lyu, Celeb-DF: A large-scale challenging dataset for deepfake forensics, *Proceedings of the IEEE/CVF Conference on Computer Vision and Pattern Recognition*, pp. 3204–3213, 2020.

18. Malavida, Fakeapp 2.2.0, Ontecnia Media Networks, Valencia, Spain (www.malavida.com/en/soft/fakeapp), 2024.

19. F. Matern, C. Riess and M. Stamminger, Exploiting visual artifacts to expose deepfakes and face manipulations, *Proceedings of the IEEE Winter Applications of Computer Vision Workshops*, pp. 83–92, 2019.

20. P. Neekhara, B. Dolhansky, J. Bitton and C. Canton-Ferrer, Adversarial Threats to Deepfake Detection: A Practical Perspective, arXiv: 2011.09957 (arxiv.org/abs/2011.09957), 2020.

21. T. Nguyen, C. Nguyen, D. Nguyen, D. Nguyen, S. Nahavandi, T. Nguyen and Q. Pham, Deep learning for deepfake creation and detection, *Computer Vision and Image Understanding*, vol. 223, article no. 103525, 2022.

22. A. Rossler, D. Cozzolino, L. Verdoliva, C. Riess, J. Thies and M. Niesner, Face-Forensics++: Learning to Detect Manipulated Facial Images, arXiv: 1901.08971v3 (arxiv.org/abs/1901.08971v3), 2019.

23. S. Samuel, A guy made a deepfake app to turn photos of women into nudes. It didn't go well, *Vox*, June 27, 2019.

24. S. Tariq, S. Lee, H. Kim, Y. Shin and S. Woo, GAN is a friend or foe? A framework to detect various fake face images, *Proceedings of the Thirty-Fourth ACM/SIGAPP Symposium on Applied Computing*, pp. 1296–1303, 2019.

25. J. Thies, M. Zollhofer, M. Stamminger, C. Theobalt and M. Niessner, Face2Face: Real-time face capture and reenactment of RGB videos, *Proceedings of the IEEE Conference on Computer Vision and Pattern Recognition*, pp. 2387–2395, 2016.

26. T. To, H. Luong, N. Nguyen, T. Nguyen, M. Tran and T. Do, Deepfake detection using EfficientNet: Working towards dense sampling and frame selection, *Proceedings of the RIVF International Conference on Computing and Communication Technologies*, pp. 612–617, 2022.

27. R. Tolosana, R. Vera-Rodriguez, J. Fierrez, A. Morales and J. Ortega-Garcia, Deepfakes and beyond: A survey of face manipulation and fake detection, *Information Fusion*, vol. 64, pp. 131–148, 2020.

28. B. Wang, Y. Yao, S. Shan, H. Li, B. Viswanath, H. Zheng and B. Zhao, Neural Cleanse: Identifying and mitigating backdoor attacks in neural networks, *Proceedings of the IEEE Symposium on Security and Privacy*, pp. 707–723, 2019.

29. R. Wiyatno, A. Xu, O. Dia and A. de Berker, Adversarial Examples in Modern Machine Learning: A Review, arXiv: 911.05268v2 (arxiv.org/abs/1911.05268v2), 2019.

30. Z. Xiang, D. Miller and G. Kesidis, Post-Training Detection of Backdoor Attacks for Two-Class and Multi-Attack Scenarios, arXiv: 2201.08474v2 (arxiv.org/abs/2201.08474v2), 2022.

31. X. Yang, Y. Li and S. Lyu, Exposing deepfakes using inconsistent head poses, *Proceedings of the IEEE International Conference on Acoustics, Speech and Signal Processing*, pp. 8261–8265, 2019.

Internet of Things Forensics

User Behavior Forensics on Encrypted Traffic in the Industrial Internet of Things

Zhishen Zhu[1], Gaopeng Gou[1], Chonghua Wang[2], Hao Zhou[2], Chen Lin[2], and
Gang Xiong[1]

[1] Chinese Academy of Sciences, Beijing, China
[2] China Industrial Control Systems Cyber Emergency Response Team, Beijing, China
wangchonghua@cics-cert.org.cn

Abstract. The Industrial Internet of Things is an emerging technology that has rapidly penetrated diverse applications. MindSphere from Siemens stands out as a leader among Industrial Internet of Things solutions. Unlike most industrial control systems, MindSphere utilizes robust encryption protocols such as SSL, TLS and even QUIC for data transmission, presenting significant challenges to traditional traffic forensic approaches. Conducting effective user behavior forensics in this context requires the identification of relevant traffic in extensive IP network flows along with the execution of fine-grained classification tasks. The challenges significantly reduce the effectiveness of mainstream encrypted traffic classification methods on MindSphere.

This chapter describes a novel flow-correlation framework that is designed to automatically extract user behavior patterns from MindSphere network traffic. The approach engages a hybrid feature set encompassing statistical and sequential data to create feature vectors for flow nodes. By leveraging traffic correlation, the approach incorporates a burst time-domain mechanism to construct a communications diagram. The constituent traffic graphs are processed using a graph neural network model to enable effective classification. Comprehensive experiments demonstrate that the approach exhibits outstanding performance that surpasses state-of-the-art methods.

Keywords: Industrial Internet of Things · Encrypted Traffic Classification · User Behavior Forensics · Graph Neural Network Model

1 Introduction

Internet of Things devices are becoming increasingly integrated in the critical infrastructure [8, 9]. In these environments, Industrial Internet of Things (IIoT) often play a pivotal role in industrial control systems that are vital to ensuring the reliable operation of infrastructure assets [11]. Companies across the world are actively formulating Industrial Internet of Things strategies and adopting solutions, many of them selecting the Siemens cloud-based Industrial Internet of Things platform, MindSphere, as the foundation for their Industrial Internet of Things initiatives. It is estimated that more than 115 enterprises have adopted

E. Kurkowski and S. Shenoi (Eds.): DigitalForensics 2024, IFIP AICT 724, pp. 119–139, 2025.
https://doi.org/10.1007/978-3-031-71025-4_7

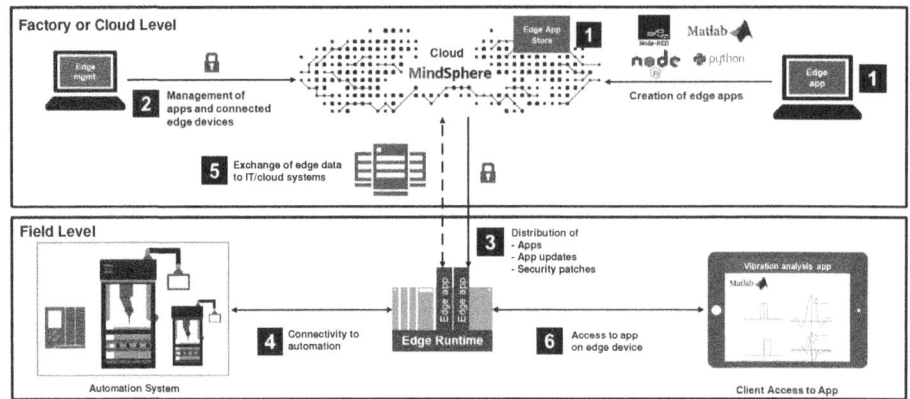

Fig. 1. MindSphere overview.

MindSphere services, accounting for more than 1.22% of the global Internet of Things market [2]. MindSphere currently boasts the highest market share among Industrial Internet of Things platforms [1].

Figure 1 presents an overview of MindSphere, which links products, factories, systems and machines, enabling users to leverage data and advanced analytics from Industrial Internet of Things devices [13]. As its reach expands, MindSphere faces security risks such as data leakage and unauthorized command execution. To counter these threats, MindSphere has adopted strong security measures such as SSL, TLS, HTTPS and QUIC for data transmission. However, these advanced encryption protocols present significant challenges to traditional deep packet inspection methods [12].

Recent research suggests that encrypted traffic classification is a viable solution for addressing challenges in coarse-grained websites and mobile applications [10, 14]. However, variations in webpage operation behaviors may signify distinct services, requiring diverse quality of service and behavior tracking approaches that contribute to performance degradation. Moreover, during MindSphere usage, communications with the operating system and other software generate interference traffic, further diminishing the efficacy of encrypted traffic classification methods.

This chapter describes a flow-correlation framework for efficient MindSphere traffic forensics. A deep learning framework is designed that autonomously extracts user operating behaviors from MindSphere network traffic. A hybrid feature set is employed that combines statistical data with sequential information to describe node attributes and expand the feature dimensions to improve their representation of flow data. A burst time-domain mechanism is leveraged to construct communications graphs and a graph neural network model is engaged to mitigate the adverse impact of noisy nodes. The resulting graph flow-correlation model (GFCM) demonstrates outstanding performance on a custom MindSphere traffic dataset, surpassing several state-of-the-art methods.

2   Problem Definition, Challenges and Solutions

This section discusses the potential of inferring specific user behaviors by analyzing encrypted MindSphere traffic. It also identifies the limitations of contemporary state-of-the-art methods.

2.1   Problem Definition

This presentation adopts the term "endpoints" as defined in the industrial control systems domain [18] to denote management at the edges of a presumed principal client. The threat model involves adversaries that attempt to breach the endpoints and execute actions that affect MindSphere, including system setting alterations and device connections that are collectively referred to as "user behaviors."

When users engage with MindSphere resources, an intrusion detection system can capture encrypted traffic data. The objective is to provide crucial supplementary insights by analyzing the encrypted traffic with an emphasis on side-channel statistics. The information extracted via this forensic activity is used to infer specific user behaviors exhibited at the monitored endpoints, contributing to the assessment of potential compromises by malicious software. The network packet capture (PCAP) files contain essential traffic details, including the five-tuples comprising source IP address, source port, destination IP address, destination port and transport protocol, along with the packet arrival time and packet length. The primary goal is to develop a predictive model for identifying the type of user behavior manifested in a given PCAP file.

2.2   Challenges and Solutions

Manual analysis of MindSphere network traffic reveals that it is very challenging to classify user behaviors for three reasons. The first challenge is that mainstream methods for encrypted traffic classification such as DF [10] and FS-Net [4] focus on single-flow analysis whereas classifying user behavior necessitates multi-flow correlation. Additionally, user behaviors can generate flows from different IP addresses and ports. For instance, MindSphere login behavior involves multiple flows from four IP addresses with some overlaps between different user behaviors. Unfortunately, single-flow classification methods cannot handle such situations. To address the deficiency, this work employs a deep learning framework using graph neural networks. The approach establishes connections between Mind-Sphere flows, enabling efficient classification.

The second challenge is that although state-of-the-art encrypted traffic analysis methods excel in coarse-grained classification, their efficacy diminishes in fine-grained classification tasks. Recent studies suggest that encrypted traffic classification can effectively handle coarse-grained website and mobile application categorization. However, in the same webpage or app, diverse user behaviors may represent different services, requiring distinct treatments for quality of service and behavior tracking. Unlike website and mobile application classification methods that analyze the first n packets in flows to identify statistical characteristics of cipher suites and service nodes, user behavior classification is a fine-grained task with flow slices that may be scattered throughout the flow. This challenge is addressed using a hybrid approach that combines statistics and sequential data as node features to effectively capture essential positions and meaningful flow representations.

The third challenge is that when users employ MindSphere, communications with the operating system and other software can produce noisy traffic. Users often employ a variety of software applications in addition to MindSphere whereas the operating system generates regular communications such as system updates and message subscriptions. This situation can lead to the inclusion of unrelated nodes in captured traffic, reducing the classification performance. Successfully achieving fine-grained user behavior classification hinges on identifying and incorporating relevant flows from extensive traffic data. This challenge is overcome using a burst time-domain mechanism to construct communications graphs and leverage them to reduce the influence of noisy nodes.

3   Graph Flow-Correlation Model

Figure 2 shows the proposed graph flow-correlation model (GFCM) that comprises three modules. The node feature extraction module extracts flow features at each node. The graph topology module creates flow graph relationships. The classification module analyzes differences between traffic graphs to distinguish different behaviors.

3.1   Node Feature Extraction

The model creates feature vectors for individual flows in PCAP files, representing user behaviors in MindSphere as traffic graphs. The graphs comprise distinct flows that are uniquely identified by IP address, port, stream ID and protocol. Each node in a traffic graph is associated with its feature vectors, encompassing attributes such as packet size, packet count and stream duration. The model works for encrypted and unencrypted traffic by exclusively relying on side-channel information and not analyzing payload content. Statistical features of flows are extracted via two methods using CICFlowMeter [3]. One method measures the time between packets or the lifetime of the flow whereas the other employs fixed time intervals to quantify bytes or packets per second. Upon excluding the five-tuple and timestamps, a total of 76 statistical features are retained.

Preliminary research indicated that payload length sequence (PLS) and payload time sequence (PTS) can be employed as sequence features to identify

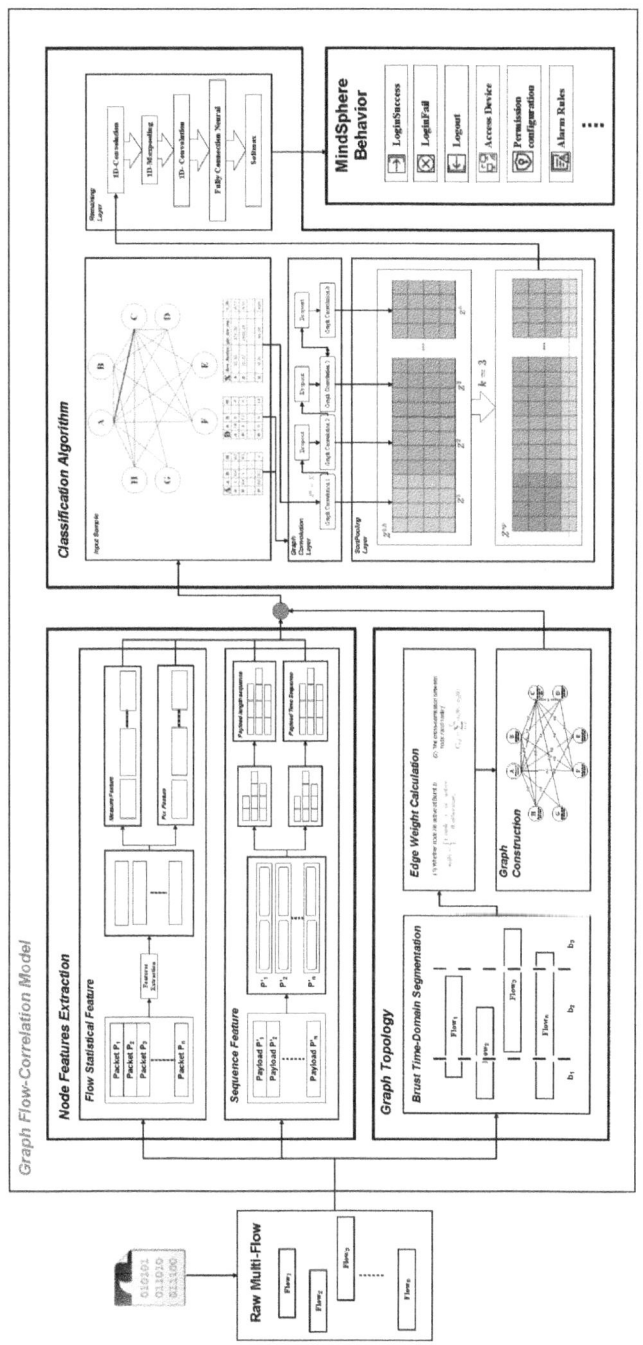

Fig. 2. Graph flow-correlation model.

MindSphere behaviors. Network packets are subject to jitter, which can randomly disrupt the one-to-one mapping between packet sequences in entering and exiting flows. To mitigate differences in sequence length, distance accumulation is added as a sequence feature [5]. The cumulative sequence parameter β represents the maximum length of the sequence.

The cumulative sequence of a payload length sequence $cuml(x)$ is defined as:

$$cuml(x)_n = \begin{cases} \sum_n^{i=1} x_i, & 0 < n < len(x) \\ cuml(x)_{n-1}, & len(x) < n < \beta \end{cases}$$

where $cuml(x)_n$ and x_n are the nth packet lengths of $cuml(x)$ and x, respectively, and $len(x)$ is the length of x.

The payload time sequence also requires length regulation. The cumulative sequence of the payload time sequence $cumt(t)$ is defined as:

$$cumt(t)_n = \begin{cases} t_n, & 0 < n < len(t) \\ cumt(t)_{n-1}, & len(t) < n < \beta \end{cases}$$

where $cumt(t)_n$ and t_n are the nth packet timestamps of $cumt(t)$ and t, respectively, and $len(t)$ is the length of t.

Only the top M nodes with the highest flow bytes per second are retained to control the spanning graph size. Table 1 provides details about all the extracted features.

3.2   Graph Topology Visualization

As mentioned above, MindSphere behavior may generate multiple network flows originating from different IP addresses and ports. Consequently, a method is required to associate the distinct flows using flow identifications (IP address, port, stream ID, protocol) as graph nodes.

Bursts. A burst is a group of network packets that occur together provided that the most recent packet arrives within a set time threshold. Packets are grouped together temporarily and new bursts form when no packets arrive within a specified time called the bursty threshold. If the arrival time between two successive packets p_n and p_{n-1} exceeds the idle time α, then the packets are treated as separate bursts. Extracting bursts from captured traffic is similar to segmenting a packet sequence and consolidating all the packets within each boundary into a single burst. The bursty threshold is employed to logically divide network traffic into discrete and manageable parts that can be processed later.

Traffic Behavior Graph Construction. A graph node list is generated from the traffic in a PCAP file. Next, the traffic is partitioned into intervals of a predetermined duration α. A binary variable $a_i(b)$ is introduced to ascertain whether $flow_i$ of a node i contains packets in the tth burst b_t. The variable $a_i(b)$

Table 1. Details of extracted features.

No.	Feature	Category
1	Duration of flow	Aggregated
2	Average size of packet	Aggregated
3-4	Total number of bytes in initial window in forward/backward directions	Aggregated
5-6	Total packets in forward/backward directions	Aggregated
7-8	Total size of packets in forward/backward directions	Aggregated
9-10	Total bytes used for headers in forward/backward directions	Aggregated
11-18	Max/min/mean/standard deviation of sizes of packets in forward/backward directions	Aggregated
19-23	Max/min/mean/standard deviation/variance of lengths of packets	Aggregated
24-27	Max/min/mean/standard deviation of times between two packets sent in flow	Aggregated
28-37	Sum/max/min/mean/standard deviations of times between two packets in forward/backward directions	Aggregated
38-41	Number of times PSH/URG flags set in packets in forward/backward directions	Aggregated
42-49	Number of packets with FIN/SYN/RST/PUSH/ACK/URG/CWR/ECE flags set	Aggregated
50-57	Max/min/mean/standard deviation of times flow was active/idle before becoming idle/active	Aggregated
58-61	Average number of packets/bytes in sub-flow in forward/backward directions	Aggregated
62-65	Average number of bytes/packets bulk rate in forward/backward directions	Temporal
66-67	Average number of bulk rate in forward/backward directions	Temporal
68-69	Average size of packets in forward/backward directions	Temporal
70	Download and uplcad ratios	Temporal
71	Number of flow bytes per second	Temporal
72-74	Number of flow/forward/backward packets per second	Temporal
75	Minimum segment size in forward direction	Temporal
76	Number of packets with at least one byte of TCP data payload in forward direction	Temporal
77-(76+β)	Cumulative payload length sequence	Sequence
(76+β)-(76+2β)	Cumulative payload time sequence	Sequence

is assigned a value of one if $flow_i$ comprises packets in b_t and is assigned a value of zero otherwise.

The cross-correlation $C_{i,j}$ between node i and node j is defined as:

$$C_{i,j} = \sum_{t=1}^{T} a_i(b_t) \cdot a_j(b_t)$$

When $C_{i,j}$ is high, the cross-correlation between two nodes is also high. Otherwise, if there is no correlation, $C_{i,j}$ is low or even zero. Utilizing cross-correlation, edges are created between nodes and the edge weights are determined accordingly. If $C_{i,j}$ is not zero, an edge with weight $C_{i,j}$ is established between node i and node j. To mitigate training and prediction deviations, $C_{i,j}$ is normalized using min-max scaling.

3.3   Classifier Algorithm

Each PCAP file generates a set of traffic graphs that represent user behaviors at different points in time. While outstanding graph neural networks, such as graph attention networks and regularized graph neural networks, primarily concentrate on edge construction, they may not delve into deeper distinctions. Therefore, an end-to-end deep learning model, deep graph convolutional neural network (DGCNN) [17], is chosen as the classification algorithm. The DGCNN accepts raw graphs as input without the need for preprocessing, making it well-suited for network traffic graphs that encompass combined features and burst time-domain relationships.

Preliminaries. A graph $G = (V, E)$ is a set of nodes $V = \{v_1, v_2, \ldots, v_N\}$ and a set of edges $E \subseteq V \times V$ that connect nodes in V. Node features are stored in a matrix $X \subseteq \mathbb{R}^{n \times d}$ where n is the number of nodes and d is the dimension of the features. An adjacency matrix $A \subseteq \mathbb{R}^{n \times n}$ is employed to describe the directed graph G. To enable attribute propagation from nodes to themselves, an extended adjacency matrix $\tilde{A} = A + I$ is defined where I is the identity matrix. It is also required to define an augmented diagonal degree matrix $\tilde{D}$ for G where $\tilde{D}_{i,i}$ is the sum of elements in the ith row of $\tilde{A}$.

Figure 3 shows a sample graph. The DGCNN incorporates three layers for obtaining tensor representations for behavior classification in MindSphere, a graph convolution layer, sortpooling layer and remaining layer.

Graph Convolution Layer. In the first stage, the graph convolution layer propagates vertex attributes to their neighboring vertices based on structural connections. To aggregate multiscale substructure properties, multiple scroll stacks are stacked. They are recursively defined as:

$$Z^{t+1} = f \left(\tilde{D}^{-1} \tilde{A} Z^t W^t \right)$$

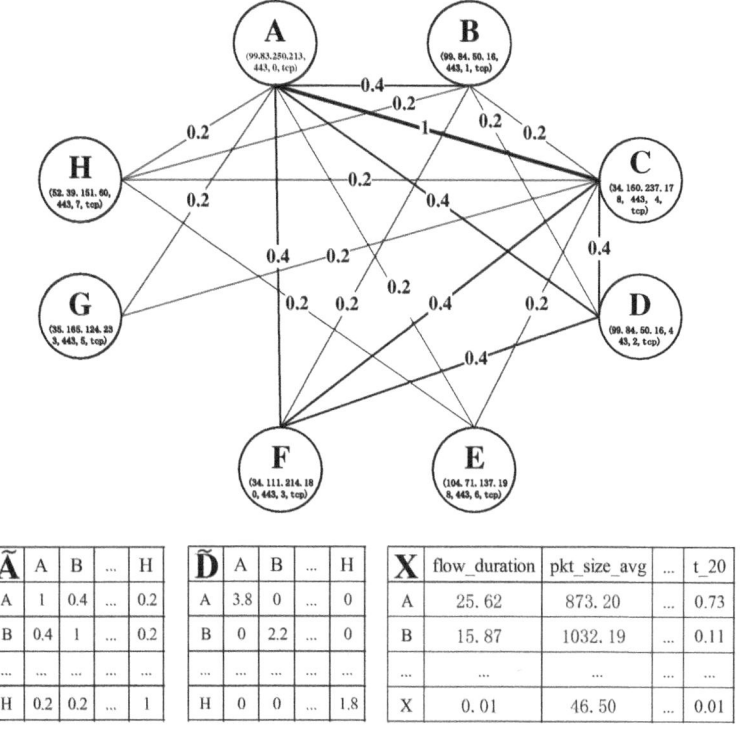

Fig. 3. Sample graph.

where $Z^0 = X$.

In the tth layer, $Z^t \in \mathbb{R}^{n \times c_t}$ is input, mapping c_t feature channels to c_{t+1} using the graph convolution parameter $W^t \in \mathbb{R}^{c_t \times c_{t+1}}$. The resulting channels for each vertex propagate to both its neighbors and to itself. This is achieved by multiplying them with the augmented adjacency matrix $\tilde{A}$ and normalizing row-wise using the augmented degree diagonal matrix $\tilde{D}$. The layer then produces element-wise activations using a nonlinear function f. After passing through h graph convolution layers, the DGCNN concatenates the output of each layer denoted as $Z^{1:h} = [Z^1, Z^2, \dots, Z^h]$.

SortPooling Layer. In the second stage, the sortpooling layer organizes vertices based on their feature descriptors as shown in Figure 4. $Z^{1:h}$ has n rows and $\sum_h^1 c_t$ columns, signifying feature descriptors at various scales. When vertices from different graphs exhibit analogous weighted feature descriptors, they cluster together. Importantly, since Z^h closely approximates the finest continuous colors in Weisfeiler-Lehman graph kernels, the sortpooling layer commences with the last layer. If the output of the last layer Z^h has c_h nodes, sorting continues with Z^{h-1} from the previous layer until all the nodes are separated. The

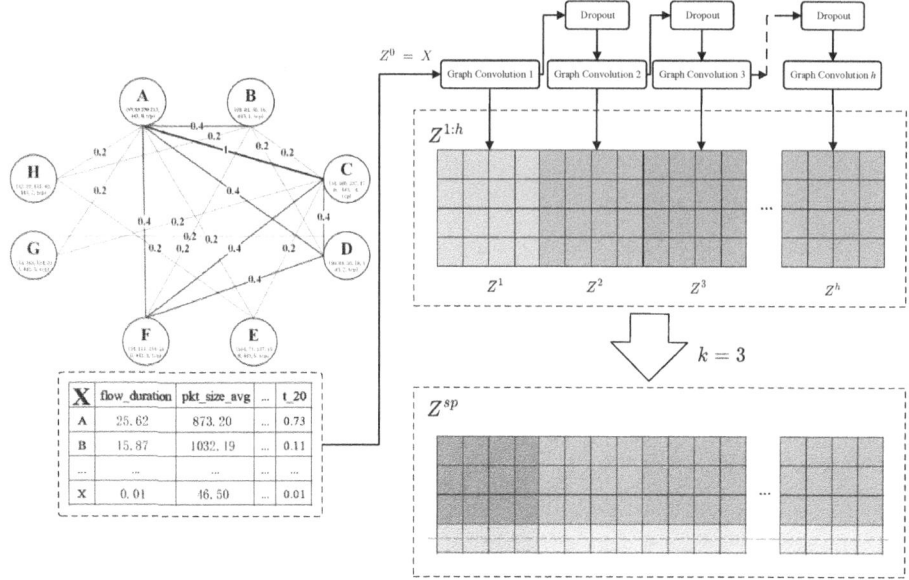

Fig. 4. Graph convolution and sortpooling layers.

sortpooling layer also adapts the sorted tensor along the first dimension, producing an output Z^{sp} with dimensions k by $\sum_h^1 c_t$. This standardizes the feature descriptor size across all graphs.

Remaining Layer. In the last stage, the DGCNN appends a one-dimensional convolution (Conv 1D) layer of kernel size $\sum_h^1 c_t$ and stride size $\sum_h^1 c_t$. If F is the number of filters in the last one-dimensional convolution layer, the sortpooling output is reduced to a one-dimensional vector of size $k \times F$, which is fed to a fully-connected one-layer perceptron for graph classification. Since the output of the model is a vector with shape $1 \times C$, where C is the number of user behavior classes in MindSphere, each value of the result vector represents the probability that the ith sample is in behavior c.

Cross-entropy loss is selected as the model loss. It is defined as:

$$\text{Loss} = -\sum_{i=1}^{B}\sum_{c=1}^{C} y_{i,c} \log\left(p_{i,c}\right)$$

where B is the batch size, $y_{i,c}$ is the ground truth and $y_{i,c}$ is one if the ith sample belongs to behavior c (otherwise it is zero) and $p_{i,c}$ is the predicted probability that the ith sample belongs to behavior c.

The stochastic gradient descent (SGD) optimization algorithm is employed with carefully chosen learning rates and momentum values to update the parameters of the DGCNN model. Table 2 presents the architecture of the classification model.

Table 2. DGCNN classification model architecture.

Layer	Output Shape
Graph Convolution Layer	
Graph Convolution 1	1,024
Dropout 1	1,024
Graph Convolution 2	1,024
Dropout 2	1,024
Graph Convolution 3	1,024
Dropout 3	1,024
Graph Convolution 4	512
SortPooling Layer	
SortPooling	(71,680, 1)
Remaining Layer	
1D Convolution	(20, 256)
1D Maxpooling	(10, 256)
1D Convolution	(5, 512)
Fully Connection Neural	1,024
Softmax Activation	1

4   Evaluation

This section describes the dataset used in the evaluation, the experiments used in the evaluation and the experimental results.

4.1   MindSphere Traffic Dataset

Due to the absence of a publicly-available MindSphere traffic dataset, an Industrial Internet of Things simulation platform was employed to create an experimental dataset comprising 15 classes. The platform facilitated remote access to a shared manufacturing resource pool, streamlined resource configuration and management with minimal effort, and reduced third-party involvement [6].

Figure 5 shows the simulation platform architecture. It comprises four layers, device layer, edge layer, platform layer and application layer:

- **Device Layer:** The device layer typically houses production equipment such programmable logic controllers, industrial motors, pumps and robots as well as monitoring systems such as human-machine interfaces, supervisory control and data acquisition systems and distributed control systems, which offer extensive human-machine interaction and functionality. From a connectivity perspective, the devices would fall in the category of traditional equipment that communicates using operational technology protocols such as S7, Profibus, Modbus and OPC. The device layer used in the simulation incorporated a Siemens S7-1512c programmable logic controller (firmware

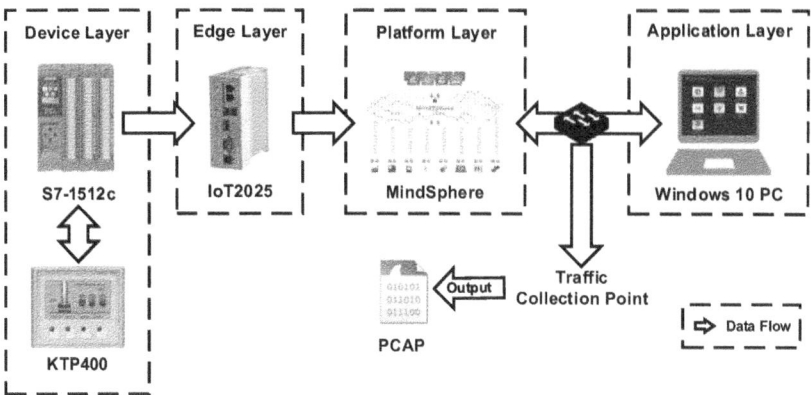

Fig. 5. Simulation platform.

v4.5) and a KTP400 human-machine interface (firmware v17.0.0.0) to simulate typical industrial control system scenarios.

– **Edge Layer:** Operating at the edge system or industrial gateway level, the edge layer collects data from the equipment layer via operational technology protocols and transmits it to the platform layer using information technology protocols such as HTTP/REST, MQTT and AMQP. These technologies implement data aggregation, filtering and cleaning mechanisms that collectively establish a device-independent model. The model serves as the foundation for decision-making and analytical logic tailored to specific device domains and types. The edge layer used in the simulation incorporated a Siemens IoT 2050 device (firmware v1.2.1 and Industrial OS v3.2.2) as the industrial gateway.

– **Platform Layer:** The platform layer serves as a centralized information repository that can accommodate vast volumes of data from diverse distributed sources. Its primary function is to enable seamless data accessibility for users in the supply chain such as logistics professionals, customers, distributors and suppliers. Concurrently, the platform layer would empower users to engage with novel devices, configure permissions, access warning data and execute various operations. To augment the authenticity of the simulation experiments, a genuine Siemens MindSphere, a cloud-based service, was employed instead of a private platform.

– **Application Layer:** To support the real-time monitoring of industrial operations, the application layer serves as the interface for presenting data collected from the platform layer to users employing personal computers or mobile devices. The application layer typically incorporates bespoke applications that leverage the services and data exposed by the platform layer and present the data in a user-friendly manner. The simulation experiments employed a 64-bit Windows 10 personal computer as the client to access the web services provided by MindSphere.

Automated scripts were employed to generate diverse user behaviors in Mind-Sphere over a period of one month. Scapy was used to capture and store the traffic in the PCAP format. Table 3 provides details of the MindSphere dataset.

4.2 Experiment Details

This section provides details of the experiments, including the comparison methods, experimental settings and benchmarking metrics.

Comparison Methods. Three state-of the-art neural network models were employed to conduct comprehensive model comparisons, FlowPrint [15], MApp-Graph [7] and TrafficGCN [16]. FlowPrint employs temporal correlations between network traffic destinations in a semi-supervised clustering approach. MAppGraph constructs a communications graph based on node tuples of IP addresses and ports, with edges established via weighted communications correlations between nodes. TrafficGCN enhances MAppGraph by incorporating packet-level and flow-level traffic data for graph construction. Note that a dynamic graph convolutional neural network (DGCNN) was employed as the classifier in TrafficGCN instead of a graph convolutional network (GCN) because it improves TrafficGCN performance using the dataset. AppScanner is an excellent multi-flow classification method. However, it could not be used for MindSphere classification because it cannot account for irrelevant traffic in PCAP files, categorizing all flows as belonging to a single class.

Experimental Settings. The PCAP files used in the experiments contained essential packet information, including five-tuple, steam ID, packet length and payload length. The node feature extraction module employed the cumulative sequence $\beta = 20$ and maximum node count $M = 20$. The experiments relied heavily on the graph topology module for which the parameter α plays a vital role; $\alpha = 0.05$ was chosen carefully for segmenting the graph. The classification algorithm employed $k = 10$ as the output size of the sortingpool layer. Following the work of Pham et al. [7], model training spanned 150 epochs with an initial learning rate of 10^{-4} and a decay rate of 0.9 every 10 epochs. The GFCM was implemented using Stellargraph 1.2.1 and Tensorflow 2.12.0 in a Python 3.6 environment. The hyper-parameters of FlowPrint, MAppGraph and TrafficGCN were tuned using the Keras Tuner library. The experiment employed a server equipped with Intel(R) Xeon(R) Silver-4110 processors and Tesla V100 graphics cards.

Benchmarking Metrics. The overall precision, recall and F1-score were selected as the key performance indicators for model evaluation:

$$Precision = \frac{TP}{TP + FP}$$

Table 3. MindSphere dataset details.

Label/Behavior	Description	Number
User Login		
1 Successful Login	User successfully logs into MindSphere account	100
2 Failed Login	User fails to log into MindSphere account	124
3 Logout	User logs out of MindSphere account	98
Asset Manager		
4 Connect Device	User accesses new industrial gateway or equipment	154
5 Modify Configuration	User modifies device connection configuration	114
6 Query Real-Time Data	User queries real-time data uploaded by device	156
Developer Cockpit		
7 Create Application	User creates industrial application	71
8 User Authorization	User modifies roles and related permissions of industrial application	125
9 Register App	User registers industrial application and makes it open to the public	145
Monitor		
10 Query Time Series Data	User queries time series data uploaded by device	117
11 Create/Modify Alarm Rule	User creates or modifies alarm configuration	108
12 Dashboard Viewer	User enters Dashboard Viewer module	103
13 Mendix	User enters Mendix module	132
14 Upgrade	User enters Upgrade module	93
15 Visual Flow Creator	User enters Visual Flow Creator module	96

$$\text{Recall} = \frac{TP}{TP + FN}$$

$$\text{F1-Score} = \frac{2 \times \text{Precision} \times \text{Recall}}{\text{Precision} + \text{Recall}}$$

where TP denotes true positives, TN denotes true negatives, FP denotes false positives and FN denotes false negatives. To enhance the reliability of the experiments, five-fold cross-validation was employed and weighted averages were computed based on the supports, which corresponded to the numbers of true instances for the labels.

4.3   Experimental Results

The encrypted traffic classification performance of GFCM was compared against the performance of FlowPrint, MAppGraph and TrafficGCN using the Mind-Sphere dataset.

Table 4 shows the encrypted traffic classification performance for the four models (best results are in boldface). GFCM – which has the best performance for almost all the metrics – yields average performance improvements of 4.20% for accuracy, 4.27% for recall and 4.56% for Fl-score. These results indicate that FlowPrint, MAppGraph and TrafficGCN have certain shortcomings with regard to fine-grained classification. GFCM benefits from the combination features and burst time-domain relationships, correctly detecting user behaviors in multiple flows.

FlowPrint Results. Key features of FlowPrint are destination-based clustering and homogeneous traffic isolation by leveraging the differences in network targets (destination IP addresses and ports) with which the application communicates. Because different websites and applications are served by different servers, FlowPrint can achieve excellent results in coarse-grained classification tasks (e.g., websites and applications). The isolation of homogeneous traffic enhances the identification of communications traffic differences between different servers. However, classifying user behaviors is a fine-grained task. Since different user behaviors are encountered on the same server, FlowPrint isolates not homogeneous traffic, but a large amount of effective traffic. The experimental results show that FlowPrint only generated four kinds of fingerprints in the 15 datasets. As a matter of fact, the results of a feature analysis experiment described below demonstrate that the destination IP address is not a key feature of fine-grained classification.

MAppGraph Results. MAppGraph is a network traffic analysis technique that focuses on IP address and port analysis. It collects mobile application network traffic in specific time intervals to create a traffic graph by defining nodes and edges and computing the edge weights. Each graph node is represented by a tuple comprising a destination IP address and port number used by an application. Nodes have strong cross-correlation when they exhibit significant activities

Table 4. Encrypted traffic classification performance.

Label	FlowPrint			MAppGraph			TrafficGCN			GFCM		
	Pr	Re	F1	Pr	Re	F1	Pr	Re	F1	Pr	Re	F1
1	6.00	**99.00**	11.31	94.06	95.00	94.53	94.00	94.00	94.00	**95.00**	**95.00**	**95.00**
2	0.00	0.00	0.00	**95.16**	**95.16**	**95.16**	93.65	95.16	94.40	95.12	94.35	94.74
3	2.27	1.02	1.41	93.94	**94.90**	94.42	93.94	**94.90**	94.42	**94.90**	**94.90**	**94.90**
4	**100.00**	0.65	1.29	86.93	86.36	86.65	85.03	**92.21**	88.47	87.58	91.56	**89.52**
5	0.00	0.00	0.00	75.00	81.58	77.69	77.69	82.46	80.00	**85.59**	**83.33**	**84.44**
6	0.00	0.00	0.00	85.52	79.49	82.39	**89.05**	78.21	83.28	86.45	**85.90**	**86.17**
7	0.00	0.00	0.00	64.06	57.75	60.74	68.12	66.20	67.14	**76.47**	**73.24**	**74.82**
8	0.00	0.00	0.00	52.00	41.60	46.22	55.56	36.00	43.69	**68.85**	**67.20**	**68.02**
9	0.00	0.00	0.00	57.30	73.10	64.24	59.59	**79.31**	68.05	**75.00**	78.62	**76.77**
10	0.00	0.00	0.00	70.25	72.65	71.43	79.41	69.23	73.97	**82.24**	75.21	**78.57**
11	0.00	0.00	0.00	74.29	72.22	73.24	72.36	82.41	77.06	**80.51**	**87.96**	**84.07**
12	65.52	18.45	28.79	92.08	90.29	91.18	92.93	89.32	91.09	**94.00**	91.26	**92.61**
13	0.00	0.00	0.00	90.23	90.91	90.57	90.44	93.18	91.79	**92.54**	**93.94**	**93.23**
14	0.00	0.00	0.00	88.76	84.95	86.81	**91.21**	89.25	90.22	89.47	91.40	90.43
15	0.00	0.00	0.00	88.04	84.38	86.17	90.22	86.46	88.30	**91.30**	87.50	89.36
Average	13.23	6.91	2.55	80.29	80.13	80.06	81.94	81.85	81.53	86.14	86.12	86.09

Pr: Precision, Re: Recall, F1: F1-Score

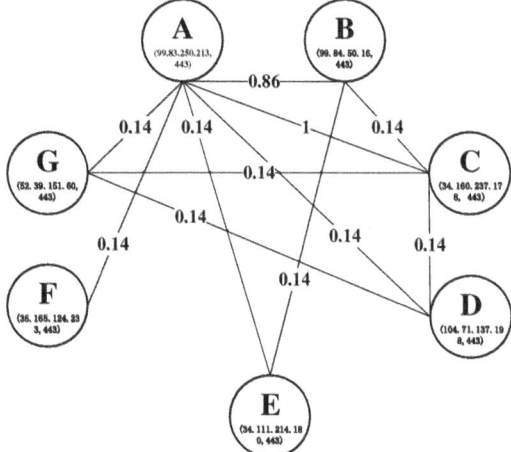

(a) MAppGraph graph topology.

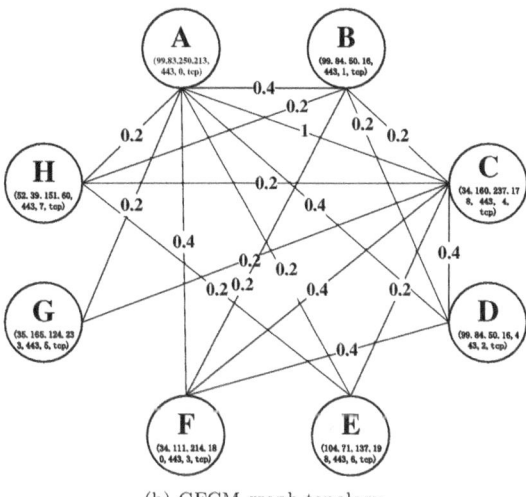

(b) GFCM graph topology.

Fig. 6. MAppGraph and GFCM graph topologies of the sample in Figure 3.

in the same time frames. While MAppGraph is effective for general classification tasks such as distinguishing between websites and applications, it struggles with detailed classification, especially the characterization of user behaviors. The primary challenge arises from the fact that identical nodes can generate multiple network flows, with only a few relevant to specific behaviors. The remaining flows are irrelevant and may disrupt the classification task. To address this problem, inspiration is drawn from MAppGraph's topology construction method to propose enhancements. As shown in Figure 6, flow identifiers (IP address, port, stream ID, protocol) are adopted as the basis for the graph nodes instead of IP address identifiers (IP address, port). The flow identifiers segment traffic into

Table 5. Performance with and without IP addresses in the node feature.

Method	Precision	Recall	F1-Score
With IP Addresses			
MAppGraph	80.29	80.13	80.06
TrafficGCN	81.44	81.45	81.34
GFCM	85.18	85.14	85.14
Without IP Addresses			
MAppGraph	80.92	80.70	80.73
TrafficGCN	81.94	81.85	81.53
GFCM	86.14	86.12	86.09

more distinct blocks, facilitating the identification of packets and flows associated with specific user behaviors.

TrafficGCN Results. As an enhancement of MAppGraph, TrafficGC combines data from various levels, including packet-level and flow-level traffic data. However, TrafficGCN relies on sliding-window sampling to collect data, which may not accurately capture user-behavior-related traffic in MindSphere and could potentially separate relevant traffic in the time domain. To address this issue, the time-window segmentation is replaced by burst segmentation, which provides more detailed depictions of flow relationships.

4.4   Feature Analysis Results

IP addresses have always been regarded as important features in coarse-grained classification. However, during fine-grained classification a counterintuitive result was obtained – the destination IP address is not the key feature of the fine classification task. On one hand, different kinds of behavior traffic may be generated by the same IP address. For example, label 1 and label 2 in the first MindSphere dataset are generated by the user login module, so the IP addresses of their traffic are essentially the same. On the other hand, due to load balancing, the IP address of a destination service may change, resulting in the same class of traffic generated by different IP addresses. The results in Table 5 demonstrate that, when IP addresses are used for training, the performance is almost the same or even slightly worse.

4.5   Ablation Study Results

Table 6 shows the results of an ablation study of the contributions of each model component and stage. Models 1 and 2 highlight the importance of both statistical and sequence features because their F1-scores drop by 22.14% and 3.63%, respectively. Model 3 shows the significance of accurate flow separation in the graph topology stage, resulting in a 3.01% F1-score drop when the burst time-domain

Table 6. Ablation results for key GFCM components.

Model	Precision	Recall	F1-Score
Complete Model: GFCM	86.14	86.12	86.09
Model 1: GFCM without Statistical Features	64.48	65.44	63.95
Model 2: GFCM without Sequence Features	82.72	82.60	82.46
Model 3: GFCM without Burst Time-Domain	83.19	83.18	83.08
Model 4: GFCM without DGCNN	78.62	78.51	78.11

is replaced with the time-window. Model 4 demonstrates that the removal of the deep model and substitution of DGCNN with a graph convolutional network (GCN) in the classification algorithm significantly reduce the F1-score by 7.98% compared with the complete model.

5 Conclusions

The popular MindSphere Industrial Internet of Things platform utilizes robust encryption protocols for data transmission, presenting significant challenges to traditional traffic forensic approaches, including deep-packet-inspection-based anomaly detection. Conducting effective user behavior forensics in this context requires the identification of relevant traffic in extensive IP network flows along with the execution of fine-grained classification tasks.

The flow-correlation framework described in this chapter is designed to automatically extract user behavior patterns from MindSphere network traffic. The approach engages a hybrid feature set covering statistical and sequential data to create feature vectors for flow nodes. By leveraging traffic correlation, the approach incorporates a burst time-domain mechanism to construct a communications diagram. The constituent traffic graphs are processed using a graph neural network model to enable effective classification. Comprehensive experiments demonstrate that the MindSphere traffic classification approach achieves impressive accuracy of up to 86% on a real-world dataset, surpassing contemporary state-of-the-art methods.

This work, which constitutes the first attempt at analyzing MindSphere from a traffic analysis perspective, contributes to protocol security and enhanced user privacy in the Industrial Internet of Things. Future research will attempt to explore other industrial platforms to foster broader and safer applications in the Industrial Internet of Things.

Acknowledgement. This research was supported by the National Key Research and Development Program of China (Grant no. 2021YFB3101400) and the National Defense Basic Scientific Research Program of China (Grant no. JCKY2021602B002).

References

1. 6sense, Siemens MindSphere, San Francisco, California (`6sense.com/tech/iot-platform/siemens-mindsphere-market-share`), 2024.
2. Gartner, Global Industrial IoT Platforms: Reviews and Ratings, Stamford, Connecticut (`www.gartner.com/reviews/market/global-industrial-iot-platforms`), 2024.
3. A. Lashkari, A. Kadir, L. Taheri and A. Ghorbani, Toward developing a systematic approach to generate benchmark Android malware datasets and classification, *Proceedings of the International Carnahan Conference on Security Technology*, 2018.
4. C. Liu, L. He, G. Xiong, Z. Cao and Z. Li, FS-Net: A flow sequence network for encrypted traffic classification, *Proceedings of the IEEE Conference on Computer Communications*, pp. 1171–1179, 2019.
5. A. Panchenko, F. Lanze, A. Zinnen, M. Henze, J. Pennekamp, K. Wehrle and T. Engel, Website fingerprinting at Internet scale, *Proceedings of the Twenty-Third Annual Network and Distributed System Security Symposium*, 2016.
6. P. Patel, M. Ali and A. Sheth, From raw data to smart manufacturing: AI and Semantic Web of Things for Industry 4.0, *IEEE Intelligent Systems*, vol. 33(4), pp. 79–86, 2018.
7. T. Pham, T. Ho, T. Truong-Huu, T. Cao and H. Truong, MAppGraph: Mobile-app classification of encrypted network traffic using deep graph convolution neural networks, *Proceedings of the Thirty-Seventh Annual Computer Security Applications Conference*, pp. 1025–1038, 2021.
8. A. Sadeghi, C. Wachsmann and M. Waidner, Security and privacy challenges in the Industrial Internet of Things, *Proceedings of the Fifty-Second Annual Design Automation Conference*, 2015.
9. U. Sendler, *The Internet of Things: Industrie 4.0 Unleashed*, Springer-Verlag, Berlin Heidelberg, Germany, 2018.
10. P. Sirinam, M. Imani, M. Juarez and M. Wright, Deep fingerprinting: Undermining website fingerprinting defenses with deep learning, *Proceedings of the ACM SIGSAC Conference on Computer and Communications Security*, pp. 1928–1943, 2018.
11. E. Sisinni, A. Saifullah, S. Han, U. Jennehag and M. Gidlund, Industrial Internet of Things: Challenges, opportunities and directions, *IEEE Transactions on Industrial Informatics*, vol. 14(11), pp. 4724–4734, 2018.
12. M. Stoyanova, Y. Nikoloudakis, S. Panagiotakis, E. Pallis and E. Markakis, A survey of Internet of Things (IoT) forensics: Challenges, approaches and open issues, *IEEE Communications Surveys and Tutorials*, vol. 22(2), pp. 1191–1221, 2020.
13. D. Sun, J. Hu, H. Wu, J. Wu, J. Yang, Q. Sheng and S. Dustdar, A comprehensive survey of collaborative data-access enablers in the IIoT, *ACM Computing Surveys*, vol. 56(2), article no. 50, 2023.
14. V. Taylor, R. Spolaor, M. Conti and I. Martinovic, AppScanner: Automatic fingerprinting of smartphone apps from encrypted network traffic, *Proceedings of the IEEE European Symposium on Security and Privacy*, pp. 439–454, 2016.
15. T. van Ede, R. Bortolameotti, A. Continella, J. Ren, D. Dubois, M. Lindorfer, D. Choffnes, M. van Steen and A. Peter, FlowPrint: Semi-supervised mobile-app fingerprinting on encrypted network traffic, *Proceedings of the Twenty-Seventh Annual Network and Distributed System Security Symposium*, 2020.

16. H. Xu, S. Li, Z. Cheng, R. Qin, J. Xie and P. Sun, TrafficGCN: Mobile application encrypted traffic classification based on GCN, *Proceedings of the IEEE Global Communications Conference*, pp. 891–896, 2022.

17. M. Zhang, Z. Cui, M. Neumann and Y. Chen, An end-to-end deep learning architecture for graph classification, *Proceedings of the Thirty-Second AAAI Conference on Artificial Intelligence, Thirtieth Innovative Applications of Artificial Intelligence Conference and Eighth AAAI Symposium on Educational Advances in Artificial Intelligence*, article no. 544, pp. 4438–4445, 2018.

18. Z. Zhu, J. Shi, C. Wang, G. Xiong, Z. Hao and G. Gou, MCFM: Discovering sensitive behavior from encrypted traffic in industrial control systems, *Proceedings of the IEEE International Conference on Trust, Security and Privacy in Computing and Communications*, pp. 897–904, 2022.

Digital Forensic Acquisition Using Private Internet of Things Cloud Application Programming Interfaces

Johannes Olegård and Stefan Axelsson

Stockholm University, Kista, Sweden
johannes.olegard@dsv.su.se

Abstract. Digital forensic practitioners face two key challenges when investigating Internet of Things devices. One is the need to reverse engineer a plethora of different devices and the other is the volatility of device data, including deleted data. This chapter attempts to address these challenges by focusing on the extraction of Internet of Things device data from the cloud by leveraging private application programming interfaces, an area that is relatively understudied in digital forensics. Specifically, this chapter presents the results of a study of decrypted traffic between six Android mobile apps (not the Internet of Things devices) and their respective cloud systems. The study results point to the feasibility of the approach and highlight the challenge involved in discovering additional application programming interface endpoints in a non-intrusive manner.

Keywords: Internet of Things Forensics · Application Programming Interface Forensics · Reverse Engineering · Transport Layer Security

1 Introduction

Digital forensic practitioners are facing multiple challenges investigating Internet of Things (IoT) devices [13, 26, 30]. Due to the diversity and lack of standardization of Internet of Things devices and their pace of development, practitioners do not have adequate resources to conduct forensic investigations as in the case of conventional computer forensics where personal computer hard drives have standardized interfaces. The only solution is to reverse engineer and experiment with individual devices in order to develop evidence acquisition techniques. However, these tasks are very time-consuming and it is difficult to keep up with myriad new Internet of Things devices that enter the market.

Another challenge is the limited storage capacity of most Internet of Things devices. This often means that fewer forensically-relevant artifacts are stored and the stored artifacts tend to be highly volatile because they are overwritten by newer data.

Yet another challenge is that Internet of Things devices of interest in investigations are often not available to forensic practitioners. The devices are difficult to locate; often there is little indication that they even exist in crime scenes.

E. Kurkowski and S. Shenoi (Eds.): DigitalForensics 2024, IFIP AICT 724, pp. 141–163, 2025.
https://doi.org/10.1007/978-3-031-71025-4_8

The devices may also be damaged or destroyed, in accidents or intentionally to cover evidence of criminal activity. The problems are multiplied at large enterprises that deploy numerous and diverse Internet of Things devices. Locating, accessing and extracting evidence from the devices is impractical.

Of course, high-end Internet of Things devices such as smart camera hubs that store video data on standard hard drives are common. But these are exceptions because Internet of Things devices are typically designed to be small, cheap and Internet-connected. Forensic practitioners routinely receive device models they have not encountered before, situations that are exacerbated by the huge examination backlogs faced by law enforcement agencies.

Fortunately, there is a tendency for Internet of Things device artifacts to be stored in a cloud or edge system. This implies that some of the digital forensic challenges could be partially addressed by downloading forensic artifacts from the cloud using application programming interfaces (APIs). The artifacts could supplement those retrieved physically from Internet of Things devices and smartphones and potentially even supersede them in triage scenarios.

Certain facts support this line of reasoning. First, the cloud likely maintains artifacts of forensic relevance longer than the devices that produce them. Second, Internet of Things vendors likely reuse cloud services for multiple device models, which means than reverse engineering a single private cloud API would be much more useful and much less time-consuming than reversing multiple device models. Third, modern web APIs are typically text-based and easy to interpret – more so than binary dumps of Internet of Things devices – and would significantly reduce the time required for reverse engineering and data analysis. Fourth, consumer-grade Internet of Things systems such as smart homes are typically controlled by mobile apps and mobile device forensics could be leveraged to conduct cloud API forensics, speeding up the digital forensic efforts.

The notion of retrieving Internet of Things device data from the cloud is by no means novel [30]. Four main approaches are available for obtaining evidence from a cloud system. First, pursuant to a warrant, a forensic practitioner could gain administrative access to a cloud system and perform the acquisition. Second, backed by a subpoena, the cloud owner could be required to acquire and provide the artifacts. Third, open APIs provided by the cloud owner could be used to obtain the artifacts. Fourth, a forensic practitioner could leverage private APIs that are not intended to be used by external parties.

The first (warrant) approach is the most complete, but is impractical due to big data, privacy and jurisdictional challenges [26]. In fact, this level of legal authorization would be available only for serious criminal cases.

The second (subpoena) approach is perhaps the most common cloud forensic method used by law enforcement in most countries, but it can be time-consuming depending on the cloud provider and jurisdiction. A small and/or new cloud provider may not have the technical and personnel resources to support the request. Also, the completeness of forensic acquisition would not be guaranteed if the provider is not fully aware about the data stored by contracted (outsourced) companies.

The two API-based approaches would be the fastest and would potentially provide more evidence than the subpoena approach. However, they are relatively understudied in the digital forensics domain. Most API forensics research has focused on open APIs (third approach), especially cloud storage APIs and social media network APIs. However, it should be noted that not all systems have open APIs, which limits the applicability of the approach. Furthermore, some cloud artifacts are not available via open APIs, but are available via private APIs.

The limited amount of research on API forensics and lack of a scientific consensus on how to perform forensics via APIs brings forensic soundness into question. More research is warranted given that several European countries have legalized remote API forensics in law enforcement investigations. Indeed, it appears that the speed of API-based approaches may be necessary to keep up with the demand for cloud-based data in digital forensic investigations and, if successful, they could be the staple of investigations just as mobile device forensics is today.

This chapter presents the results of monitoring cloud API communications of six Android mobile apps related to Internet of Things devices, each with a different cloud backend. The goal is to understand the forensically-useful artifacts that are uploaded to the cloud and how to retrieve the artifacts in a forensically-sound manner for use as digital evidence. The monitoring process involves the decryption of Transport Layer Security (TLS) traffic, which helps associate events such as Internet of Things sensor readings and user actions in the app with API endpoints used to transfer the information between the app and the cloud. The identified API requests are then imitated on a separate computer to download forensic artifacts from the cloud systems. This imitation process involves using authentication tokens extracted from the mobile app files.

2   Legality of API Forensics

Legal issues pertaining to API forensics vary in countries across the world. This section highlights the situation in some important jurisdictions where API forensics may be employed by law enforcement under the right circumstances. Note that the General Data Protection Regulation (GDPR) of the European Union and cloud provider terms of service cover relationships between consumers and companies, not law enforcement. Therefore, they have no bearing on the intended use case involving API forensics conducted by law enforcement.

Germany. German law allows for "covert remote investigations" for certain serious crimes [6] (see Sections 100b and 110(3)). This is interpreted to mean that API forensics would be lawful if the prerequisites are fulfilled.

Sweden. A recent Swedish law [28, 29] may be used to grant Swedish law enforcement authorization to perform "remote investigations" under certain circumstances. The new legislation is intended for law enforcement to access social media accounts using suspects' credentials even when the servers are physically located outside Sweden.

Norway. Norwegian law does not appear to clearly distinguish between local computing systems and remote computing systems [19] (see Sections 199a and 200a). The Norwegian Supreme Court has ruled in favor of remote forensics [27]. The case involved a law enforcement investigation of Tidal Music, a music streaming company, when remote downloads were executed of source code on a server hosted abroad on Amazon Web Services and emails hosted abroad on Google Gmail. The downloads were performed without alerting Amazon and Google. However, Tidal Music was involved and provided access.

United Kingdom. The United Kingdom Law Commission has published a recommendation [16] for updating the laws governing search warrants to allow for, among other things, the seizure of cloud data stored in other countries. However, at this time, the recommendation has not yet been enacted as a law.

3   Related Work

Roussev et al. [22, 23] introduced the use of web-based APIs in digital forensics. Specifically, they employed open web APIs to execute remote acquisition scripts for various cloud file storage services. Since then, researchers have conducted similar work involving other cloud services, including file storage and social media [21, 31].

However, retrieving forensic data from remote services via "web APIs" predates the work of Roussev et al. [22]. Notably, research on web scraping for digital forensics dates back to at least 2011, when Huber et al. [11] used it to extract data from Facebook. In the interim, other researchers have web-scraped additional social media platforms [9, 10].

The exact difference between web scraping and web API forensics mainly concerns the shift in how websites have been developed. Early websites would simply send pre-rendered HTML pages to web browsers. In contrast, a modern web page is typically rendered by a JavaScript application that runs in the web browser and calls APIs in the background to dynamically populate the local HTML page (referred to as "client-side rendering"). Therefore, web scraping techniques from the pre-rendered era would not adequately reconstruct modern web pages. This modern use of web technology to construct backend APIs has also influenced mobile and Internet of Things device development. A modern mobile app or Internet of Things device app works similarly to a web app – a local client, not necessarily written in JavaScript, sends web API requests in the background to populate the local interface that may or may not use HTML.

Previous research has also focused on the use of private web APIs in digital forensics. Notably, Chung et al. [4] reverse engineered Amazon Alexa web APIs and employed the APIs to perform remote acquisitions from the Amazon Echo

Internet of Things cloud system. This work was subsequently expanded upon by Youn et al. [32]. Other authors have applied similar techniques to other Internet of Things cloud systems [3] with varying success [24]. It is relevant to note that API forensics can also be applied to edge systems [17]. Indeed, since the protocols are typically the same, there is little difference between using APIs for local, edge and cloud systems. API reverse engineering is employed in Internet of Things security research. For example, Fereidooni et al. [7] dynamically instrumented Fitbit APIs to develop attacks on user health data in the cloud.

4   API Reverse Engineering

Several approaches have been proposed for API reverse engineering. Perhaps the easiest is to instrument a client to record the requests it sends. A client could be a web app [4], mobile app or program running on an Internet of Things device [24]. The instrumentation of web apps is often supported out-of-the-box by modern web browsers, but the process is more complicated for mobile devices and Internet of Things devices. Typically, web requests are made via secure TLS tunnels. Accessing a tunnel using a client involves tricking the client into employing an insecure tunnel by leveraging certificate injection, certificate unpinning and a man-in-the-middle attack. Alternatively, key material may be leaked from memory using a debugger or a memory dump. Both approaches require gaining elevated privileges on the device, which can be challenging due to mandatory security.

Shin et al. [24] attempted to use certificate injection attacks on various Internet of Things smart speakers, but had some problems bypassing the certificate pinning settings used by the speakers. Certificate pinning is also quite common in Android apps, rendering certificate injection mostly deprecated and ineffective for capturing traffic on modern mobile devices, especially given the changes in protections since 2016 [8]. In some situations, it may be possible to configure the client to use a proxy willingly [14], but apps and Internet of Things devices may or may not provide this functionality.

These issues suggest that the memory-reading approach to TLS decryption may be the most broadly applicable approach, assuming, of course, that elevated privileges can be obtained. For example, Dorazio et al. [5] demonstrated how to disable certificate validation on iOS devices by modifying TLS library code in live memory using a debugger. The work described in this chapter opted for a similar approach, but used a debugger to extract TLS secret keys instead of undoing certificate pinning. A reviewer of this chapter mentioned that the friTAP tool [1, 2] automates this process. Although friTAP was not employed in this work, it may be of interest to readers.

5   Methodology

Six Internet of Things systems were selected for the experiments, each system comprises one or more apps, an Internet of Things device and a cloud system.

Table 1. Internet of Things systems used in the experiments.

Internet of Things Systems
System 1
Huawei Health App (`com.huawei.health`)
Huawei Core App (`com.huawei.hwid`)
Huawei Appmarket App (`com.huawei.appmarket`)
Huawei Band 6 Smartwatch
System 2
Suunto App (`com.stt.android.suunto`)
Suunto 3 Smartwatch
System 3
Mydlink App (`com.dlink.mydlinkunified`)
D-Link W115 Smart Plug
System 4
Kasa App (`com.tplink.kasa_android`)
TP-Link HS100 Smart Plug
System 5
Imou Smartlife App (`com.mm.android.smartlifeiot`)
Imou NVR1104HS-W-S2 Smart Hub (Recorder)
Imou Bullet 2 Smart Cameras (4 Cameras)
System 6
Home Connect App (`com.bshg.homeconnect.android.release`)
Siemens SN43HW88CS/13 Dishwasher

System selection was based on availability with the goal being to cover as many different cloud systems as possible ($n = 6$) with less focus on obtaining popular devices or a representative sample of Internet of Things device types.

Table 1 shows the apps and Internet of Things devices comprising the six Internet of Things systems used in the experiments. Figure 1 shows images of the Internet of Things devices. Note that the Huawei Health app required Huawei Core/ID and Huawei Appmarket apps to be running simultaneously, so all three were monitored during the captures. All apps, except for the Huawei apps, were installed using the Google Play Store.

Repeated experiments were performed on each Internet of Things system. Each experiment involved mimicking regular user interactions with the app and with the corresponding Internet of Things device, but in a systematic manner. Modern mobile apps behave similarly to websites and have logical pages that link to each other. The pages and links form a graph and the process of systematically exploring the app involves traversal of the graph. This is similar to performing a forensic manual acquisition with unhindered network connectivity.

A page can essentially be viewed as a presentation of a subset of the cloud backend state and, in order to display the page, the app must retrieve the state. Thus, the process of coercing the app into making API calls of interest involves

Fig. 1. Internet of Things devices used in the experiments.

perturbing the cloud backend state using the app or Internet of Things device and performing a traversal of the page graph. This may not work if the app locally caches state, but it can usually be bypassed by reinstalling the app and logging in with the same account, which often exposes useful bulk download API endpoints. The entire experimental process may be summarized as leaving evidence in the cloud, reinstalling the app with the same account and performing a manual acquisition on the app.

The experimental results comprised the encrypted network traffic generated throughout the experimental process, not just the traffic during the last step. In order to capture and decrypt the traffic, the experiments had to be performed inside a network capture setup. For all devices except the smartwatches, the experiments were repeated in two networking topologies: with the mobile device and Internet of Things device on the same or separate local area networks. The latter case forced the app to use the cloud instead of directly communicating with the Internet of Things device over the local area network. The smartwatches used Bluetooth and could only be directly connected to the mobile devices.

Once the network traffic was decrypted, it was trivial (with some exceptions) to imitate the API calls. Detailed performance measurements were not taken; however, most calls took a fraction of a second whereas calls with large responses took multiple seconds. The storage locations of API credentials were identified by comparing the traffic to a logical acquisition of the app files. The ability to mimic API calls could then be tested by reinstalling the app, which resulted in the use of a new token. Some apps stored the tokens with encryption, requiring the apps to be partially reverse engineered to decrypt the tokens. This was accomplished using JADX (`www.github.com/skylot/jadx`) and then the open-source Frida reverse engineering toolkit (`www.frida.re`) to perform decryption from within the apps.

```
var SSL_CTX_set_keylog_callback = new NativeFunction(
    Module.getExportByName('libssl.so', 'SSL_CTX_set_keylog_callback'),
    'void', ['pointer', 'pointer']);

var example_callback = new NativeCallback(
    function(ssl, line)
    {
    console.log(line.readCString());
    },
    'void', ['pointer', 'pointer']);

Interceptor.attach(Module.getExportByName("libssl.so", "SSL_CTX_new"),
    {
    onLeave: function(ctx)
        {
        SSL_CTX_set_keylog_callback(ctx, example_callback);
        }
    });
```

Fig. 2. Frida snippet that leaks OpenSSL TLS keys from inside an Android app.

Note that while the page graphs can be potentially infinite, especially with scrolling pages, this was never an issue because there was always a clear stopping point. It is, for example, not meaningful to scroll further back in a diagram of heart rate data than the start of the experiment. It was also assumed that developers do not intentionally hide behavior in their apps and that all the relevant pages in graphs could be found by tapping, pulling and scrolling.

The experiments focused on the settings found in the app – advertised Internet of Things device features (sensor data and actuator commands) and uploaded data observed in traffic from previous experiments. The experimental hypothesis was that using an app as described above should yield API calls to download data. If API endpoints for downloading the data were observed, then the experiment was considered to be successful. Failure to find the endpoints usually indicated an incomplete page graph traversal or that the app did not have pages to display the data (see, e.g., results for the Suunto app below).

5.1   Traffic Capture

The experimental setup consisted of a Samsung S9 smartphone running Android 10 (Firmware PDA G960FXXSHFUJ2, NEE region www.sammobile.com). The smartphone was rooted before the experiments using Magisk (www.github.com/topjohnwu/Magisk). A Linux laptop was configured to act as a Wi-Fi access point for the smartphone to access the Internet. The laptop ran Wireshark to capture all the network traffic from the smartphone.

The Frida reverse engineering toolkit was employed to "attach" to the app of interest (including all its processes) on the smartphone and extract client-side TLS secrets. Figure 2 shows a minimal Frida JavaScript snippet the achieves key extraction. The snippet instructs Frida to react to calls to a specific function in the OpenSSL library (`libssl.so`). Specifically, whenever a new SSL "Context" object is created, another built-in debugging function [20] is used to register a callback for outputting a log in "NSS key log format" [18]. The keylog combined with the raw traffic capture enables Wireshark to decrypt the TLS traffic in the capture.

Python APIs of Frida were also employed to enable the "spawn gating" and "child gating" functionalities of Frida, which ensure that the background processes of an app are also instrumented in the same way as the main process. For efficiency, the keylog files are written to the app directory (/data/data/{app}/*) and later extracted using an Android Debug Bridge (ADB).

The approach is mostly protocol-agnostic and works if the protocol embedded in TLS-embedded is HTTP, HTTP2, WebSockets, MQTT or another protocol. This feature is unlike most non-debugger-based, man-in-the-middle tools that would otherwise require knowledge about the embedded protocol. For example, tools such as Burpsuite and `mitmproxy` intercept the HTTP host headers to determine the destination IP addresses and ports. The tools do not function properly if the header is misconfigured in the app, for example, if a non-standard port is used and not specified in the header.

The approach was verified by checking for connections with missing TLS keys. Wireshark also captures irrelevant traffic from other apps that are not instrumented by Frida. To address this, the Socket Statistics (`ss`) preinstalled as `/system/bin/ss` on the smartphone was employed during the experiment to correlate TCP connections with their originating apps. After the experiment, all three types of artifacts (from Frida, Wireshark and `ss`) were used to verify that Frida successfully obtained all the TLS key material from the app of interest.

The rooted state of the smartphone was hidden from the investigated apps using the Zygisk and "Hide Magisk App" features of Magisk. These features were adequate to bypass the checks done by the root detection app Rootbeer-Fresh (`www.github.com/KimChangYoun/rootbeerFresh`). It was assumed that this was also adequate for the other five investigated apps.

6 Case Studies

This section describes the six Internet of Things systems, experimental observations and experimental results.

6.1 Huawei Health App

The Huawei Band 6 smartwatch has two main sensors, a photoplethysmograph (PPG) for heart pulse monitoring and an accelerometer for movement tracking. The Huawei smartwatch also has an oxymeter that measures the "SPO2" blood oxygen level. The sensor data is used by the smartwatch to derive several other metrics, including heart rate (beats/min), steps taken (number over a timespan) and sleep (timestamps and depth of sleep). These metrics are computed using proprietary algorithms (with a potential for inaccuracy that must be considered in investigations).

The smartwatch was connected directly to the smartphone using Bluetooth; a mobile app on the smartphone provided communications. The smartwatch does not have a GPS radio, but in the "exercise mode," the app complements the smartwatch readings with the GPS data from the smartphone. During the exercise mode, the app also records metrics at a higher frequency. The app was denied an Internet connection during the exercise mode to perform exercises without a portable traffic capture setup.

Huawei Health stores most of its relevant local data in SQLCipher-encrypted SQLite databases. The primary database, `hihealth003.db`, has been studied by Kudera [15]. This database stores smartwatch data and the token used to make most API requests. The database password, encrypted using the Android keystore, is stored in a separate file. It was possible to extract the decrypted database password using Frida by intercepting calls to the SQLCipher function `getWritableDatabase(password)` when the app was starting. It is also possible to copy a decrypted version of the database to a file as demonstrated by Kudera [15].

Results. It was possible to obtain all the health data – pulse, steps, sleep, GPS locations during exercises, etc. – using cloud APIs. While health data is also cached in files on the smartphone, it was possible to request historical data via the APIs. This included data generated from a previous smartphone that may not be cached on the new smartphone unless the user scrolls back in history to view it.

6.2   Suunto App

The Suunto 3 smartwatch has almost the same functionality as the Huawei Band 6 smartwatch, but without an oxymeter. As in the case of the Huawei Band 6, the app was denied Internet access during exercises and access was granted after the exercises. The access token is stored unencrypted in the "user" table in `databases/amer_app.db`.

Results. Like the Huawei Band 6 smartwatch, health and exercise data were extracted using APIs. The stored access token was also recovered. The Suunto 3 smartwatch uses the `Amplitude.com` third party analytics service and regularly uploads GPS location data passively, even outside the exercise mode. However, it was not possible to retrieve the GPS coordinates because the relevant (open) API endpoint requires an administrator access token.

6.3   Mydlink App

The D-Link smart plug sits between an appliance such as a lamp and a wall socket. The smart plug can then be used, via the app, to turn the appliance on or off (this is referred to as "turning the smart plug on or off"). The smart plug can be controlled in three main ways from the app, manually, as part of a group of devices (one button can be pushed to turn the devices on/off at once) or on a schedule. Note that the smart plug does not measure the power consumed by the appliance.

The D-Link smart plug is on-boarded (given its initial configuration) using a temporary Wi-Fi connection created by the smart plug. After on-boarding, the smart plug directly communicates with its backend cloud system without the aid of an Internet of Things hub.

The access token is stored in a slightly obfuscated shared preferences file named `com.dlink.mydlinkunified_preferences.xml`. The location in the file is labeled with hexadecimal md5-sum of the string "access_token." The token is stored as a base64-encoded Java serialization object. After base64-decoding, it is only necessary to retrieve the last 32 bytes to obtain the token.

Results. It was not possible to retrieve logs of smart plug on/off state changes (toggle on/off). However, it was possible to retrieve logs of when the smart plug lost Internet connectivity because the app sends the user a notification when this occurs. The user could also view this log in the app. It was also possible to retrieve the password for the Wi-Fi network used by the smart plug. The app uses a mix of HTTP, HTTP2 and WebSockets.

6.4   Kasa (TP-Link) App

The Kasa app works almost exactly as the Mydlink app, and the two smart plugs have similar features. Kasa stores the access token needed to make requests in the file `shared_prefs/aria_sp.xml`, but the token is encrypted using keys stored in the Android Keystore. The token, which was retrieved from memory using Frida, is an Java object of type `com.tplink.cloud.context.TCAccountBean`.

Results. It was not possible to retrieve a log of the smart plug on/off state changes. However, it was possible to retrieve a log of the "scene" (devices controlled as a group) and "automation" (scheduled) control events as shown in Figure 1. This log was viewable in the app by the user and retrieved on demand. The Kasa app uses HTTP and WebSockets, and the WebSocket messages match those previously found by Softscheck [25].

6.5   Imou Smart Life App

The Imou Smart Life camera system comprises a local hub ("recorder") that acts as a Wi-Fi access point for (in this case) four cameras. The hub has Internet access via an Ethernet cable. One of the features of the camera system and app is motion detection. App users can choose to receive a notification (including video) when motion is detected by a camera. A log of the events up to a week old can be viewed in the app. The hub contains a hard disk drive that stores videos for roughly three weeks. Imou Smart Life also provides a cloud storage service for a fee, but this was not used in the experiments. However, even without the service, the user can remotely access the recording device via the cloud using

```
{"id": "59HqDpiIf1JJ5SCekqWcTZ", "timestamp": 1682970575, "smartId":
"96nSHbWS", "chainOfSmartIds": ["96nSHbWS"], "smartName": "sc1",
"avatarUrl": "SmartOneClick", "triggerId": "1NBO7wDwIomsrOUq8bRyEx",
"triggerCount": 0, "code": 0, "triggerSetting": {"isManual": true},
"actionSetting": { "thing": {"category": "plug", "nickname":
"cXdnNg==", "avatarUrl": "", "thingName":
"8006B171FCDD4B788A049E084165F6FB1A263C17", "isSubThing": false,
"service": {"serviceId": "reverseStatus", "inputParams": {}},
"delaySeconds": 0, "deviceType": "IOT.SMARTPLUGSWITCH", "hwVer":
"2.0", "model": "HS100(EU)"}}}
```

Fig. 3. Kasa scene log event recovered via a reconstructed API request.

the app and stream video even when not on the same local area network as the hub.

Unlike the other Internet of Things systems, the Imou Smart Life system was tested as-is without performing the on-boarding process anew. The system owner account can share access to the camera system with other app accounts (e.g., accounts of family members). However, the experiments only investigated the access of one of the shared accounts, not the system owner account.

Results. The Imou Smart Life app uses a mix of HTTP, HTTP2, MQTT and a proprietary UDP-based video transfer protocol. The last protocol was used to communicate directly with the hub, even when not on the same local area network. The cloud also seems to relay MQTT-based commands to the hub, but does not necessarily store these events in the cloud. The most recent motion detection events can be retrieved via cloud APIs, but the videos themselves are requested from the hub. Similarly, motion detection events up to a week old were requested from the hub rather than the cloud. However, thumbnails of motion-detected-event videos were retrieved from the cloud rather than the hub.

The Imou Smart Life API requires a complicated hashing scheme to "sign" the HTTP headers of requests. While there was enough information in the app files to reproduce the calls, doing so required more reverse engineering than the other apps.

6.6 Home Connect App

The Siemens dishwasher can be started (or scheduled to start later) using the Home Connect app. The app also provides a notification when the machine needs maintenance. The access token is stored as a cookie in a SQLite file named app_webview/Default/Cookies.

Results. It was possible to retrieve a list of notifications. One of the notifications indicates the time when the dishwasher finished a run (including runs started physically at the dishwasher instead of via the app). However, details about the dishwasher run (when the user scheduled the run, start time of the

Table 2. Internet of Things system servers and hosts.

Huawei Health App	
huawei1	sportdata-dre.things.hicloud.com
huawei2	metrics2.data.hicloud.com:6447
huawei3	metrics-dre.dt.dbankcloud.cn
huawei4	oauth-login-dre.platform.dbankcloud.com
huawei5	connect-drcn.dbankcloud.cn
huawei6	connect-dre.dbankcloud.cn
huawei7	hwid-dre.platform.hicloud.com
Suunto App	
suunto1	247.sports-tracker.com
suunto2	api.sports-tracker.com
suunto3	analytics.sports-tracker.com
suunto4	firebaselogging-pa.googleapis.com
suunto5	sdk.fra-01.braze.eu
suunto6	songun-logs.azurewebsites.net
suunto7	api.amplitude.com
Mydlink App	
mydlink1	mp-eu-ead98f12.s3.dualstack.eu-west-1.amazonaws.com
mydlink2	mp-eu-dcdca.auto.mydlink.com
mydlink3	api.auto.mydlink.com
mydlink4	mp-eu-openapi.auto.mydlink.com
Kasa App	
kasa1	api.tplinkra.com
kasa2	euw1-app-cloudgateway.iot.i.tplinknbu.com
kasa3	euw1-app-server.iot.i.tplinknbu.com
kasa4	euw1-security.iot.i.tplinknbu.com
kasa5	eu-wap.tplinkcloud.com
kasa6	n-da.tplinkcloud.com
kasa7	n-euw1-wap.tplinkcloud.com
kasa8	n-wap.tplinkcloud.com
Imou Smartlife App	
imou1	app-fk.easy4ipcloud.com
imou2	app-v2.easy4ipcloud.com
imou3	logreport-v2.easy4ipcloud.com
imou4	ali-picture-private-fk.oss-eu-central-1.aliyuncs.com
imou5	imou-fk3-ali-online-paas-private-picture.oss-eu-central-1.aliyuncs.com
imou6	imou-fk4-ali-online-paas-private-picture.oss-eu-central-1.aliyuncs.com
imou7	imou-fk-ali-online-paas-private-picture.oss-eu-central-1.aliyuncs.com
imou8	s3.dualstack.eu-central-1.amazonaws.com
Home Connect App	
homec1	api.home-connect.com
homec2	app.adjust.com
homec3	in.appcenter.ms
homec4	prod.reu.rest.homeconnectegw.com

run and details about the program, etc.) were not available. Based on the work of Hudson [12], it is known that the app uses a special library (statically linked with OpenSSL) to communicate directly with the dishwasher (the cloud possibly acts as a relay). Some app connections could not be decrypted; this was likely due to the special library. Since the library appears to be primarily intended to communicate with the dishwasher directly rather than cloud storage, it was decided not to investigate the issue.

Table 2 shows the Internet of Things system servers and hosts. Tables 3 through 7 show the API endpoints for the six apps. Only endpoints interpreted as being useful are included in the tables.

Table 3. Huawei Health app API endpoints.

Server	API Endpoint	Description
huawei1	POST /dataQuery/common/getSyncVersions	List upload timestamps (can use as key to retrieve historical data)
huawei1	POST /dataQuery/health/getHealthDataByVersion	Retrieve historical data by upload timestamp
huawei1	POST /dataQuery/health/getHealthData	Retrieve health data (heart rate, sleep, step count, etc.)
huawei1	POST /dataQuery/health/getHealthStatistics	Retrieve special summary statistics for specific device
huawei1	POST /dataQuery/health/getHealthStat	Retrieve summary statistics (e.g., daily average)
huawei1	POST /dataQuery/path/getMotionPathByVersion	Retrieve exercise GPS path
huawei1	POST /dataQuery/sequence/getSampleSequenceByVersion	List types of data recorded during an exercise
huawei1	POST /dataQuery/sport/getSportsDataByVersion	Retrieve exercise data
huawei1	POST /dataQuery/sport/getSportsDataByTime	Retrieve exercise data by upload timestamp
huawei1	POST /dataQuery/sport/getSportsDimenStat	Retrieve exercise summary statistics for all devices
huawei1	POST /dataQuery/sport/getSportsStat	Retrieve exercise summary statistics for specific device
huawei1	POST /dataSync/health/addHealthData	Upload passive health data
huawei1	POST /dataSync/health/addHealthStatistics	Upload special passive health data summary statistics
huawei1	POST /dataSync/health/addHealthStat	Upload passive health data summary statistics
huawei1	POST /dataSync/path/addMotionPathData	Upload exercise GPS path
huawei1	POST /dataSync/sport/addSportsData	Upload exercise data
huawei1	POST /dataSync/sport/addTotalSportsData	Upload exercise data summary statistics
huawei1	POST /profile/device/bindDevice	Register device (smartphone or smartwatch)
huawei1	POST /profile/device/getBindDevice	Retrieve device information (smartphone or smartwatch)
huawei1	POST /profile/device/updateBindDevice	Change device information (smartphone or smartwatch)
huawei1	POST /profile/user/getUserProfile	Retrieve general app settings (also height, weight and gender)
huawei1	POST /profile/user/setUserProfile	Change app settings
huawei2	POST /common/hmshimaintqrt	Upload analytics events (events are partially encrypted)
huawei2	POST /common/hmshioperqrt	Upload analytics events (events are partially encrypted)
huawei2	POST getPublicKey?keytype=2	Download public key used to encrypt analytics events
huawei3	POST /common/hmshimaintqrt	See metrics2.data.hicloud.com:6447
huawei3	POST getPublicKey?keytype=2	See metrics2.data.hicloud.com:6447
huawei4	POST oauth2/v3/silent_token	Renew access token
huawei5	POST agc/apigw/oauth2/v1/token	Login to get 48h access token
huawei6	POST agc/apigw/oauth2/v1/token	Login to get 48h access token
huawei7	POST /AccountServer/IUserInfoMng/getUserInfo	(HTTP2) Retrieve user account information
huawei7	POST /AccountServer/IUserInfoMng/stAuth	(HTTP2) Authenticate HTTP2 session
huawei7	POST IdmClientApi/IDM/getUserInfo	(HTTP2) Retrieve user account information and smartphones
huawei7	POST IdmClientApi/IDM/loginV3	(HTTP2) Login using userid and (hashed) password
huawei7	POST IdmClientApi/IDM/stAuth	(HTTP2) Authenticate HTTP2 session

Table 4. Suunto app API endpoints.

Server	API Endpoint	Description
suunto1	GET /v1/activity/export	Download historical passive health data
suunto1	GET /v1/recovery/export	Download stress health data
suunto1	GET /v1/sleep/export	Download historical sleep data
suunto1	POST /v1/activity	Upload passive health data
suunto1	POST /v1/recovery	Upload stress data
suunto1	POST /v1/sleep	Upload sleep data
suunto2	GET /apiserver/v1/gear/	List smartwatches registered to the account
suunto2	GET /apiserver/v1/user	Retrieve user information (some settings, also last login time)
suunto2	GET /apiserver/v1/user/settings	Retrieve user app settings (also weight and gender)
suunto2	GET /apiserver/v1/workouts/{exerciseID}/bin	Download exported exercise in binary format
suunto2	GET /apiserver/v1/workouts/{exerciseID}/sml	Download exported exercise in SML format
suunto2	GET /apiserver/v1/workouts/comments/{workoutID}	Retrieve comments on public workout by other users
suunto2	GET /apiserver/v1/workouts	List exercises in a time interval, including summary statistics, approximate GPS path and metadata
suunto2	POST /apiserver/v1/login2	Log in with username and password to obtain access token
suunto2	POST /apiserver/v1/user/settings	Change user settings
suunto2	POST /apiserver/v1/workout/extensions/{exerciseId}	Retrieve special exercise data (special metrics implemented as "extensions"/"plugins")
suunto2	POST /apiserver/v1/workouts/comment/{exerciseId}	Post comment to exercise
suunto2	POST /apiserver/v1/workouts/header	Upload exercise summary statistics (e.g., total calories burned)
suunto2	POST /apiserver/v1/workout/sml	Upload exercise data in SML format
suunto2	PUT /apiserver/v1/gear/{smartwatchSerialNumber}	Register smartwatch
suunto3	POST /events	Upload smartwatch (debugging?) events (e.g., error events)
suunto4	POST /v1/firelog/legacy/batchlog	Upload debugging logs and metrics (fireperf, etc.)
suunto5	POST /api/v3/data	Upload user analytics events (e.g., time certain pages in the app were viewed and debugging logs)
suunto6	POST /api/loguploader	Upload debugging logs (triggered by user action)
suunto7	POST	(HTTP2) Upload analytics data, including GPS coordinates

Table 5. Mydlink app API endpoints.

Server	API Endpoint	Description
mydlink1	GET /event/...	Retrieve IoT online/offline events
mydlink2	GET /SwitchCamera	Start WebSockets
mydlink2	{"command":"sign_in", ...}	(WebSockets) Login with access token at start of new WebSockets session
mydlink2	{"command":"get_setting", ...}	(WebSockets) Read IoT device settings (e.g., Wi-Fi password of LAN used by device); unclear if data is retrieved from cloud storage or directly from the device in real time
mydlink3	GET /oauth/authorize2	(HTTP2) Login using username and (hashed) password, get refresh token in return
mydlink4	GET /oauth/access_token	(HTTP2) Retrieve access token
mydlink4	GET /me/device/list	(HTTP2) List IoT devices on account (IDs and some metadata)
mydlink4	GET /me/user/info	(HTTP2) Retrieve account information and app settings
mydlink4	POST /me/device/info	(HTTP2) Retrieve IoT device information and settings
mydlink4	POST /me/nvr/event/index	(HTTP2) List event indices (YYYYMMDD dates)
mydlink4	POST /me/nvr/event/list	(HTTP2) List online/offline events (given time interval)
mydlink4	POST /me/schedule/get	(HTTP2) Get device automation schedule/scenes (both words are used to mean the same thing)
mydlink4	POST /me/schedule/put	(HTTP2) Change IoT device automation schedule/scenes
mydlink4	POST /me/user/add	(HTTP2) Create account
mydlink4	POST /me/user/update	(HTTP2) Change account information and app settings

Table 6. Kasa app API endpoints.

Server	API Endpoint	Description
kasa1	POST /v1/auth/createLocation	Create "place" (e.g., home or office) to group devices based on location
kasa1	POST /v1/auth/retrieveAccountSetting	Retrieve account information (ID, region, creation timestamp); Covers less than updateAccountSetting
kasa1	POST /v1/auth/retrieveLocation	Retrieve place information (ID, creation timestamp)
kasa1	POST /v1/auth/updateAccountSetting	Change account information (ID, region, creation timestamp)
kasa2	GET /mqtt	Open WebSockets to relay messages (formatted like MQTT) directly to device
kasa3	GET /v1/families	List "places" (families, homes, offices, etc.) with different rooms
kasa3	GET /v1/smarts/logs	List manually triggered automation events
kasa3	GET /v2/things	List IoT devices on account (more information than getDeviceList)
kasa3	POST /v1/families/thing-settings	Register device to place
kasa3	GET /v1/smarts	List automation (scenes, "oneclick" and schedules)
kasa3	POST /v1/smarts/{automationID}/exec	Manually start automation (e.g., "scene")
kasa3	PUT /v1/smarts	Create/change automation
kasa4	POST /v1/auth/app	Get JWT token from access token
kasa5	POST /api/v2/common/passthrough	See n-euw1-wap.tplinkcloud.com
kasa5	POST /api/v2/common/setAlias	See n-euw1-wap.tplinkcloud.com
kasa6	POST /api/data/app/uploadBasicData	Upload analytics (e.g., when user viewed different pages in the app)
kasa7	POST /api/v2/account/getTerminalInfoListByPage	Retrieve information about an app running on a smartphone
kasa7	POST /api/v2/account/login	Login with username and password to receive access token
kasa7	POST /api/v2/account/register	Register account
kasa7	POST /api/v2/common/getDeviceList	List IoT devices on account
kasa7	POST /api/v2/common/passthrough	Send command via relay directly to IoT device
kasa7	POST /api/v2/common/setAlias	Set IoT device display name
kasa8	POST /api/v2/account/login	Login using username and password to receive access token

Table 7. Imou Smartlife app API endpoints.

Server	API Endpoint	Description
imou1	POST /pcs/v1/cloud.message.GetDeviceAlarmMixMessageByAlarmId	Retrieve motion detected event ("alarm")
imou1	POST /pcs/v1/cloud.message.GetDeviceLatestAlarmMixMessage	List recent motion detected events
imou1	POST /pcs/v1/cloud.message.GetUserPushMessageList	List user management notifications (e.g., invitations)
imou1	POST /pcs/v1/device.info.BasicInfoGet	List IoT devices related to a recorder and their settings
imou1	POST /pcs/v1/device.list.BasicInfoQuery	List IoT devices and their settings
imou1	POST /pcs/v1/device.list.BasicList	List IoT devices, without detailed settings
imou1	POST /pcs/v1/device.list.DetailInfoQuery	List IoT devices and their settings
imou1	POST /pcs/v1/device.list.DeviceDetailsInfoGetByDeviceId	Retrieve settings for specific devices
imou1	POST /pcs/v1/transfer.alarm.MotionDetectParamGet	Retrieve motion detection sensitive settings for a camera
imou1	POST /pcs/v1/user.account.Login	Login
imou1	POST /pcs/v1/user.info.GetUserInfo	Retrieve account information
imou1	POST /pcs/v1/family.manager.UserFamilyGet	List "places" (families, homes, offices, etc.)
imou1	POST /pcs/v1/family.manager.UserFamilyUpdate	Change "place"
imou2	POST /pcs/v1/user.account.GetToken	Login
imou2	POST /pcs/v1/user.account.Register	Create account
imou3	POST /pcs/v1/log.event.TouristEventLogReport	Upload analytics
imou3	POST /pcs/v1/log.event.UserEventLogReport	Upload analytics
imou4	GET /{hub}_Biging/Alarm/{cam}/{event}_big.jpg	Motion detected thumbnail
imou4	GET /{hub}_img/Alarm/{cam}/{event}_big.jpg	Motion detected thumbnail
imou5	GET /{hub}_img/Alarm/{cam}/{event}_big_0_thumb_qcif.dav	Motion detected thumbnail
imou5	GET /{hub}_Biging/Alarm/{cam}/{event}_big_0_thumb_qcif.dav	Motion detected thumbnail
imou6	GET /{hub}_img/Alarm/{cam}/{event}_big.jpg	Motion detected thumbnail
imou6	GET /{hub}_Biging/Alarm/{cam}/{event}_big_0_thumb_qcif.jpg	Motion detected thumbnail
imou7	GET /{hub}_Biging/Alarm/{cam}/{event}_big_0_thumb_qcif.jpg	Motion detected thumbnail
imou7	GET /{hub}_img/Alarm/{cam}/{event}_big.jpg	Motion detected thumbnail
imou8	GET /imou-fk-aws-online-paas-private-picture/{path}	Motion detected thumbnail

Table 8. Home Connect app API endpoints.

Server	API Endpoint	Description
homec1	POST /security/oauth/token	Login
homec2	POST /event	Upload analytics
homec2	POST /sdk_click	Upload analytics (start of HTTP session)
homec2	POST /session	Upload analytics/debugging logs
homec3	POST /logs	Upload analytics/debugging logs
homec4	GET /account/details	Retrieve account metadata and list of registered devices
homec4	GET /account/notifications	Retrieve notifications (e.g., notification dishwasher finished running, including timestamp)
homec4	GET /account/notifications/status	Check for existence notifications (before retrieval)

7   Discussion

The experimental results demonstrate that interesting Internet of Things system artifacts are stored in the cloud that could be downloaded without the assistance of the cloud provider.

The main limitation of the experiments is that only a few configurations of the Internet of Things systems could be tested. Given that dynamic analysis is highly context-sensitive, it may not have been possible to observe all the app requests that could be made. An app may behave differently when installed on a different smartphone or with a different combination of account settings. For example, when installing the Huawei Health app, the user is prompted to specify a country (before creating an account or logging in). Depending on the chosen country, the app uses a different server, settings and API; it may not even use the cloud at all.

Nevertheless, given that the same APK file is used regardless of settings, the API endpoints should be discoverable in the binary. Therefore, future work should consider employing static analysis to find more API endpoints without increasing the human labor significantly. Furthermore, static analysis could also be used to automatically produce API-based acquisition scripts using the decompiled app code. This would help with instances such as the Imou Smart Life app, where the process of generating a request is somewhat complicated. It is also possible to uncover additional API endpoints by brute force (e.g., by guessing HTTP paths), but this could be construed as an attack by the cloud backend provider. For this reason, it is better to develop less intrusive methods for finding more API endpoints, such as by narrowing down the possibilities using machine learning.

Other future work includes capturing network traffic from Internet of Things devices themselves (instead of just mobile apps) and from additional mobile apps (other Internet of Things systems and also the Apple iOS versions of the apps investigated in this work). The debugger-based approach applied to Android devices should be applicable to Internet of Things devices, but may require more work to set up. In theory, Frida can run on Internet of Things devices, but there might not be enough flash memory or live memory to store the binary.

Another limitation of the proposed capture method is that it assumes that the system OpenSSL library is used for all TLS traffic. This is typically the situation as it was for all the investigated apps except a few cases with Home Connect). However, some apps have separate TLS implementations and possibly even hide them using static linking. Dorazio et al. [5] show how to circumvent this protection.

At this point, it is necessary to reverse engineer apps on a case-by-case basis, perhaps focusing time and effort on the most worthwhile apps. This research opted not to reverse the Home Connect app because the requests it sends were deemed unlikely to query cloud storage. However, future work may need to account for this and tools such as friTAP can certainly help.

8   Conclusions

This research has sought to evaluate the possibility of extracting Internet of Things device evidence from the cloud using private APIs. To reveal the APIs, traffic from Android apps in six smart home Internet of Things systems was captured and decrypted. Access tokens stored locally by the apps were located, which enabled API requests to be imitated successfully. As a result, it was possible to download forensically-sound data from the cloud and, in some cases, more data (e.g., historical data) than is stored locally by apps. Dynamic analysis revealed a limited number of API endpoints, mainly dictated by the features of the apps. For example, if a user could only view logs, then an app could be observed to call API endpoints to retrieve the logs.

The experimental results suggest that API forensics could be a useful addition to mobile forensics. It could even be a substitute when the user password is known and the mobile device is not accessible. However, further research is needed to develop methods for uncovering hidden API endpoints to obtain more evidence.

The experiments also revealed that user analytics data may contain unexpected artifacts, such as GPS location data. This is useful beyond API forensics because it may put law enforcement in a better position when requesting cloud data from providers. Indeed, leveraging APIs to obtain cloud artifacts is a promising area of inquiry.

Acknowledgement. The authors wish to thank Professor Inger Marie Sunde of the Norwegian Police University College, Oslo, Norway for valuable discussions about API forensics in Norwegian law.

References

1. D. Baier and F. Egner, friTap: Decrypting TLS on the fly, *lolcads tech blog* (lolcads.github.io/posts/2022/08/fritap), 2022.
2. D. Baier, F. Egner and M. Ufer, friTap: Decrypting TLS traffic on the fly, presented at the *OSDFCon Webinar* (www.youtube.com/watch?v=GODCq53zgmk), 2023.
3. Y. Brhan, API-Based Cloud Data Acquisition and Analysis from Smart Home IoT Environments, M.S. Thesis, Institute of Legal Informatics and Forensic Science, Hallym University, Chuncheon, South Korea, 2019.
4. H. Chung, J. Park and S. Lee, Digital forensic approaches for the Amazon Alexa ecosystem, *Digital Investigation*, vol. 22(S), pp. S15–S25, 2017.
5. C. D'Orazio and K. Choo, A technique to circumvent SSL/TLS validations on iOS devices, *Future Generation Computer Systems*, vol. 74, pp. 366–374, 2017.
6. Federal Office of Justice, German Code of Criminal Procedure, Federal Ministry of Justice, Berlin, Germany (www.gesetze-im-internet.de/englisch_stpo/englisch_stpo.html), 2023.
7. H. Fereidooni, J. Classen, T. Spink, P. Patras, M. Miettinen, A. Sadeghi, M. Hollick and M. Conti, Breaking fitness records without moving: Reverse engineering and spoofing Fitbit, in *Research in Attacks, Intrusions and Defenses*, M. Dacier, M. Bailey, M. Polychronakis and M. Antonakakis (Eds.), Springer, Cham, Switzerland, pp. 48–69, 2017.

8. Google, Changes to Trusted Certificate Authorities in Android Nougat, Mountain View, California (`android-developers.googleblog.com/2016/07/changes-to-trusted-certificate.html`), July 7, 2016.

9. C. Howden, L. Liu, Z. Ding, Y. Zhan and K. Lam, Moments in time: A forensic view of Twitter, *Proceedings of the IEEE International Conference on Green Computing and Communications, IEEE International Conference on Internet of Things and IEEE International Conference on Cyber, Physical and Social Computing*, pp. 899–908, 2013.

10. C. Howden, L. Liu, Z. Li, J. Li and N. Antonopoulos, Virtual vignettes: The acquisition, analysis and presentation of social network data, *Science China Information Science*, vol. 57, article no. 032104, 2014.

11. M. Huber, M. Mulazzani, M. Leithner, S. Schrittwieser, G. Wondracek and E. Weippl, Social snapshots: Digital forensics for online social networks, *Proceedings of the Twenty-Seventh Annual Computer Security Applications Conference*, pp. 113–122, 2011.

12. T. Hudson, Hacking your dishwasher or cloudless Home Connect appliances, presented at the *SEC-T Conference* (`www.youtube.com/watch?v=rhbLgg8mWxs`), 2023.

13. T. Janarthanan, M. Bagheri and S. Zargari, IoT forensics: An overview of the current issues and challenges, in *Digital Forensic Investigation of Internet of Things (IoT) Devices*, R. Montasari, H. Jahankhani, R. Hill and S. Parkinson (Eds.), Springer, Cham, Switzerland, pp. 223–254, 2021.

14. O. Kayode and A. Tosun, Analysis of IoT traffic using an HTTP proxy, *Proceedings of the IEEE International Conference on Communications*, 2019.

15. C. Kudera, All your fitness data belongs to you: Reverse engineering the Huawei Health Android app, presented at *Easterhegg 2019* (`www.youtube.com/watch?v=xQflFhj8Z2w`), 2019.

16. Law Commission, Search Warrants, Law Commission no. 396, HC 852, London, United Kingdom (`www.lawcom.gov.uk/project/search-warrants`), 2020.

17. M. Mazdadi, I. Riadi and A. Luthfi, Live forensics on RouterOS using API services to investigate network attacks, *International Journal of Computer Science and Information Security*, vol. 15(2), pp. 406–410, 2017.

18. Mozilla Foundation, NSS Key Log Format: Firefox Source Docs, San Francisco, California (`firefox-source-docs.mozilla.org/security/nss/index.html`), 2024.

19. Norwegian Ministry of Justice and Public Security, Act on Procedure in Criminal Matters (Criminal Procedures Act): Chapter 15 (in Norwegian), Oslo, Norway (`lovdata.no/dokument/NL/lov/1981-05-22-25/KAPITTEL_4#KAPITTEL_4`), 2023.

20. OpenSSL Project Authors, SSL_CTX_set_keylog_callback (`www.openssl.org/docs/man1.1.1/man3/SSL_CTX_set_keylog_callback.html`), 2018.

21. D. Pawlaszczyk, M. Bochmann, P. Engler, C. Klaver and C. Hummert, API-based evidence acquisition in the cloud – A survey, *Open Research Europe*, vol. 2, article no. 69, 2022.

22. V. Roussev, A. Barreto and I. Ahmed, API-based forensic acquisition of cloud drives, in *Advances in Digital Forensics XII*, G. Peterson and S. Shenoi (Eds.), Springer, Cham, Switzerland, pp. 213–235, 2016.

23. V. Roussev and S. McCulley, Forensic analysis of cloud-native artifacts, *Digital Investigation*, vol. 16(S), pp. S104–S113, 2016.

24. Y. Shin, H. Kim, S. Kim, D. Yoo, W. Jo and T. Shon, Certificate-injection-based encrypted traffic forensics in AI speaker ecosystem, *Forensic Science International: Digital Investigation*, vol. 33(S), article no. 301010, 2020.

25. Softscheck, Reverse engineering the TP-Link HS110, Sankt Augustin, Germany (`www.softscheck.com/en/blog/tp-link-reverse-engineering`), 2016.

26. M. Stoyanova, Y. Nikoloudakis, S. Panagiotakis, E. Pallis and E. Markakis, A survey of Internet of Things (IoT) forensics: Challenges, approaches and open issues, *IEEE Communications Surveys and Tutorials*, vol. 22(2), pp. 1191–1221, 2020.

27. Supreme Court of Norway, HR-2019-610-A (Case no. 19-010640STR-HRET), Criminal Case, Appeal Against Order: Tidal Music AS v. The Public Prosecution Authority, Oslo, Norway (`www.domstol.no/globalassets/upload/hret/decisions-in-english-translation/hr-2019-610-a.pdf`), 2019.

28. Swedish Parliament, Modernized Regulations on the Use of Coercive Measures (in Swedish), Stockholm, Sweden (`www.riksdagen.se/sv/dokument-lagar/arende/betankande/modernare-regler-for-anvandningen-av-tvangsmedel_H901JuU15`), 2022.

29. Swedish Social Democratic Party, Modernized Regulations on the Use of Coercive Measures (in Swedish), Swedish Parliament, Stockholm, Sweden (`www.regeringen.se/rattsliga-dokument/proposition/2022/02/prop.-202122119`), 2022.

30. T. Wu, F. Breitinger and I. Baggili, IoT ignorance is digital forensics research bliss: A survey to understand IoT forensics definitions, challenges and future research directions, *Proceedings of the Fourteenth International Conference on Availability, Reliability and Security*, article no. 46, 2019.

31. J. Yang, J. Kim, J. Bang, S. Lee and J. Park, CATCH: Cloud data acquisition through comprehensive and hybrid approaches, *Forensic Science International: Digital Investigation*, vol. 43(S), article no. 301442, 2022.

32. M. Youn, Y. Lim, K. Seo, H. Chung and S. Lee, Forensic analysis of AI speaker with display Echo Show 2nd generation as a case study, *Forensic Science International: Digital Investigation*, vol. 38(S), article no. 301130, 2021.

Malware Forensics

Fingerprinting Malware Families Under Uncertainty

Cayden Dunn and Krishnendu Ghosh

College of Charleston, Charleston, South Carolina, USA
ghoshk@cofc.edu

Abstract. The majority of attacks on the information technology infrastructure are executed by sets of malware that are variants of each another. Therefore, it is critical to identify malware and their variants based on their behavior captured in trace data. This chapter presents a methodology for grouping malware and their variants based on similar behavior using traces that are imprecise and incomplete. Inspired by biological sequence analysis, the methodology represents traces as discrete-time Markov chains. Kullback-Leibler divergence and Jensen-Shannon divergence are computed as similarity metrics for pairwise comparisons of the discrete-time Markov chains and edge-labeled graphs based on the traces and similarities are constructed. Following this, minimum spanning tree and community detection algorithms are successively applied to the edge-labeled graphs to construct malware families. The features extracted from the malware families and their variants are employed in machine learning models for automated malware detection and classification. The results of experiments conducted to validate the methodology demonstrate its efficacy at fingerprinting malware families.

Keywords: Malware Fingerprinting · Discrete-Time Markov Chain · Minimum Spanning Tree · Unsupervised Learning · Community Detection

1 Introduction

Malware poses serious and growing threats to the information technology and communications infrastructure [22]. Major types of malware include computer viruses, ransomware and spyware. Malware creators often create malware variants from the same codebase for obfuscation. Traditional static analysis methods for malware detection based on syntactic signatures are rendered ineffective by obfuscation and polymorphism, and are unable to identify malware variants effectively [8, 12, 34].

Studies have shown that dynamic analysis methods are less vulnerable compared with static analysis methods [12, 13, 32]. Dynamic analysis integrates behavioral characteristics of malware from system call logs. Malware behavior is typically manifested in trace data comprising sequences of application programming interface (API) system calls. Features are extracted from the data to identify malware and their recent variants [4]. Several researchers have extracted behavioral features via the runtime analysis of malware [5, 11, 13].

© IFIP International Federation for Information Processing 2025
Published by Springer Nature Switzerland AG 2025
E. Kurkowski and S. Shenoi (Eds.): DigitalForensics 2024, IFIP AICT 724, pp. 167–182, 2025.
https://doi.org/10.1007/978-3-031-71025-4_9

A malware family comprises malware variants that exhibit similar functionality and share the same codebase [45]. Constructing malware families advances the study of behavioral characteristics of malware and their variants. However, creating automated predictive classification models via machine learning is a major challenge due to the lack of adequate ground truth data, which is typically uncertain and incomplete.

State-of-the-art methods predominantly utilize supervised learning to train models on large datasets of malware traces that are pre-classified into families. However, assembling comprehensive labeled datasets is extremely challenging due to the evolving nature of malware. Furthermore, the dependence on labeled data hinders the discovery of new malware families.

To overcome the limitations, this work seeks to employ unsupervised learning for malware classification. Specifically, clusters of related malware are created from datasets of unlabeled malware traces using community detection algorithms, which identify clusters of densely-interconnected nodes in network graphs. The hypothesis is that the identified malware families encapsulate the vital characteristics needed for accurate malware classification, potentially uncovering novel families without complete dependence on pre-labeled data.

Malware trace data collected in the wild is uncertain and incomplete because it is unlikely that all the malicious system calls are captured. Additionally, the sizes of the traces are not uniform. The challenges are exacerbated because data modeling should be performed with minimal assumptions.

The proposed methodology constructs malware families with minimal assumptions. It performs data-dependent fingerprinting of malware families and subsequently classifies unknown malware traces in a predefined set of malware families. Eliminating the dependence on labeled data renders the unsupervised approach highly adaptable to ever-evolving malware. The goal is to mitigate the damage caused by unknown malware variants by leveraging the remedial measures deployed for known malware families.

2   Related Work

This section discusses related work on malware lineage, biological sequence analysis, machine learning and community detection.

2.1   Malware Lineage

The study of malware variants draws on the concept of malware lineage [9, 21, 24]. Malware lineage is relevant because malware variants are often constructed from the same codebases as their ancestors. This is akin to biological models in phylogeny studies of evolution, which is why it is referred to as the malware phylogeny problem [25, 29].

Unfortunately, there is limited understanding of the temporal relationships between original malware and variants that share parts of the same source code. A previous study attempts to employ the similarities between malware traces to construct malware families [18]. Similarities between traces are computed using concepts from biological sequence analysis. For each trace, a discrete-time Markov chain is constructed and compared using metrics such as Kullback-Leibler divergence (KLD) [15, 38] and Jensen-Shannon divergence (JSD) [33]. Edge-labeled graphs are created with nodes representing traces and edge weights based on Kullback-Leibler and Jensen-Shannon divergence values. Threshold values are used to prune the edges and the nodes linked by similar edges are identified.

Black et al. [6] have studied the similarities between malware variants across version histories of malware families. Other researchers [26, 28] have employed natural language processing techniques to identify malware families based on behavioral data. However, these methods do not fully address the imprecision and uncertainty inherent in the data.

2.2   Biological Sequence Methods for Malware Analysis

Several researchers have employed phylogenetic methods to construct malware families [1, 9, 30, 31]. At the heart of these methods is a biological sequence analysis algorithm. However, applying sequence alignment in malware trace analysis is problematic due to significant variations in the system calls made by different malware authors [30].

While biological sequence alignment algorithms often require information on point accepted mutations [14], alignment-free algorithms for constructing phylogenetic trees have been proposed [44]. Khoo and Lio [30] have aligned sequences based on functional similarities. Durbin et al. [16] have employed hidden Markov models traditionally used for modeling biological sequences to construct phylogenetic trees. Anderson et al. [2] have used discrete-time Markov chains to model system call traces.

2.3   Machine Learning in Malware Detection

The application of machine learning to malware detection is a well-researched area [40, 43, 46]. Techniques include transforming binary malware data to grayscale images and algorithms such as k-nearest neighbors and random forest [23]. Machine-learning-based methods improve on traditional signature-based detection techniques. However, they do not fully address the challenges posed by static malware detection.

San and Thwin [39] have attempted malware family classification using API system call data, utilizing features like unigrams and bigrams from seven malware families, including benign examples. They classify malware samples as benign or malicious using k-nearest neighbors, random forest and support vector machines, achieving classification accuracy up to 99%. However, their study does not fully account for new malware. Nikolopoulos and Polenakis [35] have also analyzed system calls, constraining the classification problem to a set of known malware families for which they report an accuracy of 69.28%. Severi et al. [41] have conducted a comprehensive study involving a fine-grained malware family of 66,301 samples for classification purposes.

2.4   Community Detection

In graph theory, community detection refers to the identification of clusters or groups of nodes that are more closely connected to each other than to nodes in other groups [17]. The Girvan-Newman algorithm identifies communities in a graph by computing the edge-betweenness of nodes [20]. The algorithm determines the edges that are most frequently traversed between node pairs, the idea being that edges connecting different communities have larger betweenness values. Edges with high betweenness scores are then eliminated to reveal distinct communities. However, the Girvan-Newman algorithm is computationally intensive for large datasets.

Another approach involves the use of the Louvain community detection algorithm, which iteratively computes the modularity of communities [7]. Modularity measures the strength of division of a network into communities, indicating the connectedness within communities as opposed to between communities. Community detection algorithms based on random walks have been explored; they utilize methods that simulate random paths in graphs to identify community structures [37, 42].

3   Preliminaries

This section describes the mathematical constructs used for comparing traces.

Discrete-Time Markov Chain. A discrete-time Markov chain [3] is a tuple $\mathcal{M}\langle S, S_o, \tau_{init}, R, \mathbf{P}, L\rangle$ where S is a finite set of states; S_0 is the set of initial states; R is a transition relation, $R \subseteq S \times S$, and for each state $s \in S$, there is at least one state $s' \in S$ where $(s, s') \in R$; $\mathbf{P} : S \times S \rightarrow [0, 1]$ where $\mathbf{P}$ represents the probability matrix and $\sum_{s,s' \in S} \mathbf{P}(s, s') = 1$; $\iota_{init} : S \rightarrow [0, 1]$ where $\sum_{s \in S} \iota_{init}(s) = 1$ is the initial distribution; and $L : S \rightarrow 2^{AP}$ where AP is the set of atomic propositions.

Two discrete-time Markov chains may be compared using Kullback-Leibler divergence [15, 38]. The divergence must be computed on identical state spaces.

Kullback-Leibler Divergence. Let P and Q be two probability distributions over the random variable X. The Kullback-Leibler divergence [36] denoted by $H(P, Q)$ of P with respect to Q is:

$$H(P,Q) = \sum_{x \in X} P(x) \log \frac{P(x)}{Q(x)}$$

Note that Kullback-Leibler divergence $H(P, Q)$ is not a distance metric because $H(P, Q) \neq H(Q, P)$. In contrast, Jensen-Shannon divergence is a distance metric [33] constructed from Kullback-Leibler divergence.

Jensen-Shannon Divergence. Let P and Q be two probability distributions over the random variable X. The Jensen-Shannon divergence [33] denoted by $H(J,Q)$ of P with respect to Q is:

$$J(P,Q) = \frac{1}{2}H(P,Q) + \frac{1}{2}H(Q,P)$$

A malware trace is a set of system calls.

Malware Trace. Let Σ be a finite alphabet set that represents system calls. A malware trace is a sequence $T = a_0, a_1, a_2, .., a_n$ where $a_i \in \Sigma$ and $i \in \mathbb{N}$.

Some researchers [2, 19] have represented malware traces as discrete-time Markov chains. Assume that $\mathcal{T}$ is the set of malware traces. The pairwise comparison of traces in $\mathcal{T}$ is computed as the Kullback-Leibler divergence of the two discrete-time Markov chains that represent the two malware traces.

The discrete-time Markov chains for traces $T_1, T_2 \in \mathcal{T}$ are computed as follows:

- Identify the unique system calls in T_1 and T_2 and store them in sets SC_1 and SC_2, respectively.
- Compute $SC_{12} = SC_1 \cup SC_2$, the union of the sets of system calls in traces T_1 and T_2.
- For the state space SC_{12}, construct discrete-time Markov chains $\mathcal{M}_1$ and $\mathcal{M}_2$ for traces T_1 and T_2 where the probabilities are weighted using the number of occurrences of consecutive pairs of system calls of the form (a_i, a_{i+1}).
- Compute the Kullback-Leibler divergence and Jensen-Shannon divergence on the Markov chains $\mathcal{M}_1$ and $\mathcal{M}_2$.

Algorithm 1 describes the construction of a discrete-time Markov chain $\mathcal{M}_1$ for trace T_1 compared with another trace T_2. The algorithm input $G(V, E, E_l)$ is a complete directed-edge labeled graph with nodes labeled with systems calls for traces from SC_{12} and each edge label $e_l \in E_l$ is one. The input graph has directed edges from each node to every other node. The nested for-loops in the algorithm compute the frequencies of pairs of system calls (a_1, a_2) in T_1. The edge labels connecting the vertices (a_1, a_2) in G are updated to $m + 1$ where m is the number of occurrences of (a_1, a_2) in T_1. In the last for-loop, each edge label from a state is weighted with the sum of the edge labels from the outgoing edges of each node such that the sum of probabilities of the node edges is one.

The algorithm output is the discrete-time Markov chain $\mathcal{M}_1$ for trace T_1. Similarly, the algorithm is used to construct the discrete-time Markov chain $\mathcal{M}_2$ for trace T_2. The Kullback-Leibler divergence values are subsequently computed on the discrete-time Markov chains $\mathcal{M}_1$ and $\mathcal{M}_2$.

4 Fingerprinting Malware Families

This section describes the fingerprinting of malware families using unsupervised learning. The primary goal is to extract distinctive features from malware families for classification purposes. The malware family fingerprinting methodology

---

Algorithm 1: Construction of discrete-time Markov chain.

Input: Edge-labeled directed graph $G(V, E, E_l)$ and trace T_1.
Output: Discrete Markov chain $\mathcal{M}_1$ representing trace T_1.

$S \leftarrow V$
$R \leftarrow E$
for *each successive transition* $(s \rightarrow s')$ *in* T_1 **do**
    for *each edge* $(v \rightarrow v')$, $v, v' \in V$ **do**
        if $(s = v \wedge s' = v')$ **then**
            $e_l(v, v') \leftarrow e_l + 1$
        end
    end
end
for *each* $v \in V$ **do**
$$\mathbf{P}(v_i, v_j) = \frac{e_l(v_i . v_j)}{\sum_j e_l(v_i, v_j)} \text{ where } 1 \leq j \leq |V| \text{ and } j \neq i.$$
end
return $\mathcal{M}_1 \langle S, R, \mathbf{P}, L \rangle$.

---

involves six steps, data preparation, malware trace graph creation, minimum spanning tree creation and community detection in the minimum spanning tree, community evaluation and machine learning model creation.

4.1   Data Preparation

This work employed the Mal-API-2019 malware dataset compiled by Catak et al. [10]. The publicly-available dataset comprises 7,107 dynamic malware execution traces generated using the Cuckoo Sandbox on a Windows operating system. Each trace captures the behavioral properties of malware, providing insights into different malware families.

The dataset contains traces from eight malware families: Adware (394 traces), Backdoor (1,001), Downloader (1,001), Dropper (891), Spyware (832), Trojan (1,001), Virus (1,001) and Worm (1,001). These traces, which are sequences of Windows API calls, provide behavioral profiles that reflect the inherent structures of the malware families.

As detailed in Section 3, computing the similarities between traces involves comparing system call sequences pairwise by constructing discrete-time Markov chains. The similarity measures between the discrete-time Markov chains are computed using Kullback-Leibler and Jensen-Shannon divergence.

4.2   Malware Trace Graph Creation

A complete weighted graph, MT-graph, is created for the malware traces. Nodes in the graph represent malware traces and edge weights express the similarities between associated pairs of nodes (traces). Note that a directed edge-labeled graph is created when using Kullback-Leibler divergence because the divergence values are not symmetric. In contrast, the Jensen-Shannon divergence is symmetric and yields an undirected edge-labeled graph. Since the dataset has 7,107 traces, the two MT-graphs have 7,107 nodes. However, the number of edges in a Kullback-Leibler directed graph is twice the number of edges in a Jensen-Shannon undirected graph because Kullback-Leibler divergence values are not symmetric.

4.3 Minimum Spanning Tree Creation

A minimum spanning tree (MST) is an established tool in community detection, often employed to reduce edge densities in graph-based models. Its applications extend to biological studies of proteins and genes [27].

The minimum spanning tree MST_{mt} of the MT-graph is computed to focus on the strongest relationships between traces. Kruskal's algorithm is employed to construct MST_{mt} due to its efficiency and effectiveness at handling dense graphs. The construction reduces a high-density MT-graph to a subgraph that expresses the most significant connections represented by the nodes. In the context of malware trace analysis, MST_{mt} connects all nodes (traces) in the most efficient manner, minimizing the sum of the edge weights (which represent divergence values).

Specifically, MST_{mt} includes edges with the lowest divergence values, implying these edges connect traces with the most similarity. This approach is instrumental for identifying closely-related malware traces in a dataset. Two MST_{mt} graphs are constructed using Kullback-Leibler and Jensen-Shannon divergence values. The resulting MST_{mt} graphs capture the subsets of traces that exhibit the highest similarities to each other, highlighting potential malware family groupings.

4.4 Community Detection in Minimum Spanning Trees

A minimum spanning tree does not collect nodes based on their similarity or proximity. Therefore, a community detection algorithm is applied to cluster nodes representing malware traces in an MST_{mt} graph based on their similarities. It is important to note that the communities are required to be complete subgraphs. Therefore, the features extracted from the subgraphs of malware families should correspond to the strongest node relationships.

The Girvan-Newman [20] and Louvain [7] community detection algorithms are applied to the two MST_{mt} graphs. Community detection algorithms are computationally intensive for large graphs. Constructing the minimum spanning trees reduces the sizes of the two graphs, enabling the extraction of the similar nodes (traces) corresponding to a malware family.

The community detection algorithms yield four scenarios whose outputs are compared against the original dataset of malware families:

- **KLD Girvan-Newman (KGN):** This scenario employs Kullback-Leibler divergence in an MST_{mt} graph and applies the Girvan-Newman community detection algorithm.
- **KLD Louvain (KL):** This scenario employs Kullback-Leibler divergence in an MST_{mt} graph and applies the Louvain community detection algorithm.
- **JSD Girvan-Newman (JGN):** This scenario employs Jensen-Shannon divergence in an MST_{mt} graph and applies the Girvan-Newman community detection algorithm.
- **JSD Louvain (JL):** This scenario employs Jensen-Shannon divergence in an MST_{mt} graph and applies the Louvain community detection algorithm.

4.5 Community Evaluation

The qualities of the constructed communities are evaluated by comparing them against the original labeled malware families. The malware family label for each community is determined by identifying the majority family label in the original dataset. This enables the creation of a confusion matrix to quantify the accuracy of the community detection methodology using unsupervised learning. The goal of the unsupervised learning is to obtain the top features that correspond to family signatures, not to predict the maximum traces in a family. The methodology can be modified to add adjacent nodes to the nodes in the constructed communities.

4.6 Machine Learning Model Construction

To evaluate the predictive power of the constructed communities, features are identified for evaluation during classification using machine learning algorithms. For each MST_{mt} graph and the original Mal-API-2019 malware dataset, pairwise frequencies of elements within each trace are treated as independent variables. The dependent variable is the malware family label, constructed or original. This enables machine learning models to be trained to quantify how predictions based on the constructed communities compare with the malware families in the Mal-API-2019 dataset labels. The experiments employed three machine learning models, naive Bayes, random forest and decision tree, to provide quantitative assessments of how incorporating features constructed from unsupervised community detection impacts malware family classification performance.

5 Experimental Results

Two sets of experiments were conducted. The first set of experiments sought to evaluate the performance of the unsupervised learning methodology when constructing communities of malware families. The second set of experiments sought to evaluate the efficacy of using the features in the constructed malware families to classify malware families in the original labeled dataset. For brevity, the seven malware families are denoted by integers: Adware (0), Backdoor (1), Downloader (2), Dropper (3), Spyware (4), Trojan (5), Virus (6) and Worm (7).

Table 1. Performance using the Girvan-Newman algorithm on MST_{mt}.

Class	JSD Girvan-Newman				KLD Girvan-Newman			
	Ac	Sn	Sp	F1	Ac	Sn	Sp	F1
Adware	0.0	0.0	1.0	0.0	0.0	0.0	1.0	0.0
Backdoor	0.0	0.0	1.0	0.0	0.188	0.634	0.552	0.290
Downloader	0.201	0.701	0.542	0.312	0.19	0.713	0.505	0.301
Dropper	0.0	0.0	1.0	0.0	0.0	0.0	1.0	0.0
Spyware	0.0	0.0	1.0	0.0	0.0	0.0	1.0	0.0
Trojan	0.0	0.0	1.0	0.0	0.0	0.0	1.0	0.0
Virus	0.0	0.0	1.0	0.0	0.0	0.0	1.0	0.0
Worm	0.172	0.620	0.511	0.270	0.0	0.0	1.0	0.0

5.1   Malware Family Construction Performance

This section describes the results of comparing the performance of the Girvan-Newman and Louvain community detection algorithms on MST_{mt} graphs created using Kullback-Leibler and Jensen-Shannon divergence values. The performance of the unsupervised method was evaluated using the metrics, accuracy (Ac), sensitivity (Sn), specificity (Sp) and F1-score (F1). Note that the communities with the maximum sizes were selected for computing the metrics because the largest communities contain nodes (traces) that are similar.

Table 1 shows the accuracy, sensitivity, specificity and F1-score metrics for all the families using the Girvan-Newman community detection algorithm with Kullback-Leibler and Jensen-Shannon divergence values. The accuracy metrics for the Downloader and Worm families using Jensen-Shannon divergence values are better than those for the other malware families. However, the accuracy metric for the Backdoor family is better with Kullback-Leibler divergence values whereas the accuracy metric for the Downloader family is better with Jensen-Shannon divergence values. The Backdoor, Downloader and Worm families have the largest number of samples (1,001). In general, malware families with larger samples have slightly better performance.

Table 2 shows the accuracy, sensitivity, specificity and F1-score metrics for all the malware families using the Louvain community detection algorithm with Kullback-Leibler and Jensen-Shannon divergence values. The accuracy metrics for the Adware, Backdoor, Dropper and Spyware malware families are higher using Jensen-Shannon divergence than Kullback-Leibler divergence. The F1-scores for all the families excluding Downloader are higher for Jensen-Shannon divergence than Kullback-Leibler divergence. All the malware families have accuracy values above 0.2. The specificity metrics are high because the community detection algorithms were applied to the minimum spanning trees, not the original MT-graphs. Large numbers of edges were removed during the construction of the minimum spanning trees.

In Tables 1 and 2, higher specificity values rule out the traces that are not in a family. The higher F1-score metrics for Jensen-Shannon divergence values imply

Table 2. Performance using the Louvain algorithm on MST_{mt}.

Class	JSD Louvain				KLD Louvain			
	Ac	**Sn**	**Sp**	**F1**	**Ac**	**Sn**	**Sp**	**F1**
Adware	0.431	0.074	0.995	0.126	0.309	0.077	0.990	0.123
Backdoor	0.351	0.047	0.986	0.083	0.343	0.024	0.992	0.045
Downloader	0.391	0.045	0.989	0.081	0.473	0.052	0.991	0.094
Dropper	0.321	0.038	0.988	0.068	0.233	0.024	0.989	0.043
Spyware	0.396	0.050	0.990	0.090	0.272	0.026	0.991	0.048
Trojan	0.278	0.032	0.986	0.057	0.293	0.024	0.991	0.044
Virus	0.455	0.081	0.984	0.137	0.491	0.052	0.991	0.094
Worm	0.203	0.042	0.973	0.070	0.419	0.026	0.994	0.049

that they contribute to better accuracy across the malware families compared with Kullback-Leibler divergence values. The Jensen-Shannon divergence values contribute to better metrics because Jensen-Shannon divergence graphs are not bidirectional and they have half as many edges as Kullback-Leibler divergence graphs.

Table 2 demonstrates that the Louvain algorithm outperforms the Girvan-Newman algorithm and is a more accurate representation of how the malware families are related compared with the original dataset. Compared with Table 1, the F1-score metrics in Table 2 are higher for all the malware families excluding Downloader. The performance metrics could potentially be improved if the overlapping communities (with identical nodes) were combined. However, as far as feature extraction was concerned, the focus was on the nodes with the strongest similarities based on the Kullback-Leibler and Jensen-Shannon divergence values, which created the communities.

5.2   Machine Learning Model Results

The features from the constructed communities using the MST_{mt} trees comprised unigram, bigram and trigram. The frequencies of occurrences of unigrams, bigrams and trigrams were considered for the traces that were used to construct the communities for the malware families. The top 15 features of the constructed communities are available at zenodo.org/record/8226703. With regard to the plots of the top 15 features, the frequencies of system calls for the malware families were completely different. Nevertheless, fingerprinting each community significantly reduced the number of features used from the large feature spaces of unigrams, bigrams and trigrams for each malware family.

Additional experiments were conducted to evaluate the effects of data partitioning (training-testing splits) on model classification for the top 15 features. Three machine learning models, naive Bayes (NB), decision tree (DT) and random forest (RF), were employed. The performance metrics include the F1-score (F1), precision (P) and recall (R).

Table 3. Effects of data partitioning on model classification with the top 15 features.

Data Split	Model	Metric	0	1	2	3	4	5	6	7
70-30	NB	F1	0.86	0.51	0.63	0.46	0.47	0.43	0.67	0.49
		P	0.70	0.53	0.63	0.46	0.44	0.44	0.64	0.56
		R	0.86	0.51	0.63	0.46	0.47	0.43	0.67	0.49
	DT	F1	0.86	0.51	0.63	0.46	0.47	0.43	0.67	0.49
		P	0.70	0.53	0.63	0.46	0.44	0.44	0.64	0.56
		R	0.86	0.51	0.63	0.46	0.47	0.43	0.67	0.49
	RF	F1	0.86	0.59	0.69	0.54	0.52	0.46	0.76	0.62
		P	0.91	0.56	0.72	0.52	0.54	0.46	0.73	0.64
		R	0.82	0.63	0.66	0.56	0.51	0.45	0.79	0.60
80-20	NB	F1	0.86	0.51	0.63	0.46	0.47	0.43	0.67	0.49
		P	0.70	0.53	0.63	0.46	0.44	0.44	0.64	0.56
		R	0.86	0.51	0.63	0.46	0.47	0.43	0.67	0.49
	DT	F1	0.86	0.51	0.63	0.46	0.47	0.43	0.67	0.49
		P	0.70	0.53	0.63	0.46	0.44	0.44	0.64	0.56
		R	0.86	0.51	0.63	0.46	0.47	0.43	0.67	0.49
	RF	F1	0.87	0.64	0.58	0.55	0.46	0.52	0.73	0.63
		P	0.93	0.62	0.78	0.57	0.51	0.47	0.74	0.66
		R	0.86	0.64	0.65	0.57	0.54	0.49	0.81	0.64
90-10	NB	F1	0.82	0.56	0.63	0.45	0.49	0.41	0.66	0.53
		P	0.75	0.48	0.70	0.41	0.42	0.50	0.67	0.59
		R	0.82	0.56	0.63	0.45	0.49	0.41	0.66	0.53
	DT	F1	0.86	0.51	0.63	0.46	0.47	0.43	0.67	0.49
		P	0.70	0.53	0.63	0.46	0.44	0.44	0.64	0.56
		R	0.86	0.51	0.63	0.46	0.47	0.43	0.67	0.49
	RF	F1	0.85	0.67	0.71	0.60	0.57	0.55	0.72	0.62
		P	0.88	0.65	0.80	0.56	0.53	0.52	0.72	0.68
		R	0.85	0.67	0.71	0.60	0.57	0.55	0.72	0.62

Table 3 shows the results obtained with training-testing data splits of 70-30, 80-20 and 90-10. The metrics show that the random forest model yields the best classification performance for all the malware families.

The performance of the machine learning models are captured by receiver operating characteristic (ROC) curves. Figure 1 shows the ROC curves of the machine learning models using the three training-testing data splits. The curves clearly demonstrate that malware families Backdoor (1), Downloader (2) and Spyware (4) are classified better than the other families. It appears that the trace data in the labeled dataset captures the significant features for these three malware families. However, the higher specificity metrics in Table 2 prove that the models perform well by not labeling unknown traces to malware families to which they do not belong.

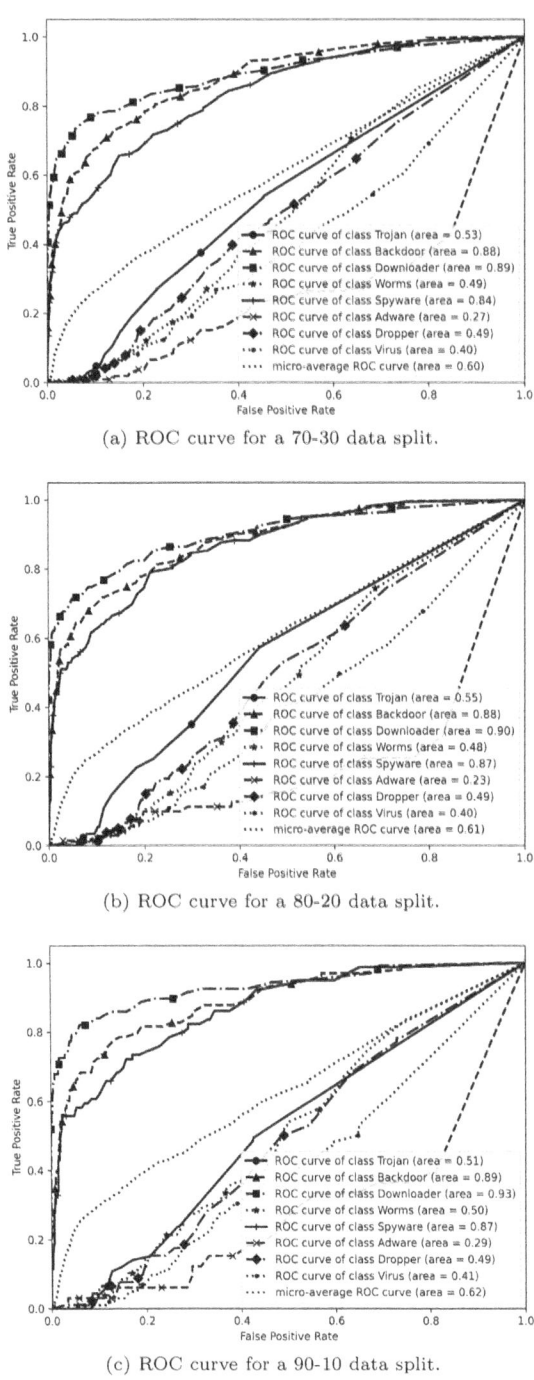

(a) ROC curve for a 70-30 data split.

(b) ROC curve for a 80-20 data split.

(c) ROC curve for a 90-10 data split.

Fig. 1. ROC curves for various training-testing data splits.

Features in the experiments were constructed using Kullback-Leibler divergence values in the MST_{mt} graph. Experiments were conducted using top 5, top 8, top 10, top 13 and top 15 features. The ROC curve results are consistent for the top 10, top 13 and top 15 features. However, the ROC curve results for the top 5 and top 8 features are poor.

Interested readers are referred to a supplementary data site for analysis, scripts and data (zenodo.org/record/8226703). The proposed methodology was able to fingerprint families with reasonable accuracy despite the presence of uncertain and incomplete data. Indeed, the constructed fingerprints provided useful features for the machine learning models.

6 Conclusions

Current malware detection methods have severe limitations and often incorporate drastic simplifications. The challenges of gathering malware data from the wild exacerbates the problem of identifying malware families because the data is of poor quality. The methodology described in this chapter groups malware and their variants based on similar behavior using traces that are imprecise and incomplete. Inspired by biological sequence analysis, traces are represented as discrete-time Markov chains. Kullback-Leibler and Jensen-Shannon divergence are computed as similarity metrics for pairwise comparisons of the discrete-time Markov chains and to create edge-labeled graphs based on traces and their similarities. Next, minimum spanning tree and community detection algorithms are applied to the edge-labeled graphs to construct similar malware traces. The features constructed from communities of malware and their variants are employed in machine learning models for automated malware detection and classification. The best model of malware family construction using unsupervised learning was obtained using the Louvain algorithm community detection algorithm with Jensen-Shannon divergence.

The unsupervised learning accuracy was different for malware families due to the different sizes of data for the families. Using larger, diverse datasets would have improved the classification accuracy. The machine learning model performance could be improved by increasing the numbers of edges in the minimum spanning trees by adding more edges to each node. For example, if the top 5 percentages of edges were to be chosen, the communities would be larger and the feature coverage broader.

This work is intended to serve as a foundation and the methodology can be improved in multiple ways. For example, the Girvan-Newman and Louvain community detection algorithms applied to large dense graphs often do not construct small subgraphs accurately. Algorithms such as Walktrap [37] and Synwalk [42] that use random walks to construct communities hold promise; they will be evaluated in future work. Future research will also seek an alternative to minimum spanning trees whose creation prunes considerable information that could improve the quality of the constructed communities; a solution is to use graphs with Jensen-Shannon divergence directly as inputs to community detection algorithm-

s. Deep neural networks also offer opportunities for improvement. Nevertheless, the methodology presented in this chapter is viable for constructing malware families with minimal assumptions from uncertain and incomplete data.

References

1. B. Anderson, T. Lane and C. Hash, Malware phylogenetics based on the multiview graphical lasso, *Proceedings of the Thirteenth International Symposium on Intelligent Data Analysis*, pp. 1–12, 2014.
2. B. Anderson, D. Quist, J. Neil, C. Storlie and T. Lane, Graph-based malware detection using dynamic analysis, *Journal in Computer Virology*, vol. 7(4), pp. 247–258, 2011.
3. C. Baier and J. Katoen, *Principles of Model Checking*, MIT Press, Cambridge, Massachusetts, 2008.
4. U. Bayer, C. Kruegel and E. Kirda, TTAnalyze: A tool for analyzing malware, *Proceedings of the Fifteenth Annual Conference of the European Institute for Computer Antivirus Research*, pp. 180–192, 2006.
5. U. Bayer, A. Moser, C. Kruegel and E. Kirda, Dynamic analysis of malicious code, *Journal in Computer Virology*, vol. 2(1), pp. 67–77, 2006.
6. P. Black, I. Gondal, P. Vamplew and A. Lakhotia, Evolved similarity techniques in malware analysis, *Proceedings of the Eighteenth IEEE International Conference on Trust, Security and Privacy in Computing and Communications and Thirteenth IEEE International Conference on Big Data Science and Engineering*, pp. 404–409, 2019.
7. V. Blondel, J. Guillaume, R. Lambiotte and E. Lefebvre, Fast unfolding of communities in large networks, *Journal of Statistical Mechanics: Theory and Experiment*, article no. P10008, 2008.
8. D. Canali, A. Lanzi, D. Balzarotti, C. Kruegel, M. Christodorescu and E. Kirda, A quantitative study of accuracy in system-call-based malware detection, *Proceedings of the International Symposium on Software Testing and Analysis*, pp. 122–132, 2012.
9. E. Carrera and G. Erdelyi, Digital genome mapping -âĂŞ Advanced binary malware analysis, *Proceedings of the Virus Bulletin Conference*, pp. 187–197, 2004.
10. F. Catak, J. Ahmed, K. Sahinbas and Z. Khand, Data-augmentation-based malware detection using convolutional neural networks, *PeerJ Computer Science*. vol. 7, article no. e346, 2021.
11. S. Chaba, R. Kumar, R. Pant and M. Dave, Malware Detection Approach for Android Systems Using System Call Logs, arXiv: 1709.08805v1 (arxiv.org/abs/1709.08805v1), 2017.
12. C. Christodorescu, S. Jha, S. Seshia, D. Song and R. Bryant, Semantics-aware malware detection, *Proceedings of the IEEE Symposium on Security and Privacy*, pp. 32–46, 2005.
13. M. Christodorescu and S. Jha, Static analysis of executables to detect malicious patterns, *Proceedings of the Twelfth Conference on USENIX Security*, 2003.
14. M. Dayhoff, R. Schwartz and B. Orcutt, A model of evolutionary change in proteins, *Atlas of Protein Sequence and Structure*, vol. 5(3), pp. 345–352, 1978.
15. K. Deng, Y. Sun, P. Mehta and S. Meyn, An information-theoretic framework to aggregate a Markov chain, *Proceedings of the American Control Conference*, pp. 731–736, 2009.

16. R. Durbin, S. Eddy, A. Krogh and G. Mitchison, *Biological Sequence Analysis: Probabilistic Models of Proteins and Nucleic Acids*, Cambridge University Press, Cambridge, United Kingdom, 1998.

17. S. Fortunato, Community detection in graphs, *Physics Reports*, vol. 486(3-5), pp. 75–174, 2010.

18. K. Ghosh and J. Mills, Automated construction of malware families, in *Security, Privacy and Anonymity in Computation, Communication and Storage*, G. Wang, J. Feng, M. Bhuiyan and R. Lu (Eds.), Springer, Cham, Switzerland, pp. 465–474, 2019.

19. K. Ghosh, J. Mills and J. Dorr, Phylogenetic-inspired probabilistic model abstraction in detection of malware families, *Proceedings of the 2017 AAAI Fall Symposium Series, Deep Models and Artificial Intelligence for Military Applications: Potentials, Theories, Practices, Tools and Risks*, 2017.

20. M. Girvan and M. Newman, Community structure in social and biological networks, *Proceedings of the National Academy of Sciences*, vol. 99(12), pp. 7821–7826, 2002.

21. L. Goldberg, P. Goldberg, C. Phillips and G. Sorkin, Constructing computer virus phylogenies, *Journal of Algorithms*, vol. 26(1), pp. 188–208, 1998.

22. L. Gordon, M. Loeb, W. Lucyshyn and R. Richardson, 2005 CSI/FBI Computer Crime and Security Survey, Computer Security Institute, San Francisco, California, 2005.

23. H. Guo, S. Huang, M. Zhang, Z. Pan, F. Shi, C. Huang and B. Li, Classification of malware variants based on ensemble learning, *Proceedings of the International Conference on Machine Learning for Cyber Security*, pp. 125–139, 2020.

24. I. Haq, S. Chica, J. Caballero and S. Jha, Malware lineage in the wild, *Computers and Security*, vol. 78, pp. 347–363, 2018.

25. M. Hayes, A. Walenstein and A. Lakhotia, Evaluation of malware phylogeny modeling systems using automated variant generation, *Journal in Computer Virology*, vol. 5(4), pp. 335–343, 2009.

26. A. Jackson and K. Ghosh, Unsupervised learning approaches for construction of malware families, *Proceedings of the IEEE International Conference on Big Data*, pp. 2989–2996, 2022.

27. M. Joseph and S. Ashok, Minimum-spanning-tree-based community detection for biological data analysis, *Journal of Engineering and Applied Sciences*, vol. 12(21), pp. 5452–5456, 2017.

28. E. Karbab and M. Debbabi, MalDy: Portable, data-driven malware detection using natural language processing and machine learning techniques on behavioral analysis reports, *Digital Investigation*, vol. 28(S), pp. S77–S87, 2019.

29. M. Karim, A. Walenstein, A. Lakhotia and L. Parida, Malware phylogeny generation using permutations of code, *Journal in Computer Virology*, vol. 1(1-2), pp. 13–23, 2005.

30. W. Khoo and P. Lio, Unity in diversity: Phylogenetic-inspired techniques for reverse engineering and detection of malware families, *Proceedings of the First Systems Security Workshop*, pp. 3–10, 2011.

31. H. Kim, W. Khoo and P. Lio, Polymorphic attacks against sequence-based software birthmarks, presented at the *Second ACM SIGPLAN Workshop on Software Security and Protection*, 2012.

32. J. Kolter and M. Maloof, Learning to detect and classify malicious executables in the wild, *Journal of Machine Learning Research*, vol. 7, pp. 2721–2744, 2006.

33. J. Lin, Divergence measures based on Shannon entropy, *IEEE Transactions on Information Theory*, vol. 37(1), pp. 145–151, 1991.

34. A. Moser, C. Kruegel and E. Kirda, Limits of static analysis for malware detection, *Proceedings of the Twenty-Third Annual Computer Security Applications Conference*, pp. 421–430, 2007.

35. S. Nikolopoulos and I. Polenakis, A graph-based model for malware detection and classification using system-call groups, *Journal of Computer Virology and Hacking Techniques*, vol. 13(1), pp. 29–46, 2017.

36. T. Pham and J. Zuegg, A probabilistic measure for alignment-free sequence comparison, *Bioinformatics*, vol. 20(18), pp. 3455–3461, 2004.

37. P. Pons and M. Latapy, Computing communities in large networks using random walks, *Journal of Graph Algorithms and Applications*, vol. 10(2), pp. 191–218, 2006.

38. Z. Rached, F. Alajaji and L. Campbell, The Kullback-Leibler divergence rate between Markov sources, *IEEE Transactions on Information Theory*, vol. 50(5), pp. 917–921, 2004.

39. C. San and M. Thwin, Selecting prominent API calls and labeling malicious samples for effective malware family classification, *International Journal of Computer Science and Information Security*, vol. 17(5), pp. 89–105, 2019.

40. M. Schultz, E. Eskin, F. Zadok and S. Stolfo, Data mining methods for detection of new malicious executables, *Proceedings of the IEEE Symposium on Security and Privacy*, pp. 38–49, 2001.

41. G. Severi, T. Leek and B. Dolan-Gavitt, Malrec: Compact full-trace malware recording for retrospective deep analysis, *Proceedings of the Fifteenth International Conference on Detection of Intrusions and Malware, and Vulnerability Assessment*, pp. 3–23, 2018.

42. C. Toth, D. Helic and B. Geiger, Synwalk: Community detection via random walk modeling, *Data Mining and Knowledge Discovery*, vol. 36, pp. 739–780, 2022.

43. D. Ucci, L. Aniello and R. Baldoni, Survey of machine learning techniques for malware analysis, *Computers and Security*, vol. 81, pp. 123–147, 2019.

44. S. Vinga and J. Almeida, Alignment-free sequence comparison – A review, *Bioinformatics*, vol. 19(4), pp. 513–523, 2003.

45. C. Willems, T. Holz and F. Freiling, Toward automated dynamic malware analysis using CWSandbox, *IEEE Security and Privacy*, vol. 5(2), pp. 32–39, 2007.

46. Y. Ye, T. Li, D. Adjeroh and S. Iyengar, A survey of malware detection using data mining techniques, *ACM Computing Surveys*, vol. 50(3), article no. 41, 2017.

Improving Android Malware Detection in Imbalanced Data Scenarios

Shengzhi Qin and Kam-Pui Chow

University of Hong Kong, Hong Kong, China
chow@cs.hku.hk

Abstract. The massive storage capacity of electronic devices has significantly increased the volume of evidentiary data encountered in digital forensic investigations. As a result, the automation of digital evidence analysis employing deep learning techniques has become a trend. The training data distributions for deep learning techniques are typically balanced, which means that the data size of each class is roughly the same. However, in the digital forensics domain, evidence is mostly imbalanced, containing a large proportion of normal data and a small proportion of anomalous data. As a result, deep learning algorithms have to be enhanced to achieve good performance on imbalanced evidentiary data. This chapter focuses on a common digital evidence analysis task – identifying Android malware dispersed in a large number of normal files. An imbalance tuning method leveraging bidirectional encoder representations from transformers (BERT) is employed to overcome the imbalanced data problem. The BERT model is trained with balanced training data and subsequently tuned using imbalanced data. The model achieves a low false positive rate and a high malware detection rate with an overall performance (F-score) of 90.26% when the positive sample population in the testing set is set to 1%.

Keywords: Digital Evidence Analysis · Android Malware Detection · Deep Learning · Imbalanced Learning Model

1 Introduction

The proliferation of electronic devices with massive storage capacity has contributed to an explosion in the volume of digital evidence encountered in investigations. This situation has significantly impacted digital evidence analysis, a task that is time-consuming and labor-intensive. A promising strategy is to automate digital evidence analysis to reduce the burden on human digital forensic practitioners and the massive backlogs in digital forensic investigations.

Employing deep learning techniques in digital forensic investigations offers several benefits. Deep learning models can reduce human labor by automating surveying and analysis tasks [3]. Deep learning models have obvious speed advantages when processing large volumes of data, reducing the time required to complete investigative tasks [10]. Deep learning models are also less prone to

E. Kurkowski and S. Shenoi (Eds.): DigitalForensics 2024, IFIP AICT 724, pp. 183–200, 2025.
https://doi.org/10.1007/978-3-031-71025-4_10

making mistakes compared with humans [3, 10]. Another key advantage is privacy protection. Digital investigations routinely involve large amounts of sensitive, personally-identifiable information. Deep learning models have the potential to protect the privacy of victims and suspects by reducing human access to sensitive data during investigations [11].

A key technical challenge to applying deep learning in digital forensic investigations is the skewed distributions of evidentiary data. The problem is that general deep learning techniques adopt balanced training methods. Balanced training uses similar numbers of positive and negative samples for training and, as expected, yields good performance with balanced testing data. However, imbalanced data is common in digital forensic scenarios where normal data samples greatly outnumber anomalous data samples. In general, class imbalance arises when one or more classes are underrepresented in a dataset, with significantly fewer instances compared with other classes.

This work focuses on a common imbalanced evidence analysis task – identifying malicious files from among a large number of normal files extracted from an Android device. Two training methods have been proposed for deep-learning-based Android malware detection. The first method, balanced training, employs equal numbers of malware and benign samples. While this method could achieve high malware identification rates in imbalanced testing scenarios, it is associated with high false positive rates. A high false positive rate indicates that there is a significant likelihood of a benign file being incorrectly identified as malware. As a result, it is required to invest considerable effort in eliminating false positives.

The second method, imbalanced training, intentionally employs a small number of malware samples. The idea is to simulate an imbalanced data distribution that could effectively reduce the false positive rates in imbalanced testing scenarios. However, due to the limited amount of malware data used for training, the malware identification rate is low, which is also unacceptable.

Current deep learning techniques cannot achieve low false positive rates and high malware identification rates simultaneously in imbalanced scenarios. To address this issue, an imbalance tuning method is employed with a bidirectional encoder representations from transformers (BERT) model for use in imbalanced Android malware detection scenarios. The proposed model undergoes balanced and imbalanced training to improve malware detection performance.

2   Related Work

Deep learning methods have been employed to improve classical malware detection. Chen et al. [5] have proposed an Android malware detection method that employs bidirectional long short-term memory (Bi-LSTM) and multi-head attention. The method attempts to cover global feature information with partial timing relationships between compressed features. Millar et al. [16] have developed a convolutional neural network model for zero-day Android malware detection based on low-level opcodes, app permissions and proprietary Android application package interface (API) package usage. Xu et al. [22] have leveraged

BERT [6] in malware detection. They train an empty BERT from scratch using API sequence data and employ the pre-trained model to detect malware.

The methods of Chen et al., Millar et al. and Xu et al. adopt balanced training, which yields good malware identification performance if sufficient malware samples are provided. However, the methods produce high false positive rates when datasets contain few malware samples interspersed with large numbers of benign samples. The high false positive rates require considerable verification effort on the part of digital forensic practitioners.

Several researchers have studied the imbalanced data problem. According to Leevy et al. [14], methods for addressing the imbalanced data problem include data-level (e.g., data sampling) and algorithm-level (e.g., cost-sensitive and hybrid/ensemble) approaches. Data sampling approaches are commonly used for dealing with data imbalance problems. Random over-sampling approaches generally yield better overall performance. One example is RHSBoost that employs random under-sampling and random over-sampling under a boosting scheme [9]. Johnson and Khoshgoftaar [12] have observed that traditional methods for class imbalance using data sampling and cost-sensitive learning are effective at deep learning and methods that exploit neural network feature learning abilities provide satisfactory results. Rajabi et al. [19] have demonstrated that using specialized loss functions improves BERT performance on imbalanced data.

Dhalaria and Gandotra [7] have proposed a cost-sensitive forest algorithm (containing a group of decision trees) for malware detection. The tree group engages a cost-sensitive voting technique to classify Android malware families. Dhalaria and Gandotra mention the imbalanced data problem, but do not provide experimental results pertaining to the performance of minority classes. In fact, the overall performance may not capture the data imbalance. This is because perfect majority class performance dominates the overall performance in imbalanced data scenarios.

Almomani et al. [1] have proposed an Android ransomware detection method that employs several key techniques. A binary particle swarm optimization algorithm is used for tuning classification hyperparameters and selecting features. A support vector machine (SVM) is employed as the classifier and the synthetic minority oversampling technique (SMOTE) [4] is used to address data imbalance.

McDonnell et al. [15] have classified eight types of malware using a BERT-based model with API call sequences as input. Random oversampling of minority class data is employed to address the data imbalance problem. Notably, Zuech et al. [23] have shown that random under-sampling improves the classification performance of ensemble learning on imbalanced web attack data. Ding et al. [8] have proposed an imbalanced malware classification method that takes opcode sequences as input features. Oak et al. [17] have employed BERT for Android malware detection and discuss the performance under scenarios with different data imbalance rates.

The four works described above leverage imbalanced training to effectively reduce false positive rates in imbalanced scenarios. However, the malware identification rates are not high enough due to the presence of limited malware

```
<apk_api>
  <Suspicious_Action_Monitored Details="setRepeating
      (alarm_type: 1, trigger_at_millis:
      1495514599078, api_name:
      android.app.AlarmManager->setRepeating,
      interval_millis: 60000, intent: { intent:
      [{'data_type': u'', 'extra': {}, 'data_uri': u'',
      'comp_class_name':
      u'com.mopub.OMFWoYHbEsnpqAIQJdIZ',
      'action': u'', 'comp_pkg_name':
      u'ua.throw.score.coffee.pacific'}], type:service})"
      Action="APK file set up an alarm"/>
  <Suspicious_Action_Monitored Details="traffic: SSL,
      using_ssl, TLS1.0,
      10.0.2.15:35352->216.58.195.238:443,"
      Action="APK file used SSL"/>
  <Suspicious_Action_Monitored Details=
      "setCompontentEnabledSetting
      (new_state: 2, component_name:
      ua.throw.score.coffee.pacific/com.mopub.uLC
      Action="APK file removed the launcher icon"/>
```

Fig. 1. Sample dynamic analysis report.

samples. The malware detection model described in this chapter employs an imbalance tuning method to reduce the false positive rate while increasing the malware identification rate.

3   Imbalance-Tuning Malware Detection Model

Android malware detection is a binary imbalanced data classification task in digital forensic scenarios. In the classification task, the majority class is benign whereas the minority class is malware. The model input comprises action sequences extracted from the dynamic analysis reports of Android APK files. The model output is the classification result – benign or malware. This section provides details about the Android malware detection data, the Android malware detection model and the proposed imbalance tuning method.

3.1   Android Malware Detection Data

The data [2] used in this research was obtained from Palo Alto Networks and Shodan. Android APK files were processed by WildFire [18], a malware analysis engine from Palo Alto Networks. XML reports were generated after the dynamic analysis.

Figure 1 shows a sample dynamic analysis report. The report records the suspicious malware action in the Action field. The action sequence is extracted by mapping the action to action ID and keeping the action order. A sample action sequence extraction is shown in Section 4. The extracted action sequence may be used as input to a malware detection model.

3.2   Android Malware Detection Model

The proposed Android malware detection model is based on the BERT model [6] and the initial model weight was set to the default pre-trained configuration. The BERT model is pre-trained on a large corpus of English data such as BooksCorpus and Wikipedia and has demonstrated good performance in several natural language processing tasks. Although the base BERT model is pre-trained on natural language data, the pre-training gives it the ability to capture context information that is suitable for sequence classification in other domains.

The BERT model employs a transformer encoder [21]. The transformer encoder uses self-attention to embed context information. The self-attention mechanism computes the attention score for all the words in a sentence that encodes context information. In addition to the attention mechanism, pre-training enables the model to enhance its ability to understand the context. One of the BERT pre-training steps employs a masked language model (MLM). The masked language model provides a sentence with a masked token for BERT and asks BERT to predict the masked token by optimizing the model weights. Researchers have demonstrated that the BERT model, pre-trained on natural language, converges faster and performs better than randomly-initialized models in other domains. For example, Kao and Lee [13] have verified this conclusion for the amino acid, DNA and music domains and Oak et al. [17] have verified good performance in the case of malware detection.

After being pre-trained with a large corpus, the BERT model is able to capture context knowledge and apply it to malware detection in digital forensic scenarios. In the original BERT design, two special tokens, CLS and SEP, are added to the input sequence. CLS is a special symbol added in front of every input example for the classification task. SEP is a special separator token (e.g., separating questions and answers). In the malware detection implementation, the CLS token is added to the action sequence but a SEP token is not added. The CLS token is added because the output of CLS by BERT represents the entire malware action sequence and is input to the classification layer. The SEP token is not added because no single model input contains multiple samples.

Figure 2 provides details of the BERT model for Android malware detection. The model comprises 12 transformer layers. The input to the first layer is a 50-dimension action sequence. Each layer is input 50 token embeddings and the output embedding list has the same length. The output embedding of the CLS token from layer 12 is classified by the classifier layer.

3.3   Imbalance Tuning Method

Figure 3 shows the imbalance-tuning malware detection model workflow. The action sequence data is split into three parts, balanced training data, imbalanced tuning data and imbalanced testing data. The first two datasets are used for

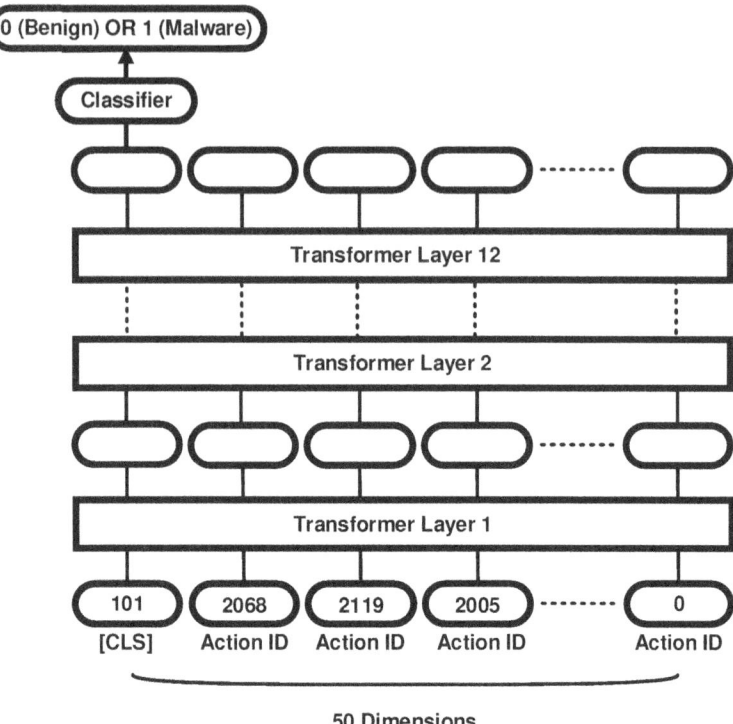

Fig. 2. BERT action sequence classification.

model training. The testing data simulates the imbalanced data distribution for better evaluating model performance in digital forensic scenarios.

The imbalance tuning method has two steps. The first step, balanced training, trains the base BERT model (BERT-Base) with the balanced training data. The training data is balanced and contains adequate data, around 90% of the total training data size. The BERT-Base model is initialized with the default parameters learned from massive natural language corpora. The model parameters are adjusted during the balanced training process. The trained model with the new parameters is called BERT-Bal.

The balanced training step enables the BERT-Bal model to learn sufficient action sequence data from the benign and malware classes. Balanced training provides the model with sufficient malware samples to improve its ability to identify malware.

The second step involves imbalance tuning. The BERT-Bal model is tuned using the imbalanced tuning data. The amount of imbalanced tuning data is small, around 10% of the total training data size. The ratio of malware samples to benign samples is determined by the real digital forensic scenario. In this work, the ratio was set to same value as the imbalanced testing data. The imbalanced

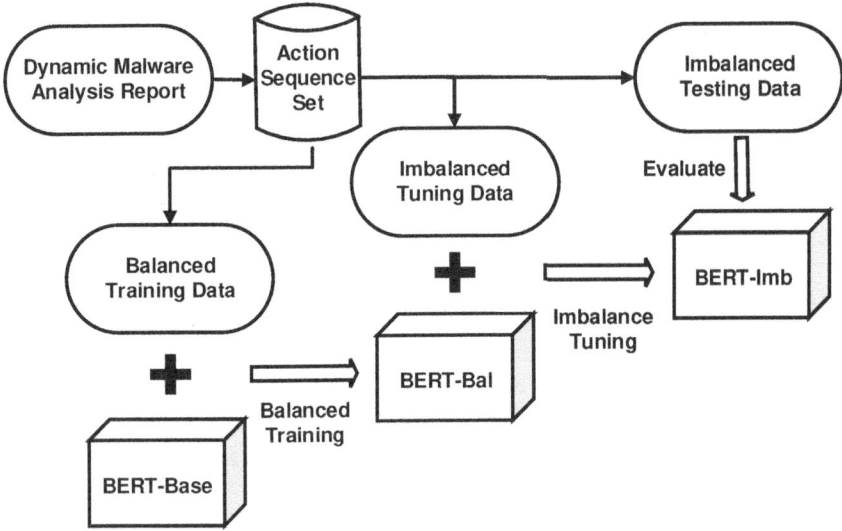

Fig. 3. Imbalance-tuning malware detection model workflow.

tuning data is employed to adjust the BERT-Bal model parameters. The model with tuned parameters is called the BERT-Imb model.

The imbalance tuning step provides the model with the same malware-benign ratio as in the testing scenario. This step fills the data distribution gap between the balanced training data in the first step and the imbalanced data encountered in a real digital forensic scenario. The imbalance tuning step is designed to decrease the false positive rate of malware detection.

4 Experiments and Results

This section describes the experiments and results for the Android malware detection model based on action sequences. Specifically, the performance of the proposed imbalance-tuning malware detection model is compared with the performance of other training methods.

4.1 Experimental Setup

The first step was to extract action sequences from the dynamic analysis results in the XML format [2]. Figure 4 shows sample extracted action sequence data. The value in the Action field was extracted in order from the dynamic analysis report of an Android APK file. Each action was mapped to a unique action ID by the <Action-ID> map table. For example, the action "APK file set up an alarm" mapped to ID 2068. The table contained 175 different actions. The

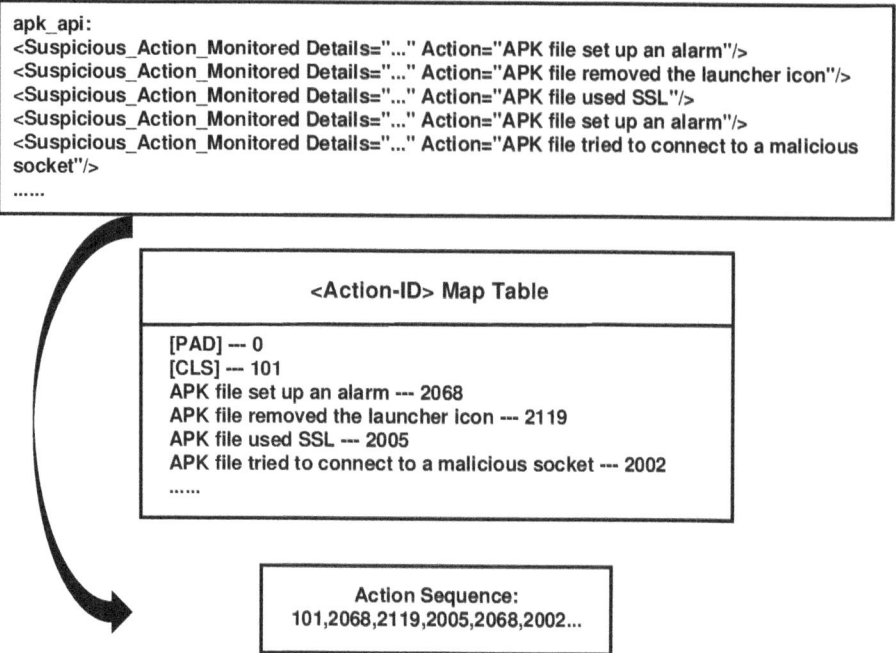

Fig. 4. Sample extracted action sequence data.

mapped action IDs comprised action sequences for Android APK files. The action sequence set contained the action sequences extracted from all the samples.

After the action sequence set was extracted, the special CLS token was prepended to each action sequence based on the BERT model requirement. The CLS token was associated with ID 101. The length of the sequence was set to 50 as recommended by Oak et al. [17]. Samples with action sequence length less than 50 had their action sequences padded with zeros. Samples with long action sequences had their action sequences truncated to 50 dimensions. The final action sequence set comprised 104,158 malware samples and 67,759 benign samples, a total data size of 171,917.

The BERT-Base model was employed as the initial malware detection model. This 12-layer BERT model had the hyperparameter settings: learning rate = 2×10^{-5}, optimizer = Adam, epochs = 3, batch size = 32 and dropout value = 0.1. The split rate of the training-validation set was 0.1, implying that 90% of the data was used for training and 10% of the data was used for validation. The split process did not change the benign-malware ratio in the data.

Due to the accuracy paradox [20], accuracy is not a good metric in imbalanced scenarios. Therefore, it was decided to employ precision, recall and F1-score to evaluate malware detection performance:

$$\text{Precision} = \frac{TP}{TP + FP}$$

$$\text{Recall} = \frac{TP}{TP + FN}$$

$$\text{F1-Score} = 2 \times \text{Precision} \times \frac{\text{Recall}}{\text{Precision} + \text{Recall}}$$

where TP (true positive) denotes malware identified as malware, FN (false negative) denotes malware identified as benign and FP (false positive) denotes benign identified as malware.

High precision corresponds to a low false positive rate. High recall corresponds to a high malware identification rate. The F1-score, which considers precision and recall, is a comprehensive measure of malware detection performance.

4.2   Malware Detection Experiments

The performance results of different training methods are presented as baselines to demonstrate the effectiveness of the imbalance tuning method. To support comparisons, all the training methods were supplied with training data of the same size (40,000 samples). The positive rate was set to 1% for the imbalanced testing data to simulate the ratios encountered in digital forensic scenarios. The default imbalanced testing set Dt used in the experiments comprised 15,000 samples – 14,850 benign samples and 150 malware samples. The testing data, corresponding to the holdout data, had a null intersection with the training data in all the experiments.

Baseline 1. The default setting for deep learning was set to balanced training for the classical malware detection task. In classical malware detection, a model is trained and tested using balanced data. However, the testing data should be imbalanced to model a digital forensic scenario. Therefore, Baseline 1 captures how a balanced training model performs in an imbalanced testing data scenario.

Baseline 1.1 corresponds to the BERT-Base model trained with 20,000 benign and 20,000 malware samples. For comparison, balanced and imbalanced testing data were used to evaluate the trained model. The balanced test data comprised the imbalanced testing set Dt augmented with 14,700 extra malware samples, resulting in a total of 14,850 benign and 14,850 malware samples. As mentioned above, Dt comprised 14,850 benign and 150 malware samples.

Table 1 compares the performance of the balanced training model with balanced and imbalanced testing data. As expected, the balanced training model performed well on balanced test data. However, when imbalanced testing data was supplied, the balanced training model achieved a high malware detection rate (high recall) but a high false positive rate (low precision). The high false positive rate is unacceptable in digital forensic scenarios.

Table 1. Baseline 1 performance.

ID	Training Method	Testing Data	Precision	Recall	F1-Score
1.1	Balanced	Balanced	0.9816	0.9742	0.9779
		Imbalanced	0.3532	0.9867	0.5202

The experimental result can be explained using a mathematical proof. The performance of a malware detection model on balanced testing data T is expressed in terms of precision and recall. Using the equations for precision (p) and recall (r) above, the false positive rate FP is expressed as:

$$FP = TP \times (\frac{1}{p} - 1)$$

Assume that malware samples are randomly removed from the balanced testing data T to produce a new testing set T'. The number of benign samples is Nb. The number of malware samples before removal is Nm and the number of malware samples remaining after removal is Nm'. Since T is balanced, $Nb = Nm$.

The imbalance ratio α is defined as:

$$\alpha = \frac{Nm}{Nm'} = \frac{Nb}{Nm'}$$

where $\alpha > 1\%$.

Furthermore, the following equations hold:

$$Nm = TP + FN$$
$$Nm' = TP' + FN'$$

Since malware samples are randomly removed from T, the following equations hold:

$$\frac{TP}{TP'} = \alpha$$
$$\frac{FN}{FN'} = \alpha$$
$$TN' = TN$$
$$FP' = FP$$

The performance of the same model on T' is expressed in terms of precision p' and recall r'. The following equations hold:

$$p' = \frac{TP'}{TP' + FP'}$$
$$= \frac{\frac{TP}{\alpha}}{\frac{TP}{\alpha} + FP}$$
$$= \frac{\frac{TP}{\alpha}}{\frac{TP}{\alpha} + TP * (\frac{1}{p} - 1)}$$
$$= \frac{TP}{TP + \alpha * TP * (\frac{1}{p} - 1)}$$
$$= \frac{p}{p + \alpha - \alpha * p}$$

$$r' = \frac{TP'}{TP' + FN'}$$
$$= \frac{\frac{TP}{\alpha}}{\frac{TP}{\alpha} + \frac{FN}{\alpha}}$$
$$= \frac{TP}{TP + FN}$$
$$= r$$

Figure 5 shows graphs of precision p' versus precision p in the range $[0, 1]$ for two values of α. The figure shows large drops in precision p' due to malware removal. One of the typical points for $\alpha = 100$ is $(p = 0.99, p' = 0.497)$. The imbalance ratio $\alpha = 100$ is the focus of this work. Although the precision for the balanced testing set T is as high as 0.99, the precision for the imbalanced testing set T' is still below 0.5, which is unacceptable. The equation for recall $r' = r$ above demonstrates that malware removal does not affect recall.

Baseline 2. Baseline 2 corresponds to the BERT-Base model trained with imbalanced data that has the same positive sample population (1%) as the testing data. This is the common method for training deep learning models.

Baseline 2.1 corresponds to the BERT-Base model trained using 39,600 benign and 400 malware samples; the testing data used was Dt. Table 2 shows the performance. For the imbalanced training method, high precision implies that the false positive rate is low. However, the low malware identification rate (recall lower than 80%) is unacceptable in digital forensic scenarios. If the malware cannot be identified accurately, a digital forensic practitioner may not be able to find key evidence in an investigation.

The low recall is due to the high imbalanced ratio and the fact that the model was trained with insufficient malware data. The performance indicates that imbalanced training results in the classifier being overtrained for the majority class and undertrained for the minority class.

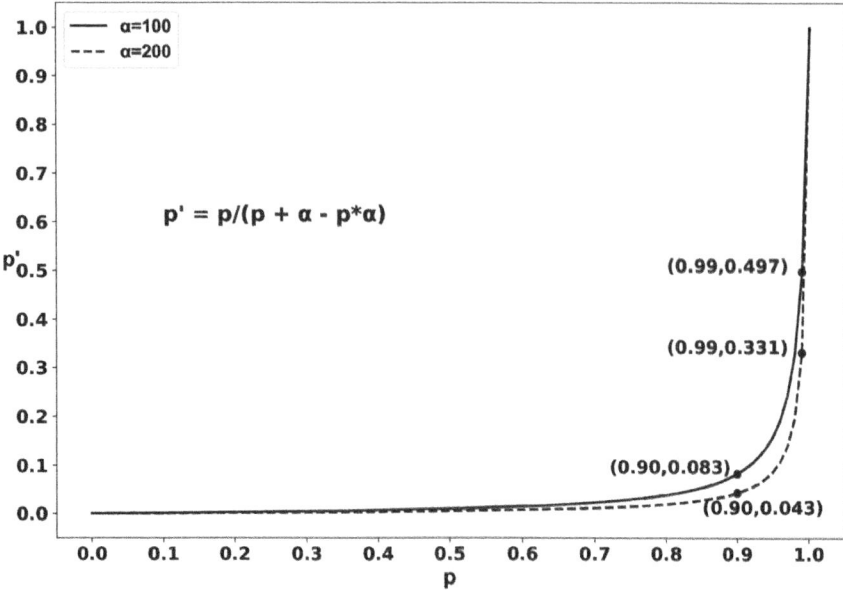

Fig. 5. Visualization of precision p' versus precision p.

Table 2. Baseline 2 performance.

ID	Training Method	Precision	Recall	F1-Score
2.1	Imbalanced	0.9514	0.7800	0.8571

Baseline 3. In order to improve malware identification seen in Baseline 2, it was necessary to balance the data appropriately and increase the proportion of malware. Baseline 3 increased the malware proportion using resampling.

The initial model in Baseline 3 was BERT-Base as in the previous baselines. The training data for Baseline 3 was generated by three resampling methods: random over-sampling, random under-sampling and synthetic minority over-sampling. Random over-sampling generates new samples by randomly sampling the available malware samples with replacement. Random under-sampling selects a random subset from the benign data. Synthetic minority over-sampling is commonly used to synthesize new exemplars. Malware samples that are close to each other in feature space are selected by drawing a line between the samples in feature space and generating a new sample at a point along the line.

The resampling data was based on the training data used for Baseline 2. Data over-sampling does not increase the training data size because it does not introduce new samples. In the experiments, different resampling ratios were employed to increase the malware proportion. Specifically, malware samples were over-sampled twice, randomly over-sampled five times and synthetic minority

Table 3. Baseline 3 performance.

ID	Training Data Size		Performance		
	Benign	Malware	Precision	Recall	F1-Score
2.1	39,600	400	0.9514	0.7800	0.8571
Random Over-Sampling					
3.1	39,600	400×2	0.9401	0.8134	0.8713
3.2	39,600	400×5	0.8913	0.8400	0.8644
Random Under-Sampling					
3.3	30,000	400	0.9786	0.7700	0.8618
3.4	20,000	400	0.9227	0.7967	0.8550
Synthetic Minority Over-Sampling					
3.5	39,600	400×2	0.9610	0.8000	0.8729
3.6	39,600	400×5	0.9520	0.7900	0.8633

over-sampled five times. In the case of under-sampling, the malware samples were decreased from 39,600 to 20,000 and 30,000. All the experiments employed *Dt* for testing.

Table 3 shows the Baseline 3 performance. Random over-sampling and synthetic minority over-sampling are effective at increasing the F1-score whereas random under-sampling is not significant. Over-sampling is better than under-sampling because the training data is more sufficient.

However, over-sampling may suffer from overfitting problems when the over-sampling ratio is high as in Baselines 3.2 and 3.6. The resampling methods do not change the fact that the malware data is insufficient, which limits the performance improvement.

Baseline 4. Ding et al. [8] have proposed a new imbalanced malware detection method that employs a self-attention mechanism. In Baseline 4, the class_weight parameter was adjusted for the imbalanced scenario. The model parameters were optimizer = Adam, epochs = 12, class_weight = (benign: 1, malware: 10) and validation split ratio = 0.2. The Baseline 4.1 model was trained using self-attention with the same training data as Baseline 2.1 and was tested on *Dt*.

Table 4. Baseline 4 performance.

ID	Training Method	Precision	Recall	F1-Score
4.1	Self-Attention	0.9126	0.6267	0.7431

Table 4 shows the Baseline 4 performance. The Baseline 4.1 model performance is not as good as the BERT model in Baseline 2.1 for the same imbalanced

Table 5. Imbalance tuning method performance.

ID	Training Method	Precision	Recall	F1-Score
5.1	Imbalanced (Tuning)	0.9433	0.8400	0.8884
5.2	Balanced	0.3655	0.9600	0.5294
5.3	Balanced (Mixed Data)	0.3775	0.9700	0.5428

training data. The reason is that the self-attention model structure is simpler than BERT and the parameters were not pre-trained.

Imbalance Tuning Method. The proposed imbalance tuning method was used in Baseline 5. The balanced training data comprised 18,000 malware samples and 18,000 benign samples. The imbalanced tuning data comprised 40 malware samples and 3,960 benign samples. The positive sample population in the imbalanced tuning data (1%) was the same as that for the testing data. The number of imbalance tuning epochs was set to 2 and the learning rate was set to 2×10^{-5}.

The control variates method was employed to demonstrate the effectiveness of the proposed method. The Baseline 5.2 model was trained using the same balanced training data (18,000 malware samples and 18,000 benign samples) as in Baseline 5.1. The training data used for the Baseline 5.3 model was drawn from the training and tuning data used in Baseline 5.1. Specifically, the data from the balanced training (18,000 benign samples and 18,000 malware samples) was mixed with the imbalance tuning data (3,960 benign samples and 40 malware samples) to yield the training data comprising 21,960 benign samples and 18,040 malware samples used in Baseline 5.3. The Baseline 5.1, 5.2 and 5.3 models were all tested using Dt.

Table 5 shows the performance of the imbalance tuning method. The F1-score is improved significantly. The model was trained with sufficient data during the balanced training process. The imbalance tuning data had the same distribution as the testing data. The performance improvements between Baseline 5.2 and Baseline 5.1 and between Baseline 5.3 and Baseline 5.1 demonstrate the effectiveness of the imbalance tuning method.

Table 6 compares the performance of the imbalance tuning method against the performance of the other baselines. Baseline 1.1 employed the balanced training method for Android malware detection – its precision (high false positive rate) is unacceptable when the testing set is imbalanced. Baseline 2.1 corresponds to the BERT model trained using the same positive sample population as the testing data – its recall (malware detection rate) is lower than 0.8, which is unsatisfactory. Baseline 3.5 has the best performance in Baseline 3, which employed synthetic minority over-sampling. This resampling method is effective at improving the performance in imbalanced scenarios. It is also a widely used imbalanced training method.

Table 6. Performance comparison.

ID	Training Method	Precision	Recall	F1-Score
1.1	Balanced	0.3532	0.9867	0.5202
2.1	Imbalanced	0.9514	0.7800	0.8571
3.5	Synthetic Minority Over-Sampling	0.9610	0.8000	0.8729
4.1	Self-Attention	0.9126	0.6267	0.7431
5.1	Imbalance Tuning	0.9433	0.8400	0.8884

Baseline 4.1 corresponds to the latest imbalanced malware detection model proposed by Ding et al. [8]. However, its performance is inferior to that of Baseline 5.1 that employed imbalance tuning. Indeed, the Baseline 5.1 model has the best overall performance (F1-score). Also, it is better in terms of the false positive rate and the malware detection rate. The proposed model was provided with sufficient malware data during balanced training as well as the appropriate imbalanced ratio from the testing set during imbalance tuning.

Figure 6 compares the F-1 scores obtained using three training data sizes (30,000, 40,000 and 50,000 samples). The x-axis contains the imbalanced training method, resampling method and imbalance tuning method. The F1-score of the resampling method is the highest score from among the random over-sampling, random under-sampling and synthetic minority over-sampling methods. The 30,000 training data splits were 13,500 benign and 13,500 malware samples for balanced training, and 2,970 benign and 30 malware samples for imbalance tuning. The 50,000 training data splits were 22,500 benign and 22,500 malware samples for balanced training, and 4,950 benign and 50 malware samples for imbalance tuning.

The best performance was achieved by the proposed method with the largest training data size of 50,000. The precision is 0.9121, recall is 0.8933 and the F1-score is 0.9026. Additionally, the false positive rate and malware detection rate are satisfied simultaneously (at least 0.9).

For a given training data size, resampling can be effective at improving the performance, while the imbalance tuning method further improves the performance. The imbalance tuning method yielded better performance that the other methods for all the training data sizes. For larger training sizes, the imbalance tuning method has an advantage because it makes better use of the malware data. The results demonstrate that the proposed imbalance-tuning model nicely accommodates imbalanced scenarios encountered in Android malware detection.

5 Conclusions

Deep learning techniques are increasingly used to automate digital evidence analysis. However, the default data distributions used to train deep learning models are balanced, which means that the data size of each class is roughly the same.

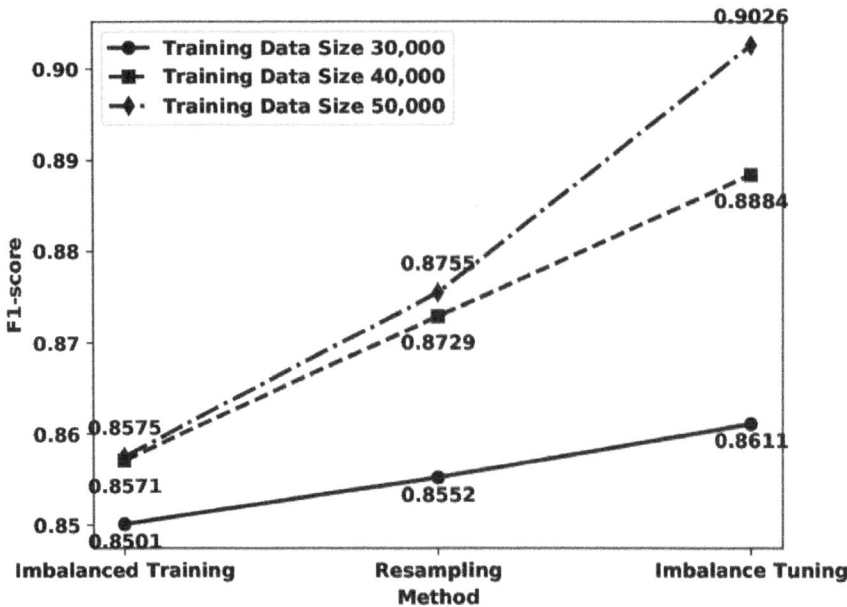

Fig. 6. Performance comparison for different training data sizes.

Unfortunately, evidence in the digital forensics domain is typically imbalanced, leading to the inadequate performance of deep learning models on imbalanced evidentiary data.

This work engages deep learning to identify Android malware in large tranches of normal Android files. An imbalance tuning method leveraging bidirectional encoder representations from transformers (BERT) is employed to address the imbalanced data problem. The BERT model is trained with balanced training data and subsequently tuned using imbalanced data. Experiments employing a variety of training methods demonstrate the superior performance of the imbalance-tuning model. Specifically, it yields a high comprehensive F1-score while satisfying the key false positive rate and malware detection rate requirements.

Although BERT is primarily a natural language model, pre-training the model with a large English corpus equips BERT with the ability to capture context information. This makes it possible to apply BERT and the proposed imbalance tuning approach to other digital evidence analysis tasks. In particular, the tasks should be convertible to sequence classification and the values comprising input feature sequences should be discrete.

Future research will extend and apply the proposed model to other digital evidence analysis tasks. Additionally, attempts will be made to adjust the loss function and add cost-sensitive learning in imbalance tuning. Also, the possibility of extending the model from input feature sequences with discrete values to sequences with continuous variables will be investigated.

References

1. I. Almomani, R. Qaddoura, M. Habib, S. Alsoghyer, A. Al Khayer, I. Aljarah and H. Faris, Android ransomware detection based on a hybrid evolutionary approach in the context of highly imbalanced data, *IEEE Access*, vol. 9, pp. 57674–57691, 2021.

2. I. Amit, J. Matherly, W. Hewlett, Z. Xu, Y. Meshi and Y. Weinberger, Machine Learning in Cyber-Security – Problems, Challenges and Data Sets, arXiv: 1812.07858v3 (`arxiv.org/abs/1812.07858v3`), 2019.

3. I. Atas, C. Ozdemir, M. Atas and Y. Dogan, Forensic dental age estimation using a modified deep learning neural network, *Balkan Journal of Electrical and Computer Engineering*, vol. 11(4), pp. 298–305, 2023.

4. N. Chawla, K. Bowyer, L. Hall and W. Kegelmeyer, SMOTE: Synthetic minority over-sampling technique, *Journal of Artificial Intelligence Research*, vol. 16(1), pp. 321–357, 2002.

5. Y. Chen, A. He, G. Chen and Y. Liu, Android malware detection system integrating block feature extraction and a multi-head attention mechanism, *Proceedings of the International Computer Symposium*, pp. 408–413, 2020.

6. J. Devlin, M. Chang, K. Lee and K. Toutanova, BERT: Pre-Training of Deep Bidirectional Transformers for Language Understanding, arXiv: 1810.04805v2 (`arxiv.org/abs/1810.04805v2`), 2019.

7. M. Dhalaria and E. Gandotra, CSForest: An approach for imbalanced family classification of Android malicious applications, *International Journal of Information Technology*, vol. 13, pp. 1059–1071, 2021.

8. Y. Ding, S. Wang, J. Xing, X. Zhang, Z. Qi, G. Fu, Q. Qiang, H. Sun and J. Zhang, Malware classification of imbalanced data through self-attention, *Proceedings of the Nineteenth IEEE International Conference on Trust, Security and Privacy in Computing and Communications*, pp. 154–161, 2020.

9. J. Gong and H. Kim, RHSBoost: Improving classification performance in imbalanced data, *Computational Statistics and Data Analysis*, vol. 111, pp. 1–13, 2017.

10. E. Hemdan and D. Manjaiah, Digital investigation of cybercrimes based on big data analytics using deep learning, in *Deep Learning and Neural Networks: Concepts, Methodologies, Tools and Applications*, Information Resource Management Association (Ed.), IGI Global, Hershey, Pennsylvania, pp. 615–632, 2020.

11. S. Iqbal and S. Alharbi, Advancing automation in digital forensic investigations using machine learning forensics, in *Digital Forensic Science*, B. Shetty and P. Shetty (Eds.), IntechOpen, London, United Kingdom, pp. 3–18, 2019.

12. J. Johnson and T. Khoshgoftaar, Survey on deep learning with class imbalance, *Journal of Big Data*, vol. 6, article no. 27, 2019.

13. W. Kao and H. Lee, Is BERT a Cross-Disciplinary Knowledge Learner? A Surprising Finding of Pre-Trained Models' Transferability, arXiv: 2103.07162v3 (`arxiv.org/abs/2103.07162v3`), 2022.

14. J. Leevy, T. Khoshgoftaar, R. Bauder and N. Seliya, A survey on addressing high-class imbalance in big data, *Journal of Big Data*, vol. 5, article no. 42, 2018.

15. S. McDonnell, O. Nada, M. Abid and E. Amjadian, CyberBERT: A deep dynamic-state session-based recommender system for cyber threat recognition, *Proceedings of the IEEE Aerospace Conference*, 2021.

16. S. Millar, N. McLaughlin, J. Martinez del Rincon and P. Miller, Multi-view deep learning for zero-day Android malware detection, *Journal of Information Security and Applications*, vol. 58, article no. 102718, 2021.

17. R. Oak, M. Du, D. Yan, H. Takawale and I. Amit, Malware detection on highly imbalanced data through sequence modeling, *Proceedings of the Twelfth ACM Workshop on Artificial Intelligence and Security*, pp. 37–48, 2019.

18. Palo Alto Networks, Advanced Wildfire, Santa Clara, California (`www.paloalto networks.com/products/secure-the-network/wildfire`), 2024.

19. Z. Rajabi, O. Uzuner and A. Shehu, Detecting scarce emotions using BERT and hyperparameter optimization, *Proceedings of the Thirtieth International Conference on Artificial Neural Networks, Part V*, pp. 383–395, 2021.

20. F. Valverde-Albacete and C. Pelaez-Moreno, 100% classification accuracy considered harmful: The normalized information transfer factor explains the accuracy paradox, *PLOS ONE*, vol. 9(1), article no. e84217, 2014.

21. A. Vaswani, N. Shazeer, N. Parmar, J. Uszkoreit, L. Jones, A. Gomez, L. Kaiser and I. Polosukhin, Attention is All You Need, arXiv: 1706.03762v7 (`arxiv.org/abs/1706.03762v`), 2023.

22. Z. Xu, X. Fang and G. Yang, Malbert: A novel pre-training method for malware detection, *Computers and Security*, vol. 111, article no. 102458, 2021.

23. R. Zuech, J. Hancock and T. Khoshgoftaar, Investigating rarity in web attacks with ensemble learners, *Journal of Big Data*, vol. 8, article no. 71, 2021.

Filesystem Forensics

Text File Recovery Using an N-Gram Model

Kaparthi Srinivas[1], Chalicheemala Gireesh[1], Eswara Sai Prasad Chunduru[2], and Venugopal Temberveni[3]

[1] Vasavi College of Engineering, Hyderabad, India
`srinivas.kaparthi@staff.vce.ac.in`
[2] Central Forensic Science Laboratory, Hyderabad, India
[3] JNTUH University College of Engineering, Jagtial, India

Abstract. This chapter describes a file carving method for recovering deleted text files without relying on file table information. Specifically, text files are reconstructed by analyzing file fragments and utilizing three n-gram language models, the absolute discounting interpolated trigram language model, absolute discounting interpolated bigram language model and Laplace bigram language model. The method selects text files and segments them into blocks that are copied to a memory buffer in random order to simulate the file allocation process. Graph theory is employed to formulate the text file recovery problem with clusters as nodes and probabilities of successor clusters as edges. The absolute discounting interpolated trigram language model yielded the highest average accuracy of 79.19%. The results underscore the effectiveness of leveraging linguistic patterns inherent in fragmented data to restore lost text content.

Keywords: File Carving · N-Gram Language Model · Text File Recovery · NLTK Library · Greedy Algorithms

1 Introduction

Large text files have numerous application areas such as big data analysis, machine learning, artificial intelligence, data mining, web scraping, log files, genomic data, geographic information systems, finance, archiving and digital libraries, textual databases, textual corpora, server logs, applications logs, e-commerce, social media analytics and academic research. A user might accidentally delete important files or an attacker might delete files for malicious reasons. In either case, the task of recovering deleted text files is important.

In order to recover deleted text files, it is important to understand the file deletion operation at the filesystem level. Although, this section uses the FAT (file allocation table) filesystem to present the fundamentals of file deletion, the method proposed for recovering deleted text files is not limited to FAT-based storage devices. Indeed, the proposed method for recovering deleted text files is general in that it works for every filesystem.

Figure 1 shows the filesystem layout of files `file1.txt` and `file2.txt` residing on typical storage media. Clusters 108, 109, 110, 114 and 115 contain `file1.txt` data and clusters 111, 112 and 113 contain `file2.txt` data.

The original version of the chapter has been revised. A correction to this chapter can be found at
https://doi.org/10.1007/978-3-031-71025-4_16

© IFIP International Federation for Information Processing 2025, corrected publication 2025
Published by Springer Nature Switzerland AG 2025
E. Kurkowski and S. Shenoi (Eds.): DigitalForensics 2024, IFIP AICT 724, pp. 203–224, 2025.
https://doi.org/10.1007/978-3-031-71025-4_11

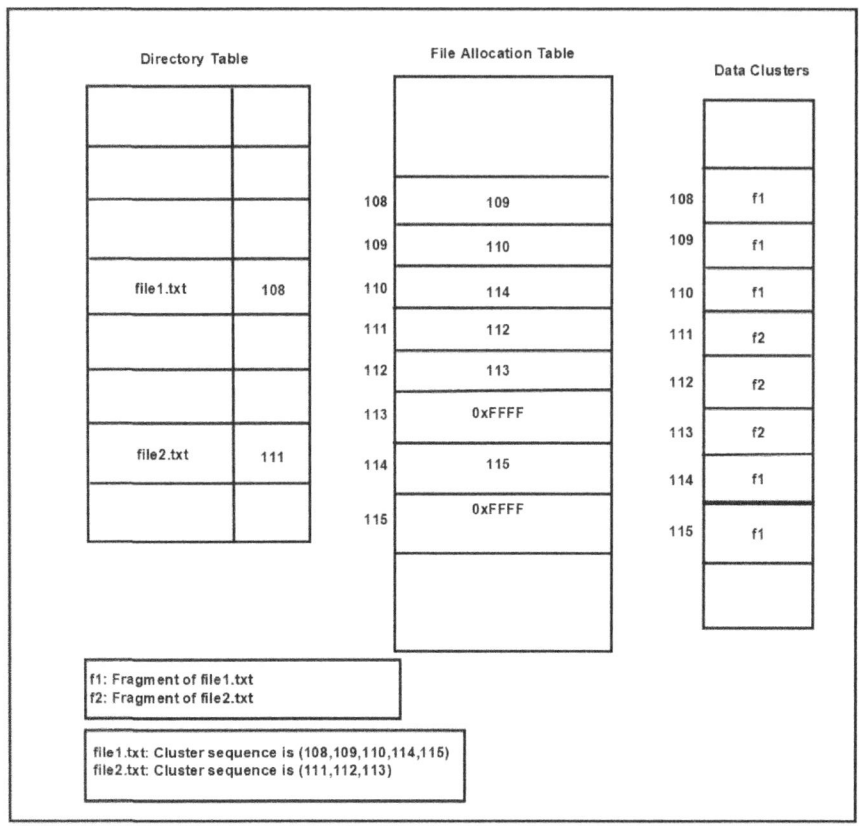

Fig. 1. FAT filesystem state before deleting `file1.txt`.

Figure 2 shows the filesystem data layout after file `file1.txt` is deleted. The first byte of the filename is changed to underscore (_). The file used clusters 108, 109, 110, 114 and 115 on the storage media.

The filesystem changes the values at locations 108, 109, 110, 114 and 115 in the file allocation table (FAT) to zeros. The zero in the file allocation table indicates a free cluster. The data in the data blocks section is intact. This data continues to be available until the filesystem allocates the clusters to other files. Although file data exists on the storage media, it is inaccessible by the conventional method of accessing files by names via the filesystem module. The residual fragments are important from a forensic point of view.

The zero values at locations 108, 109, 110, 114 and 115 in the file allocation table imply that, after file deletion, the file allocation table chain for the deleted file `file1.txt` is lost. Therefore, in the recovery process, it is necessary to rebuild the chain

$$108 \rightarrow 109 \rightarrow 110 \rightarrow 114 \rightarrow 115.$$

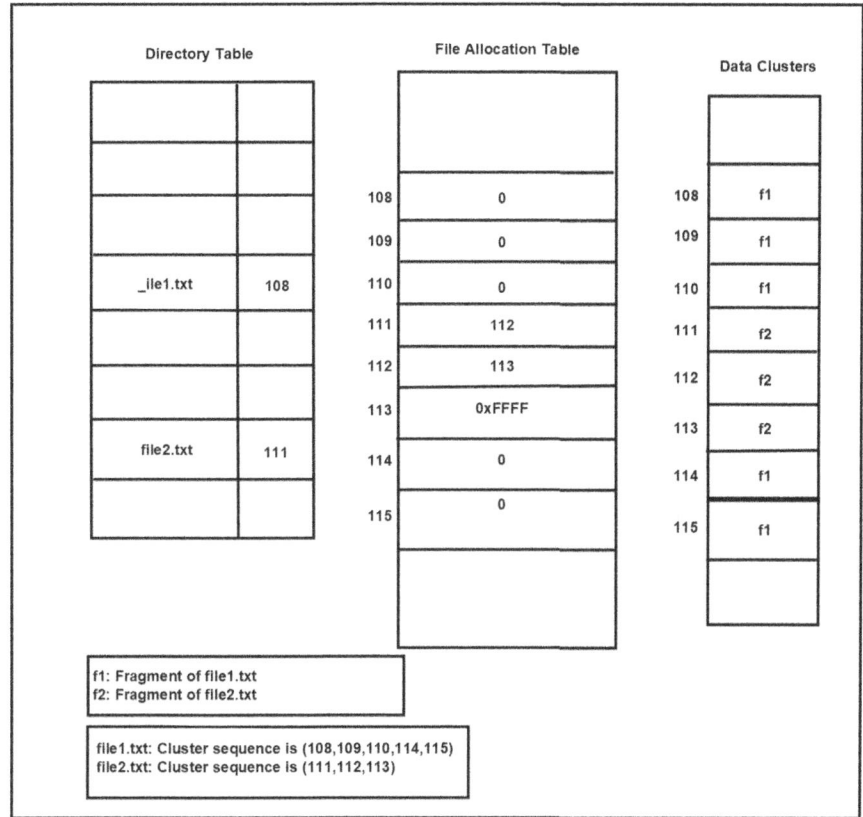

Fig. 2. FAT filesystem state after deleting `file1.txt`.

The paragraphs above describe the delete operation in a FAT filesystem. However, in every filesystem, when a file is deleted, the filesystem tables are updated and the contents of the deleted file in the clusters are left intact. Although the structure of filesystem tables may differ from one filesystem to another, the underlying principle remains the same. Specifically, the cluster linkage information is lost and the deleted file contents are intact until the free clusters are used for other files. The proposed method for deleted file recovery does not use filesystem tables. Instead, it works on the clusters containing deleted file content. Therefore, the method works for every filesystem.

Undelete tools have limited capabilities to recover deleted files. In particular, they are unable to deal with simple file recovery scenarios posed by normal file operations. This issue will be discussed later in this chapter.

Starting in 2003, research on file recovery techniques changed its focus from analyzing content available in filesystem tables to "file carving" that does not rely on filesystem tables [5]. File carving, which was initially applied to document files, analyzes the data present in the clusters of deleted files (unallocated clusters). It is a file-type-specific approach whereas undeleting is a general approach. Since the early document file recovery research, significant progress has been made in developing file recovery techniques for several file types, including images and video. However, little attention has focused on text file recovery and no efforts have been made to leverage natural language processing in file recovery. This chapter presents a file carving method for recovering text files using an n-gram language model.

2   Related Work

File recovery using the undelete command of Microsoft's Disk Operating System (DOS) [5] leverages two filesystem tables, the directory table and file allocation table. Given a deleted filename, the directory table is scanned to identify the starting cluster c. Next, the list of free clusters starting at c in the file allocation table is obtained. It is assumed that the deleted file contains data in these consecutive clusters. Accordingly, the file allocation table chain starting at c is rebuilt. This recovery method works if the deleted file was not fragmented when the file was created; otherwise, the file is partially recovered. The method also fails if two consecutive files on the disk were deleted and the undelete command was used to recover the first deleted file. In this case, the recovered file comprises data belonging to both the deleted files. The disadvantage with this method is that it does not analyze cluster data to locate the successor cluster.

Digital forensic practitioners often employ recovery tools such as Scalpel, PhotoRec and Bulk Extractor. These tools analyze the data present in clusters to determine whether the data can be part of a recovered file. However, these tools fail when the file to be recovered is fragmented on the storage media. File carving methods have been developed to address this important issue.

Memon and Pal [4] have addressed the issue of file fragmentation when attempting to recover deleted image files. They proposed a set of eight greedy algorithms for reassembling deleted image file fragments. Poisel and Tjoa [6] evaluated around 130 publications related to file carving, identifying 70 key articles with major file carving contributions. Tang et al. [11] employed the coherence of Euclidian distance metric to detect fragmentation points on storage media. The metric outperforms the sum of differences metric even when the differences fluctuate in different areas of images. Srinivas and Venugopal [9, 10] have designed and implemented an algorithm that generates datasets in a virtual (challenge) drive for testing file carving methods.

Sencar and Memon [8] have proposed a method for efficiently identifying successor fragments of a deleted JPEG file and recovering orphaned JPEG file fragments. Durmus et al. [2] have developed a method that leverages the underlying camera fingerprint (camera sensor noise) to find the positions of fragments in image frames; the method is suitable for carving images captured using a given mobile phone camera. Uzun and Sencar [12] employed a large database of JPEG images from the Flickr website to obtain characteristics of JPEG image headers used for file carving. The method decompresses incomplete data (i.e., JPEG image blocks without the corresponding header blocks) to obtain the spatial parameters.

Durmus et al. [1] have designed an algorithm that carves orphaned JPEG file fragments. The algorithm, which employs an interval data structure, improves the time complexity for the same tasks performed by the algorithms developed by Uzun and Sencar [12]. In subsequent work, Uzun and Sencar [13] developed the Jpg Scraper tool that carves JPEG file fragments with missing headers. The tool, which uses a specialized decoder to handle orphaned JPEG fragments, has the ability to differentiate JPEG blocks from other types of blocks with 97% accuracy. Wu et al. [14] have shown that pixel-based analysis improves the performance of orphaned file fragment carving.

However, researchers have paid little attention to text file recovery. Ravi et al. [7] have proposed a dictionary-based method for carving text files. The method constructs a word w across two clusters c_i and c_j. Specifically, w is constructed by concatenating the starting word of cluster c_j with the ending word of cluster c_i. If the word w appears in the dictionary, then clusters c_i and c_j are predicted to contain consecutive blocks of text from the original text file. The method of Ravi and colleagues works correctly when words are split across two clusters. However, it does not work when words are not split across two clusters. The n-gram language model method presented in this chapter addresses this issue. In particular, it considers phrases across two clusters to determine if the two clusters contained consecutive blocks of text from the original text file.

3   Text File Recovery

This section describes the proposed text file recovery method. First, deleted text file recovery is formulated as a directed graph problem. Next, an n-gram language model is developed. Following this, the n-gram language model is employed to compute the edge weights of the graph. The final step is to reconstruct the deleted text file.

3.1   Graph Problem Representation

The important task in text file recovery is to restore the links between two clusters that were lost when a file was deleted. Figure 3 shows the status of the links between clusters. The first row in the figure shows that the successors of clusters 108, 109, 110 and 114 are clusters 109, 110, 114 and 115, respectively. The second row shows the same information with the help of arrows. The third row shows that the successor cluster entries are changed to zeros when the file is deleted. Specifically, the links shown in the second row of Figure 3 are lost.

The problem of restoring the links is formulated as a graph problem. Figure 4 shows the directed complete graph representation of the text file recovery problem for eight clusters. Each node in the graph represents a cluster. The weight of an edge between two nodes (clusters) c_i and c_j expresses the probability of

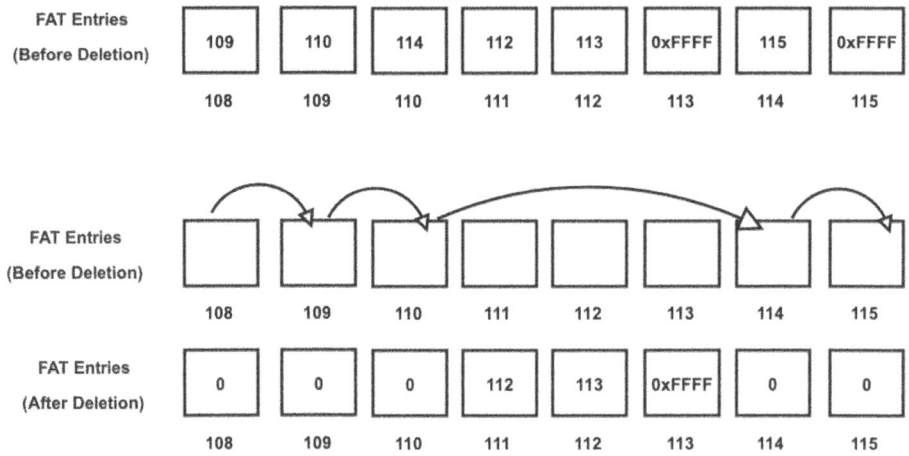

Fig. 3. Status of links between clusters.

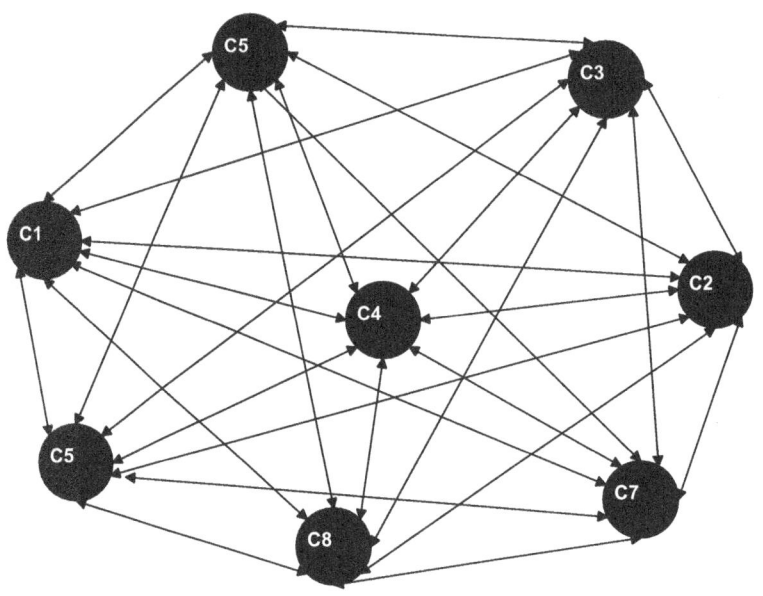

Fig. 4. Directed complete graph representation.

cluster c_j being the successor cluster of cluster c_i. An n-gram language model is employed to compute the edge weights in the graph.

Let $\{c_1, c_2, \ldots, c_M\}$ be a set of used clusters (i.e., presently unallocated clusters of deleted files) on a secondary storage device. The used clusters contain raw text data belonging to multiple deleted text files. It is required to find the successor of each cluster, which corresponds to the actual allocated order of the clusters containing the deleted text files. Each cluster contains a sequence of bytes that are decoded as a string of characters. The character string corresponding to each cluster is converted to a sequence of tokens. The number of tokens k varies from cluster to cluster.

The list of tokens $Tokens_{c_i}$ corresponding to cluster c_i is given by:

$$Tokens_{c_i} = [t_1^i, t_2^i, \ldots, t_k^i]$$

where the first and last tokens t_1^i and t_k^i can be a complete word or part of a word or a punctuation symbol.

For a cluster c_i, the most probable successor cluster $successor(c_i)$ is computed as:

$$successor(c_i) = argmax_j\{P(c_i, c_j)\}$$

where P is the probability of cluster adjacency.

Let $TailTokens_{c_i}$ and $HeadTokens_{c_j}$ be the lists of tail tokens and head tokens of the clusters c_i and c_j, respectively:

$$TailTokens_{c_i} = [\ldots, t_{k-1}^i, t_k^i]$$
$$HeadTokens_{c_j} = [t_1^j, t_2^j, \ldots]$$

The tail tokens of cluster c_i are connected to the head tokens of cluster c_j to create $JoinedTokens_{c_{i,j}}$, a new list of tokens across the clusters c_i and c_j:

$$JoinedTokens_{c_{i,j}} = [\ldots, t_{k-1}^i, t_k^i, t_1^j, t_2^j, \ldots]$$

The edge weight between clusters c_i and c_j, i.e., the probability that cluster c_j is the successor of cluster c_i, is given by:

$$P(c_i, c_j) = \begin{cases} P(t_{k-1}^i, t_k^i, t_1^j, t_2^j) & \text{if } condition \text{ 1 holds} \\ P(t_{k-1}^i, t_k^i \cdot t_1^j, t_2^j) & \text{if } condition \text{ 2 holds} \end{cases}$$

where $\cdot$ denotes concatenation, $condition$ 1 is the first condition in which the end token t_k^i of cluster c_i is a complete word or punctuation character or white space character and $condition$ 2 is the second condition in which the end token t_k^i of cluster c_i is a partial word.

The complete graph is used to reassemble the text file fragments to recover the deleted text files. The greedy path algorithms presented by Memon and Pal [4] can be used for file reassembly.

3.2   N-Gram Language Model Development

An n-gram language model is a probabilistic model that is used for natural language processing. An n-gram is a sequence of words; 1-gram, 2-gram and 3-gram are often referred to as unigram, bigram and trigram, respectively.

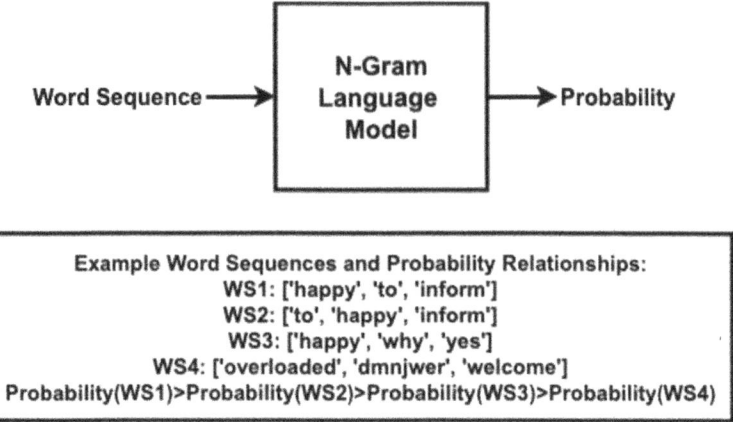

Fig. 5. Probability relationships of word sequences.

A language model has two functions. The first function is: given a sequence of words, it outputs the probability of occurrence of the word sequence in a natural language. The second function is: given a partial sentence, it predicts the next word.

The first function is used for text file recovery – obtaining the probabilities of given word sequences. Figure 5 shows four example word sequences and the relationships between their probabilities. The word 'dmnjwer' does not exist in the English language. However, such words are commonly produced by concatenation in file recovery scenarios. For example, consider the English words 'happy' and 'inform.' If they are split as ('ha' and 'ppy') and ('inf' and 'orm'), respectively, the concatenation of 'ha' and 'inf' yields 'hainf' and the concatenation of 'orm' and 'ha' yields 'ormha.' The words 'hainf' and 'ormha' do not exist in the English language. As shown in Figure 5, the probability of occurrence of the word sequence ['happy', 'to', 'inform'] is greater than the probability of occurrence of the word sequence ['to', 'happy', 'inform']. This is because the phrase 'happy to inform' is more likely to occur in English text than the phrase 'to happy inform.'

The probabilities are computed as follows. Let the P denote the joint probability of each word in a sequence having a particular value:

$$P(X_1 = w_1; X_2 = w_2; \ldots; X_n = w_n)$$

A simplified representation of this joint probability is:

$$P(w_1, w_2, \ldots, w_n)$$

which is represented in shorthand as $P(w_{1:n})$.

The probability of an entire sequence $P(w_{1:n})$ is computed by decomposing it using the chain rule of probability:

$$P(w_{1:n}) = P(w_1)P(w_2|w_1)P(w_3|w_{1:2})\ldots P(w_n|w_{1:n-1})$$

which can be rewritten as:

$$P(w_{1:n}) = \Pi_{k=1}^{n} P(w_k|w_{1:k-1})$$

The Markov assumption states that the probability of a word depends only on the previous word. A Markov model is a probabilistic model that assumes that the probability of a future outcome can be predicted without looking too far into the past [3]. When a bigram model is employed to predict the conditional probability of the next word, the following bigram approximation is made:

$$P(w_n|w_{1:n-1}) \approx P(w_n|w_{n-1})$$

The probability of an entire word sequence can be computed using the bigram assumption. Accordingly, the probability of the sequence $P(w_{1:n})$ is approximated as:

$$P(w_{1:n}) \approx \Pi_{k=1}^{n} P(w_k|w_{k-1})$$

An intuitive method for estimating probabilities is to use maximum likelihood estimation. The maximum likelihood estimates of the parameters of an n-gram model are obtained by extracting word counts from a corpus and normalizing the counts so that they lie between zero and one as follows:

$$P(w_n|w_{n-1}) = \frac{Count(w_{n-1}w_n)}{\Sigma_w Count(w_{n-1}w)}$$

The experimental work employed the Brown, Reuters and Gutenberg corpora for training language models. The corpora collectively comprise 4.45 million words. NLTK library functions were employed to compute the probabilities of word sequences.

Some words in a corpus appear in a test set in a previously-unseen context. For example, they appear after words they never appeared before (during training). In these instances, a bit of the probability mass must be shaved from some more frequent instances and given to the unencountered instances. This modification is called smoothing or discounting.

Laplace smoothing adds one to each count, which is why it is often called one-smoothing. If there are V words in a vocabulary and each word was incremented, it is also necessary to adjust the denominator to take into account the extra V observations. The probability using Laplace smoothing P_{LS} is computed as:

$$P_{LS}(w_n|w_{n-1}) = \frac{Count(w_{n-1}w_n) + 1}{\Sigma_w(Count(w_{n-1}w) + 1)}$$
$$= \frac{Count(w_{n-1}w_n) + 1}{Count(w_{n-1}) + V}$$

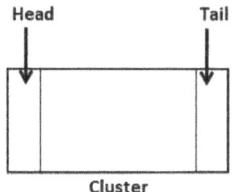

Fig. 6. Cluster head and tail.

Discounting the counts of frequent bigrams is necessary to save some probability mass for the smoothing algorithm to distribute to unseen bigrams. Absolute discounting formalizes this intuition by subtracting a fixed discount d from each count. This discounting can help solve the problem of zero frequency n-grams. However, the concept of interpolation must be addressed. If it is required to compute $P(w_n \mid w_{n-2} \, w_{n-1})$, but no examples of a particular trigram $w_n \mid w_{n-2} \, w_{n-1}$ are encountered, the probability can be estimated using the bigram probability $P(w_n \mid w_{n-1})$. Similarly, if there are no counts to compute $P(w_n \mid w_{n-1})$, the unigram probability $P(w_n)$ can be employed.

The absolute discounting interpolated probability P_{ADI} is computed as:

$$P_{ADI}(w_n|w_{n-1}) = \frac{Count(w_{n-1}w_n) - d}{\Sigma_w Count(w_{n-1}w)} + \lambda(w_{n-1})P(w_n)$$

where the first term is the discounted bigram with $0 \leq d \leq 1$ and the second term is the unigram with an interpolation weight λ.

3.3   Edge Weight Computation

The n-gram language model takes word sequences as input, analyzes the inputs with the help of a large corpus and outputs the probabilities that the word sequences appear in a natural language. This section shows how the probabilities – edge weights in the directed graph – are computed in order to restore the links between clusters containing deleted text files.

In order to compute an edge weight between clusters c_i and c_j, it is necessary to obtain a word sequence across the two clusters. This is accomplished by first defining the term head as the starting l number of bytes of a cluster and the term tail as the ending l number of bytes of a cluster. Figure 6 illustrates the head and tail of a cluster.

Figure 7 shows how the tail of a cluster c_i and the head of another cluster c_j are concatenated to obtain a string S across the two clusters. If cluster c_j is, in fact, the successor of cluster c_i comprising a deleted text file, then the string S would contain a meaningful phrase (word sequence) in the natural language.

The string S is tokenized to obtain a list of words. The list is then sliced to retain a sequence of the required number of complete words that span across clusters c_i and c_j. Also, the remaining portions at the beginning and at the

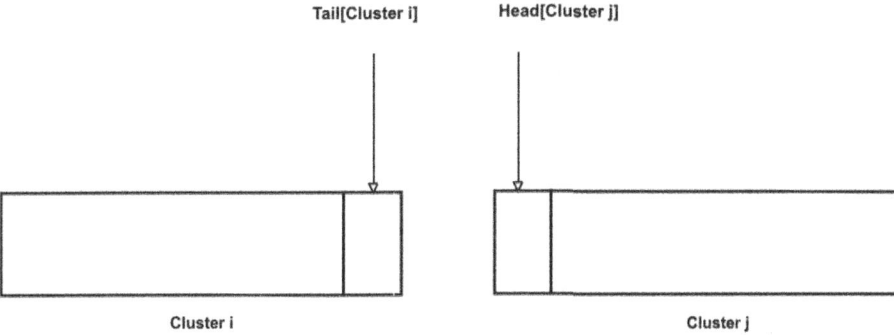

Fig. 7. Using tail and head to obtain a word sequence across two clusters.

end of the list are eliminated. The sliced word sequence is input to the n-gram language model to obtain the probability of the word sequence appearing in the natural language. The above operations are repeated for every pair of clusters in the directed graph. This yields the entire directed graph with edge weights for recovering deleted files.

3.4   Deleted Text File Recovery

Memon and Pal [4] have developed several greedy path algorithms for recovering deleted image files. These algorithms, with some changes, are applied to the directed graph used to recover deleted text files.

4   Experiments and Results

This section describes the experimental setup, language model training and experimental results.

4.1   Experimental Setup

The blocks of a document were read sequentially and stored in a fragmented memory buffer. The size of a fragment was equal to the block size. The order of the blocks in the buffer was random. Each buffer fragment corresponds to a cluster.

To explain the experimental setup, assume that the text file blocks are $[b_0, b_1, b_2, b_3, b_4, b_5]$ and the clusters are $[c_0, c_1, c_2, c_3, c_4, c_5]$. A block sequence order of a document is the order of storage of its blocks in the memory buffer. Let [b3, b2, b0, b1, b5, b4] be the block sequence order generated by a random process. The text file blocks are placed in clusters according to the block sequence order. Figure 8 shows the placement of text file blocks in the clusters.

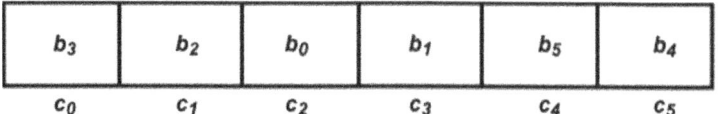

Fig. 8. Placement of text file blocks in clusters.

A cluster sequence order of a text file is the order in which blocks are re-assembled to obtain the original text document. The cluster sequence order is $[c_2, c_3, c_1, c_0, c_5, c_4]$.

If the block sequence order of a document is known, it is trivial to determine the cluster sequence order. First, it is necessary to identify the successor clusters of all the clusters except the cluster that contains the last block. In this case the successor of cluster c_0 is c_5 because c_0 contains b_3 and c_5 contains b_4. Similarly, the successor of cluster c_1 is c_0, and so on.

Clusters are modeled as directed graph nodes and cluster successor relationships as directed edges. The successor set is the set of directed edges:

$$\{c_0 \rightarrow c_5, c_1 \rightarrow c_0, c_2 \rightarrow c_3, c_3 \rightarrow c_1, c_5 \rightarrow c_4\}$$

where $c_i \rightarrow c_j$ denotes that cluster c_j is the successor of cluster c_i. Given the successor set, the cluster sequence order of a document is obtained and the text document is reconstructed.

If the block sequence order of a text document is not known, then it is necessary to compute the successor set from the text data available in the clusters. In the experiments, trained n-gram language models were applied to text document blocks to obtain the predicted successor sets. The accuracy of a predicted successor set is computed as:

$$\text{Accuracy} = \frac{\text{Number of Edges Common in Predicted and True Successor Sets}}{\text{Total Number of Edges}}$$

If the predicted successor set is equal to the true successor set, then the cluster sequence order is computed correctly. The document can be reassembled by concatenating the blocks in the order of the cluster sequence order.

4.2   Language Model Training

The NLTK library was used to generate bigrams and trigrams for the training corpus using the Brown, Reuters and Gutenberg corpora that were downloaded from www.nltk.org. The absolute discounting interpolated and Laplace language models were fitted on bigrams. The absolute discounting interpolated language model was also fitted on trigrams.

Table 1. Text files used in the experiments and their sizes in blocks.

File Name	File Size (KB)	Blocks (4 KB/Block)
text1.txt	64	16
text2.txt	96	24
text3.txt	103	26
text4.txt	108	27
text5.txt	113	29
text6.txt	109	28
text7.txt	111	28
text8.txt	105	27
text9.txt	106	27

4.3   Experimental Results

Table 1 shows the text files used in the experiments and their sizes in blocks. The processing of text file text1.txt is used as an exemplar to demonstrate the evaluation approach. File text1.txt contained 16 blocks $[b_0, b_1, \ldots, b_{15}]$. The block sequence order generated by a random process was:

$$[b_{11}, b_{14}, b_4, b_{15}, b_{13}, b_6, b_5, b_3, b_{10}, b_{12}, b_8, b_9, b_0, b_2, b_1, b_7]$$

The file blocks were read sequentially and stored in memory buffer clusters $[c_0, c_1, \ldots, c_{15}]$ according to the block sequence order.

The true successor set for file text1.txt was:

$$\{(0, 9), (1, 3), (2, 6), (3, 16), (4, 1), (5, 15), (6, 5), (7, 2),$$

$$(8, 0), (9, 4), (10, 11), (11, 8), (12, 14), (13, 7), (14, 13), (15, 10)\}$$

The remaining eight text files were processed in a similar manner.

Extracting Cluster Heads and Tails. Each cluster of 4 KB size of each text document was processed to extract 60 bytes of head and tail portions that were decoded as ASCII characters. The character strings were tokenized to obtain the respective HeadTokens and TailTokens word lists. Figure 9 shows the HeadTokens and TailTokens lists of text1.txt.

Concatenating TailTokens and HeadTokens Lists. Each token in the Tail-Tokens list of cluster c_i was concatenated with each token in the HeadTokens list of cluster c_j to create the JoinedTokens list of words across the two clusters. The index i varied from 0 to $n-1$, where n is the number of clusters of the text document. For each index i value, the index j varied from 0 to $n-1$. This created a total of $n \times n$ JoinedTokens lists per text document. During this process, the

```
Cluster0, Block11:
HEAD:['stolen', 'shoes', ',', 'and', 'Laughing', 'Jim', ',', 'the', 'strange', 'admixture', 'of', 'e']
TAIL:['stered', 'trademark', '.', 'It', 'may', 'only', 'be', 'used', 'on', 'or', 'associated', 'in', 'a']
Cluster1, Block14:
HEAD:['Gutenberg', 'electronic', 'works', ',', 'and', 'the', 'medium', 'on', 'which', 'the']
TAIL:['and', 'ensuring', 'that', 'the', 'Project', 'Gutenberg', 'collection', 'will']
Cluster2, Block4:
HEAD:['lenced', 'by', 'the', 'chairman', ',', 'who', 'calmly', 'stated', 'that', 'for', 'purposes']
TAIL:['issipated', ',', 'he', 'slipped', 'the', 'gun', 'back', 'into', 'its', 'worn', 'holster', 'an']
Cluster3, Block15:
HEAD:['remain', 'freely', 'available', 'for', 'generations', 'to', 'come', '.', 'In', '2001', ',', 't']
TAIL:['subscribe', 'to', 'our', 'email', 'newsletter', 'to', 'hear', 'about', 'new', 'eBooks', '.']
Cluster4, Block13:
HEAD:['rg', 'License', 'for', 'all', 'works', 'posted', 'with', 'the', 'permission', 'of', 't']
TAIL:['ect', 'Gutenberg', 'collection', '.', 'Despite', 'these', 'efforts', ',', 'Project']
Cluster5, Block6:
HEAD:['om', 'George', ',', 'doffed', 'his', 'hat', ',', 'brought', 'his', 'heels', 'together', ',', 'and']
TAIL:['merry', 'over', 'it', ',', 'this', 'last', 'day', ',', 'and', 'played', 'pranks', ',', 'and', 'loiter']
Cluster6, Block5:
HEAD:['d', 'whispered', 'to', 'us', ',', 'his', 'partners', ':', 'Come', 'on', ',', 'boys', '!', 'Ive', 'g']
TAIL:['emphatic', 'fist', 'on', 'the', 'bar', '.', 'Quite', 'mockingly', 'he', 'backed', 'away', 'fr']
Cluster7, Block3:
HEAD:['en', 'now', 'into', 'a', 'broad', 'ribbon', 'of', 'ice', ',', 'snow', '-', 'covered', ',', 'and', 'restin']
TAIL:['hom', 'was', 'Phil', 'Mahoney', ',', 'began', 'shouting', 'arguments', ';', 'but', 'were', 'si']
Cluster8, Block10:
HEAD:['ad', '.', 'Mahoney', '.', 'But', 'I', 'got', 'him', '!', 'Hes', 'over', 'there', '!', 'H']
TAIL:['es', 'its', 'beaten', 'winter', 'trails', ',', 'Phil', 'Mahoney', ',', 'the', 'thief', ',', 'in', 'his']
Cluster9, Block12:
HEAD:['ny', 'way', 'with', 'an', 'electronic', 'work', 'by', 'people', 'who', 'agree', 'to', 'be', 'bo']
TAIL:['der', '.', 'Additional', 'terms', 'will', 'be', 'linked', 'to', 'the', 'Project', 'Gutenbe']
Cluster10, Block8:
HEAD:['owl', ',', 'and', 'saw', 'him', 'swing', 'one', 'ponderous', 'fist', 'into', 'a', 'palm', '.']
TAIL:['l', 'hundred', 'miles', 'to', 'do', 'it', 'in', '.', 'Two', 'of', 'us', 'better', 'rustle', 'a', 'boat']
Cluster11, Block9:
Ln 1, Col 1     3,606 characters
```

```
TAIL:['ect', 'Gutenberg', 'collection', '.', 'Despite', 'these', 'efforts', ',', 'Project']
Cluster5, Block6:
HEAD:['om', 'George', ',', 'doffed', 'his', 'hat', ',', 'brought', 'his', 'heels', 'together', ',', 'and']
TAIL:['merry', 'over', 'it', ',', 'this', 'last', 'day', ',', 'and', 'played', 'pranks', ',', 'and', 'loiter']
Cluster6, Block5:
HEAD:['d', 'whispered', 'to', 'us', ',', 'his', 'partners', ':', 'Come', 'on', ',', 'boys', '!', 'Ive', 'g']
TAIL:['emphatic', 'fist', 'on', 'the', 'bar', '.', 'Quite', 'mockingly', 'he', 'backed', 'away', 'fr']
Cluster7, Block3:
HEAD:['en', 'now', 'into', 'a', 'broad', 'ribbon', 'of', 'ice', ',', 'snow', '-', 'covered', ',', 'and', 'restin']
TAIL:['hom', 'was', 'Phil', 'Mahoney', ',', 'began', 'shouting', 'arguments', ';', 'but', 'were', 'si']
Cluster8, Block10:
HEAD:['ad', '.', 'Mahoney', '.', 'But', 'I', 'got', 'him', '!', 'Hes', 'over', 'there', '!', 'H']
TAIL:['es', 'its', 'beaten', 'winter', 'trails', ',', 'Phil', 'Mahoney', ',', 'the', 'thief', ',', 'in', 'his']
Cluster9, Block12:
HEAD:['ny', 'way', 'with', 'an', 'electronic', 'work', 'by', 'people', 'who', 'agree', 'to', 'be', 'bo']
TAIL:['der', '.', 'Additional', 'terms', 'will', 'be', 'linked', 'to', 'the', 'Project', 'Gutenbe']
Cluster10, Block8:
HEAD:['owl', ',', 'and', 'saw', 'him', 'swing', 'one', 'ponderous', 'fist', 'into', 'a', 'palm', '.']
TAIL:['l', 'hundred', 'miles', 'to', 'do', 'it', 'in', '.', 'Two', 'of', 'us', 'better', 'rustle', 'a', 'boat']
Cluster11, Block9:
HEAD:['.', 'The', 'others', 'arrange', 'for', 'some', 'one', 'to', 'keep', 'an', 'eye', 'on', 'our', 'cab']
TAIL:['George', ',', 'still', 'supporting', 'the', 'dying', 'mans', 'shoulders', 'and', 'he']
Cluster12, Block0:
HEAD:['The', 'Project', 'Gutenberg', 'eBook', 'of', 'Gratitude', 'This', 'ebook', 'i']
TAIL:['s', ',', 'the', 'persistent', 'clacking', 'of', 'chips', 'and', 'markers', 'at', 'the', 'bank']
Cluster13, Block2:
HEAD:['tedly', ',', 'on', 'that', 'evening', ',', 'it', 'was', 'the', 'means', 'of', 'saving', 'the', 'life']
TAIL:[',', 'regardless', 'of', 'streets', ',', 'on', 'the', 'flat', 'facing', 'the', 'river', '--', 'froz']
Cluster14, Block1:
HEAD:[',', 'and', 'the', 'clattering', 'of', 'dice', 'where', 'chuck', '-', 'a', '-', 'luck', 'held', 'forth', '.']
TAIL:['who', 'knew', 'him', 'up', 'and', 'down', 'the', 'long', 'Northwestern', 'coast', '.', 'Undoub']
Cluster15, Block7:
HEAD:['ed', ',', 'and', 'threw', 'the', 'last', 'shovelfuls', 'with', 'something', 'of', 'regret', ',']
TAIL:['and', 'I', 'saw', 'the', 'hurt', 'look', 'on', 'his', 'face', 'give', 'way', 'to', 'an', 'angry', 'sc']
Ln 1, Col 1     3,606 characters
```

Fig. 9. HeadTokens and TailTokens lists of text1.txt clusters.

TailTokens-join-HeadTokens

File   Edit   View

Cluster0_Tail join Cluster0_Head:
['stered', 'trademark', ',', '_', 'It', 'may', 'only', 'be', 'used', 'on', 'or', 'associated', 'in', 'a', 'stolen', 'shoes', ',', ',', 'and', 'Laughing', 'Jim', ',', ',', 'the', 'strange', 'admixture', 'of', ',', 'e']
Cluster0_Tail join Cluster1_Head:
['stered', 'trademark', ',', '.', 'It', 'may', 'only', 'be', 'used', 'on', 'or', 'associated', 'in', 'a', 'Gutenberg', 'electronic', 'works', ',', ',', 'and', 'the', 'medium', 'on', 'which', 'the']
Cluster0_Tail join Cluster2_Head:
['stered', 'trademark', ',', ',', 'It', 'may', 'only', 'be', 'used', 'on', 'or', 'associated', 'in', 'a', 'alenced', 'by', 'the', 'chairman', ',', ',', 'who', 'calmly', 'stated', 'that', 'for', 'purposes']
Cluster0_Tail join Cluster3_Head:
['stered', 'trademark', ',', 'It', 'may', 'only', 'be', 'used', 'on', 'or', 'associated', 'in', 'a', 'remain', 'freely', 'available', 'for', 'generations', 'to', 'come', ',', '.', 'In', '2001', ',', ',', 't']
Cluster0_Tail join Cluster4_Head:
['stered', 'trademark', ',', 'It', 'may', 'only', 'be', 'used', 'on', 'or', 'associated', 'in', 'arg', 'license', 'for', 'all', 'works', 'posted', 'with', 'the', 'permission', 'of', 't']
Cluster0_Tail join Cluster5_Head:
['stered', 'trademark', ',', 'It', 'may', 'only', 'be', 'used', 'on', 'or', 'associated', 'in', 'aom', 'George', ',', ',', 'doffed', 'his', 'hat', ',', ',', 'brought', 'his', 'heels', 'together', ',', ',', 'and']
Cluster0_Tail join Cluster6_Head:
['stered', 'trademark', ',', 'It', 'may', 'only', 'be', 'used', 'on', 'or', 'associated', 'in', 'ad', 'whispered', 'to', 'us', ',', ',', 'his', 'partners', ':', ':', 'Come', 'on', ',', ',', 'boys', '?', 'ive', 'g']
Cluster0_Tail join Cluster7_Head:
['stered', 'trademark', ',', 'It', 'may', 'only', 'be', 'used', 'on', 'or', 'associated', 'in', 'aen', 'now', 'into', 'a', 'broad', 'ribbon', 'of', 'ice', 'snow', ',', 'covered', ',', 'and', 'restin']
Cluster0_Tail join Cluster8_Head:
['stered', 'trademark', ',', 'It', 'may', 'only', 'be', 'used', 'on', 'or', 'associated', 'in', 'aad', ',', 'Mahoney', ',', ',', 'But', 'I', 'got', 'him', '!', 'hes', 'over', 'there', '!', 'H']
Cluster0_Tail join Cluster9_Head:
['stered', 'trademark', ',', 'It', 'may', 'only', 'be', 'used', 'on', 'or', 'associated', 'in', 'any', 'way', 'with', 'an', 'electronic', 'work', 'by', 'people', 'who', 'agree', 'to', 'be', 'bo']
Cluster0_Tail join Cluster10_Head:
['stered', 'trademark', ',', 'It', 'may', 'only', 'be', 'used', 'on', 'or', 'associated', 'in', 'aowl', ',', ',', 'and', 'saw', 'him', 'swing', 'one', 'ponderous', 'fist', 'into', 'a', 'palm', '.']
Cluster0_Tail join Cluster11_Head:

Ln 1, Col 1   58,378 characters   100%   Windows (CRLF)   UTF-8

Fig. 10. JoinedTokens lists for cluster c_0.

Phrase0-0:	['or', 'associated', 'in', 'a', 'stolen', 'shoes', ',']
Phrase0-1:	['or', 'associated', 'in', 'a', 'Gutenberg', 'electronic', 'works']
Phrase0-2:	['or', 'associated', 'in', 'alenced', 'by', 'the', 'chairman']
Phrase0-3:	['or', 'associated', 'in', 'a', 'remain', 'freely', 'available']
Phrase0-4:	['or', 'associated', 'in', 'arg', 'License', 'for', 'all']
Phrase0-5:	['or', 'associated', 'in', 'aom', 'George', ',', 'doffed']
Phrase0-6:	['or', 'associated', 'in', 'ad', 'whispered', 'to', 'us']
Phrase0-7:	['or', 'associated', 'in', 'aen', 'now', 'into', 'a']
Phrase0-8:	['or', 'associated', 'in', 'aad', '.', 'Mahoney', '.']
Phrase0-9:	['or', 'associated', 'in', 'any', 'way', 'with', 'an']
Phrase0-10:	['or', 'associated', 'in', 'aowl', ',', 'and', 'saw']
Phrase0-11:	['or', 'associated', 'in', 'a', '.', 'The', 'others']
Phrase0-12:	['or', 'associated', 'in', 'aThe', 'Project', 'Gutenberg', 'eBook']
Phrase0-13:	['or', 'associated', 'in', 'atedly', ',', 'on', 'that']
Phrase0-14:	['or', 'associated', 'in', 'a', ',', 'and', 'the']
Phrase0-15:	['or', 'associated', 'in', 'aed', ',', 'and', 'threw']

Fig. 11. Phrases across cluster c_0 and the other 15 clusters.

last word in the TailTokens list and the first word in the HeadTokens list were validated for concatenation.

File text1.txt contained 16 clusters. For each cluster, 16 JoinedTokens lists were generated. A total of 256 (= 16 × 16) JoinedTokens lists were generated for file text1.txt. Figure 10 shows the JoinedTokens lists for cluster c_0.

Extracting Phrases Across Clusters. Each text1.txt cluster had 16 Joined-Tokens lists. A phrase of tokens was extracted from each JoinedTokens list by slicing the list at both ends. A PhraseTokens list with all the tokens from these phrases was created. The PhraseTokens list contained tokens spanning two clusters. A total of 256 PhraseTokens lists were created for the 16 text1.txt clusters. Figure 11 shows the phrases across cluster c_0 and the other 15 clusters.

Applying Trained Language Models. For each cluster of each text file, the probabilities of all the PhraseTokens lists were computed using n-gram language models. Three language models were employed: (i) absolute discounting inter-polated trigram language model (ADITGLM), (ii) absolute discounting inter-polated bigram language model (ADIBGLM) and (iii) Laplace bigram language model (LBGLM).

Figure 12 shows the 16 × 16 probability matrix generated for file text1.txt by the absolute discounting interpolated trigram language model. The maximum of each row of the probability matrix was computed. If i is the row index and

Probabilty(PhraseTokens) of all clusters of test1.txt

	C0	C1	C2	C3	C4	C5	C6	C7	C8	C9	C10	C11	C12	C13	C14	C15
C0	8.07E-18	2.44E-19	0	8.30E-17	0	0	2.31E-22	0	0	5.14E-10	0	1.63E-19	0	0	5.96E-14	0
C1	7.71E-22	6.71E-23	0	6.60E-14	0	3.49E-26	6.46E-24	1.23E-25	1.49E-27	4.78E-26	9.99E-21	8.15E-24	5.23E-21	0	1.11E-16	2.65E-23
C2	1.20E-20	1.04E-21	0	3.55E-19	0	0	1.55E-12	0	0	0	0	4.57E-21	0	0	3.39E-16	0
C3	8.69E-18	7.56E-19	0	2.57E-16	0	3.93E-22	7.28E-20	1.39E-21	1.68E-23	5.38E-22	1.13E-16	3.31E-18	9.51E-17	0	2.46E-13	2.99E-19
C4	1.98E-17	2.87E-13	0	5.84E-16	0	0	0	0	0	0	0	1.28E-17	0	0	1.36E-12	6.48E-20
C5	2.24E-19	1.95E-20	0	6.64E-18	0	0	0	0	0	0	0	8.56E-20	0	0	6.35E-15	3.41E-14
C6	0	0	0	0	0	2.21E-13	0	0	0	0	0	0	0	0	0	0
C7	1.46E-22	1.27E-23	1.45E-13	4.83E-21	0	0	0	0	0	0	0	5.58E-23	0	0	4.14E-18	0
C8	2.54E-12	2.33E-17	0	7.91E-15	0	0	0	0	0	0	0	2.66E-18	0	0	2.32E-11	0
C9	0	0	0	0	2.14E-10	0	0	0	0	0	0	0	0	0	0	0
C10	1.67E-17	1.46E-18	0	4.95E-16	0	0	0	0	0	0	0	2.40E-18	0	0	4.96E-16	3.05E-21
C11	1.05E-20	9.16E-22	0	5.46E-19	0	0	0	0	6.20E-20	0	0	7.87E-23	0	0	4.46E-15	1.62E-19
C12	5.81E-17	5.06E-18	0	1.72E-15	0	0	0	0	0	0	0	1.51E-17	0	0	5.78E-11	6.00E-17
C13	0	0	0	0	0	0	0	2.35E-12	0	0	0	0	0	0	0	0
C14	0	0	0	0	0	0	0	0	0	0	0	0	0	1.30E-18	0	0
C15	0	0	0	0	0	0	0	0	0	0	2.79E-14	0	0	0	0	0

Fig. 12. Phrase token probabilities generated by ADITGLM for file `text1.txt`.

j is the column index of the probability matrix, then for each cluster c_i, the column index j with the maximum probability would correspond to the predicted successor cluster c_j.

Based on the probability matrix in Figure 12, the predicted successor set for file `text1.txt` is:

$$\{(0,9),(1,3),(2,6),(3,14),(4,14),(5,15),(6,5),(7,2),$$

$$(8,14),(9,4),(10,14),(11,14),(12,14),(13,7),(14,13),(15,10)\}$$

Figure 13 shows the predicted successor cluster graph for file `text1.txt`. Cluster c_{14} is predicted as the successor for multiple clusters. This ambiguity can be resolved by a greedy method that is apparent in Figure 12. Specifically, the highest probability value in the column for cluster c_{14}, which lies in the row corresponding to cluster c_{12} is used. Future research will develop a greedy algorithm that resolves such ambiguity to maximize accuracy. Additionally, future research will conduct experiments on real storage media with large deleted text files.

The accuracy obtained for file `text1.txt` was $12/16 = 0.75$ (75%). The above procedure was repeated for the remaining text files. The outputs for all the files are available at `github.com/CGNaidu/TextFileCarving_N-Gram_LM`.

Table 2 shows the accuracy results for the three natural language models for individual files and the average accuracy results over the nine text files considered in the experiments. The absolute discounting interpolated trigram language model yielded the best average accuracy of 79.19% over the nine text files.

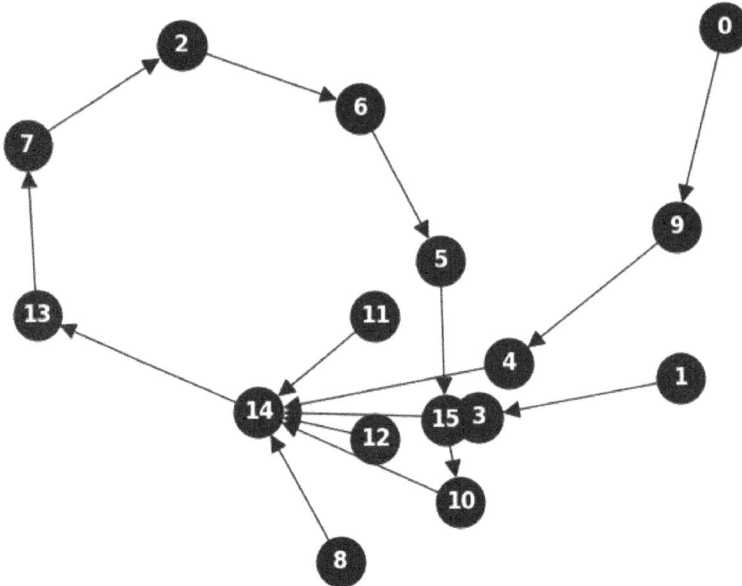

Fig. 13. Predicted successor cluster graph for file `text1.txt`.

Table 2. Accuracy results for the natural language models.

File Name	ADITGLM	ADIBGLM	LBGLM
text1.txt	75.00%	50.00%	12.50%
text2.txt	87.50%	50.00%	29.16%
text3.txt	69.23%	53.84%	23.08%
text4.txt	74.07%	51.85%	14.81%
text5.txt	75.86%	58.62%	24.14%
text6.txt	82.14%	46.42%	14.28%
text7.txt	78.57%	42.86%	32.14%
text8.txt	81.48%	62.96%	7.40%
text9.txt	88.88%	59.26%	37.03%
Average	79.19%	52.87%	21.62%

Figures 14 and 15 show the results for the best-performing absolute discount-ing interpolated trigram language model. The graphs compare the predicted successor clusters against the true successor clusters for the nine text files considered in the experiments.

Figure 16 compares the average accuracy results obtained for the three natural language models.

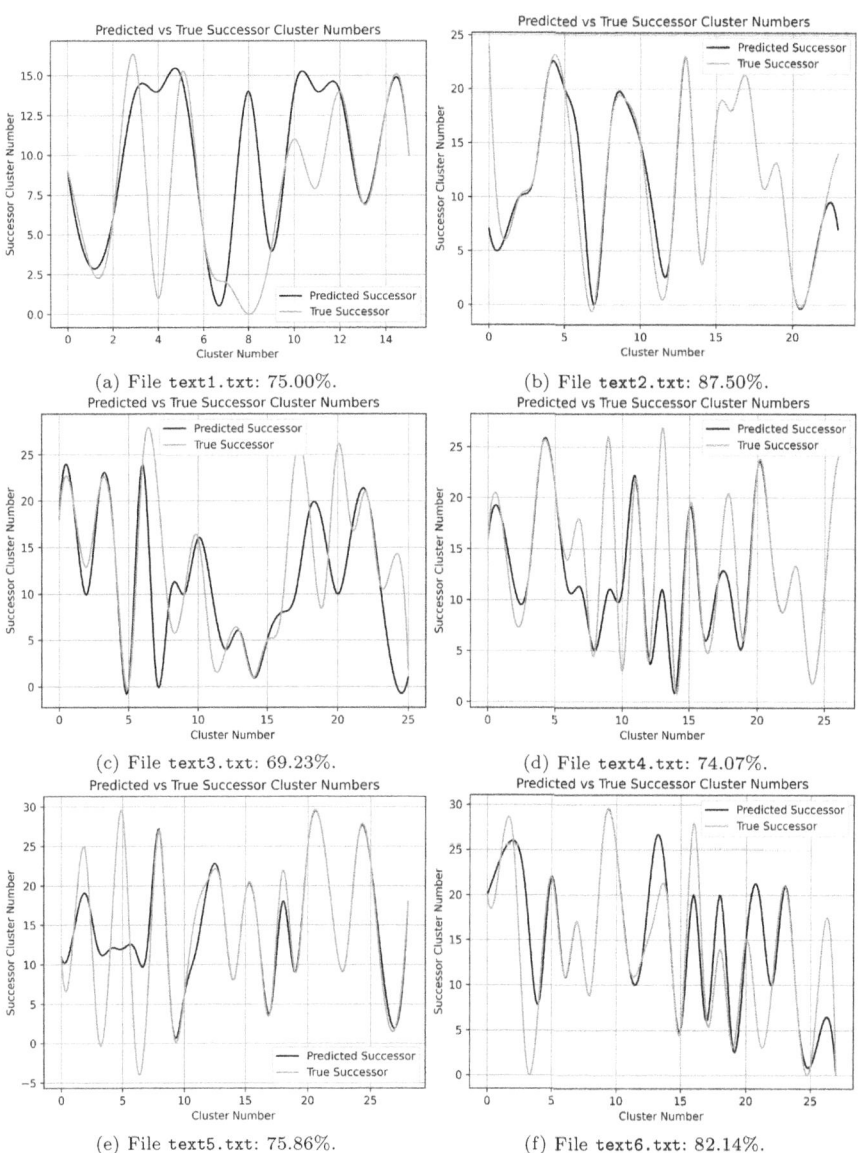

(a) File `text1.txt`: 75.00%.

(b) File `text2.txt`: 87.50%.

(c) File `text3.txt`: 69.23%.

(d) File `text4.txt`: 74.07%.

(e) File `text5.txt`: 75.86%.

(f) File `text6.txt`: 82.14%.

Fig. 14. ADITGLM predicted versus true successor clusters.

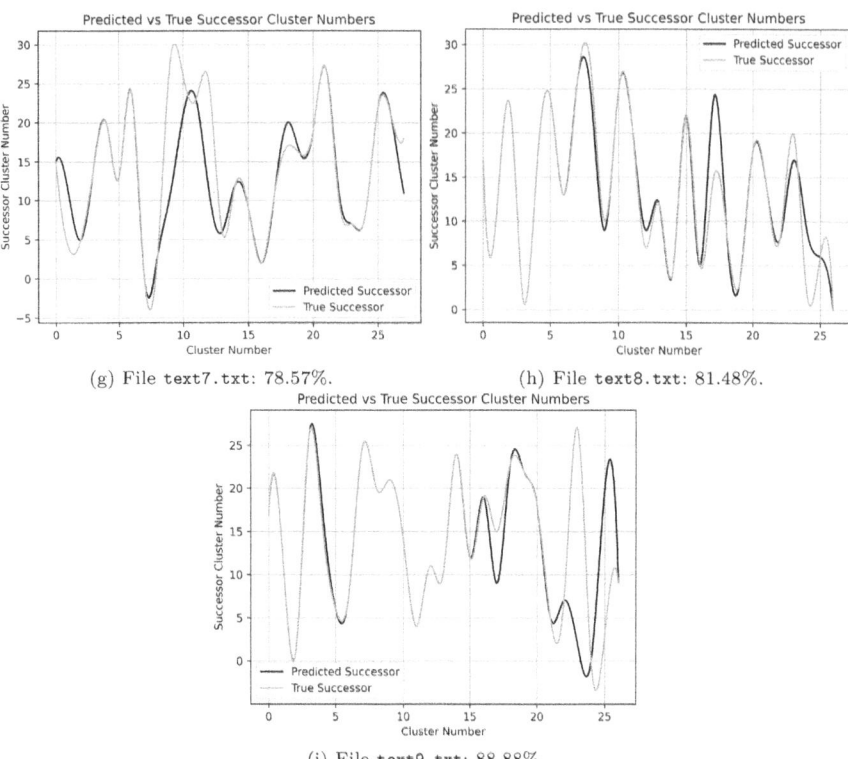

(g) File text7.txt: 78.57%.   (h) File text8.txt: 81.48%.

(i) File text9.txt: 88.88%.

Fig. 15. ADITGLM predicted versus true successor clusters (continued).

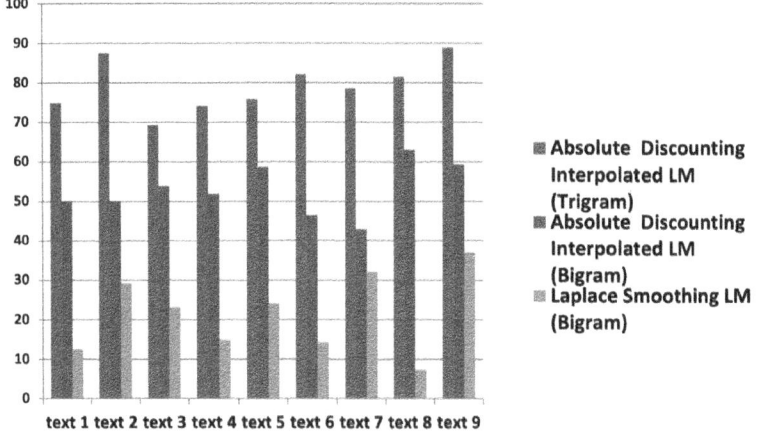

Fig. 16. Average accuracy results for the natural language models.

5 Conclusions

This chapter describes a text file carving method that leverages n-gram language models to reestablish the connections between filesystem clusters that are lost upon file deletion or corruption of the file allocation table. Graph theory is employed to capture the text file recovery problem with clusters as nodes and probabilities of succession as edges. The method was evaluated using three n-gram language models, the absolute discounting interpolated trigram language model, absolute discounting interpolated bigram language model and Laplace bigram language model. Experimentation revealed that the absolute discounting interpolated trigram language model yields the highest average accuracy of 79.19%. The results underscore the effectiveness of leveraging linguistic patterns inherent in fragmented data to reconstruct lost text content.

Analysis has revealed that additional processing of the generated probabilities could enhance accuracy. Future research will focus on processing the generated probabilities and developing greedy algorithms to maximize accuracy. Additionally, future research will conduct experiments on real storage media with large deleted text files.

References

1. E. Durmus, P. Korus and N. Memon, Every shred helps: Assembling evidence from orphaned JPEG fragments, *IEEE Transactions on Information Forensics and Security*, vol. 14(9), pp. 2372–2386, 2019.
2. E. Durmus, M. Mohanty, S. Taspinar, E. Uzun and N. Memon, Image carving with missing headers and missing fragments, *Proceedings of the IEEE Workshop on Information Forensics and Security*, 2017.
3. D. Jurafsky and J. Martin, *Speech and Language Processing: An Introduction to Natural Language Processing, Computational Linguistics and Speech Recognition*, Third Edition Draft (web.stanford.edu/ jurafsky/slp3/ed3book.pdf), February 3, 2024.
4. N. Memon and A. Pal, Automated reassembly of file-fragmented images using greedy algorithms, *IEEE Transactions on Image Processing*, vol. 15(2), pp. 385–393, 2006.
5. A. Pal and N. Memon, The evolution of file carving: The benefits and problems of forensic recovery, *IEEE Signal Processing Magazine*, vol. 26(2), pp. 59–71, 2009.
6. R. Poisel and S. Tjoa, A comprehensive literature review of file carving, *Proceedings of the International Conference on Availability, Reliability and Security*, pp. 475–484, 2013.
7. A. Ravi, T. Kumar and A. Mathew, A method for carving fragmented document and image files, *Proceedings of the International Conference on Advances in Human Machine Interaction*, 2016.
8. H. Sencar and N. Memon, Identification and recovery of JPEG files with missing fragments, *Digital Investigation*, vol. 6(S), pp. S88–S98, 2009.
9. K. Srinivas and T. Venugopal, Automated generation of a natural challenge file for file carving algorithms, *Proceedings of the International Conference on Applied Sciences, Engineering, Technology and Management*, pp. 18–24, 2017.

10. K. Srinivas and T. Venugopal, Testing a file carving tool using realistic datasets generated with openness, *International Journal of Data Analysis Techniques and Strategies*, vol. 12(2), pp. 155–171, 2020.

11. Y. Tang, J. Fang, K. Chow, S. Yiu, J. Xu, B. Feng, Q. Li and Q. Han, Recovery of heavily fragmented JPEG files, *Digital Investigation*, vol. 18(S), pp. S108–S117, 2016.

12. E. Uzun and H. Sencar, Carving orphaned JPEG file fragments, *IEEE Transactions on Information Forensics and Security*, vol. 10(8), pp. 1549–1563, 2015.

13. E. Uzun and H. Sencar, Jpg Scraper: An advanced carver for JPEG files, *IEEE Transactions on Information Forensics and Security*, vol. 15, pp. 1846–1857, 2020.

14. X. Wu, Q. Han, X. Niu, H. Zhang, S. Yiu and J. Fang, JPEG image width estimation for file carving, *IET Image Processing*, vol. 12(7), pp. 1245–1252, 2018.

Generating Usable and Assessable Datasets Containing Anti-Forensic Traces at the Filesystem Level

Thomas Göbel, Harald Baier, and Jan Türr

University of the Bundeswehr, Munich, Germany
`thomas.goebel@unibw.de`

Abstract. Digital forensics and anti-forensics are essential to security because they provide vital information to institute preventive and reactive measures. Diverse and realistic datasets that reflect anti-forensic measures are needed to validate digital forensic tools and advance digital forensics education and research. However, datasets are increasingly created in a synthetic manner due to privacy and legal constraints. The work described in this chapter contributes to improving the digital forensic process by assessing anti-forensic measures at the filesystem level and providing a means for synthesizing datasets containing anti-forensic artifacts. Specifically, it provides an in-depth analysis of anti-forensic data hiding techniques in the evolving Linux-based B-tree filesystem (Btrfs). Also, it presents a methodology for generating anti-forensic traces at the filesystem level in a *post mortem* storage device dataset. The methodology links the `ForTrace` data synthesis framework and `fishy` anti-forensic data hiding framework. A data synthesis tool is developed for generating anti-forensic data hiding traces for three common filesystems, NTFS, ext4 and Btrfs, and providing essential data synthesis functionality to simulate the expected behavior of the operating system. Additionally, a validation model comprising three complexity levels is presented for assessing the implemented anti-forensic data hiding techniques. Overall, the research provides a powerful approach for generating datasets that reflect anti-forensic artifacts potentially used by attackers.

Keywords: Data Synthesis · Data Generation · B-Tree Filesystem · Filesystem Forensics · Anti-Forensics · Data Hiding

1   Introduction

The increased reliance on Internet-connected devices and traditional computers in personal and business environments has led to significant increases in attack vectors, attacks and potential victims. Forensic analyses of attacked and manipulated systems are vital to implementing mitigations that minimize damage, attribute attacks and institute proactive measures to prevent future attacks. Education and research in digital forensics are therefore of high importance.

E. Kurkowski and S. Shenoi (Eds.): DigitalForensics 2024, IFIP AICT 724, pp. 225–246, 2025.
https://doi.org/10.1007/978-3-031-71025-4_12

A key component for digital forensic education and research is the availability of diverse forensically-relevant data [31]. However, real data is often outdated, incomplete, unrealistic and/or not publicly accessible and, most importantly, often has missing labels [2, 14, 39]. Collecting and curating new and complete real-world datasets, especially for law enforcement purposes, is often not possible due to data protection laws [17]. To bypass privacy laws and other constraints on real-world data collection, several attempts have been made to generate synthetic forensic datasets [6, 8, 15, 16]. In particular, efforts seek to facilitate data synthesis by simulating user interactions because manual data synthesis involves significant effort [8, 14, 15].

An accurate understanding of anti-forensic measures is important for training digital forensic practitioners and developing high-functionality forensic tools. Anti-forensic methods are designed to obscure, destroy and/or mislead digital forensic investigations [10, 18]. The taxonomy by Conlan et al. [7] starts with the four original anti-forensic categories (data hiding, artifact wiping, trail obfuscation and attacks against computer forensic processes and tools) [33] and augments them with additional sub-categories of anti-forensic behavior. This work focuses on data hiding, one of the largest anti-forensic fields because it encompasses many types of manipulations with different levels of complexity [7, 25]. However, most data hiding algorithms and tools are often inaccessible due to missing source code and documentation or are focused on specific filesystems or data hiding techniques.

A promising approach is to deploy and maintain a modular and extensible framework capable of manipulating multiple filesystems, including a variety of data hiding techniques. Therefore, the work described in this chapter focuses on manipulating filesystem structures to hide data. Data hiding methods that leverage filesystem vulnerabilities attempt to obfuscate data using reserved, unchecked or unused parts of a filesystem without impairing filesystem functionality [3]. Sometimes, even data structures ordinarily used by a filesystem are abused to make it difficult to detect and reconstruct the hidden data. The goal is to develop an understanding of the extent to which attackers can conceal traces at the filesystem level.

This chapter provides a detailed analysis of anti-forensic data hiding techniques in the evolving Linux-based B-tree filesystem (Btrfs). It presents a methodology for generating anti-forensic traces at the filesystem level by leveraging the ForTrace data synthesis framework and fishy anti-forensic data hiding framework. A data synthesis tool is developed for generating anti-forensic data hiding traces in three common filesystems, NTFS, ext4 and Btrfs, and providing essential data synthesis functionality to simulate the expected behavior of the operating system. Additionally, a validation model comprising three complexity levels, basic, specialist and white box levels, is presented for assessing the implemented anti-forensic data hiding techniques.

2   Related Work

This section discusses related work on anti-forensic dataset generation with a focus on data hiding and data synthesis tools.

2.1   Data Hiding Tools

Using filesystem structures to hide data is not a new idea. StegFS, a filesystem that employed steganographic channels to hide data, was introduced in 2000 [26]. In 2005, Eckstein and Jahnke [9] identified several methods for hiding data. Several early anti-forensic tools such as FragFS, MAFIA, bmap and RuneFS are either no longer accessible or poorly documented and only accessible via third-party publications [24].

Huebner et al. [21] have described methods for hiding data in NTFS filesystem structures. Berghel et al. [3] have investigated NTFS and Linux-based filesystems for potential hiding places. Göbel and Baier [12] and Neuner et al. [29] have discussed the data hiding potential of timestamps (especially nanosecond timestamps) in the ext4 and NTFS filesystems, respectively. Heeger et al. [19] have developed the exHide tool that implements multiple methods for hiding data in exFAT filesystem structures.

Abduhalil et al. [1] proposed a somewhat different variant of data hiding. Specifically, they duplicated files in NTFS using index entries. After deleting the files, the duplicate files remained in the filesystem.

Other researchers have analyzed the capabilities and vulnerabilities of Btrfs. Bhat and Wani [4] and Juch [23] partially base their analyses of Btrfs on the work of Rodeh et al. [32] and mention potential vulnerabilities and features of Btrfs. Wani et al. [38] provide an overview of potential data hiding methods for Btrfs. Gehrke [11] has studied Btrfs timestamps as a forensically-relevant structure. Schneider et al. [35] have shown that entire filesystems can be hidden in Btrfs.

2.2   Data Synthesis Tools

The early data synthesis tool Forensig[2] [27, 28] generates filesystem images by simulating user interactions via Python scripts. The EviPlant [34] framework is used to create forensically-relevant datasets. It produces a base system with a set amount of potential actions to create forensic artifacts. The differences between the base and manipulated systems are combined into an evidence package. The evidence package is then applied to the base system to create a forensically-relevant dataset. The VMPOP data synthesis framework employs virtual machines [30], which it populates with forensically-relevant artifacts by scripting interactions with the virtual machine interfaces.

The Python-based hystck framework [16] generates network and hard drive traces automatically using Python scripts or via YAML configuration files. Automated synthesis makes it possible to create a variety of traces with little effort in virtual machines. In parallel to the synthesis process, a log file is created that contains and retains the ground truth of a scenario.

TraceGen [8] emulates user interactions to synthesize forensic artifacts. It employs scripts running on a virtual machine as well as scripts interacting with the virtual machine as in the case of VMPOP. Unfortunately, the source code of the TraceGen framework is not publicly available.

The FADE tool [6] synthesizes forensically-relevant Android device images. Specifically, it uses Android emulators to create forensic artifacts. Unfortunately, the FADE source code is also not available.

The ForGeOSI (`github.com/maxfragg/ForGeOSI`) and ForGen (`github.com/Jjk422/ForGen`) tools also generate forensically-relevant images. ForGeOSI acts as a wrapper for the Python virtualization environment `pyvbox` and uses the connection to synthesize data whereas ForGen uses FTK Imager and VirtualBox to generate images.

Although there is consensus in the digital forensics community on the importance of synthetic datasets [2, 17, 39], combining a data synthesis approach with forensically-relevant anti-forensic techniques is relatively uncommon. This is curious because the resulting images would be good candidates for testing forensic tools and use in educational/training environments. Only the ForGe tool [36] is able to create NTFS images and enable data hiding in file slack or via steganographic channels. However, ForGe has not been updated since 2015.

3   Data Hiding in Btrfs

Btrfs is a filesystem that is gaining importance in Linux systems [5]. The origin of the acronym remains open; one is its B-tree directory representation whereas another is that it is simply a better filesystem. The following sections describe parsing Btrfs to find data structures that could hide data and discuss data hiding in Btrfs data structures.

3.1   Parsing Btrfs

As in the case of modern filesystems, it is necessary to find and understand the basic filesystem data structure of a Btrfs partition, i.e., superblock, to identify additional relevant filesystem structures.

Figure 1 presents the steps involved in parsing a Btrfs filesystem to find data structures that could be used to hide data. One component of interest is the filesystem interface that recognizes the filesystem and helps locate and interpret all the relevant filesystem structures. The second component comprises two chosen data hiding techniques, timestamp (nanoseconds) data hiding and file slack data hiding. These techniques are responsible for hiding, reading and removing hidden data as well as creating metadata objects and computing the checksums of filesystem structures changed by hiding or deleting data.

- **Step 0:** The filesystem of interest has to be identified as an instance of Btrfs. The filesystem type is checked by finding the expected superblock location

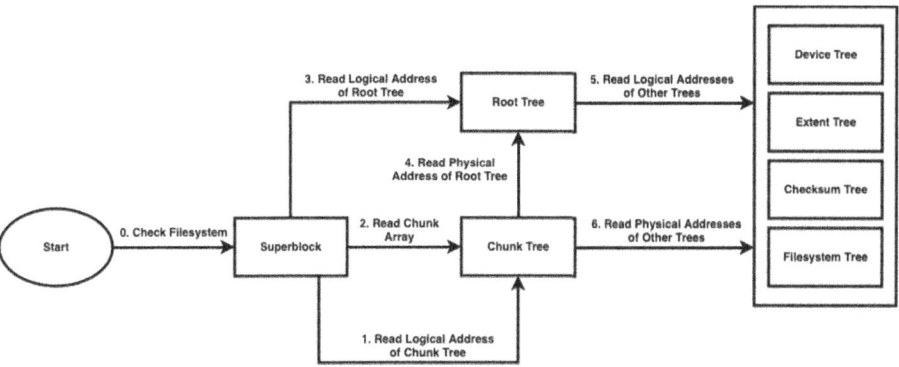

Fig. 1. Parsing Btrfs filesystem to find data structures for data hiding.

at offset 64 KiB in the partition and validating the superblock by checking its magic signature string _BHRfS_M at offset 0x40 of the superblock, i.e., at offset 0x10040 of the partition [5].

- **Step 1:** The superblock contains essential information about the filesystem, such as the size of the allocation units (blocks) and nodes that must be known in order to work with the filesystem. This is why the rest of the superblock is parsed. The chunk tree is an important data structure that is identified during this step. Btrfs mainly uses logical addresses and the chunk tree is used to translate the logical addresses to their physical addresses to access data structures. During Step 1, the logical address of the chunk tree at offset 0x58 of the Btrfs superblock is extracted.

```
1   POST http://android.clients.google.airpush.com/login
2   if logical_adr >= key_variable
3   AND logical_adr < key_variable + chunk_size:
4   physical_adr = stripe_adr
  + (logical_adr-key_variable)
```

Fig. 2. Pseudocode for the addressing process.

- **Step 2:** The chunk tree physical address is computed from its logical address and a partial copy of the chunk tree, which is stored at offset 0x32B of the superblock. Figure 2 shows the pseudocode that translates logical addresses to physical addresses.
- **Step 3:** The logical address of the root tree is read from offset 0x50 of the superblock. The root tree is important because it contains the logical addresses of the entry points of all the other trees in Btrfs [20].

Table 1. Data fields of Btrfs inodes for hiding data [5].

Offset	Size (Bytes)	Description
0x00	8	Inode generation
0x70	8	Access timestamp
0x78	4	Access timestamp (nanoseconds)
0x7c	8	Change timestamp
0x84	4	Change timestamp (nanoseconds)
0x90	4	Modified timestamp (nanoseconds)
0x9c	4	Inode creation timestamp (nanoseconds)

- **Step 4:** Using the chunk tree located in Step 2, the logical address of the root tree is converted to its corresponding physical address, providing access to the root tree.
- **Step 5:** The root tree is analyzed and the logical addresses of all the other relevant trees are extracted.
- **Step 6:** As in Step 4, the physical addresses of the trees can be computed as needed. At this point, access is available to all the relevant Btrfs data structures.

3.2   Btrfs Data Hiding Techniques

This section analyzes the Btrfs filesystem data structures that can be leveraged to hide data. It begins with classic locations such as timestamps and slack areas and finally examines Btrfs-specific locations.

Btrfs Timestamp Hiding Technique. Inodes in Linux-based filesystems are the data structures that store metadata of filesystem objects such as directories and files. Table 1 shows the important data fields of Btrfs inodes for hiding data.

While the fine-grained structure of a Btrfs inode differs from the specifications of other filesystems, there are some similarities. A similarity with the ext4 filesystem is the presence of nanosecond timestamps. Unlike ext4 and APFS timestamps, which only allow 30 bits of the entire timestamp to be used to ensure the integrity of the rest of the timestamp [12], the Btrfs variant of the hiding technique can use the entire four-byte sub-second timestamp portion due to the separation of the timestamp parts shown in Table 1. However, manipulating the eight-byte main timestamp should be avoided because a simple filesystem check would detect a broken timestamp [11].

Figure 3 shows the workflow of the `write` function of the Btrfs timestamp hiding technique as implemented in the `fishy` anti-forensic framework. The filesystem is parsed as explained in Figure 1 to create a list of inode offsets. Additionally, the data input stream, whether from a file or the console, is read. For every entry in the list of inode addresses, 16 bytes of the input stream are

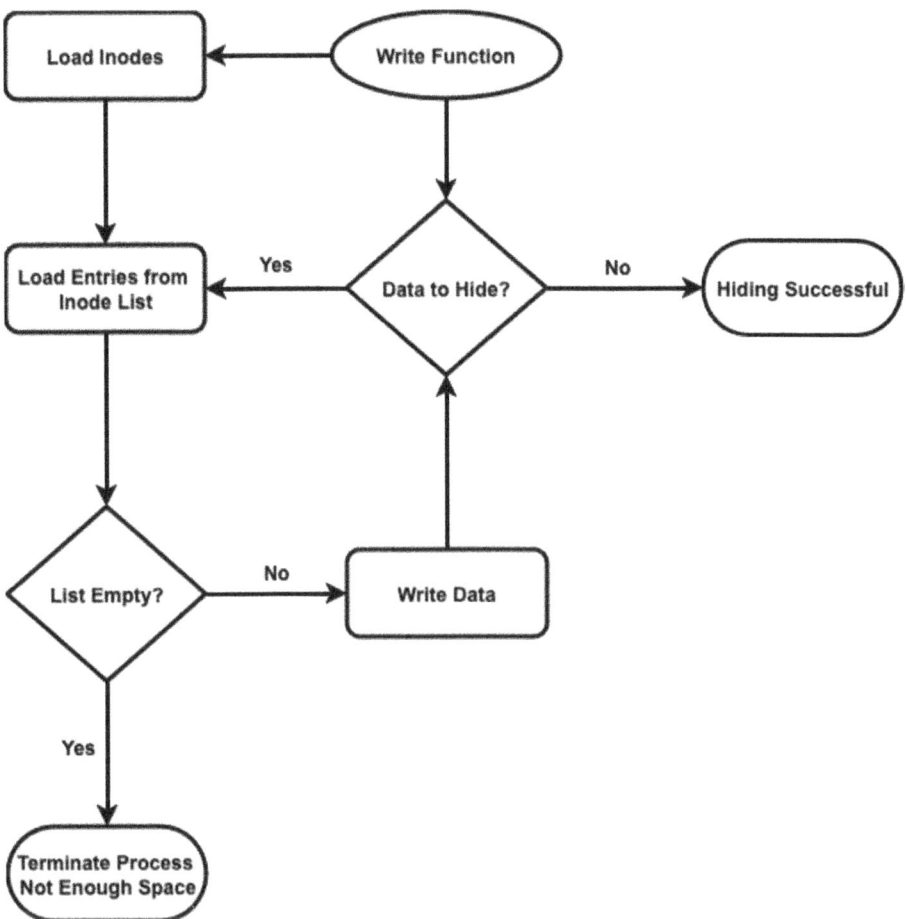

Fig. 3. Btrfs timestamp hiding technique workflow.

read. If the list of inode addresses is empty, but the input stream has not yet ended, the process terminates due to the lack of hiding space. After writing data to the four timestamps of an inode, the new checksum corresponding to the inode is computed and replaced.

Btrfs File Slack Hiding Technique. A slack space is created when more space is allocated to an object than is needed. Different types of slack spaces arise in filesystems, for instance, between the end of the file content and its allocated space. Because the slack space does not store content, it may be used to hide data.

The workflow of the write function of the Btrfs file slack hiding technique is similar to that of the Btrfs timestamp hiding technique (Figure 3). The filesystem

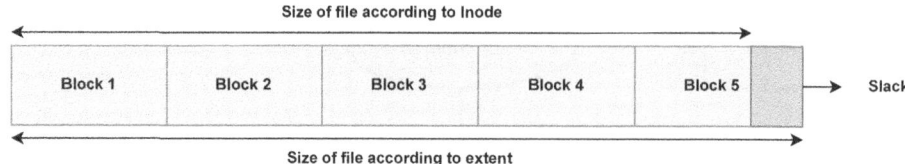

Fig. 4. Computation of Btrfs file slack space.

is parsed to create lists of extent and inode offsets. The lists are then used to find slack areas. If the lists are empty, but the input stream of data continues, the process terminates. Unlike the timestamp hiding technique, the potential hiding space existing in file slack space is more difficult to compute. The reason is that while timestamps offer a fixed amount of hiding space, file slack space is volatile and therefore has variable size.

Figure 4 illustrates the computation of Btrfs file slack space. The extent and inode structures tied to a file are required. The extent specifies the size of a file in terms of the number of allocated filesystem units (blocks). For example, the file in Figure 4 allocates five filesystem blocks of typical size 4 KiB = 4,096 bytes. Thus, the extent shows a file size of $5 \times 4\,\text{KiB} = 20\,\text{KiB} = 20{,}480$ bytes. However, as indicated by the respective inode, the actual file size may be any number of bytes between 16,385 and 20,480 bytes. The file slack size is simply the difference between 20,480 and 16,385 bytes. Similarly, the offset of the file slack location is computed by adding the file size found in the inode to the physical address of the file. The logical file address found in the inode is computed as described in Figure 2.

An additional challenge compared with timestamp-based hiding is updating the checksums in different Btrfs filesystem structures. First, the file content checksum in the checksum tree has to be recomputed and replaced. The entry is found using the starting position of file data located in the extent. Additionally, the file data checksum is contained in a node, similar to a node that contains multiple inodes. Therefore, after recomputing a file data checksum, the checksum of the corresponding node has to be computed and replaced as well.

Additional Btrfs Hiding Techniques. Ahead of every superblock in the filesystem is a 64 KiB unused space. This space is not traditional slack space, but it can be used in a similar manner. Even better, data hiding does not present the challenges posed by slack space hiding because the unused space never changes. However, the data hiding is easily detected. This is because of the limited number of superblocks in a filesystem and manual investigations commonly performed on important structures such as superblocks would detect the data hiding. In any case, since the area ahead of the superblock is usually empty, it could be paired with another hiding space [38].

Btrfs node structures also provide space for hiding data. Both types of n-odes, internal nodes and leaf nodes, have default allocation sizes of 16 KiB and

Fig. 5. Internal node slack area.

contain slack areas too. Internal nodes, shown in Figure 5, often only fill the first 1,000 bytes of the nodes to locate the node headers and the key pointers to child nodes, leaving up to 150,00 bytes of slack area if the node sizes are set to the default size of 16 KiB.

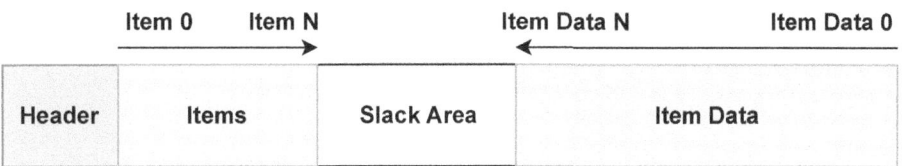

Fig. 6. Leaf node slack area.

Leaf nodes usually have smaller slack areas than internal nodes because they contain filesystem metadata. While the internal node slack is always located at the end of a node, the leaf node slack corresponds to the space between the node item metadata and the actual node item data (Figure 6).

The storage capacity of node-based hiding techniques increases with filesystem size – in depth (more files) as well as in width (more volumes) – because both options scale with the amount of metadata and, therefore, the number of nodes [37].

4 Dataset Generation with Anti-Forensic Traces

This section describes how anti-forensic data hiding practices are integrated in a data synthesis framework. The goal is to provide an easy-to-use method for generating datasets that contain hidden forensic traces and assessing the extent to which data hiding can actually be detected by forensic tools and digital forensic practitioners. The section describes the workflow and capabilities of the `fishy` filesystem anti-forensics framework [13] and the `ForTrace` data synthesis framework [15]. Following this, insights are provided into Btrfs data hiding techniques and the implementation of the interface between the two frameworks.

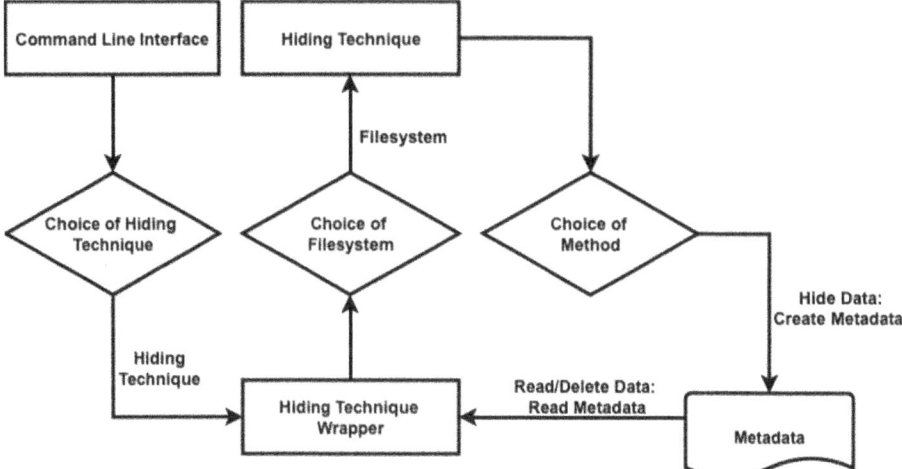

Fig. 7. fishy framework architecture.

4.1 fishy Framework

fishy [13] is a modular open-source framework that enables users to hide, read and delete data using reserved areas and other vulnerabilities in various filesystems. The framework was selected as the data hiding component for the data synthesis environment for several reasons. First, fishy is not restricted to specific anti-forensic methods or filesystems. In particular, the tool provides wrappers for common filesystems and also enables existing anti-forensic modules to be extended and new modules to be added (e.g., new filesystems and new hiding techniques). The framework is comprehensively documented and still maintained. Additionally, all the data hiding techniques offered by the framework have similar structures and are, therefore, easy to use. Also, the modular architecture of the framework facilitates the creation of a uniform interface.

Figure 7 shows a simplified version of the fishy framework architecture. The framework has three principal components that regulate the workflow:

- **Command Line Interface:** The command line interface parses user inputs and determines the target image, chosen techniques, methods and metadata options. As described later, when fishy is integrated with ForTrace, the command line interface is skipped because the new interface directly calls the second component, the hiding technique wrappers.
- **Hiding Technique Wrappers:** A wrapper exists for every implemented data hiding technique. The wrappers employ filesystem detectors to determine the implementations of the hiding techniques that need to be called. The wrappers also handle organizational tasks such as reading metadata files if they are needed by the called functions. Additionally, the wrappers handle input and output data streams.

– **Hiding Techniques:** Data hiding techniques are implemented in the corresponding filesystem modules. The filesystem modules parse filesystem structures and offer the requested information about them to the actual techniques to be used. Every hiding technique has three basic functions: `write` that inserts data to be hidden (Figure 3), `read` that recovers hidden data and `clear` that wipes hidden data using zero bytes.

Additional functions can be implemented. Most modules also provide an `info` function that displays the corresponding filesystem and data hiding technique information.

Before the integration of the new Btrfs module, `fishy` had modules for the NTFS, ext4, FAT32, exFAT and APFS filesystems. Note that the FAT32, exFAT and APFS modules are not included in the data synthesis integration effort described in this chapter.

– **NTFS Module:** This module parses the common NTFS Windows filesystem. The NTFS module has four implemented hiding techniques. Two of the techniques, badcluster and addcluster, manipulate filesystem cluster management. The third technique computes the offsets and sizes of slack areas in master file table (MFT) records. The fourth technique hides data in the ordinary file slack area of a regular file (as in the case of Btrfs, this technique is present in all the `fishy` modules except for the APFS module). The filesystem interface and parser are realized by employing The Sleuth Kit and its Python bindings `pytsk3` (`pypi.org/project/pytsk3`) and `Construct` (`construct.readthedocs.io/en/latest`) to detect and model the filesystem structures.

– **ext4 Module:** This module parses the common ext4 Linux and Android filesystem. In addition to the almost universal file slack hiding technique, the ext4 module supports five hiding techniques. One uses nanosecond locations in the inode tables to hide data [12]. Other techniques leverage other areas in the inodes (such as the `osd2` and `obso_faddr` fields), backup copies of group descriptor tables and slack areas connected to filesystem superblocks. Unlike the NTFS module, the ext4 module employs an additional internal filesystem parser in combination with the `pytsk3` library.

All the `fishy` modules relevant to the interface implementation are presented in more detail in Section 4.3. Table 2 shows all the hiding techniques that can be used via the new interface as part of the data synthesis framework `ForTrace`.

4.2 `ForTrace` **Framework**

`ForTrace` [15] is a data synthesis framework based on `hystck` [16]. As shown in Figure 8, the architecture supports the simulation of human-computer interactions by leveraging a client-server architecture connected through a private network so that the collected network traffic is not affected by `ForTrace`-specific orchestration artifacts [15].

Table 2. Integrated `fishy` and `ForTrace` data hiding techniques.

Hiding Technique	NTFS	Btrfs	ext4	Description
file slack	✓	✓	✓	Uses file slack
mftslack	✓			Uses master file table entry slack
addcluster	✓			Adds clusters to files for hiding data
badcluster	✓			Marks bad clusters for hiding data
reserved_gdt_blocks			✓	Uses reserved group descriptor table blocks
superblock_slack			✓	Uses superblock slack
osd2			✓	Uses osd2 entries in inodes
obso_faddr			✓	Uses obso_faddr entries in inodes
nanoseconds		✓	✓	Uses nanosecond parts of timestamps

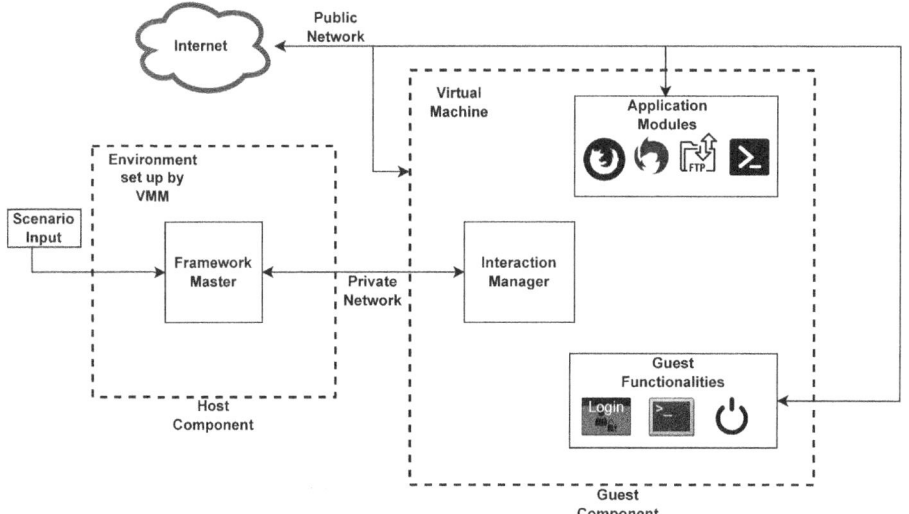

Fig. 8. `ForTrace` framework architecture [15].

The server-side components handle organizational tasks. The Virtual Machine Monitor (VMM) class generates the client-side components by cloning a previously installed and configured template. Additionally, sockets for communications are created and maintained by the class. The Guest class handles the actual communications between the server and client components. It transfers commands and parameters to the client. This component is called the framework master in Figure 8. The client side is a virtual machine cloned by the Virtual Machine Monitor class that is referred to as the interaction manager in Figure 8. It executes the client-side modules corresponding to the commands sent by the Guest class and returns status updates to the server components.

The `ForTrace` workflow is briefly summarized as follows. First, the Virtual Machine Monitor class clones a template. Next, the client and server components attempt to connect over the private network. Following this, the created scenario

	Slot	Start	End	Length	Description
000:	Meta	0000000000	0000000000	0000000001	Primary Table (#0)
001:	-------	0000000000	0000002047	0000002048	Unallocated
002:	000:000	0000002048	0000104447	0000102400	NTFS / exFAT (0x07)
003:	000:001	0000104448	0124781196	0124676749	NTFS / exFAT (0x07)
004:	-------	0124781197	0124782591	0000001395	Unallocated
005:	000:002	0124782592	0125825023	0001042432	Unknown Type (0x27)
006:	-------	0125825024	0125829119	0000004096	Unallocated

Fig. 9. Typical image partitioning created by ForTrace.

is communicated to the client. The client executes all the necessary actions. After completing the scenario, a network dump and an optional memory dump are created. A hard disk image with all the new traces is also created. Finally, the client is shut down. If specified, the client is deleted. In addition, during the data synthesis process, the reporting component of ForTrace logs all the interactions to preserve the ground truth.

4.3   Data Synthesis Framework Integration

The integration of the two frameworks provides the ability to invoke fishy functions directly without having to invoke fishy from a different console while attempting to create a highly realistic image simultaneously using all the ForTrace data synthesis functions. Like the existing framework components, the new interface is also constructed in a modular manner, meaning that module extensions and new modules can be added easily using the new specifications. The usual first step of command line interaction with fishy is skipped because the interface directly invokes the hiding technique wrappers with the appropriate parameters.

The new interface is designed to fulfil three goals:

- The principal functionality of the new interface is that ForTrace can invoke the fishy hiding techniques. fishy could have been implemented like other ForTrace modules, but this would leave additional framework artifacts on the guest machine, which must always be avoided in a data simulation environment. Instead, the new interface is implemented as a exclusive server-side utility that can be used like regular modules during data synthesis.
- Another key functionality is that service on the synthesized virtual machine need not be interrupted. This is important because disruption of service due to the use of data hiding techniques would constitute high detectability of manipulation. To achieve this goal, changes were made in fishy to allow for specific starting point offsets, which are also included in every function in the filesystem parsers and hiding techniques. Additionally, checks are implemented to see how running guest machines react to the use of hiding techniques.
- Compatible hiding techniques must work despite the presence of additional partitions. By default, fishy only works with single filesystem partitions. However, virtual machines created by ForTrace have additional partitions such as the additional default Windows reserved partition (Figure 9). The

hiding techniques would attempt their workflows starting at the first marked partition, resulting in immediate failure. Therefore, the actual offset of the correct partition is added to every offset computation in fishy to find the correct partition and filesystem structure.

The interface implementation involved three steps. First, fishy was adapted so that the potential additional offset of a specific partition in an image could be interpreted and added to all the necessary functions. This change was realized by adding an additional parameter to all the functions that compute offsets in the filesystem.

Second, fishy was integrated with ForTrace by implementing a utility class that allows direct invocations of hiding technique wrappers to support running filesystems, i.e., the operations of a manipulated virtual machine are not disturbed by hiding data. When called, the class has to be initialized with the path to the synthesized image and the partition offset containing the filesystem the user intends to manipulate.

Third, an additional change to ForTrace was an optional second template and client-side component creation process. ForTrace only created qcow2 images. However, to use fishy, a raw image file is needed. Therefore, an installation script for raw templates was added along with optional create_guest_raw and create_raw functions to create and start raw guest images, respectively.

5   Validation Model and Evaluation

This section evaluates the data hiding techniques. It introduces the validation model for assessing the difficulty of detecting anti-forensic data hiding techniques. Next, the model is employed to evaluate Btrfs data hiding techniques. Finally, the framework interface functionality is assessed.

5.1   Validation Model

The validation model for evaluating the difficulty of discovering Btrfs hiding techniques has three levels of complexity:

- **Basic Level:** The first level provides an entry barrier for hiding techniques and is, therefore, the weakest validation level. A hiding technique that fails to succeed at the basic level is disqualified from hiding data and would only be usable in another context such as creating falsified evidence [7]. The basic level simulates an uneducated user without forensic knowledge and tools. The only available knowledge is that a hiding incident has occurred and the only tool available at the basic level is a filesystem check. The goal is to confirm the existence of a data hiding incident.
- **Specialist Level:** The second level is equivalent in difficulty to a cryptanalytic chosen plaintext attack [40]. The specialist level assumes that the digital forensic practitioner knows that hidden data is in the system. However, the practitioner does not know the actual hiding technique used. In addition to

knowledge about the incident, additional tools such as The Sleuth Kit are available. Due to the availability of knowledge and tools, the goals at this level are increased. In addition to confirming the data hiding incident, it is necessary to find and clear the system of hidden data.

- **White Box Level:** The third level is comparable in difficulty to a crypt-analytic white box attack [22, 41]. The level assumes knowledge about the hiding technique as well as access to all possible tools, including Btrfs foren-sic tools. The only limitations are the lack of knowledge about the size or type of hidden data and no direct access to the specific hiding technique. Due to the increased capabilities at this level, the goals increase in complexity. In addition to confirming the data hiding incident and locating the hidden data, it is required to perform a complete or at least partial reconstruction of the hidden data. However, it is assumed that the hidden data is not encrypted.

5.2   Btrfs Hiding Technique Evaluation

This section evaluates data hiding in the Btrfs file slack and timestamp data structures. It also evaluates the new interface that integrates the `fishy` anti-forensic framework with the `ForTrace` data synthesis framework.

Btrfs File Slack Hiding. Typically, file slack hiding techniques offer the greatest potential data hiding capacity [24]. While this is also true for the Btrfs implementation, there is a caveat regarding reduced storage capacity. Files that are small enough to fit within the extent items are marked as inline and leave no usable slack because they are integrated in metadata structures [38]. Additionally, the stability of this data hiding technique is low because file sizes change. Therefore, it is possible that growing files may overwrite hidden data. Methods for increasing stability include filling slack areas backwards and hiding data in files that are rarely used. However, both methods would reduce the storage capacity.

The basic validation level can only employ filesystem checks. Since the data hiding technique computes and replaces the checksums of used file data blocks, it is not possible to confirm the data hiding incident at the basic level.

The specialist validation level has a much better chance at finding hidden data. While there is no direct way to find the hidden data, sampling file contents using the `icat` tool can lead to discovery. Figure 10 shows that hidden text is easily detected, confirming the data hiding incident and enabling the removal of the hidden data.

In the case of less recognizable data, such as binary image data in Figure 11, achieving the specialist level goal is more complex. Additional steps would have to be taken to confirm hidden data. This could be accomplished in the same way as the data hiding technique. Specifically, `istat` would be used to obtain the file size to be compared with the `icat` file size that includes the slack space. Hidden data is confirmed when the `icat` output is larger than the `istat` output.

Since the data hidden in file slack can be discovered at the specialist level, the same process can be applied at the more powerful white box level. Since the

```
♪�€€€p€€U€^9tB€d€LI€€8>€€€€€€M€r€R§-€H€€€€}€€m€mw€\€€G€€Cw.€▓€€€€F€€Y&▓▓d€€€€H[€o€€\€€€€I€6{€tH€€w€%-€€€;€J{
ia€€€€€43-€€!S€E€,rY/€€`€€,€7€$€Ri€i€B€€€N=€L€€u.X^€;€€z3€€€€€€!€T€pA€;Zm[€€    m€€€€w€U5b)ia€i€VV1U€9€€€I€€
<c\♭$€€{w€U`>uV€€{€}Gxl€€€#sU€o€}€€-€€6Vu|z€ PK
]    €R`€€j€,              MalwareBot-master/MalwareBot/packages.configUTm`€`{€{€€}En€BYjQqf-€€€€€€€Bj^r-Jf^€€R
]    €RúY€    '           MalwareBot-master/MalwareBot/upload.txtUTm`€`Dies ist eine hochgeladene DateiPK
]    €R        MalwareBot-master/UTm`€`PK
]    €R€€n€€              9MalwareBot-master/.gitattributesUTm`€`PK
]    €R€€
q    4MalwareBot-master/.gitignoreUTm`€`PK
MalwareBot-master/CommandTest/UTm`€`PK
MalwareBot-master/CommandTest/CommandLineParser.cppUTm`€`PK
]    €R€€3€- ZMalwareBot-master/CommandTest/CommandTest.cppUTm`€`PK
]    €R$6C€5h$1        oMalwareBot-master/CommandTest/CommandTest.vcxprojUTm`€`PK
]    €R€cb:€9           €MalwareBot-master/CommandTest/CommandTest.vcxproj.filtersUTm`€`PK
]    €Rû    €y€,        rMalwareBot-master/CommandTest/CryptoTest.cppUTm`€`PK
]    €R7X0€7,           >MalwareBot-master/CommandTest/ParserTest.cppUTm`€`PK
]    €R€€"€€%           tMalwareBot-master/CommandTest/pch.cppUTm`€`PK
]    €R€&€€€€#          €MalwareBot-master/CommandTest/pch.hUTm`€`PK
]    €Re€€Q-            €!MalwareBot-master/MalwareBot/MalwareBot.slnUTm`€`PK
]    €R        €$MalwareBot-master/MalwareBot/UTm`€`PK
]    €R€€€>
€$      ^$MalwareBot-master/MalwareBot/Bot.cppUTm`€`PK
]    €R€€€€              .MalwareBot-master/MalwareBot/Command.cppUTm`€`PK
]    €RI€€€'&           2MalwareBot-master/MalwareBot/Command.hUTm`€`PK
2    N4MalwareBot-master/MalwareBot/CommandLineParser.cppUTm`€`PK
]    €R€q€
            $S€        €8MalwareBot-master/MalwareBot/CommandLineParser.hUTm`€`PK
]    €R€#l`f8['         (:MalwareBot-master/MalwareBot/Crypto.cppUTm`€`PK
]    €R3€#€,%           €IMalwareBot-master/MalwareBot/Crypto.hUTm`€`PK
]    €R€€€€X+           €€MalwareBot-master/MalwareBot/Executions.cppUTm`€`PK
]    €R€€t€€ G }        €gMalwareBot-master/MalwareBot/Executions.hUTm`€`PK
]    €R%6Z€C/           -qMalwareBot-master/MalwareBot/InternetHelper.cppUTm`€`PK
]    €R;€€€H-           €MalwareBot-master/MalwareBot/InternetHelper.hUTm`€`PK
]    €R€€€€U%/          dMalwareBot-master/MalwareBot/MalwareBot.vcxprojUTm`€`PK
]    €RK    €€r         7       F€MalwareBot-master/MalwareBot/MalwareBot.vcxproj.filtersUTm`€`PK
]    €R€€Cc    '        €MalwareBot-master/MalwareBot/Parser.cppUTm`€`PK
]    €Ru)€`€€%          €€MalwareBot-master/MalwareBot/Parser.hUTm`€`PK
]    €R€€€ €€(          .MalwareBot-master/MalwareBot/constants.hUTm`€`PK
]    €R`€€j€,           €€MalwareBot-master/MalwareBot/packages.configUTm`€`PK
]    €RúY€    '         l€MalwareBot-master/MalwareBot/upload.txtUTm`€`PK

                                                   6685)↲cc0659050001aa1d4fbc26f3a9
Thou art more lovely and more temperate:
Rough winds do shake the darling buds of May,
And summer's lease hath all too short a date;
Sometime too hot the eye of heaven shines,
And often is his gold complexion dimm'd;
And every fair from fair sometime declines,
By chance or nature's changing course untrimm'd;
But thy eternal summer shall not fade,
Nor lose possession of that fair thou ow'st;
Nor shall death brag thou wander'st in his shade,
When in eternal lines to time thou grow'st:
    So long as men can breathe or eyes can see,
    So long lives this, and this gives life to thee.
```

Fig. 10. icat output of a hidden text file in Btrfs file slack.

white box level has no restrictions, a data reconstruction is also possible using similar methods as at the specialist level. However, manipulation that is harder to detect involves hidden data in slack space that has been deleted. Since file slack areas filled with zeros are not out of the ordinary, it would be impossible to determine if hidden data existed in the past at all three validation levels.

Btrfs Timestamp Hiding. The Btrfs timestamp hiding technique is more powerful than the comparable methods for the ext4 and APFS filesystems because all four Btrfs nanosecond bytes can be used to hide data. Of course, the storage capacity of this technique is significantly lower than the file slack hiding technique. Each timestamp has only four bytes available and all four timestamps

Fig. 11. `icat` output of a hidden image file in Btrfs file slack.

of the inode can be employed to hide data. Thus, there is a maximum of 16 bytes of available data hiding space per inode. The stability of the timestamp hiding technique can be improved by reducing the number of timestamps used because some timestamps are changed more frequently than others. But this would significantly decrease the storage capacity of the timestamp technique.

The base validation level would fail to find hidden data in the timestamps because the checksums would have been modified after the data was hidden. Therefore, the data hiding incident could not be confirmed at the base level.

At the specialist level, single inodes with hidden data could be discovered. While the hidden data shown in Figure 12 is difficult to distinguish, the presence of deleted data shown in Figure 13 would be discovered because it would be very unusual for multiple timestamps to have their nanosecond parts filled with zeros.

However, an anomaly would be identified at the specialist level if the u-naffected timestamps in Figure 14 were to be compared against the affected timestamps in Figure 12. Therefore, the data hiding incident could be confirmed at the specialist level, but it would not be possible to find all the hidden data. Nevertheless, at the specialist level it would be possible to find all the former hiding places in the case of deleted data.

At the white box level, the first goal of confirming the data hiding incident would be accomplished in the same way as at the specialist level. Similarly, all the locations with deleted hidden data would be identified. However, reconstructing the hidden data would be complicated. If the hidden data was simple text, manually investigating all the timestamps using a hex or disk editor could restore

```
Inode (virtual): 1
Subvolume: 0x5
Inode (real): 257
Allocated: yes
Compressed: no
Generation: 8
UID / GID: 0 / 0
Mode: drwxr-xr-x
Size: 0
Num of Links: 1

Flags:

Inode Times:
Accessed:      2023-01-14 19:23:21.1701144692 (UTC)
Created:       2023-01-14 19:23:25.544175136 (UTC)
Modified:      2023-01-14 19:23:25.1970479201 (UTC)

Extended attributes:
```

Fig. 12. istat output of inode timestamps affected by write.

```
Inode (virtual): 1
Subvolume: 0x5
Inode (real): 257
Allocated: yes
Compressed: no
Generation: 8
UID / GID: 0 / 0
Mode: drwxr-xr-x
Size: 0
Num of Links: 1

Flags:

Inode Times:
Accessed:      2023-01-14 19:23:21.000000000 (UTC)
Created:       2023-01-14 19:23:25.000000000 (UTC)
Modified:      2023-01-14 19:23:25.000000000 (UTC)

Extended attributes:
```

Fig. 13. istat output of inode timestamps affected by clear.

the hidden data. However, if the hidden data was binary data or encrypted data, this process would not work because the recovered hidden data would be indistinguishable from legitimate timestamps.

5.3 Framework Interface Functionality

The correct functionality of the new interface between the fishy and ForTrace frameworks is validated by showing that the three goals stated above are accomplished:

– ForTrace is able to use the hiding techniques provided by fishy. This fundamental functionality is realized by the newly-implemented DataHiding utility class.

```
Inode (virtual): 1
Subvolume: 0x5
Inode (real): 257
Allocated: yes
Compressed: no
Generation: 8
UID / GID: 0 / 0
Mode: drwxr-xr-x
Size: 0
Num of Links: 1

Flags:

Inode Times:
Accessed:       2023-01-14 19:23:21.908000000 (UTC)
Created:        2023-01-14 19:23:25.748000000 (UTC)
Modified:       2023-01-14 19:23:25.748000000 (UTC)

Extended attributes:
```

Fig. 14. istat output of unaffected inode timestamps.

- Service on the manipulated virtual machine must not be interrupted. All the hiding techniques presented in Table 2 can be used to hide data on running machines and shutdown machines without interrupting running machines or preventing shutdown machines from being started. This is accomplished by incorporating the filesystem partition offset as a parameter of the interface function that invokes the hiding technique wrappers.
- Compatible hiding techniques must work despite the presence of additional partitions. The changes that address the previous goal also help accomplish this goal. A new parameter -area has been added to account for different starting offsets and multiple filesystems available in the partitioning. The separate use of fishy in the traditional manner is not affected because the new parameter is initialized to zero by default.

6 Conclusions

This work has attempted to improve the digital forensic process by assessing anti-forensic measures at the filesystem level and providing a means for synthesizing datasets containing anti-forensic artifacts. Additionally, three validation models for assessing anti-forensic data hiding techniques have been developed.

The research has demonstrated that the Btrfs filesystem is resilient to some data hiding methods due to its robust checksums and filesystem protections such as its logical addressing structure and reducing the number of files capable of producing slack space. However, Btrfs is still susceptible to data hiding methods. The new interface that integrates the fishy anti-forensic framework and the ForTrace data synthesis framework makes it possible to evaluate data hiding techniques for Btrfs as well as for the popular ext4 and NTFS filesystems. Due to its modular design, the interface component can be extended to include additional anti-forensic data hiding techniques and other filesystems. Furthermore,

ForTrace can be used to generate complex scenarios involving hidden data at the filesystem level over and above its existing data synthesis functions.

Future research will enhance compatibility by synthesizing datasets using additional fishy-compatible filesystems such as APFS, FAT32 and exFAT. A viable APFS interface requires a ForTrace macOS implementation that is missing, but introducing FAT32 and exFAT compatibility is relatively simple. This would permit the simulation of anti-forensic manipulations of USB devices during data synthesis.

Future research will also focus on the Btrfs filesystem. Certain other slack and reserved areas are known to exist in Btrfs, some of which have been considered unusable due to checksums and other filesystem protections [37, 38]. However, experiments conducted during this research revealed that some of the reserved areas in the filesystem could be used to hide data. Key features that have not been implemented for Btrfs with regard to this research are using multiple hard drives and addressing multiple subvolumes. Structures and parsing functions needed to address these issues are present in the current Btrfs module. Future research will attempt to implement this functionality.

References

1. G. Abduhalil, M. Obid and Y. Rakhmatulla, Algorithm for steganographic hiding of information using a filesystem, *Proceedings of the International Conference on Information Science and Communications Technologies*, 2021.
2. S. Abt and H. Baier, Are we missing labels? A study of the availability of ground truth in network security research, *Proceedings of the Third International Workshop on Building Analysis Datasets and Gathering Experience Returns for Security*, pp. 40–55, 2014.
3. H. Berghel, D. Hoelzer and M. Sthultz, Data hiding tactics for Windows and Unix filesystems, *Advances in Computers*, vol. 74, pp. 1–17, 2008.
4. W. Bhat and M. Wani, Forensic analysis of the B-tree filesystem (Btrfs), *Digital Investigation*, vol. 27, pp. 57–70, 2018.
5. Btrfs Contributors, *Wikipedia: The Free Encyclopedia* (en.wikipedia.org/wiki/Btrfs), 2024.
6. A. Ceballos Delgado, W. Glisson, G. Grispos and K. Choo, FADE: A forensic image generator for Android device education, *Wiley Interdisciplinary Reviews: Forensic Science*, vol. 4(2), article no. e1432, 2022.
7. K. Conlan, I. Baggili and F. Breitinger, Anti-forensics: Furthering digital forensic science through a new extended, granular taxonomy, *Digital Investigation*, vol. 18(S), pp. S66–S75, 2016.
8. X. Du, C. Hargreaves, J. Sheppard and M. Scanlon, TraceGen: User activity emulation for digital forensic test image generation, *Digital Investigation*, vol. 38(S), article no. 301133, 2021.
9. K. Eckstein and M. Jahnke, Data hiding in journaling filesystems, presented at the *Digital Forensic Research Workshop*, 2005.
10. D. Forte, Dealing with forensic software vulnerabilities: Is anti-forensics a real danger? *Network Security*, vol. 2008(12), pp. 18–20, 2008.

11. A. Gehrke, Forensic Analysis of Timestamps in Selected Filesystems (in German), Bachelor of Engineering Thesis, IT Forensics, Hochschule Wismar, University of Applied Sciences: Technology, Business and Design, Wismar, Germany (it-forensik.fiw.hs-wismar.de/images/9/95/BT_AGehrke.pdf), 2020.
12. T. Göbel and H. Baier, Anti-forensics in ext4: On secrecy and usability of timestamp-based data hiding, Digital Investigation, vol. 24(S), pp. S111–S120, 2018.
13. T. Göbel and H. Baier, fishy – A framework for implementing filesystem-based data hiding techniques, in Digital Forensics and Cyber Crime, F. Breitinger and I. Baggili (Eds.), Springer, Cham, Switzerland, pp. 23–42, 2019.
14. T. Göbel, H. Baier and F. Breitinger, Data for digital forensics: Why a discussion on "how realistic is synthetic data" is dispensable, Digital Threats: Research and Practice, vol. 4(3), article no. 38, 2023.
15. T. Göbel, S. Maltan, J. Türr, H. Baier and F. Mann, ForTrace – A holistic forensic dataset synthesis framework, Forensic Science International: Digital Investigation, vol. 40(S), article no. 301344, 2022.
16. T. Göbel, T. Schäfer, J. Hachenberger, J. Türr and H. Baier, A novel approach for generating synthetic datasets for digital forensics, in Advances in Digital Forensics XVI, G. Peterson and S. Shenoi (Eds.), Springer, Cham, Switzerland, pp. 73–93, 2020.
17. C. Grajeda, F. Breitinger and I. Baggili, Availability of datasets for digital forensics – And what is missing, Digital Investigation, vol. 22(S), pp. S94–S105, 2017.
18. R. Harris, Arriving at an anti-forensics consensus: Examining how to define and control the anti-forensics problem, Digital Investigation, vol 3(S), S44–S49, 2006.
19. J. Heeger, Y. Yannikos and M. Steinebach, Exhide: Hiding data within the exFAT filesystem, Proceedings of the Sixteenth International Conference on Availability, Reliability and Security, article no. 77, 2021.
20. J. Hilgert, M. Lambertz and S. Yang, Forensic analysis of multiple device Btrfs configurations using The Sleuth Kit, Digital Investigation, vol. 26(S), pp. S21–S29, 2018.
21. E. Huebner, D. Bem and C. Wee, Data hiding in the NTFS filesystem, Digital Investigation, vol. 3(4), pp. 211–226, 2006.
22. M. Joye, On white-box cryptography, in Security of Information and Networks, A. Elci, S. Ors and B. Preneel (Eds.), Trafford Publishing, Victoria, Canada, pp. 7–12, 2008.
23. A. Juch, Btrfs Filesystem Forensics, Master's Thesis, Software Engineering/Internet Program, Faculty of Informatics, Vienna University of Technology, Vienna, Austria, 2014.
24. A. Kailus, C. Hecht and T. Göbel, fishy – A framework for implementing hiding techniques in filesystems, Proceedings of the D-A-CH Security Conference, 2018.
25. X. Lin, Introductory Computer Forensics: A Hands-On Practical Approach, Springer, Cham, Switzerland, 2018.
26. A. McDonald and M. Kuhn, StegFS: A steganographic filesystem for Linux, Proceedings of the Third International Workshop on Information Hiding, pp. 463–477, 1999.
27. C. Moch and F. Freiling, The Forensic Image Generator Generator (Forensig^2), Proceedings of the Fifth International Conference on IT Security Incident Management and IT Forensics, pp. 78–93, 2009.
28. C. Moch and F. Freiling, Evaluating the Forensic Image Generator Generator, Proceedings of the International Conference on Digital Forensics and Cyber Crime, pp. 238–252, 2011.

29. S. Neuner, A. Voyiatzis, M. Schmiedecker, S. Brunthaler, S. Katzenbeisser and E. Weippl, Time is on my side: Steganography in filesystem metadata, *Digital Investigation*, vol. 18(S), pp. S76–S86, 2016.

30. J. Park, TREDE and VMPOP: Cultivating multi-purpose datasets for digital forensics – A windows registry corpus as an example, *Digital Investigation*, vol. 26, pp. 3–18, 2018.

31. A. Qadir and A. Varol, The role of machine learning in digital forensics, *Proceedings of the Eighth International Symposium on Digital Forensics and Security*, 2020.

32. O. Rodeh, J. Bacik and C. Mason, BTRFS: The Linux B-tree filesystem, *ACM Transactions on Storage*, vol. 9(3), article no. 9, 2013.

33. M. Rogers and M. Lockheed, Anti-Forensics, Center for Education and Research in Information Assurance and Security, Department of Information and Computer Technology, Purdue University, West Lafayette, Indiana, 2005.

34. M. Scanlon, X. Du and D. Lillis, EviPlant: An efficient digital forensics challenge creation, manipulation and distribution solution, *Digital Investigation*, vol. 20(S), pp. S29–S36, 2017.

35. J. Schneider, M. Eichhorn and F. Freiling, Ambiguous filesystem partitions, *Forensic Science International: Digital Investigation*, vol. 42(S), article no. 301399, 2022.

36. H. Visti, S. Tohill and P. Douglas, Automatic creation of computer forensic test images, in *Computational Forensics*, U. Garain and F. Shafait (Eds.), Springer, Cham, Switzerland, pp. 163–175, 2015.

37. M. Wani, A. AlZahrani and W. Bhat, Filesystem anti-forensics – Types, techniques and tools, *Computer Fraud and Security*, vol. 2020(3), pp. 14–19, 2020.

38. M. Wani, W. Bhat and A. Dehghantanha, An analysis of anti-forensic capabilities of the B-tree filesystem (Btrfs), *Australian Journal of Forensic Sciences*, vol. 52(4), pp. 371–386, 2020.

39. K. Woods, C. Lee, S. Garfinkel, D. Dittrich, A. Russell and K. Kearton, Creating realistic corpora for security and forensic education, *Proceedings of the Sixth Annual Conference on Digital Forensics, Security and Law*, 2011.

40. U. Wurst, Use of Cryptographic Methods on Highly Resource-Limited Devices (in German), Ph.D. Thesis, Faculty of Computer Science, University of Stuttgart, Stuttgart, Germany (`d-nb.info/1042941734/34`), 2003.

41. B. Wyseur, W. Michiels, P. Gorissen and B. Preneel, Cryptanalysis of white-box DES implementations with arbitrary external encodings, *Proceedings of the Fourteenth International Workshop on Selected Areas in Cryptography*, pp. 264–277, 2007.

Forensic Investigations

Leveraging Client-Side User Account Data in Digital Forensic Investigations

Pulkit Garg[1], Vishal Srivastava[1], Nitesh Bharadwaj[2], and Gaurav Gupta[3]

[1] Indian Institute of Technology, Jodhpur, India
[2] National Institute of Technology, Raipur, India
[3] Ministry of Electronics and Information Technology, New Delhi, India
`gauravg@gov.in`

Abstract. Smartphones have become integral to daily routines, generating a wealth of user data with every interaction. Client-side data from smartphones is invaluable in digital forensic investigations, especially data generated while using social media apps and Google services. However, large volumes of the generated data – called user account data – are not stored on the mobile devices, but on enterprise servers.

This chapter explores the user account data maintained by three prominent service providers, Meta Platforms, Google and Microsoft, and highlights its pivotal role in digital forensic investigations. Additionally, the chapter describes the Information Extraction and Collation Tool, an automated solution designed to extract relevant information from large user account datasets. The tool facilitates comparisons with data from other users, enabling the identification of shared activities and enhancing the efficiency of investigations.

Keywords: User Account Data · Android Data Forensics · Forensic Tool

1 Introduction

Smartphones were designed to revolutionize communications via phone calls and text messages. However, as the Internet and other digital services became popular, smartphones have become powerful, ubiquitous devices that are integral to our daily lives. They enhance convenience and productivity by providing information access, entertainment, navigation, payment capabilities, and more. Smartphones are equipped with high-resolution cameras that eliminate the need for dedicated cameras and video recording devices, enabling users to effortlessly capture, store and share their cherished moments. At this time, there are approximately 6.93 billion smartphone users worldwide [12], highlighting the massive reach and importance of smartphones in modern society.

The pervasive use of smartphones renders them invaluable in digital forensic investigations because they provide access to vast repositories of client-side data. The diverse data includes call records, photos, videos, chat transcripts, browsing history, location coordinates, and more. The widespread utilization of smartphones to access social media and several Google services elevates app usage

E. Kurkowski and S. Shenoi (Eds.): DigitalForensics 2024, IFIP AICT 724, pp. 249–269, 2025.
https://doi.org/10.1007/978-3-031-71025-4_13

data to a source of indispensable information in digital forensic investigations. However, only a small amount of this information is stored on smartphones, which complicates the evidence extraction process. Fortunately, user and activity data generated during interactions with smartphone apps are preserved on enterprise servers as user account data (UAD), which digital forensic practitioners can conveniently retrieve and utilize.

Google, the primary creator of the popular Android smartphone operating system, offers several Internet-based services such as Gmail, Google Drive, Google Maps and Google Play. What is intriguing is that all these services can be managed via a single Google account on a smartphone or computer. Due to their widespread availability and user-friendly features, Google services are extremely popular among smartphone users, exceeding five billion app downloads. Users also engage in online activities related to Google Maps, browsing the Internet and using email. All these activities generate massive amounts of digital data pertaining to users and their activities. Google consistently collects and stores all this data and links the data to Google user accounts.

Smartphone users install many other apps, especially social media apps such as Facebook, Instagram and LinkedIn, that enable them to connect with friends, share information and post images. These and other user interactions generate massive amounts of user account data of value in digital forensic investigations because they provide insights into users' lives. Clearly, leveraging user account data from multiple service providers can enhance the effectiveness of digital forensic investigations.

Digital forensic professionals have begun to utilize client-side user account data in criminal investigations. However, efficiently leveraging user account data is challenging due to the large volumes and presence of numerous irrelevant details. Additionally, different service providers store user data in different formats, rendering the extraction of information very challenging. There is a great need to identify and automatically extract relevant information from multiple user account data sources in order to streamline and expedite digital forensic investigations.

This chapter analyzes user account data as potential sources of crucial client-side information. It sheds light on the extensive records of user activities preserved by tech giants such as Meta Platforms (Facebook and Instagram), Google and Microsoft (LinkedIn). Additionally, the chapter describes the Information Extraction and Collation Tool, an automated solution designed to extract relevant information from diverse user account datasets provided by the four platforms. The tool facilitates user profiling based on location history, organizational affiliations and contacts. Additionally, it supports the collation of data associated with multiple users to provide insights into their shared activities.

2   User Account Data Analysis

Over the past few years, smartphones and their services have experienced a substantial increase in user engagement. Service providers store the information

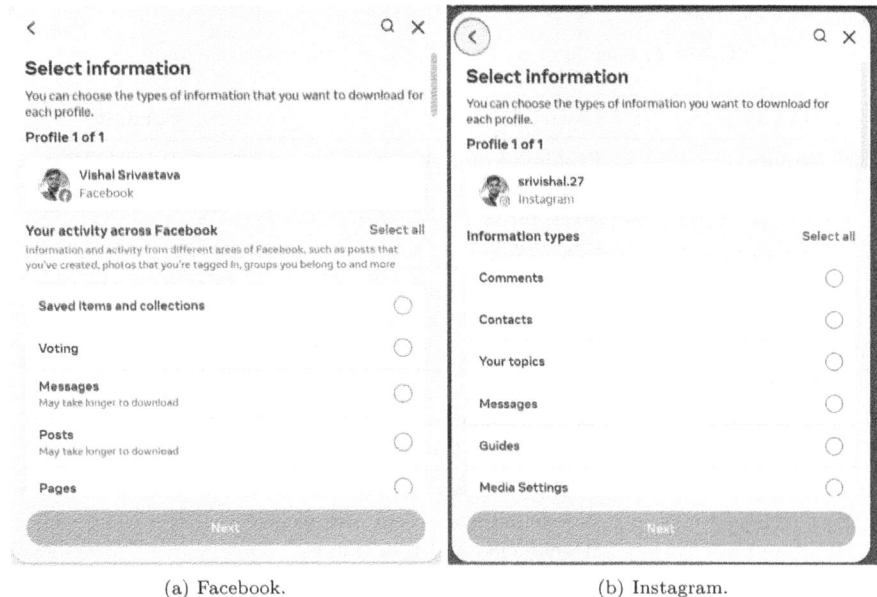

(a) Facebook.   (b) Instagram.

Fig. 1. User account data downloading options for Facebook and Instagram.

provided by the users to access services and their interactions as user account data at enterprise servers. This is done to enhance user experience, deliver personalized advertisements and provide convenient backup solutions. Most service providers enable users to download user account data via apps. The apps considered in this work include Facebook and Instagram from Meta Platforms, various Google services and LinkedIn from Microsoft.

2.1   Facebook and Instagram

Facebook and Instagram are two of the most popular social media platforms. Originally designed for users to connect with friends and family, they now enable users to share their thoughts and deeds via text, images and videos. Importantly, within the content shared by users on these platforms, there may exist information pertinent to forensic investigations.

Figure 1 shows that the Facebook and Instagram social media platforms provide users with the option to download their user account data stored at Meta Platforms [3]. Tables 1 and 2 show the diverse user account data stored by Facebook and Instagram, respectively, along with the supported formats. The data includes the user profiles, photos and videos, messages, account settings, and more.

Table 1. Facebook services, data and supported formats.

Service	Data	Format
Profile	Profile information, username, bio, posts, followers, following, posts liked, saved posts, IGTV videos, stories, synced contacts, comments, messages	JSON, ZIP
Photos and Videos	Media files of uploaded photos and videos, including captions and timestamps	JPG, MP4
Stories	Shared and archived stories, including images and videos with captions and timestamps	MP4, JSON
Messages	Direct messages, including conversations, messages sent and received, attachments and timestamps	JSON
Activity	User activity, including likes, comments, follows, unfollows and other interactions	JSON
Followers	Followers, including usernames and timestamps	JSON
Following	Followed usernames and timestamps	JSON
Saved Posts	Posts saved to collections, including post details and timestamps	JSON
IGTV Videos	IGTV videos uploaded, including video files and video information	MP4, JSON
Comments	Comments on user posts, comments on other users' posts	JSON
Likes	Posts liked by user, likes received for user posts	JSON
Explore Activity	Activity related to content user has seen on explore pages	JSON
Profile Interactions	Interactions with user profile such as profile visits and follow requests	JSON
Hashtags	Posts associated with specific hashtags and hashtags used by user	JSON
Geotags	Posts tagged with locations, posts user has tagged with locations	JSON
Account Settings	Account settings and preferences	JSON

Table 2. Instagram services, data and supported formats.

Service	Data	Format
Profile	About, posts, friends list, photos, videos, events, messages, likes, comments, groups, marketplace activity, ad activity, payment history, account activity, security, login information	HTML, JSON
Friends	Friends list, including names, profile URLs and timestamps	JSON, CSV
Posts	User posts, including text, photos, videos and timestamps	HTML, JSON
Messages	Messaging history, including sent and received messages, attachments and timestamps	HTML, JSON
Likes and Reactions	Posts and content liked by user, including reaction types	JSON
Groups	Groups joined, including posts, discussions and members	HTML, JSON
Events	Events attended or interested in, including event details and RSVPs	HTML, JSON
Marketplace Activity	Activity in Facebook Marketplace, including listings, inquiries and purchases	JSON
Ad Activity	Ad interactions, including ad details, clicks and impressions	JSON
Pages	Pages managed or administered, including posts and page insights	HTML, JSON
Videos	Videos uploaded or shared by user including details, captions and timestamps	JSON
Photos	Photos uploaded and shared by user, including details and timestamps	JSON
Comments	Comments made about user posts, user comments about other posts	JSON
Account Settings	Account settings and preferences	HTML, JSON
Account Activity	Account logs, logins and locations	JSON
Payment History	Facebook transactions	JSON

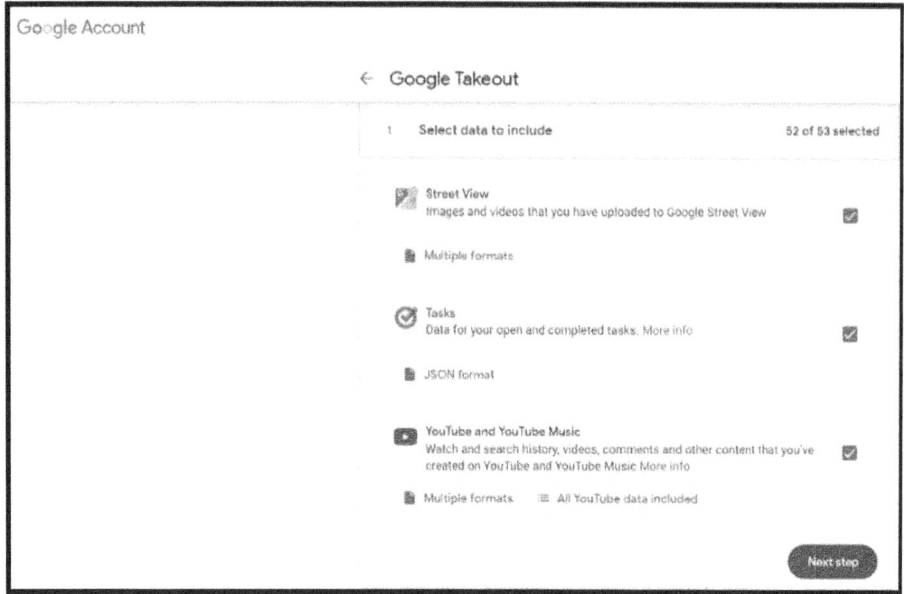

Fig. 2. User account data download options for Google services.

2.2   Google Services

Google Takeout [4] is a service that empowers users to export and download comprehensive copies of their account data accumulated by Google. Since the data collected and maintained by different Google services differs, users may select specific services to include in their user account data downloads. Figure 2 shows the user account data download options for Google services. For example, Calendar offers data related to appointments and reminders whereas Contacts provides contact information along with profile images. Fit logs daily activities and the Google Photos repository of images, videos and maps offers valuable insights into user location history and commuting routes. Collectively, Google user account data provides a comprehensive profile of user behavior, daily routines, visited locations and social connections.

Tables 3 through 6 provide detailed breakdowns of the services integrated in Google Takeout, along with the corresponding data and supported formats. The tables showcase the diverse user data that can be brought to bear in digital forensic investigations.

2.3   LinkedIn

LinkedIn, a subsidiary of Microsoft, stands out as a specialized social media platform tailored for professionals and the business community. It offers users

Table 3. Google services, data and supported formats.

Service	Data	Format
Android Device Configuration Service	Device attributes, performance data, software versions, account identifiers	HTML
Arts and Culture	Google Arts and Culture galleries created by user and user favorites	HTML, CSV
Bookmarks Bookmarks	User bookmarks (located at www.google.com/bookmarks)	HTML
Calendar	Calendar data, appointments, reminders	iCalendar
Chrome	Autofill, bookmarks, browser history, dictionary, extensions, search engines, sync settings	JSON, HTML, CSV
Classroom	Posts, submissions, roster	JSON
Contacts	Google account contacts and photos (My Contacts), contacts saved from Google product interactions such as Gmail (All Contacts)	vCard, CSV
Crisis User Reports	Answers to yes/no user report questions related to crises	CSV
Data Shared for Research	Crowdsourced donated images, Crowdsourced donated labels	JPG, TXT
Drive	Documents, drawings, forms, presentations, spreadsheets, uploads	DOX, JPG, XLSX, PPTX
Fit	Activities, daily aggregations	TCX, CSV
G Suite Marketplace	Application listings, reviews	JSON
Google Help Communities	Posted text, attachments (user's ask and reply contributions to the Google Help Communities, including text and images posted)	CSV, JSON
Google Input Tools	Learned words, input tokens and typed times	JSON
Google My Business	Information posts, reviews and replies, messaging settings, photos, videos, bookings, website (if created using Google My Business), verification address, accounts, hotel (if location is a hotel)	JSON

Table 4. Google services, data and supported formats (continued).

Service	Data	Format
Google Pay	Money sent and requested, My Activity, saved passes, Google transactions	HTML, PDF, CSV
Google Photos	Photos, videos, album metadata, photo metadata	Original Format, PNG, JPG, MP4, WEBP, JSON
Google Play Books	Purchased book metadata, content uploaded to Google Play Books	HTML, JSON
Google Play Game Services	`avatar.png`, player data, scores, achievements, quests, experience, activity, cover image, `Data.bin`, metadata, `name.bin`	PNG
Google Play Movies and TV	Linked services, notification preferences, ratings, streaming services, watchlist	CSV, JSON
Google Play Store	Installs, redemption history, library, reviews, purchase and order history, devices, subscriptions, play settings, play point details	JSON
Google Shopping	Order history, loyalty, addresses, product reviews, user and collection point data	CSV, JSON
Google+ Stream	Posts, activity log, photos, collections	Original Format, JSON, HTML
Groups	Group information, group memberships, group posts	CSV, MBOX
Hands Free	Transaction history	CSV
Hangouts	Chat history, chat attachments	Original Format, JSON
Home App	Device, room and home information	JSON
Keep	Note content, image and voice attachments	3GP, AMR, HTML
Hangouts on Air	Questions asked about user's and other users' events	CSV

Table 5. Google services, data and supported formats (continued).

Service	Data	Format
Location History	User location data while opted in	JSON, KML
Mail	Messages and attachments in user's Gmail account	MBOX
Maps	Commute routes and settings, food and drink preferences, labeled places, user personalization feedback, added dishes, products, activities	CSV, JSON
Maps (Places)	Starred places, place reviews	GeoJSON
My Activity	Timestamped activity records across Google products, image attachments, audio attachments	HTML, JSON, JPEG, MPEG
My Maps	Maps, layers, features, media	KMZ
News	Topics, articles, magazines, topics followed or saved on Google News	TXT
Google Posts	Google Posts and Cameos text content, Posts on Google Images, Cameos videos	JSON, JPG, MP4
Profile	Profile settings, directory of previous profile and cover photos, current profile and cover photos	Original Format, JSON
Purchases and Reservations	Upcoming and past purchases and reservations from Google services, including transactions, deliveries, online orders, upcoming and past reservations from services such as Assistant and Gmail, recurring subscription payments	JSON
Saved	URLs and titles of saved items (e.g., images, places, web pages) from Google Search and Maps	CSV
Search Contributions	Commentaries on sports and other search results, thumb ratings for movies, TV shows, music albums, etc., tags and reviews added to movies and search results	JSON

Table 6. Google services, data and supported formats (continued).

Service	Data	Format
Shopping Lists	Items added to lists, shopped on Google or checked off	CSV
Street View	Video files, uploaded spherical images, sensor data	Video, Image, Sensor Data
Tasks	Open and completed tasks	JSON
Textcube Blog	Blog files from Textcube, blog URL mappings, blog file mappings	CSV
YouTube	Video media and metadata, history, subscriptions, playlists, comments, live chats, community posts and attachments, stories, chats, community contributions	HTML, JSON
YouTube Gaming	Uploaded emojis and sponsorship badges	Original Format, PNG

a unique avenue for personal branding, job exploration and networking by enabling them to create and craft profiles that serve as their digital resumes. The profiles showcase users' professional trajectories, academic and work histories, affiliations, noteworthy accomplishments, and more [5].

Figure 3 shows the user account data download options for LinkedIn. Table 7 shows that LinkedIn provides users with comprehensive user account data, including user profiles, connections and messages, in the CSV format. LinkedIn user account data can have significant relevance in digital forensic investigations, especially when dealing with professional or business cases.

3   Privacy and Security Challenges

In light of technological advancements and the growing dependence of modern society on electronic devices, digital forensic professionals leverage new information sources to extract forensic artifacts. These sources encompass electronic devices as well as electronic data, including user account data, stored on the devices and at service provider systems.

Section 65(B) of the Indian Evidence Act addresses the admissibility of electronic records as evidence in legal proceedings. Under this section, it is not mandatory to present a certificate of admissibility for electronic evidence from a responsible authority during judicial proceedings. This provision authorizes the utilization of user account data in criminal investigations and considers it as admissible records in courts of law. However, leveraging user account data in

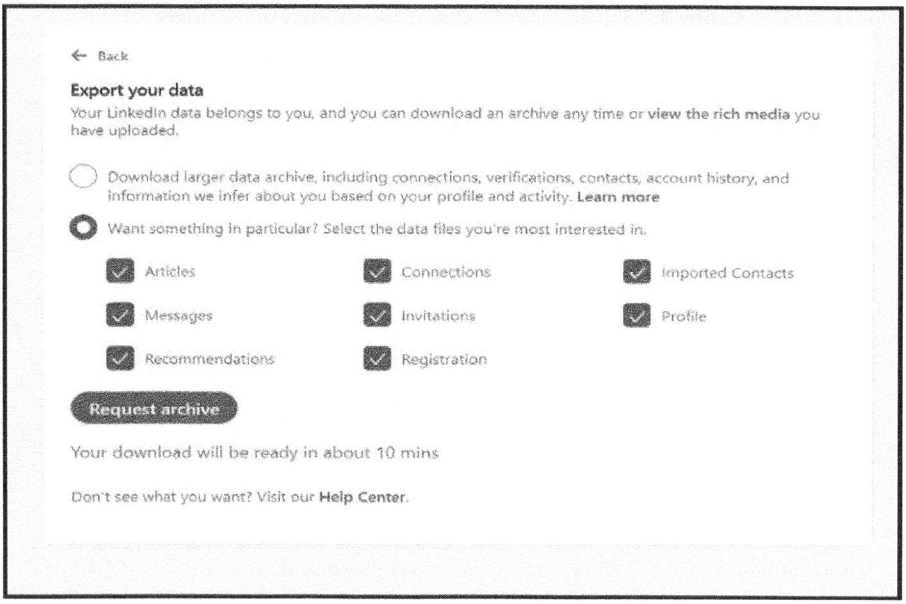

Fig. 3. User account data download options for LinkedIn.

digital forensic investigations raises privacy and security concerns that must be addressed carefully.

As demonstrated above, user account data encompasses a broad spectrum of information, including personal information, that raises significant privacy concerns when subjected to analysis, even for legitimate purposes. Digital forensic practitioners frequently encounter challenges in accessing and analyzing user account data due to the need to obtain legal authorizations, which can be complex and time-consuming. Additionally, it is vital to secure the collected user account data over the entire digital forensics process. Security lapses and breaches can lead to the release, misuse and abuse of sensitive user account information that could result in severe consequences to users as well as legal repercussions for digital forensic practitioners and prosecutors. Therefore, all the individuals involved in the digital forensic process and prosecution must adhere to rigorous protocols and implement strict measures to safeguard the privacy and security of sensitive user account data.

4 Related Work

Modern digital forensic investigations depend heavily on client-side information to piece together the facts and better understand the circumstances of cases. Maus et al. [6] have discussed the examination of Android device logs to acquire geodata with corresponding timestamps. Spreitzenbarth et al. [11] have

Table 7. Linkedin services, data and supported formats.

Service	Data	Format
Profile	Profile and contact information, summary, experience, education, skills, recommendations, interests, accomplishments	CSV
Connections	Connections, including names, connection dates, current positions	CSV
Messages	Messaging history, including sent and received messages, attachments and timestamps	CSV
Posts and Activities	Posts, articles, comments, likes, shares and activities in user's feed	CSV
Groups	Information about joined groups, including posts, discussions and members	CSV
Recommendations	Recommendations given and received, including text and endorsements	CSV
Job Applications	Positions applied, application dates and status	CSV
Ads and Sponsored Content	Ads and sponsored content interacted with, including details and click-through data	CSV
Account Settings	Account settings and preferences	CSV
Endorsements	Endorsements given and received, including skills endorsed	CSV
Events	Events attended and shown interest in	CSV
Followed Companies	Companies followed, updates from followed companies	CSV
Education and Positions	Education details and positions	CSV
Articles	Published articles, drafts saved by user	HTML

extracted location data from Android smartphone apps using the Android Data Extractor Lite forensic tool; their experiments demonstrate that Android apps provide more accurate information than network operators. Scrivens and Lin [10] and Zhang et al. [14] have analyzed the information stored by the instant messaging apps and have developed procedures from extracting forensically-relevant data. Bays and Karabiyik [2] have explored the forensic potential of two popular location-sharing apps on iOS and Android devices, focusing on locally-stored data for previous location tracking. However, these techniques primarily extract information from local device storage and logs, posing persistent risks of data tampering.

To reduce the data tampering risks, researchers have focused on device data stored in cloud platforms. Roussev et al. [9] have highlighted the incompatibility of established forensic techniques and tools with the software as a service (SaaS) model; responding to this deficiency, they developed a tool for cloud data extraction using Google Docs APIs. Williams and Yerby [13] raised privacy concerns about Facebook and Google apps by demonstrating the recovery of social interactions, pictures, documents and location tracking information. Arshad et al. [1] have demonstrated the challenges faced in analyzing social media data due to its vastness, diversity and unstructured nature. To address the challenges, they developed a multilayer semantic framework for integrated forensic acquisition from social media.

While cloud approaches extract more forensically-relevant information than can be obtained from local device storage, few efforts have attempted to leverage user account data, which is a valuable information source. Additionally, existing forensic tools lack the ability to examine information about multiple users and extract evidence regarding shared activities, functionality that is often required in digital forensic investigations. This research has attempted to address the need by developing an information extraction and collation tool that is tailored to process user account data effectively and efficiently.

5 Information Extraction and Collation Tool

The Information Extraction and Collation Tool (IECT) is designed to gather relevant information from multiple user account data sources, in particular, Facebook, Instagram, Google services and LinkedIn. The tool generates a comprehensive list of user data and activities required for user profiling. Additionally, given user account data for multiple users, the tool provides an option for comparing their user profiles and identifying shared records and activities, such as mutual friends, common social connections (followers and followed users) and locations where they might have met. These details can assist digital forensic practitioners in inferring and validating the linkages of individuals involved in incidents.

5.1 Information Sources

Social media and other service providers routinely gather and retain vast quantities of user account data, of which only a small fraction is of forensic relevance. Given that the storage format of user account data is consistent across all the users associated with a service provider, it is possible to pre-determine the locations that hold critical data. The tool harnesses the inherent structural uniformity of user account data to pinpoint and extract relevant data while efficiently filtering extraneous data. The targeted information sources include Facebook, Instagram, Google services and LinkedIn.

Facebook and Instagram. The Facebook and Instagram social media platforms have significant user engagement, resulting in the generation of large amounts of user account data on a daily basis. The tool discerns and extracts the following forensically-relevant data from the two platforms:

- **Friends and Followers:** Friends and followers are connections on social media platforms that include individuals known to a user and with whom the user engages in information sharing. The information is valuable in forensic investigations because it helps establish relationships, communications patterns and potential associations between individuals of interest.
- **Posts:** A significant portion of social media posts involve travel and dining experiences, offering insights into a user's recent whereabouts. When a user tags a city or restaurant in posts, social media platforms store the corresponding locations. Additionally, the images uploaded by the user often contain metadata, allowing for the extraction of precise timestamps. The tool systematically iterates through all the posts involving a user, extracting coordinates and timestamps for further analysis.

Google Services. Google Takeout provides vast amounts of user account data. The tool identifies and extracts the following forensically-relevant data from Google services:

- **Contacts:** Users store the contact information of friends and family members. Similar to Facebook friends and Instagram followers, the contact information provides valuable information about associations between individuals of interest in an investigation.
- **Google Photos:** Images uploaded by users to Google Photos contain location coordinates and associated timestamps, indicating the presence of the users at specific locations and times. The tool iterates over all the images and filters their metadata to extract location coordinates. The information enables digital forensic practitioners to map the movements of users and potentially establish crucial timelines and patterns of behavior relevant to investigations.
- **Maps:** Google collects user locations periodically when users opt in for location history. This process operates independently of user activity on smartphones and continuously gathers location data in the background. The collected location history is stored on Google servers as Place Visited and Activity Segment. Place Visited contains information about the places a user has visited, including coordinates and starting and ending times of each visit whereas Activity Segment records the user trips from one location to another, including the starting and ending coordinates of the trips and their starting and ending times.
  The tool extracts location information from Google servers to identify user position at different timestamps. This data can be crucial in digital forensic investigations, providing insights into user movements and activities over time.

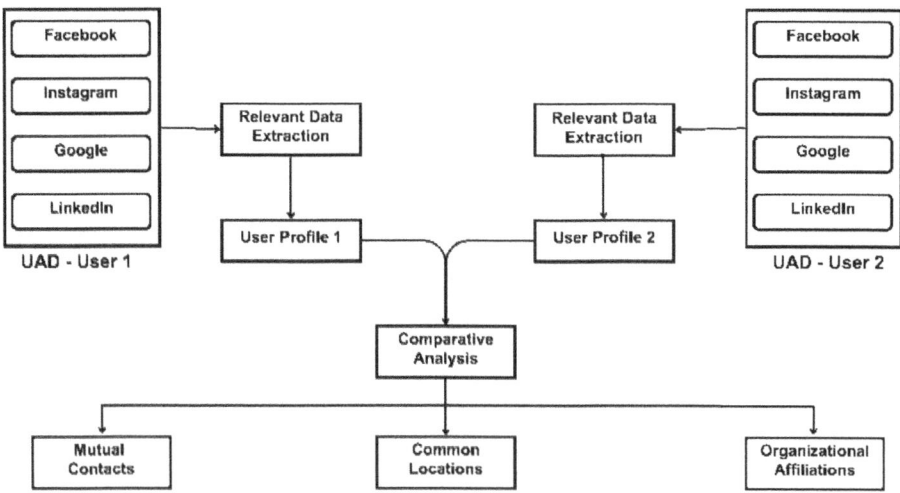

Fig. 4. Tool workflow for generating and comparing user profiles.

LinkedIn. LinkedIn provides insights into user career trajectories and professional associations that are valuable in professional- and business-related cases. LinkedIn user account data contains diverse information from which the tool identifies and extracts the following forensically-relevant data:

- **Profiles:** As mentioned above, retrieving a user's past associations with various organizations is useful in social network analysis. A user's Positions file accessible via LinkedIn user account data lists the user's previous and current organizations, along with the user's positions and position start dates and end dates.
- **Connections:** LinkedIn connections provide information about professional colleagues and associates who may differ from the personal contacts identified in social media and other services. Importantly, the information provided includes the names of the individuals as well as their current and previous job positions and employers.

5.2 Implementation Details

The Information Extraction and Collation Tool is been developed as an installable desktop application using Python 3 [8] and the Tkinter library [7] to ensure full compatibility with the Windows operating system. The tool is designed to perform two functions, profiling users and comparing multiple user profiles. Figure 4 shows the workflow for generating and comparing user profiles.

User Profiling. The tool excels at profiling multiple users simultaneously, requiring only the number of users and user account data file paths as inputs as

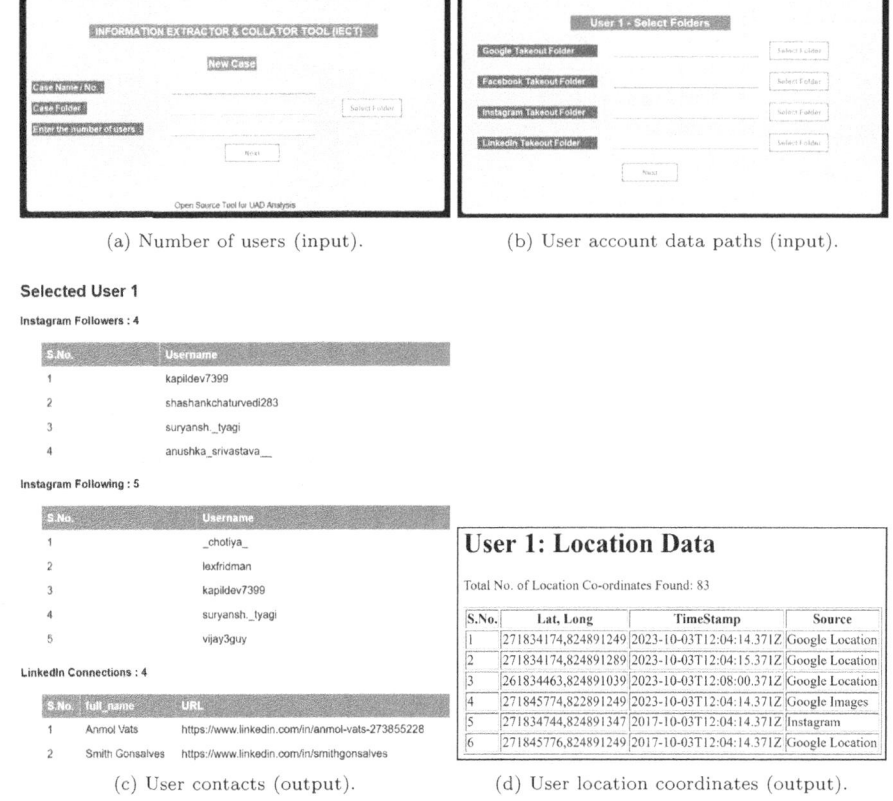

(a) Number of users (input).   (b) User account data paths (input).

(c) User contacts (output).   (d) User location coordinates (output).

Fig. 5. Information Extraction and Collation Tool inputs and outputs.

shown in Figures 5(a) and 5(b). For each user, the tool employs JSON/HTML parsers and CSV readers (as needed) to extract forensically-relevant data from multiple user accounts. If similar information is found in multiple user accounts, the tool consolidates and compiles them to create a comprehensive list. Essentially, the tool provides an all-encompassing contact list along with detailed user location histories with timestamps and a comprehensive record of current and past and user affiliations. These files are stored in the system for further analysis and comparison of multiple users.

Figures 5(c) and 5(d) show the generated user's contact file and location history file, respectively. The tool also helps track the previous movements of users by visualizing them on maps utilizing the data obtained from the Activity Segment in Google user account data.

The tool provides digital forensic practitioners with the ability to query the generated files according to their needs, enhancing flexibility and customization. For example, practitioners can refine the location results by specifying time periods and the distances from specific location coordinates. These additional parameters can be input directly to the tool to obtain precise tailored results. This functionality enables digital forensic practitioners to extract relevant information efficiently, facilitating targeted data interpretation and analysis.

Comparing Multiple User Profiles. In digital forensic investigations, it is often necessary to establish connections between multiple users of interest. The tool supports this important feature by identifying mutual contacts, pinpointing shared location coordinates at specific timestamps and uncovering shared organizational affiliations. As shown in Figure 6(a), the user provides the required parameters for comparison, ultimately yielding the following results:

- **Mutual Contacts:** The tool systematically scans the contact list for all users, computing the frequency of each contact. When the computed frequency matches the total number of users, the contact is identified as a mutual contact. The results are stored as HTML files (Figure 6(b)).
- **Common Locations:** To determine whether two or more users shared a common location at a specific timestamp, it is necessary to accommodate potentially minute variations in the location coordinates. The tool computes calculates the distance d between the (ψ_1, λ_1) and (ψ_2, λ_2) latitude-longitude coordinates using the Haversine formula:

$$\Delta\psi = \psi_2 - \psi_1$$
$$\Delta\lambda = \lambda_2 - \lambda_1$$
$$x = \sin^2\left(\frac{\Delta\psi}{2}\right) + \cos(\psi_1) \cdot \cos(\psi_2) \cdot \sin^2\left(\frac{\Delta\lambda}{2}\right)$$
$$d = 2 \cdot r \cdot \sin^{-1}\left(\sqrt{x}\right)$$

The tool analyzes the location data of a user, specifically the location coordinates obtained from social media posts, images and Places Visited from Google, searching for instances where other users' location data is recorded within a 15-minute time window. When such data is found, the Haversine formula is employed to measure the distance between the corresponding coordinates. The tool identifies two coordinates as a match if they are no more than 100 meters apart. The coordinates that satisfy the timestamp and location criteria are considered as potential meeting points. These results are also stored in HTML files as shown in Figure 6(c). To enhance understanding, the location coordinates are also visually represented on maps that are presented in an interactive format.
- **Organizational Affiliations:** The tool identifies shared organizational affiliations in much the same way as it does for mutual contacts. However, it extends the analysis by considering the start and end dates of the individuals' positions in organizations.

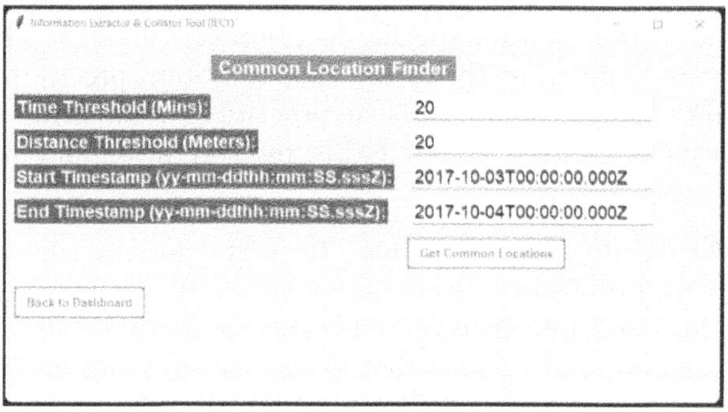

(a) User comparison functionality.

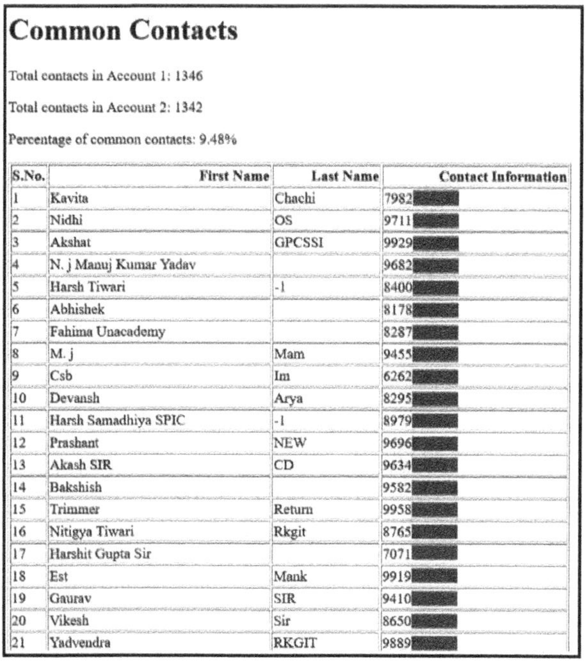

(b) Common User 1 and User 2 contacts (output).

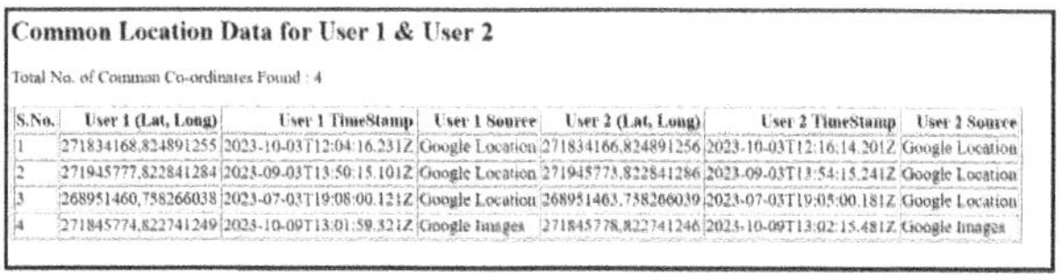

(c) Common User 1 and User 2 location coordinates (output).

Fig. 6. Information Extraction and Collation Tool snapshots.

6   Application Scenarios

The tool offers automated user profiling and facilitates the identification of shared records and activities among multiple users, a capability essential in forensic investigations. The following application scenarios highlight several tool use cases:

- **Missing Person Search:** When searching for a missing person (user), it is very useful to know their previous locations and daily routines. The tool utilizes user account data to expedite the search, providing essential location and activity details along with the user's known contacts.
- **Comprehensive Analysis:** The use of multiple user account data sources in user profiling enables the collection of comprehensive details about a user. This is important because valuable information resides in multiple sources. By consolidating data from multiple sources and preventing potential tampering when accessing data across different platforms, the tool can provide accurate information even in complex scenarios. This multi-source approach enhances the completeness and reliability of the collected data.
- **Intelligence Gathering:** The tool provides a comprehensive overview of a user's social network and other activities, providing insights into behavior patterns and highlighting connections with other individuals of interest.
- **Intellectual Property Theft:** The tool provides information about a user's past and present organizational affiliations as well as skills and accomplishments related to potential intellectual property theft. Moreover, the user's contacts and social network activities can reveal associations with competitors and/or co-conspirators.
- **Witness Validation:** Information provided by the tool can be used to validate the statements of witnesses and defendants by establishing timelines, verifying sequences of events and detecting activity patterns and behaviors. Comparing multiple users simultaneously can help identify potential discrepancies.
- **Data Recovery:** When a smartphone malfunctions or is damaged, the tool offers an alternative means for extracting forensically-relevant information.

7   Conclusions

User engagement with smartphone apps has increased significantly in recent years. This generates massive amounts of user account data that are valuable in digital forensic investigations. However, not all the data is permanently stored on smartphones, posing challenges for digital forensic professionals who need to extract pertinent client-side information. Fortunately, the service providers of smartphone apps such as Meta Platforms, Google and Microsoft maintain user account data on their servers to make it easily accessible to users.

This chapter has examined the importance of user account data from Facebook, Instagram, Google services and LinkedIn, highlighting the various types of user account data and the supported formats. It also describes the Information Extraction and Collation Tool, an automated solution designed to pinpoint and extract relevant client-side information from large user account datasets. It provides a comprehensive user profile that includes users contacts, location history and organizational affiliations. By capitalizing on the structural similarities of user account datasets, the tool anticipates potential information sources in advance. The tool also facilitates comparisons with data from other users, enabling the identification of shared activities and enhancing the efficiency of investigative processes.

Future research will extend the tool to analyzing chats and messages stored in user account datasets. By leveraging natural language understanding techniques, this extension will support advanced user profiling. Additionally, measures will be implemented to ensure the integrity and confidentiality of processed user account data, bolstering the overall veracity and security of digital forensic investigations.

References

1. H. Arshad, A. Jantan, G. Hoon and A. Butt, A multilayered semantic framework for integrated forensic acquisition from social media, *Digital Investigation*, vol. 29, pp. 147–158, 2019.
2. J. Bays and U. Karabiyik, Forensic analysis of third party location applications in Android and iOS, *Proceedings of the IEEE Conference on Computer Communications Workshops*, 2019.
3. Facebook Help Center, Download a copy of your information on Facebook, Meta Platforms, Menlo Park, California (facebook.com/help/212802592074644), 2024.
4. Information and Technology Services, Getting started with Google Takeout, University of Michigan, Ann Arbor, Michigan (documentation.its.umich.edu/google-takeout), 2024.
5. LinkedIn Help, Download your account data, LinkedIn, Sunnyvale, California (linkedin.com/help/linkedin/answer/a1339364/downloading-your-account-data), 2024.
6. S. Maus, H. Hofken and M. Schuba, Forensic analysis of geodata in Android smartphones, *Proceedings of the Third International Conference on Cybercrime, Security and Digital Forensics*, 2011.
7. Python Software Foundation, Graphical User Interfaces with Tk, Wilmington, Delaware (docs.python.org/3/library/tk.html), 2024.
8. Python Software Foundation, Python 3.12.4 Documentation, Wilmington, Delaware (docs.python.org/3), 2024.
9. V. Roussev, I. Ahmed, A. Barreto, S. McCulley and V. Shanmughan, Cloud forensics – Tool development studies and future outlook, *Digital Investigation*, vol. 18, pp. 79–95, 2016.
10. N. Scrivens and X. Lin, Android digital forensics: Data, extraction and analysis, *Proceedings of the ACM Turing 50th Celebration Conference*, article no. 26, 2017.
11. M. Spreitzenbarth, S. Schmitt and F. Freiling, Comparing sources of location data from Android smartphones, in *Advances in Digital Forensics VIII*, G. Peterson and S. Shenoi (Eds.), Springer, Berlin Heidelberg, Germany, pp. 143–157, 2012.
12. A. Turner, How many smartphones are in the world? (2024), *Bankmycell* (bankmycell.com/blog/how-many-phones-are-in-the-world), March 13, 2024.

13. E. Williams and J. Yerby, Google and Facebook data retention and location tracking through forensic cloud analysis, *Proceedings of the Sixteenth Southern Association for Information Systems Conference*, 2019.

14. H. Zhang, L. Chen and Q. Liu, Digital forensic analysis of instant messaging applications on Android smartphones, *Proceedings of the International Conference on Computing, Networking and Communications*, pp. 647–651, 2018.

Honeypot-Based Data Collection for Dark Web Investigations Using the Tor Network

Krishan Pal Singh, Emmanuel Pilli, and Vijay Laxmi

Malaviya National Institute of Technology, Jaipur, India
espilli.cse@mnit.ac.in

Abstract. The Dark Web presents a challenging and complex environment where cyber criminals conduct illicit activities with high degrees of anonymity and privacy. This chapter describes a honeypot-based data collection approach for Dark Web browsing that incorporates honeypots on three isolated virtual machines, including production honeypots, an onion-website-based research honeypot (Honey Onion) offering illegal services and a log server that collects and securely stores the honeypot logs. Experiments conducted over 14 days collected more than 250 requests on the Honey Onion service and in excess of 28,000 chat records from the Dark Web forum. The log server also monitored Honey Onion traffic, providing details such as packet types, timestamps, network data, and HTTP requests. The data collection results provide valuable insights into Dark Web activities, including malicious, benign and uncategorized activities. The data analysis identified common user categories such as malicious actors, researchers and security professionals, and uncategorized actors. The experimental results demonstrate that honeypot-based data collection can advance Dark Web investigations as well as enable the development of effective cyber security strategies and efforts to combat cyber crime in the Dark Web.

Keywords: Dark Web Investigations · Data Collection · The Onion Router · Honey Onion Service · Production Honeypot · Research Honeypot

1 Introduction

The Dark Web is a cryptic domain that exists below the Surface Web and Deep Web and operates outside the purview of traditional search engines [13]. The Dark Web is deliberately obscured and is only accessed via specialized means such as Freenet [6], Invisible Internet Protocol (I2P) [2], The Onion Router (Tor) [7] and ZeroNet [36]. Tor, the most widely used method for accessing the Dark Web, is a decentralized network that enables anonymous communications by routing Internet traffic through volunteer-operated servers or nodes, encrypting and re-encrypting the data multiple times. Tor utilizes an open-source infrastructure that incorporates a sophisticated multi-layer encryption mechanism called onion routing, which is why Tor is named The Onion Router [7].

© IFIP International Federation for Information Processing 2025
Published by Springer Nature Switzerland AG 2025
E. Kurkowski and S. Shenoi (Eds.): DigitalForensics 2024, IFIP AICT 724, pp. 271–290, 2025.
https://doi.org/10.1007/978-3-031-71025-4_14

The Dark Web thrives in the depths of encrypted networks, giving users anonymity and protecting them from surveillance, unlike the Surface Web that comprises pages that are indexed and accessible using conventional search engines [17]. Privacy plays a crucial role in safeguarding the principles of free expression and enabling individuals to evade oppressive regimes [32]. However, the Dark Web is also a fertile environment for cyber criminals, illicit marketplaces and malicious activities. Indeed, with an estimated 2.5 million users daily, the Dark Web has become a hive of nefarious activity [29]. Unfortunately, law enforcement entities and cyber security professionals encounter considerable obstacles when investigating and monitoring illegal activities conducted on the Dark Web [3].

Honeypots are cyber security systems that attract and deceive malicious actors into interacting with simulated environments [38]. In the context of the Dark Web, honeypots can play a crucial role in data collection and analysis, enabling law enforcement entities and researchers to gain insights into the patterns, trends and tactics of malicious actors [15]. Honeypots also facilitate the passive acquisition of data about malicious actor behaviors while operating within ethical and legal constraints [24].

This chapter describes an innovative approach that leverages Tor to identify and investigate Dark Web activities. The approach employs a production honeypot deployed as a Honey Onion service that gathers intelligence about malicious activities by closely monitoring a highly-secure Dark Web chat forum. Also, it employs a research honeypot that focuses on discerning the intentions of malicious actors and identifying potential threats.

2   Background and Related Work

This section describes background information and examines the literature on Dark Web investigations and data collection using honeypots.

2.1   Background

Modern society relies heavily on the Surface Web for numerous purposes such as social networking, online shopping, video streaming, news and research [28]. In contrast, the anonymous Deep Web comprises intranets, networks and websites that are intentionally made inaccessible to regular browsing [13]. It operates as a globally-untraceable network that caters to individuals with potentially illegal intentions as well as profitable enterprises dealing with malware services, child sex abuse material and numerous other contraband goods and services [37].

While anonymizing tools such as I2P and Freenet provide decentralized communications options with guaranteed anonymity [15, 20], Tor remains the most prominent gateway to the Dark Web. Figure 1 shows the Tor architecture. It leverages onion routing, in which data packets are encrypted and forwarded through numerous relays (like the layers of an onion) before arriving at their destinations.

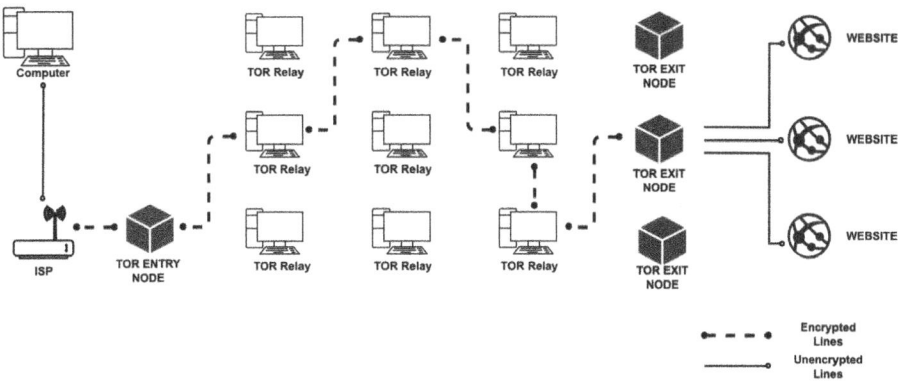

Fig. 1. Tor architecture [3].

Researchers have conducted investigations of the social effects of the Dark Web and how governments and security organizations can manage Dark Web activities to protect society [19]. Tazi et al. [33] have focused on configurations, programs and authorization strategies to access the Dark Web, emphasizing safety measures, particularly for new users to cope with threats posed by malware and identity theft. Nazah et al. [26] have studied the Dark Web, its criminal activities and potential crime control methods.

The Dark Web serves as platform for myriad illicit activities. It is used very effectively by terrorist organizations such as the Islamic State to disseminate misinformation, recruit individuals and distribute materials that support terrorism [12]. On average, daily transactions in Dark Web markets involving diverse goods and services exceed $2 million [5, 29]. Common goods include child pornography, narcotics, firearms and fake passports; activities include human trafficking and hiring assassins [14]. A notorious example is the Silk Road, which operated in the Dark Web for approximately 2.5 years before being shut down by the Federal Bureau of Investigation in October 2013. During its operation, the Silk Road processed more than $1.2 billion in transactions, making it one of the most prominent illegal online marketplaces [35]. Strong law enforcement efforts have resulted in Dark Web entities remaining active for only 200 to 300 days on average [30]. Unfortunately, the increased use of cryptocurrencies such as Bitcoin and Ethereum renders online illicit markets more accessible. In fact, the three largest illicit marketplaces in the Dark Web account for 65% of all cryptocurrency market listings, enabling anonymous payments for enhanced security [35].

2.2   Honeypot-Based Data Collection

Honeypots are effective instruments for collecting data about cyber threats and attacks [21]. The systems are configured to present themselves as attractive and susceptible victims, enticing potential attackers to engage in extended interac-

Table 1. Honeypot classification.

Honeypot Basis	Honeypot Type	Examples
Purpose-Based	Production Honeypot	Cowrie, Honeyd, Snort
	Research Honeypot	Glastopf, Conpot
Interaction-Based	Low-Interaction Honeypot	Honeyd, Kippo, Glastopf
	Medium-Interaction Honeypot	Dionea, Nepenthes, Thug
	High-Interaction Honeypot	Specter, Capture-HPC

tions with them. Data collected by honeypots provides deep understanding of attacker objectives, strategies, tactics and methods [34].

Honeypots are classified according to their purpose and degree of user interactions (Table 1). With regard to their purpose, honeypots are categorized as production honeypots or research honeypots. Production honeypots draw attackers away from real systems, protecting critical assets and reducing potential damage. These simulated systems actively observe the actions of attackers to acquire up-to-date information about evolving cyber threats [22].

In contrast, research honeypots serve the broader purpose of acquiring knowledge about the conduct of attackers and their methodologies. They are widely used by government agencies, military entities, educational institutions and enterprises to gain insights into the strategies employed by malicious entities, enhancing proactive security measures and reducing cyber risks [24]. Leveraging honeypots in network security complements traditional security mechanisms and enhances incident detection and response. Organizations strengthen their cyber security postures by deliberately deploying and vigilantly monitoring honeypots to gain valuable expertise that advances attack protection, detection and mitigation efforts [4, 23].

Deployed honeypots engage in varying levels of interactions with malicious actors. Low-interaction honeypots simulate restricted services to gather initial information about potential security breaches. Medium-interaction honeypots provide attackers with realistic responses that provide intelligence and help redirect their activities without arousing suspicion. High-interaction honeypots offer engaging environments for collecting comprehensive data on attacker tactics, techniques and procedures; they are particularly valuable for identifying advanced zero-day attacks [16]. Honeypots gather valuable information such as attacker IP addresses, attack methods, malware samples and communications patterns, helping understand the latest cyber threats, detect emerging attack patterns and enhance security postures [11].

2.3   Data Collection in Dark Web Investigations

Honeypots play a crucial role in Dark Web investigations, attracting potential malicious actors and providing security analysts with insights into their goals, strategies and methods. This information helps understand the latest cyber threats and identify new attack patterns, contributing to improved security [18, 27]. Honeypots are particularly effective at detecting ransomware outbreaks and offering early warnings that identify and counter ransomware.

Research has shown that monitoring Tor network traffic in the Dark Web using honeypots is effective for studying criminal activities and identifying malicious behaviors [8, 31]. One study [38] evaluated the effectiveness of a honeypot set up in the Dark Web for more than seven months. It collected data on criminal activities and provided valuable insights into preventative measures. Security and flexibility were ensured by using virtual machines (VMs) to host web servers and log servers. Other studies [9, 32] have demonstrated the importance of deploying multiple honeypots to increase data collection and address problems such as insufficient comment data filtration to prevent future security breaches.

2.4 Deploying Honeypots in the Dark Web

The effective deployment of honeypots in the Dark Web requires a meticulous and comprehensive strategy for gathering data while maintaining operational security. Ethical and legal considerations are paramount when implementing these deceptive systems, necessitating adherence to ethical and legal frameworks and striking a balance between knowledge acquisition and individual rights [10, 38]. Maintaining anonymity is vital as well as ensuring that honeypots operate covertly to avoid detection and evasion [4, 18].

Robust monitoring mechanisms capturing a wide range of activities and interactions provide insights into criminal behavior, helping counter their objectives, strategies and methods [21, 34]. Collaboration between researchers and cyber security professionals is essential to adapting to the dynamic Dark Web landscape, improving data collection and combating crime [31]. Flexibility and adaptability are crucial for honeypot efficacy; continual modifications are required to outsmart targets [8]. Privacy and data protection measures such as restricted access and encryption are imperative to safeguard the data collected by honeypots [27]. Indeed, a holistic approach that considers ethical, legal, technical and operational aspects is vital to deploying honeypots in Dark Web investigations [10, 38].

2.5 Research Gaps

While honeypots have gained traction in Dark Web investigations, a notable research gap is their enduring viability and adaptability in the dynamic Dark Web landscape. Current research has focused on their effectiveness at attracting malicious actors and monitoring their activities. However, there are questions about honeypot resilience over time, especially when dealing with skilled adversaries. Expert attackers continually refine their strategies to evade honeypots, diminishing their long-term efficacy at providing consistent insights into attacker activities [1, 14]. Standardizing honeypot deployments to provide comparative and generalized findings is essential. Additionally, effective analysis and interpretation of honeypot data are critical. Resilient analytical frameworks and

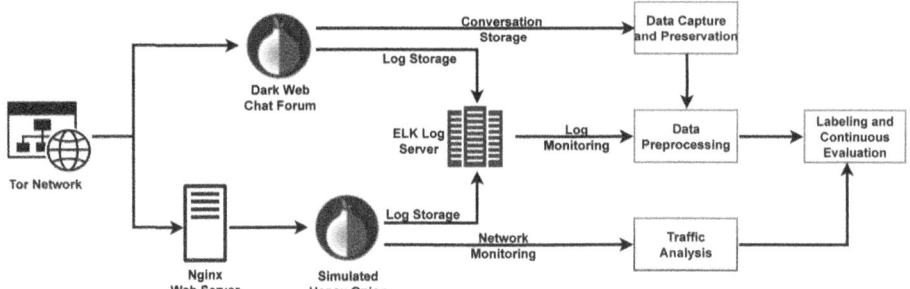

Fig. 2. Honeypot deployment environment.

specialized tools are also required for the effective analysis and interpretation of honeypot data [25].

3 Honeypot Data Collection Approach

The honeypot data collection approach for the Dark Web leveraged an onion service simulation featuring production and research honeypots. Additionally, a production honeypot was deployed in a Dark Web chat forum, its primary objective being to capture and store conversations and logs for analysis. The system engaged simulated Honey Onions to attract and interact with users in the Tor network, ensuring data collection while maintaining anonymity. The chat conversations were securely stored and analyzed using an ELK (Elasticsearch, Logstash, Kibana) log server to ensure efficient data capture and preservation. Rigorous preprocessing of the data was performed to refine its quality and utility, providing for more accurate insights.

Figure 2 provides an overview of the honeypot deployment environment. The implemented system provides unique perspectives on Dark Web browsing activities and criminal behaviors by emphasizing accurate emulation and continuous monitoring via honeypots.

3.1 Overview

This research sought to create and operate a simulated Honey Onion service designed to attract malicious actors and engage in meaningful interactions to capture valuable intelligence. This involved determining the type of onion service to be emulated and specifying situational awareness requirements, which highlighted the potential challenges and risks. To bolster honeypot credibility, a research honeypot was aligned with Honey Onion to create a research honeypot subsystem that would attract malicious actors. The research honeypot subsystem was established as a standalone virtualized environment in order to explore different implementations that would enhance attractiveness which maintaining separation from the operational Honey Onion service.

Malware and malicious actors strive to identify and evade virtualized machine environments. Detection techniques are well-documented and relatively straightforward to implement. However, the utility of these techniques has diminished as legitimate systems increasingly adopt virtualized machine environments for their resilience and cost-efficiency. Honeypots are widely deployed as virtualized systems, often exhibiting lower levels of fidelity. Virtualized machine environments allow the execution of multiple tools simultaneously, efficiently using the hardware and offering low-maintenance operations for multiple honeypots via a single connection. Depending on the resemblance of a production honeypot to an onion service, a virtualized honeypot can serve several essential functions. These include incident response and system restoration planning, system testing and validation, assessing the impacts of security measures, evaluating device security, vulnerability scanning and penetration testing.

Designing Dark Web Honeypots and Identifying Target Services. This task involves a thorough analysis of the Dark Web environment to identify valuable data sources such as illicit marketplaces and chat forums. Understanding these targets is vital to creating honeypots that attract malicious actors. The strategic placement of honeypots in locations known for malicious activities advances data collection efforts.

Mimicking Dark Web Nodes and Websites. The effectiveness of honeypots depends on their ability to mimic real Dark Web nodes and websites. The likelihood of targeted actors interacting with honeypots increases when the decoys accurately replicate visual styles and content found in the Dark Web.

The first step was to identify well-known Dark Web services for their involvement in illicit activities and understand their characteristics for accurate imitation. To entice malicious actors, Honey Onion was endowed with fictitious credentials and fake data that appeared to be genuine. Additionally, attractive bait that fit in with illicit Dark Web activities – such as hosting listings of illicit products – was dangled.

Honey Onion was equipped with a research honeypot for constant monitoring and in-depth data analysis to identify guard nodes, user patterns and possible service requests. To ensure that the honeypots continued to gather valuable data, response and mitigation strategies were instituted to isolate compromised honeypots, analyze the methods used by the targeted actors and reinforce security measures.

Attracting Malicious Tor Network Actors. Two primary strategies were implemented to attract Tor traffic and actors to Honey Onion. One was advertising the service on a popular Dark Web chat forum and the other was to emulate standard Dark Web marketplace activity patterns to avoid suspicion. The honeypot targeted specific malicious behaviors by promoting illicit substances on

Table 2. Experimental setup.

Hardware Details	
Operating System	Linux Mint
Memory	8 GB RAM
Processor	Intel Core i7 9th Gen
Virtualization Environment	VirtualBox v6.1
Software Details	
Simulated Onion Services (Honey Onion)	Nginx web server
Centralized Log Storage	Elasticsearch, Logstash, Kibana (ELK) log server
Deployment Details	
Deployment Duration	14 Days
Network Type	Virtual local area network (VLAN)

the chat forum, offering opportunities to execute data breaches and to acquire illicit goods such as hacking tools and child sex abuse material. The promotions were strategically positioned on well-known Dark Web platforms to attract malicious actors. Of course, this required the careful examination and emulation of established Dark Web services to create a sense of familiarity and enhance target interactions. By actively engaging with the chat forum community, the honeypots gathered valuable data pertaining to malicious actor interactions, messages, shared files and IP addresses. The collected data was analyzed to identify recurring patterns and emerging trends, enhancing the understanding of Dark Web activities.

Monitoring and Logging Dark Web Activities. Implementing effective monitoring and logging mechanisms is a critical aspect of data collection using honeypots in the Dark Web. This task involved capturing malicious actor requests to the Honey Onion service and logging communications and malicious actor actions in the chat forum, including dialogs, discussions and participant interactions, all the while maintaining the appearance of an authentic chat forum participant. Logged actions of activities conducted in the Honey Onion environment included user searches, actions initiated by the outlying research honeypot and details such as user identifiers, timestamps and relevant metadata.

3.2   Experimental Setup

The experimental setup comprised three fully-secured virtual machines, each with a designated role in surveilling activities in the Dark Web. The objective of the configuration was to collect extensive data while guaranteeing robust

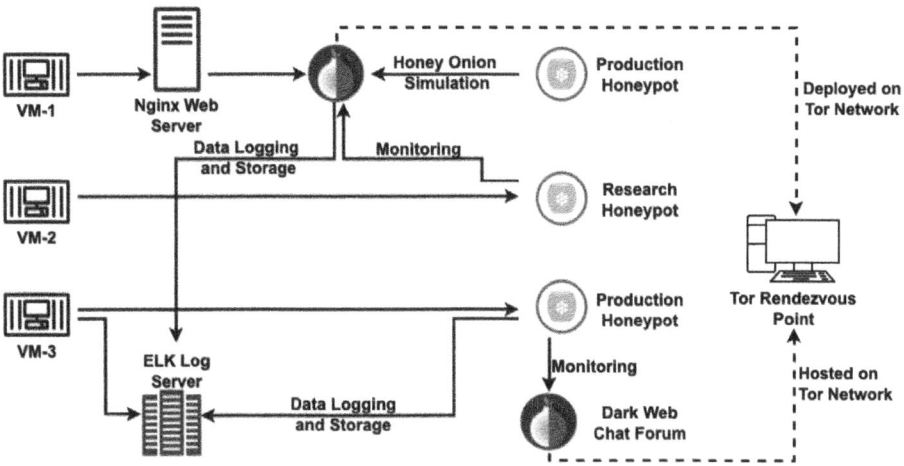

Fig. 3. Honeypot deployment in the host system.

levels of honeypot security and adaptability. Table 2 shows the experimental setup. The virtual machines were hosted on a computing system with an i7 9th Gen processor and 8 GB RAM running the Linux Mint operating system. The experimental setup was operational for fourteen days, allowing adequate time for data collection and analysis.

Honeypot Deployment. The host system in the experimental setup operated three honeypots – a low-interaction production honeypot, a research honeypot on a simulated onion service (Honey Onion) and a production honeypot positioned in a well-known Dark Web chat forum. Figure 3 shows the deployment of the three honeypots in the host system:

- **Low-Interaction Production Honeypot on Honey Onion:** The first virtual machine environment (Honey Onion) operated as a low-interaction production honeypot that replicated a variety of onion services while avoiding direct, high-risk engagements with malicious actors. In particular, Honey Onion modeled the visual and operational characteristics of well-known Dark Web marketplace platforms. Also, it captured diverse malicious actor interactions and communications passively while minimizing the detection and security risks.
- **Low-Interaction Research Honeypot on Honey Onion:** The second virtual machine environment operated as a low-interaction research honeypot strategically deployed on the Honey Onion service. The honeypot explicitly advocated illicit activities typically conducted in the Dark Web. The research honeypot passively monitored the Honey Onion service network traffic, system interactions and attacker behavior. It collected data about potential

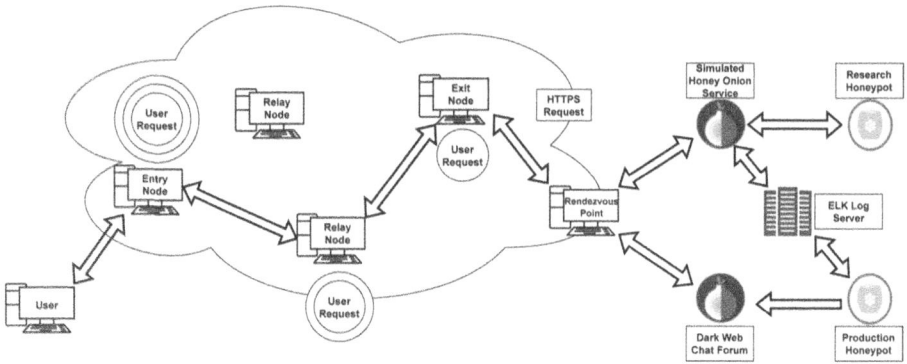

Fig. 4. User perspective of the honeypot deployment architecture.

threats by enabling actors to interact with the virtualized simulation environment. The collected data pertained to malware samples, malicious code, exploit attempts, attacker methods to identify common attack vectors, tactics used by different threat actors and emerging attack techniques.
– **Production Honeypot in Dark Web Chat Forum:** The third virtual machine environment operated as a production honeypot strategically deployed in a Dark Web chat forum visited by malicious actors. The honeypot engaged in interactions and discussions with other chat forum participants in a seamless manner. Interactions and communications were systematically recorded to enable comprehensive analysis of illicit activities.

The virtual machines hosting the honeypots were secured and updated regularly to mitigate risks posed by privilege escalation and other vulnerabilities. Comprehensive images of the virtual machines were captured daily to ensure that the honeypots could be returned to secure and pristine states in the event of compromise. These proactive measures guaranteed the integrity and security of the honeypot environments.

Data Acquisition and Preliminary Analysis. The data and metadata collected by the honeypots was acquired after their 14-day deployment and a preliminary analysis was performed. Subsequently, malicious activities and anomalies were identified. Forum discussions and requests submitted to the simulated onion service (Honey Onion) were analyzed to flag Dark Web browsing behaviors. Figure 4 shows the honeypot deployment architecture from a Dark Web user's perspective.

– **Production and Research Honeypots:** The honeypots acquired substantial data and metadata by engaging with malicious actors involved in Dark Web activities. The collected data included user interactions and communications exchanges in the Dark Web chat forum along with the actions executed in the honeypot environment. Metadata such as timestamps, user identifiers, session logs and system information provided contextual information and facilitated subsequent analysis.

IP addresses and geographical information pertaining to Tor guard nodes (entry nodes) are of significant interest because traffic is decrypted after exiting the guard nodes. The IP addresses assist in geolocating malicious actors. Geolocation data also provides valuable insights into the global distribution of illicit activities, enabling law enforcement entities to potentially track malicious actors and attribute their actions.

The Honey Onion functioned as a locally-running server process. It was crucial to ensure that the server behind the hidden service did not use a public IP address because it could lead to detection and deanonymization, especially given the availability of databases that index the entire Internet. To prevent information leakage, immediate response and mitigation strategies were implemented to isolate the Honey Onion and analyze the attacker methods to reinforce security measures.

Initial plans were to employ fake websites that mimicked hidden service websites, but this would have raised suspicion. Instead, a functional Honey Onion service was deployed. The number of visits to the Honey Onion service was limited – the daily schedule involved three two-hour deployments, a total of six hours per day. This schedule enabled the honeypots to detect malicious actors who visited the Honey Onion outside its deployment schedule. Since sophisticated Dark Web actors tend to wait longer to evade detection because the Honey Onion directory service changes periodically, the approach trades off accuracy for stealth because the hidden service's short lifespan would not engage malicious actors who wait too long.

All server requests and their timestamps were logged to enable the identification of user patterns and investigate their behavior. Requests made on port 80 were analyzed for request types and content, distinguishing between automated headless crawls and requests from Tor browsers.

- **Production Honeypot in Dark Web Chat Forum:** The production honeypot assumed the identity of a user in a Dark Web chat forum known for supporting conversations about diverse onion sites and the commodities they provide. It also followed the time schedules and security considerations mentioned earlier. The forum offers valuable information and technologies relevant to its criminal emphasis. Algorithm 1 specifies the steps involved in logging and classifying Dark Web activities.

  Processing and analyzing the raw data collected from the Dark Web chat forum involved several steps:

  - *Raw HTML Data Parsing:* Network traffic captures were performed at the interface handling Tor traffic (ports 9001 and 9030). A standard HTML parser was adapted to the Dark Web chat forum. The parser produced structured files containing only the textual information from HTML pages.
  - *Foreign Language Translation:* An automated translation process was employed to convert content in other languages to English.

Algorithm 1: Logging and classifying Dark Web activities.

Initialize sample data for demonstration purposes:
$search\_history \leftarrow$ ["hacking tools", "educational cybersecurity courses", "anonymous browsing", "exploits and vulnerabilities"]
$login\_records \leftarrow \{\}$

Function classify_dark_web_activity_and_users(*content*):
    Define keywords for each activity category
    Convert content to lowercase for case-insensitive matching
    $content \leftarrow convert\_to\_lowercase(content)$
    if *any(keyword in content for keyword in malicious_ activities)* **then**
        return *"Malicious Activities"*
    end
    else if *any(keyword in content for keyword in benign_ activities)* **then**
        return *"Potential Benign Activities"*
    end
    else
        return *"Indefinite"*
    end

Function read_data_from_file(*file_ path*):
    open *file_ path* for reading as $\overline{f}ile$
    return *list of lines from file*

Function log_connection_info(*client_ address*):
    $timestamp \leftarrow get\_current\_timestamp()$
    open "Honeypot_log.txt" for appending as log_file
    write "$\{timestamp\}-$ Connection from $\{client\_address[0]\} : \{client\_address[1]\}$" to log_file
    close log_file
    return

Function Honeypot_server():
    $Honeypot\_port \leftarrow 80$ // Port number for the web server (HTTP)
    $Honeypot\_ip \leftarrow$ "$fe80 :: fc83 : 49d9 : e7eb : fb49$" // Listen on all available network interfaces
    $Honeypot\_hardware\_address \leftarrow$ "$F4 : 8E : 38 : D3 : 1A : 02$"
    $server\_socket \leftarrow create\_socket()$
    bind $server\_socket$ to $Honeypot\_ip$ and $Honeypot\_port$
    $start\_listening(server\_socket)$
    print "Honeypot web server is listening..."
    while *True* **do**
        $client\_socket, client\_address \leftarrow accept\_connection(server\_socket)$
        log_connection_info (*client_ address*)
        $send\_http\_response(client\_socket)$
        $close\_connection(client\_socket)$
    end

Function Main():
    $data\_file\_path \leftarrow$ "dark_web_data.txt"
    $collected\_data \leftarrow$ read_data_from_file (*data_ file_path*)
    for *content in collected_ data* **do**
        $activity\_category \leftarrow$ classify_dark_web_activity_and_users (*content*)
        print "$\{content.strip()\}$" $\rightarrow \{activity\_category\}$
    end
    Honeypot_server

- *Data Cleansing:* Data was standardized via data cleansing. This involved the conversion of all characters to lower case and removing symbols, numbers and non-English words. Additional steps included the elimination of tags and extraneous punctuation marks in web page content.
- *Word Tokenization and Stop Word Removal:* Dark Web content was converted into tokens (words, symbols and numbers). Stop words, commonly occurring words in text, that contribute little or no meaning and are irrelevant to classification were removed. The collected Dark Web content was organized using the attributes: URL, title, keywords, word frequency and description.
- *Information Extraction:* Relevant information was extracted from the translated text, focusing on titles of forum threads and posted messages. A knowledge base was created that connected threads, messages and topics. The raw data and knowledge base were then stored in Elasticsearch, a tool for data exploration. Elasticsearch reads structured data, interprets timestamps and locations. It also facilitates trend analysis across different threads and forums.

4   Results and Discussion

The production honeypot provided a simulated Honey Onion service that promoted the illicit dealing of premium narcotics, firearms and hacking tools, emphasizing anonymity and covert shipping. The honeypot was designed to have a striking resemblance to the visual and operational characteristics of a popular illicit marketplace. Several scripts were developed to create and deploy Honey Onion services resembling prominent illicit marketplaces in the Dark Web. The scripts generated configuration `torrc` files for Tor relays. The `torrc` files specify essential parameters, including the SOCKS port, hidden service directory for the private key, advertised port of the hidden service and the running port of the local server. However, the deployment of Honey Onion services presented challenges, primarily due to need to preserve Tor statistics related to hidden services, especially in the presence of anomalies.

4.1   Honey Onion and Research Honeypot

The research honeypot on the Honey Onion service attracted potential malicious actors and monitored their activities using data such as the visited Honey Onion services, visit timestamps, service requests and guard node locations used to access the onion address. The subjects were categorized based on their Honey Onion activities, providing estimates of the numbers of users and identifying likely malicious actors. An HTTP server written in Python leveraged Nginx to listen on specific ports for incoming requests. The server logged all complete requests and their times.

The deployed production and research honeypots collected data from more than 250 Tor relays along with their service requests. Figure 5 shows the traffic logs captured by the Honey Onion service.

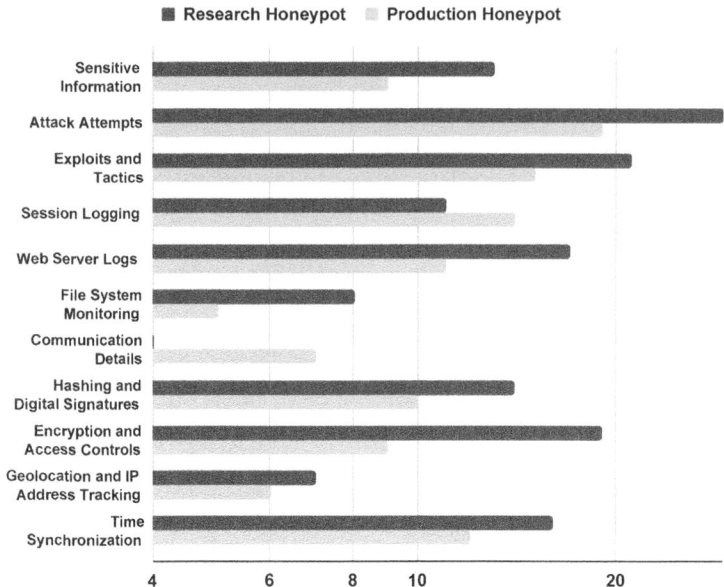

Fig. 5. Traffic logs captured by the Honey Onion service.

To prevent the overloading of single relays on the virtual machines and maintain the performance and responsiveness of the hidden service, automated scripts were executed to generate and deploy new Honey Onions on the aforementioned schedules that ran on separate virtual machines to ensure isolation.

The Honey Onion deployment in the Dark Web extended from September 22, 2023 to October 6, 2023. During this period, a few significant spikes were observed in the number of users, with the second spike being the largest. Notably, during its daily deployment schedule, Honey Onion detected user behavior before the spike in hidden services, indicating that it was not an anomaly. These observations suggest that active investigations of the hidden services were conducted by external entities. It is pertinent to mention that a ten-hour delay existed between a Honey Onion appearance and its activity, during which a total of 84 hours of activities were logged. Given the deterministic operational period and functionality of the honeypot, efforts were implemented to deceive potential attackers and keep them from identifying the honeypot as suspicious. As a result, Honey Onion obtained less, albeit adequate data, for analysis and categorization.

4.2   Dark Web Chat Forum

Analysis of the honeypot data revealed diverse activities occurring in the Dark Web chat forum involving illicit goods and services as well as benign actions pertaining to privacy. The observed activities are classified in the following three categories:

- **Malicious Activities:** Honeypot data revealed a wide range of illicit activities, including drug trafficking, stolen credit card trading, financial fraud and identity theft (fake ID document) services. The Dark Web chat forum served as a market for child sex abuse material as well as illegal firearms. Malicious actors also distributed malware and hacking tools.
- **Potentially Benign Activities:** Honeypot data revealed that some individuals are attracted to the Dark Web chat forum for clandestine communications, privacy and anonymity, especially in regions with Internet restrictions. Individuals concerned with digital privacy sought information and engaged in discussions about safeguarding their data. Other benign activities included online education and research and support groups focused on online banking, e-commerce, crowdfunding and whistleblowing. Not all interactions in the Dark Web chat forum were malicious.
- **Uncategorized Activities:** The Dark Web chat forum hosts diverse activities. Journalists, activists, whistleblowers and others seeking to evade surveillance for legitimate reasons employed it for anonymous communications. Others used the chat forum to bypass local restrictions without engaging in illicit activities. Privacy-conscious individuals sought security solutions and discussions to protect their online privacy lawfully. Identifying and categorizing these activities was challenging due to the absence of identifying information, underscoring the need to balance privacy protection and vigilance with regard to potential malicious activities.

Analysis of Dark Web chat forum interactions and activities revealed three main types of users:

- **Malicious Actors:** Several malicious actors exploited the anonymity of the Dark Web chat forum for the illicit trade of goods and services. These included narcotics, firearms, weapons, stolen credit card data, fake IDs and child sex abuse material, as well as malware and hacking tools. The malicious actor category included potential attackers, unauthorized users (individuals accessing restricted areas without proper authorization), flagged attackers and unknown external visitors whose identities and motives were not discerned.
- **Researchers and Security Professionals:** Researchers and security professionals participated in the Dark Web chat forum to obtain insights about illicit goods and services being traded. Their efforts sought to obtain threat intelligence that would advance their cyber security postures as well as crime prevention efforts. The participants included academic researchers, penetration testers, web crawlers, threat intelligence teams and cyber security professionals actively focused on understanding Dark Web dynamics, identifying vulnerabilities and mitigating threats.
- **Uncategorized Actors:** Some Dark Web chat forum participants had ambiguous motives and utilized the privacy features for various purposes. Some

sought to bypass geo-restrictions and censorship whereas others engaged in discussions about privacy and security resources. The paucity of information made it challenging to ascertain the intentions of these participants, underscoring the need for continuous monitoring and analysis to differentiate between legitimate and potentially harmful actors.

Dark Web chat forum content typically has a hierarchical structure, with participants posting messages (posts) that form collections known as threads. Threads are often categorized, such as "Drugs or Pills," "Exploits" and "Notifications." Posts comprise message content and also provide meta information about users (usernames/pseudonyms, registration dates) and the dates and times of posts. User profiles were crawled to enhance information retrieval, providing insights into passive users and the chat forum community at large. The profiles contain valuable information including the registration dates and last visited times.

HTML parsers were implemented to process posts and user profiles during the extraction process. The parsers transformed the HTML representations of posts to a unified JSON format, each post represented as a JSON object with attributes such as forum, category, thread, username, timestamp and message. Objects from non-English web forums were supplemented with their English translations. User profiles were transformed to JSON objects with attributes such as forum, username, registration date and, when available, last visited time. All this information was stored in the ELK log server.

The dominant languages in the Dark Web chat forum were English, Russian and German. The Dark Web chat forum hosted several interest groups, including news, pornography, software, drug and other marketplaces, cryptocurrency, hacking, gaming, leaks, cracking, monetizing techniques, tutorials, frauds, conspiracy theories, drugs, crime, security, hacking and distributed denial-of-service services.

Table 3 provides details about the Dark Web chat forum users and their activities. A total of 28,799 communications were collected and analyzed, providing valuable insights into the motives and behaviors of chat forum users. User pseudonyms, languages of communication and relevant identification artifacts were recorded. These items are useful for attribution and geolocation purposes.

5   Conclusions

The innovative honeypot data collection system described in this chapter leverages Tor to identify and investigate Dark Web activities. The system incorporates an onion service simulation featuring production and research honeypots. Additionally, it incorporates a production honeypot deployed in a Dark Web chat forum to capture and store conversations and logs for analysis. Simulated Honey Onions were designed to attract and interact with users in the Tor network, ensuring effective data collection while maintaining anonymity. The chat conversations were securely stored and analyzed using an ELK (Elasticsearch, Logstash, Kibana) log server. Rigorous preprocessing of the data was performed

Table 3. Dark Web chat forum users and activities.

User Activities	Malicious Actors	Researchers and Security Professionals	Uncategorized Actors
Malicious Activities			
Illegal Drugs	972	835	214
Stolen Credit Card Data	873	418	241
Malware and Hacking Tools	1,058	778	595
Weapons (Illegal Firearms)	755	525	128
Fake IDs	749	642	400
Child Sex Abuse Material	922	654	43
Assassination Services	777	281	17
Potentially Benign Activities			
Online Education	38	153	469
Support Groups and Forums	197	562	732
Access to Public Information and Research	823	785	482
Online Banking and Financial Management	954	318	573
E-commerce and Online Shopping	209	432	783
Crowdfunding	1,063	874	850
Whistleblowing and Anonymity	82	246	613
Uncategorized Activities			
Anonymous Communications	478	417	255
Privacy and Security Seekers	969	835	942
Bypassing Geo-Restrictions	842	554	392

to refine its quality and utility, helping provide insights into Dark Web actors and their activities.

Future research will focus on the use of deep learning for user attribution and geolocating Tor network relays to extract nuanced insights from the data while maintaining the privacy of legitimate users. It is paramount to ensure that data collection, analysis and use are rooted in research ethics, with the sole focus being the identification and mitigation of malicious actors and services in the Dark Web. The commitment to responsible, ethical, legal and privacy-preserving research practices will contribute to the broader understanding of Dark Web activities while ensuring that the privacy of legitimate users is safeguarded.

References

1. A. Alaidi, R. Alairaji, S. Alrikabi, I. Aljazaery and S. Abbood, Dark Web illegal activities crawling and classifying using data mining techniques, *International Journal of Interactive Mobile Technologies*, vol. 16(10), pp. 122–139, 2022.

2. F. Astolfi, J. Kroese and J. Van Oorschot, I2P – The Invisible Internet Project, Web Technology Report, Media Technology, Leiden University, Leiden, The Netherlands, 2015.

3. O. Bamsey and R. Montasari, A critical analysis of the Dark Web challenges to digital policing, in *Social Media Analytics, Strategies and Governance*, H. Jahankhani, S. Kendzierskyj, R. Montasari and N. Chelvachandran (Eds.), CRC Press, Boca Raton, Florida, pp. 192–202, 2022.

4. O. Catakoglu, M. Balduzzi and D. Balzarotti, Attack landscape in the dark side of the web, *Proceedings of the Symposium on Applied Computing*, pp. 1739–1746, 2017.

5. J. Chan, S. He, D. Qiao and A. Whinston, Shedding light on the dark: The impact of legal enforcement on Darknet transactions, *Information Systems Research*, vol. 35(1), pp. 145–164, 2023.

6. I. Clarke, O. Sandberg, B. Wiley and T. Hong, Freenet: A distributed anonymous information storage and retrieval system, in *Designing Privacy-Enhancing Technologies*, H. Federrath (Ed.), Springer, Berlin Heidelberg, Germany, pp. 46–66, 2001.

7. R. Dingledine, N. Mathewson and P. Syverson, Tor: The second-generation Onion Router, *Proceedings of the Thirteenth USENIX Security Symposium*, pp. 303–320, 2004.

8. W. Fan, Z. Du, D. Fernandez and V. Villagra, Enabling an anatomic view to investigate honeypot systems: A survey, *IEEE Systems Journal*, vol. 12(4), pp. 3906–3919, 2018.

9. F. Gallo-Serpillo and J. Valls-Prieto, Analysis of CSEM offenders on the Dark Web using honeypots to geolocate IP addresses from Spain, *Computers in Human Behavior*, vol. 154, article no. 108137, 2024.

10. M. Ghanem, P. Mulvihil, K. Ouazzane, R. Djemai and D. Dunsin, D2WFP: A novel protocol for forensically identifying, extracting and analyzing Deep and Dark Web browsing activities, *Journal of Cybersecurity and Privacy*, vol. 3(4), pp. 808–829, 2023.

11. A. Ghourabi, T. Abbes and A. Bouhoula, Characterization of attacks collected from the deployment of a web service honeypot, *Security and Communication Networks*, vol. 7(2), pp. 338–351, 2014.

12. K. Godawatte, M. Raza, M. Murtaza and A. Saeed, Dark Web along with Dark Web marketing and surveillance, *Proceedings of the Twentieth International Conference on Parallel and Distributed Computing, Applications and Technologies*, pp. 483–485, 2019.

13. M. Hatta, Deep Web, Dark Web, Dark Net: A taxonomy of the "hidden" Internet, *Annals of Business Administrative Science*, vol. 19(6), pp. 277–292, 2020.

14. C. Horan and H. Saiedian, Cyber crime investigation: Landscape, challenges and future research directions, *Journal of Cybersecurity and Privacy*, vol. 1(4), pp. 580–596, 2021.

15. Y. Hu, F. Zou, L. Li and P. Yi, Traffic classification of user behaviors in Tor, I2P, ZeroNet and Freenet, *Proceedings of the Nineteenth International Conference on Trust, Security and Privacy in Computing and Communications*, pp. 418–424, 2020.

16. A. Jadoon, W. Iqbal, M. Amjad, H. Afzal and Y. Bangash, Forensic analysis of the Tor browser: A case study for privacy and anonymity on the web, *Forensic Science International*, vol. 299, pp. 59–73, 2019.

17. D. Kavallieros, D. Myttas, E. Kermitsis, E. Lissaris, G. Giataganas and E. Darra, Understanding the Dark Web, in *Dark Web Investigation*, B. Akhgar, M. Gercke, S. Vrochidis and H. Gibson (Eds.), Springer, Cham, Switzerland, pp. 3–26, 2021.

18. I. Koniaris, G. Papadimitriou, P. Nicopolitidis and M. Obaidat, Honeypot deployment for the analysis and visualization of malware activity and malicious connections, *Proceedings of the IEEE International Conference on Communications*, pp. 1819–1824, 2014.

19. D. Laferriere and D. Decary-Hetu, Examining the uncharted Dark Web: Trust signaling in single vendor shops, *Deviant Behavior*, vol. 44(1), pp. 37–56, 2023.

20. F. Lamy, R. Daniulaityte and S. Dudley "Pressed OXY M30 pills, Great press, potent, fast shipping!!!" Availability of counterfeit and pharmaceutical oxycodone pills in one major cryptomarket, *Journal of Psychoactive Drugs*, vol. 56(1), pp. 1–7, 2023.

21. A. Mairh, D. Barik, K. Verma and D. Jena, Honeypots in network security: A survey, *Proceedings of the International Conference on Communication, Computing and Security*, pp. 600–605, 2011.

22. I. Mokube and M. Adams, Honeypots: Concepts, approaches and challenges, *Proceedings of the Forty-Fifth Annual Southeast Regional Conference*, pp. 321–326, 2007.

23. C. Moore, Detecting ransomware with honeypot techniques, *Proceedings of the Cybersecurity and Cyberforensics Conference*, pp. 77–81, 2016.

24. J. Moubarak and C. Bassil, On Darknet honeybots, *Proceedings of the Fourth Cyber Security in Networking Conference*, 2020.

25. C. Murty, H. Rana, R. Verma, R. Pathak and P. Rughani, Building an AI/ML-based classification framework for Dark Web text data, *Proceedings of the International Conference on Computing and Communication Networks*, pp. 93–111, 2022.

26. S. Nazah, S. Huda, J. Abawajy and M. Hassan, Evolution of Dark Web threat analysis and detection: A systematic approach, *IEEE Access*, vol. 8, pp. 171796–171819, 2020.

27. A. Nursetyo, D. Setiadi, E. Rachmawanto and C. Sari, Website and network security techniques against brute force attacks using honeypots, *Proceedings of the Fourth International Conference on Informatics and Computing*, 2019.

28. Z. Omar and J. Ibrahim, An overview of Darknet, rise and challenges and its assumptions, *International Journal of Computer Science and Information Technology*, vol. 8(3), pp. 110–116, 2020.

29. T. Pavel, Malicious financial activities in the Dark Web – Prevailing information and knowledge, in *Cyber Laundering: International Policies and Practices*, N. Rebe (Ed.), World Scientific, London, United Kingdom, pp. 145–173, 2023.

30. L. Poe, Cybercrime in the age of digital transformation, rising nationalism and the demise of global governance, in *Modern Police Leadership*, M. Roycroft and L. Brine (Eds.), Palgrave Macmillan, Cham, Switzerland, pp. 109–126, 2021.

31. G. Sadasivam, C. Hota and B. Anand, Detection of severe SSH attacks using honeypot servers and machine learning techniques, *Journal of Software Networking*, vol. 2017(1), pp. 79–100, 2017.

32. J. Saleem, R. Islam and M. Kabir, The anonymity of the Dark Web: A survey, *IEEE Access*, vol. 10, pp. 33628–33660, 2022.

33. F. Tazi, S. Shrestha, J. De La Cruz and S. Das, SoK: An evaluation of the secure end user experience on the Dark Net through systematic literature review, *Journal of Cybersecurity and Privacy*, vol. 2(2), pp. 329–357, 2022.

34. E. Vasilomanolakis, S. Karuppayah, P. Kikiras and M. Muhlhauser, A honeypot-driven cyber incident monitor: Lessons learned and steps ahead, *Proceedings of the Eighth International Conference on Security of Information and Networks*, pp. 158–164, 2015.

35. L. Waller, S. Johnson, N. Satchell, D. Gordon, G. Daley, H. Reid, K. Fender, P. Llewellyn, L. Smyle and P. Linton, Woe is the Dark Web: The main challenges that governments of the Commonwealth Caribbean will face in combating Dark-Web-facilitated criminal activities, *Transforming Government: People, Process and Policy*, vol. 17(1), pp. 87–100, 2023.

36. S. Wang, Y. Gao, J. Shi, X. Wang, C. Zhao and Z. Yin, Look deep into the new deep network: A measurement study on the ZeroNet, *Proceedings of Twentieth International Conference on Computational Science*, pp. 595–608, 2020.

37. P. William, M. Jawale, A. Pawar, R. Bibave and P. Narode, Systematic approach for detection and assessment of Dark Web threat evolution, in *Using Computational Intelligence for the Dark Web and Illicit Behavior Detection*, R. Rawat, U. Kaur, S. Khan, R. Sikarwar and K. Sankaran (Eds.), IGI Global, Hershey, Pennsylvania, pp. 230–256, 2022.

38. R. Zeid, J. Moubarak and C. Bassil, Investigating the Darknet, *Proceedings of the International Wireless Communications and Mobile Computing Conference*, pp. 727–732, 2020.

Modeling Analyst Intentions Using a Markov Chain for Investigative Action Recommendations

Romain Brisse[1,2,3,4], Simon Boche[1], Frederic Majorczyk[5], and
Jean-Francois Lalande[2,3,4]

[1] Malizen, Rennes, France
[2] CentraleSupelec, Rennes, France
[3] INRIA, Rennes, France
[4] University of Rennes, Rennes, France
romain@malizen.com
[5] Direction Generale de l'Armement, Bruz, France

Abstract. Despite the availability of detection tools and the automation of cyber security tasks, analysts are in demand because they can perform complex security investigations to identify and assess threats. Due to the shortage of expert analysts, it is necessary to employ systems that simplify and speed up security tasks. A promising solution is to employ recommender systems such as those used to enable shoppers to navigate enormous amounts of heterogeneous data in online marketplaces.

This chapter describes a recommender system for incident response. The system recognizes seven analyst intentions during the investigative process and provides appropriate recommendations for an analyst's next actions based on his/her most probable objectives. The recommender system is evaluated using four experiments and five datasets. The results demonstrate the validity of the model and the relevance of the recommendations, an important first step towards recommendations based on analyst intention recognition during incident response.

Keywords: Recommender Systems · Security Investigations · Incident Response · Log Exploration · Analyst Intentions

1 Introduction

The need for cyber security has been growing significantly. Attackers are multiplying [13] and the volume of attacks registered has never been higher [6]. New advanced persistent threat groups with unique methods are discovered on a regular basis, forcing automated tools to be retrained on newer and more representative data. The attacks are more likely to evade automated tools, causing an additional burden on already-overloaded incident response teams. This chapter describes a solution that reduces analyst workloads during investigations, especially in the case of junior analysts that need guidance.

Recommender systems are a promising solution for enhancing user speed and efficiency when performing specific tasks. The systems are commonly used in e-commerce to suggest relevant items for purchase. They are also being used in

© IFIP International Federation for Information Processing 2025
Published by Springer Nature Switzerland AG 2025
E. Kurkowski and S. Shenoi (Eds.): DigitalForensics 2024, IFIP AICT 724, pp. 291–308, 2025.
https://doi.org/10.1007/978-3-031-71025-4_15

the cyber security domain, primarily for incident handling and response [7, 10]. The use cases range from attack detection and mitigation recommendations to analyzing the security standards of enterprises in order to recommend protection plans.

Incident response investigations are typically conducted by cyber security analysts. During investigations, analysts rely on their knowledge, experience and instincts to detect suspicious behaviors, find the paths followed by attackers and understand the impacts of the actions executed by the attackers. It is possible to model the manner in which analysts interact with data during investigations and employ the model to provide recommendations during investigations. The resulting recommender system would reduce the time needed for incident handling and limit incident impacts.

This chapter describes a recommender system that recognizes analyst intentions during log exploration. The system records and analyzes actions taken by analysts and offers exploration paths. The idea is to provide a decision-assistance tool integrated with the analyst workflow that enables exploration paths corresponding to analyst intentions to be evaluated rapidly and efficiently. Analysts often know what to do, but they do not always know how to translate their instincts into concrete actions. The recommender system is based on the concept of intentions – abstractions of what analysts want to do with log data, such as broadening or deepening searches. An experimental methodology that relies on the observation of investigations and the processing of analyst actions is leveraged to extract a model of analyst intentions. The model is employed to create a Markov chain that captures the next most probable intention of an analyst. This enables the system to recommend actions in agreement with analyst intentions.

The recommender system is integrated in a visualization platform for conducting investigations. Four experiments were conducted to evaluate the relevance of the Markov chain created in 80 investigations using five log datasets.

2   Use Case

This section describes a situation encountered in a threat hunting investigation in which a recommender system would be useful. The recommender system attempts to understand analyst intentions during an investigation and offer relevant actions that help attain the investigative goal.

In the use case scenario, an attacker has infiltrated a network and exploited client machines. An analyst has identified the attacks and has discovered attempts by the attacker to connect to the machine hosting the Active Directory. Log data indicates that the Active Directory has been compromised. The analyst is interested in how the attacker was able to access the Active Directory. This is accomplished by finding additional information and context about the situation to formally identify the techniques used by the attacker.

The analyst searches for data that correlates with the information already on hand. Knowing that the attacker had access to the machine, the analyst checks the running processes at the time, who ran them and their privileges. The analyst notices two strings in the logs, `powershell.exe` and `administrator`. The two strings point to the attacker gaining access to the Active Directory using a Zerologon attack. Specifically, the attacker leveraged the PowerShell task automation and configuration management utility and an administrator account without a password [9].

The use case scenario demonstrates the intention of broadening an investigative search in order to gain information about a security situation. Other analyst intentions may manifest themselves during an investigation and recognizing them and associating them with the corresponding analyst actions are the focus of this work. By anticipating analyst intent, it is possible to determine the next most probable intention and recommend the related actions to be undertaken. The recommended actions are the best way to achieve analyst goals. They enable analysts to focus their expertise on investigations instead of the platforms used in the investigations.

Returning to the scenario, the analyst knows how the privileges on the infected client machine were escalated to obtain administrator access to the Active Directory. Armed with all the context that is needed, the analyst may wish to find the exact log that identifies the attack. The recommender system would offer the analyst the option to filter the data using the value that proves the use of the Zerologon attack in order to focus on the information related to it. Next, the data would be filtered using the hostname of the machine instead of the user account because this would enable the analyst to uniquely identify a specific log entry.

3   Related Research

This section describes related research on recommender systems, incident response and understanding analyst intentions.

3.1   Recommender Systems

Recommender systems are decision-assistance tools. They incorporate engines that take input data from diverse sources, extract candidates for recommendations, rank them using scoring models and present the recommendations to users [11, 17]. The data sources used as inputs define the type of recommender system such as knowledge-based or collaborative filtering. Recommender systems are used in many domains with success [1]. The systems have been studied extensively to improve their performance [3] and hybridize them [4].

Cyber Security. Recommender systems in the cyber security domain have attracted attention [10, 14]. Most of the systems focus on cyber attack prediction [15]. Relying on usage logs, network topologies and/or threats, the systems attempt to predict which attacks are occurring or may occur in the near future. While the results are promising, the false positive rates of automated attack detection can reduce the trust that analysts place on recommender systems.

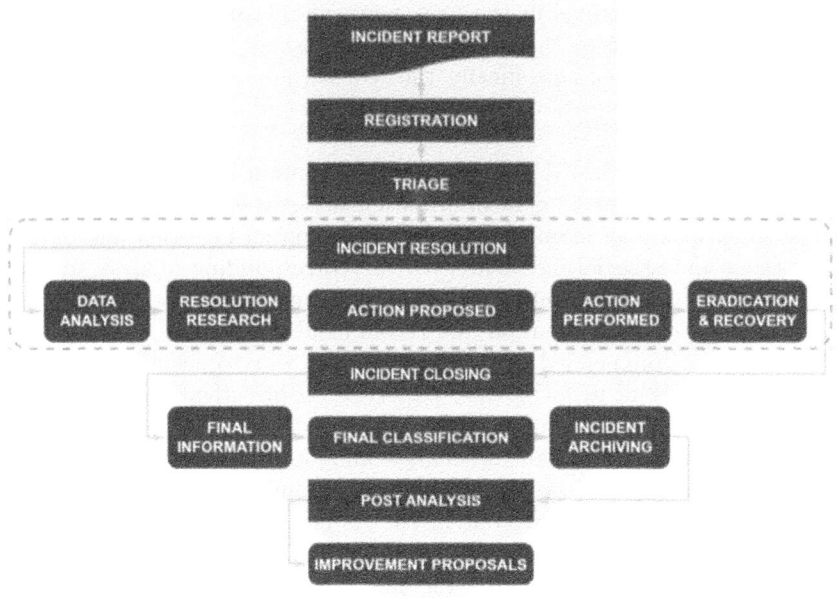

Fig. 1. Incident response workflow [6].

Other systems offer protection recommendations based on user requirements and protection services and their properties [8]. Hybrid data sources support the extraction of pertinent candidates and provide valuable services to analysts.

Incident Response. Recommender systems are increasingly employed in incident response. Figure 1 shows the incident response workflow; the principal steps are in the central column. Most recommender systems for incident response focus on data triage and incident resolution. Zimmerman [21] notes that triaging alerts in security operations centers is time-consuming and a recommender system could significantly enhance analyst efficiency. De Moura Del Esposte and colleagues [5] created a recommender system that uses alerts and network administrator ratings and preferences to dispatch alerts to the appropriate analysts.

A key task in incident resolution is to identify the best attack countermeasures and mitigations. The APIRO recommender system [19] leverages application programming interface (API) documentation and data augmentation techniques as inputs to a neural network, which provides recommendations on the appropriate application programming interfaces for understanding incidents. Other research attempts to tackle the same problem by directly recommending protection measures. For example, MENTOR [8] recommends tools for implementing defense mechanisms according to analyst needs.

Another key step in incident response is prevention and proactive protection. Several researchers have focused on this step. For example, Soldo et al. [18] have developed a novel method for predictive blacklisting. They employ blacklists of previously-banned IP addresses and their behaviors along with their interactions with victims in order to predict IP addresses that might be malicious.

However, all these contributions focus on very specific tasks in the incident response chain. Often, automating a step such as triage is interesting because errors have limited consequences. For example, an analyst who receives an incorrectly-routed alert would recognize it as such and merely redirect it to the appropriate analyst.

In contrast, this work focuses on the incident resolution step (highlighted portion in Figure 1). It would be dangerous to attempt to automate incident response as a whole because errors could have significant impacts on incident response times. Instead, the focus is on analysts who conduct incident response investigations. Since the analysts do their work after the initial detection by automated tools, a perfect opportunity exists to enable them to accomplish their tasks efficiently instead of relying on automation.

3.2   Understanding Analyst Intentions

Moskal and Yang [12] have developed a machine learning model that translates alert descriptions to a more interpretable state. Their so-called action-intent-stages model draws on expert knowledge databases such as MITRE ATT&CK, MITRE CVE and intrusion signatures to refine the meanings of alerts that are often difficult to understand at first glance. These improved descriptions are recommended to analysts. While such recommender systems help analysts understand attacker intentions, the analysts do not make use of the actions directly but, instead, work with established knowledge.

Zhong et al. [20] have sought to improve data triage performance and assist less experienced analysts in making the right decisions. They use the record-ed actions of senior analysts during the analytic process of intrusion detection and compare the similarity of the recorded situations against the new contexts encountered by junior analysts. Triage is rendered more efficient by associating resolved incidents with ongoing incidents. The work is driven by attempts to understand analysts better and help them gain cyber security situational aware-ness. They also advocate human-in-the-loop processes, especially in the cyber security domain where humans are much better than machines at interpreting data. However, the work of Zhong and colleagues is only applicable to the data triage portion of incident response.

This work focuses on inferring analyst intentions from data. Instead of using cyber security knowledge databases or directly matching previously-encountered situations to provide recommendations for specific tasks, a different approach is adopted. Specifically, the incident resolution step is considered as a whole and the focus is on analysts who perform incident resolution. Indeed, this work stands out because it is the first to model cyber security analyst intentions during investigations and make recommendations.

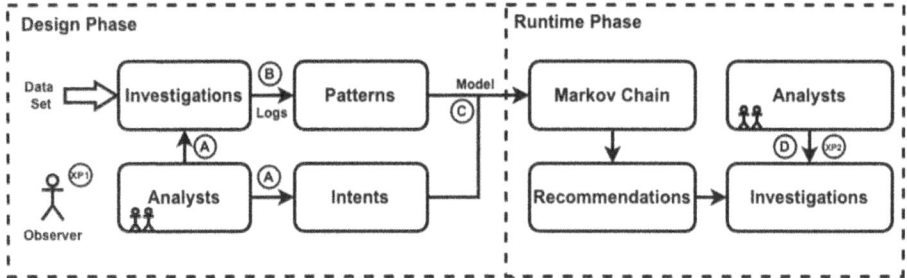

Fig. 2. Design and runtime phases.

4   Overview

The operation of the recommender system is organized around two phases, a design phase and a runtime phase. The design phase provides inputs to the recommender engine that operates during the runtime phase.

Figure 2 outlines the design and runtime phases. Note that a log investigation platform is used in both phases. The platform enables analysts to investigate data using visualizations provided by a graphical interface. The log investigation platform is described in Section 4.3.

4.1   Design Phase

The design phase involves the observation of security investigations and the extraction of the parameters of the two components needed to create the recommendation engine, patterns and intentions. Analysts (subjects) were sought to conduct investigations using the log investigation platform.

The investigations conducted by the analysts were observed and attempts were made to understand their way of thinking and how they worked during investigations. The observations provided insights into the various goals analysts have when conducting investigations. These goals are referred to as intentions (A in Figure 2).

A logging mechanism is incorporated in the investigation platform (B in Figure 2). The mechanism captures the actions performed by analysts during their investigations. Meaningful groups of actions are extracted as described in Section 5.2. The meaningful groups of actions are then matched against the previously-identified analyst intentions (C in Figure 2). The matching operation between groups of actions and analyst intentions contribute to the creation of the model that feeds the recommender system, the idea being to materialize intentions through concrete actions.

During their investigations, analysts often find field values that are somewhat, but not definitely, suspicious. During these situations, the analysts deepen their searches. These intentions can be realized by filtering the data according to the suspicious values and also filtering the timelines to focus on the particular events that led to the logging of the suspicious values. The methodology for linking an intention with a group of actions is described in Section 5.

4.2   Runtime Phase

During the runtime phase, the extracted model is used to provide recommendations. Specifically, the previously-obtained data is used to build a Markov chain (C in Figure 2). Markov chains are commonly used in decision-making and were deemed to be appropriate for modeling the probabilities of analysts going from one intention to another during investigations. Integrated with the recommendation engine, a Markov chain can recommend the patterns of actions associated with the next most probable intentions of analysts.

The recommender system is used during the runtime phase (D in Figure 2). During an investigation, the system triggers a recommendation when a pattern of actions is recognized. The associated intention is given to the recommender system that decides on the most probable analyst intention and recommends the associated pattern of actions.

4.3   Log Investigation Platform

The log investigation platform primarily assists analysts in performing log analyses for incident response and threat hunting. An analyst may input logs from any source into the platform. The platform considers each log entry as a set of fields and aggregates all the values of identical fields. Fields are identified using the Elastic Common Schema (ECS) (`www.elastic.co/guide/en/ecs/current/index.html`). This enables analysts to visualize the values contained in the logs using the ECS fields.

The log investigation platform mainly provides a graphical interface for conducting investigations. An analyst can easily investigate the logs by dragging and dropping fields from A to the board in Figure 3, and creating visualizations (C and D in Figure 3). A visualization presents an aggregation of values for a single data field. For example, visualization window C in Figure 3 shows a visualization called Top10 for the field `file.name`. Multiple visualizations can be observed concurrently and filters by value, range of values and/or time can be applied; they dynamically influence the other visualization windows. Part B in Figure 4 shows a timeline of the logs, which enables analysts to focus on time intervals of interest.

In order to select only the actions relevant to a cyber security investigation, all possible actions are filtered to produce a list of possibilities corresponding to four categories. Figure 4 shows the complete list of actions selected (AL) along with their categories. The list has three complex actions that require explanation: (i) `flag` saves a value along with the state of the tool and context to find it again and report on it easily, (ii) `change visualization` enables an analyst to switch from a Top10 to a treemap (for example) and (iii) `navigate on platform` changes pages in the platform. The recommender system is integrated with the

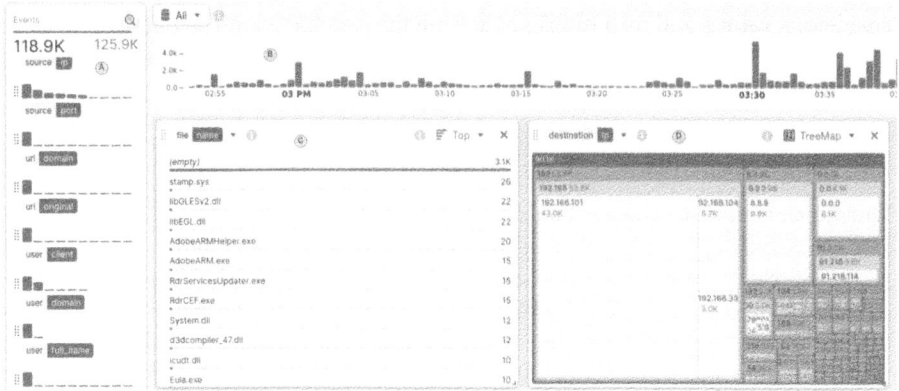

Fig. 3. Analysis portion of the log investigation platform.

Add/Remove Data	Filter Data	Report and Navigate	Use Decision Helpers
Create New Visualization	Filter Timeline	Flag	Follow Recommendation
Delete Visualization	Filter Range of Values	Change Visualization	Ask for Recommendation
Clear All Data	Filter Value	Navigate on Platform	
		End Investigation Session	

Fig. 4. Actions selected as conveying semantic intent.

log investigation platform and its recommendations are triggered according to the intentions underlying analyst actions.

5   Recommender System

This section provides details about the recommender system design process.

5.1   Collecting Intentions

Five cyber security students (subjects) were presented with two unknown datasets containing attacks. The datasets were VAST 2012 (www.vacommunity.org/VAST+Challenge+2012) and TC3 (github.com/darpa-i2o/Transparent-Computing/blob/master/README-E3.md). After a presentation about the experimental goals and use of the log investigation platform, the subjects were given 30 minutes to explore the VAST 2012 dataset and 45 minutes to explore the TC3 dataset. The subjects were asked to express their intentions during their explorations.

Their actions on the log investigation platform were observed as they carried out their intentions.

A total of ten investigations were conducted by the five subjects. Based on the oral discussions during the investigations, the following seven exploration intentions were identified:

- **Startup/Discover (S):** Intention to find an entry point in an investigation.
- **Broaden Search (B):** Intention to add new information to the current state of the investigation to contextualize it better.
- **Deepen Search (D):** Intention to deepen the search to reduce the amount of data investigated; conduct a deep dive into the data.
- **Report Findings (R):** Intention to save the analysis results; an important step in an investigation.
- **Backtrack (X):** Intention to return to a previous state in the investigation by backtracking from the last few actions.
- **Search for New Lead (L):** Intention to pursue an entirely new path in an investigation because going back to a previous state of the investigation would not help.
- **Guide by Recommendation (M):** Intention to be guided by a recommendation.

5.2   Collecting Actions and Creating Patterns

The actions performed by the subjects using the log investigation platform were collected. The platform enables an analyst to perform multiple actions. However, the actions do not provide the same information. Since a unique action can often be linked to multiple intentions, it was decided to focus on groups of actions.

In particular, the notion of a pattern was defined. A pattern is a pair of analyst actions and their associated contexts. Each action is captured as a single log entry containing the action performed by the analyst and the entire context associated with it. This is necessary because the context associated with an action can sometimes change the meaning of the action entirely.

As an example, the meaning of action filter-value is changed by its context. In this case, the context of the action is the filter state, which is enabled or disabled. If the filter is enabled, the scope of the search is restricted. If the filter is disabled, the scope of the search is broadened.

A pattern is formally described as:

$$P_{ik}^{i'k'} = ((action_i, context_k), (action_{i'}, context_{k'}))$$

$$(i, i') \in |AL|, (k, k') \in |\{contexts\}|$$

At this point, it is useful to illustrate two groups of actions using the follow-recommendation and filter-value actions. The follow-recommendation action corresponds to a recommendation made by the log investigation platform and adopted by the analyst. Two groups of actions with their associated contexts are associated with the two intentions. The first group, $((follow\text{-}recommendation, \varnothing),$

(filter-value, disable)), shows that the analyst broadens the scope of the investigation by removing a filter after receiving an exploration recommendation. The second group, ((follow-recommendation, $\varnothing$), (filter-value, enable)), shows that the analyst restricts, and thus deepens, the scope of the investigation to examine a smaller portion of the dataset after receiving an exploration recommendation.

The pattern size was empirically set to two actions. A different pattern size could have been used, but the size directly impacts the frequency of finding patterns in investigations. It was necessary to select a pattern size with frequency high enough to reappear in later investigations. Patterns of sizes three to five were evaluated, but their frequencies of appearance in investigations were too low to be significant. Upon selecting a pattern size of two and considering all combinations of possible actions and contexts, 16 unique actions were obtained with a total of 120 possible patterns.

5.3   Linking Patterns to Analyst Intentions

The ten investigations conducted by the five subjects yielded adequate material to extract patterns from the investigation traces and to determine whether or not they matched specific analyst intentions. Each pattern was matched to one intention. In rare instances, a pattern was represented by two intentions. In these situations, one pattern was chosen arbitrarily for reasons of transparency and traceability.

Two cyber security experts were consulted to evaluate the matching results. The experts, who were knowledgeable about the log investigation platform, were asked to list the maximum of number of patterns they would use to achieve each intent. The final list of patterns employed were the patterns located in the intersection of the two sets provided by the experts. This yielded a total of 39 relevant patterns associated with the seven analyst intentions. The resulting model, which links concrete actions in the log investigation platform with analyst intentions, was employed by the recommendation engine.

6   Recommendation Engine

This section describes the Markov chain used to implement the model in the recommendation engine. The goal is to detect actions while the log investigation platform is used by an analyst, grasp the underlying intention and recommend the next intention.

6.1   Using a Markov Chain to Link Intentions

Intentions must be linked to make recommendations – when the recommender system detects an intention, its goal is to suggest the next intention. However, the experimental data and observations revealed that, in a given situation, analysts do not follow the same intention, implying that there is a probability attached to going from one intention to another.

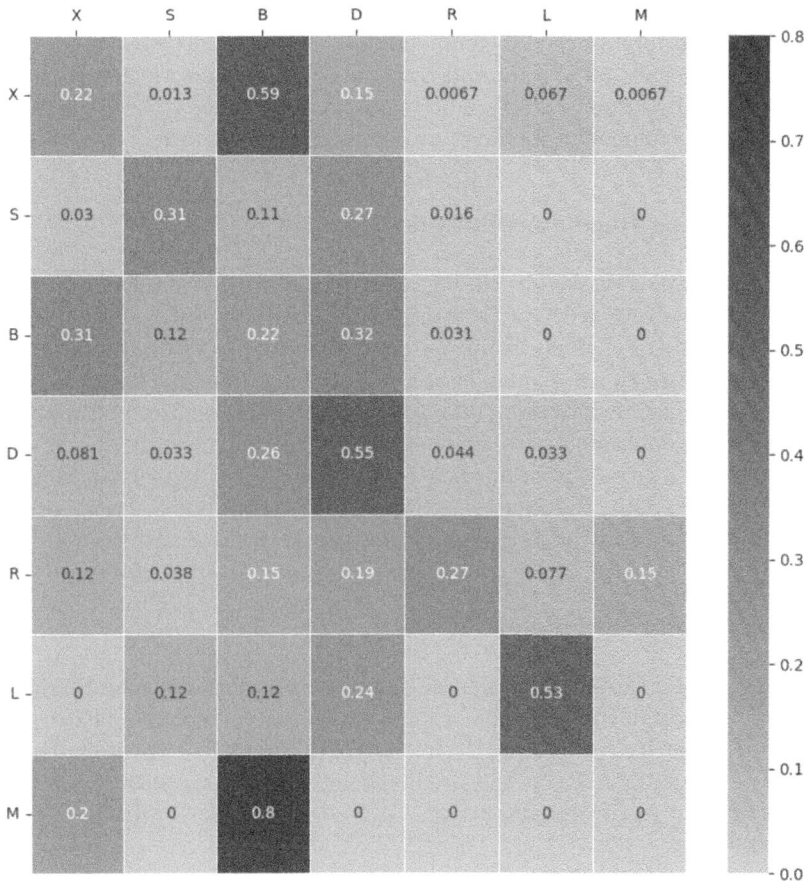

Fig. 5. Transition matrix of the Markov chain with intentions from Section 5.1

A Markov chain was deemed to be a natural representation for modeling this analyst behavior. Specifically, a discrete time Markov chain [16] was employed and the remainder of this chapter focuses on a Markov chain represented using its transition matrix. A state in a Markov chain is defined by a unique intention, meaning that there are seven possible states in the chain. Each state has a set of associated patterns that enables an analyst to realize the intention. A transition has a probability p to go from a known intention detected from a pattern to another intention.

The experimental data was analyzed to convert every investigation from actions to patterns, which were subsequently matched to intentions. The sequences of intentions yielded information about how often one intention led to another intention, enabling the construction of a transition matrix that defined a Markov chain.

Figure 5 shows the transition matrix. Given an intention, the transition matrix identifies the appropriate recommendation. For example, when the backtrack intention (X) occurs, 59% of the time an analyst performs actions corresponding to the broadening intention (B). The maximal probability of 59% conveys that it is the best recommendation after an intention to backtrack.

6.2   Triggering Recommendations

Pattern detection seeks to identify the best trigger for recommendations. Interviews of analysts revealed that they prefer unsolicited, albeit well-timed, recommendations instead of them having to make requests for recommendations.

This motivated the development of a detection module. The detection module records the last analyst action. When it detects a new action, it compares the two actions to determine if they constitute a pattern known to be associated with a specific analyst intention. If a pattern exists, the recommendation with the highest probability is triggered. Otherwise, the last known action is replaced by the new action, and the module waits for the analyst to execute a new action.

6.3   Presenting Recommendations

Recommendations are made based on the actions performed using the labels in Figure 4. A recommendation corresponds to the most probable next intention an analyst might have according to the matrix in Figure 5. The recommendation is presented to an analyst as the predicted intention along with the actions to be performed to realize the intention.

7   Evaluation

The evaluation of the recommender system was complex for two reasons. First, evaluating recommender systems is not standardized – no good method stands out. Second, evaluating a recommender system is subjective. For example, an analyst could receive a recommendation, find it relevant but decide to follow-up on it later. This would mark the recommendation as not followed despite it being of interest. As a result, different aspects of the recommender system were evaluated. In particular, the quality of the Markov chain and the effectiveness of recommendations were evaluated. For clarity of presentation, a Markov chain is referred to using its transition matrix.

7.1   Markov Chain Quality

This section describes the evaluation of Markov chain quality in terms of Markov chain validity and Markov chain relevance. First, the datasets employed in the evaluation are described.

Table 1. Dataset information.

Dataset	VAST 2012	TC3	SUPSEC	BotsV1
Events	23.7 M	19.5 M	125.9 K	33.4 M
Nature	Network Only	System Only	Network and System	Network and System
Investigations	5	5	32	48
Investigation Time	2.5 hrs	3.75 hrs	64 hrs	32 hrs
Transition Matrices	10		32	48

Datasets. This section describes the sets of analyst investigations. An investigation comprises a sequence of analyst actions. An investigation is performed on a dataset as described in the design phase (Figure 2).

Table 1 provides details about the four datasets used in the evaluation. The VAST 2012, TC3 and BotsV1 datasets (logs) are available to the public. More than 85 analysts participated in the creation of the datasets over four occasions, with various goals and timeframes for the investigations.

The investigations were grouped into three sets based on the datasets used:

- **Reference Traces:** This set comprised ten investigations, five each on the VAST 2012 and TC3 datasets. The investigations were conducted by five subjects during an experiment focused on constructing the Markov chain shown in Figure 5.
- **SUPSEC Traces:** This set comprised 32 investigations. The investigations were conducted by analysts with varying experience during a blue team exercise. Each analyst was given two hours to investigate the SUPSEC dataset. The analysts did not receive any external assistance except for a basic contextualization of the dataset at the beginning of the exercise.
- **BotsV1 Traces:** This set comprised 48 investigations created by teams during a capture the flag event in 2023. The teams included cyber security amateurs and professionals. More than 60 teams participated, but only the investigations of the 48 teams that worked seriously on the challenges were selected regardless of whether or not they succeeded.

Markov Chain Validity. This evaluation sought to confirm the validity of the approach. Specifically, it was deemed necessary to show that the Markov chain probabilities of transitions between analyst intentions make sense from a cyber security standpoint. An experiment was performed to compare the constructed Markov chain against those that were created randomly.

The experiment employed a reference matrix computed from all the investigations in the Reference Traces set along with the transition matrices computed

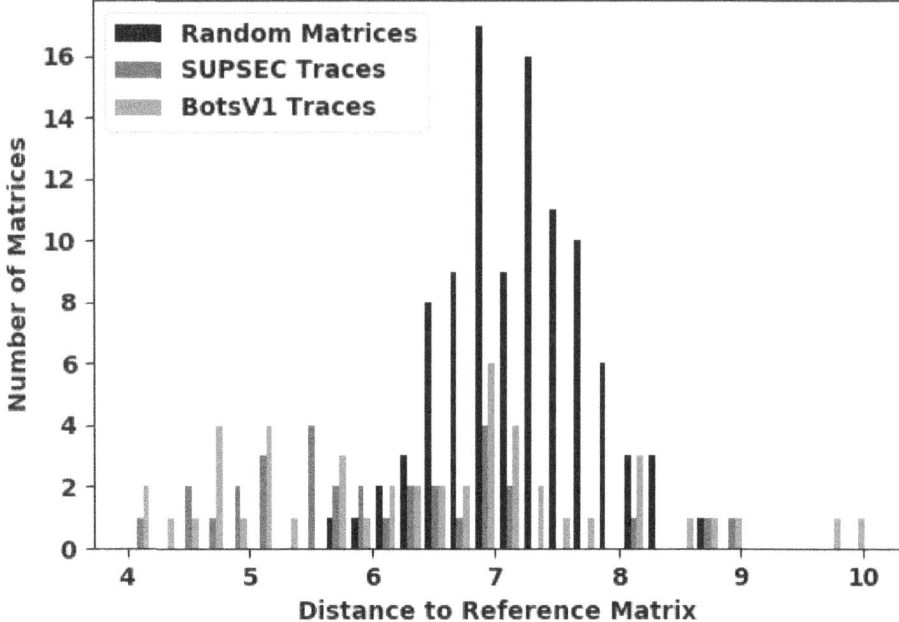

Fig. 6. Distribution of matrix distances.

from all the investigations in the SUPSEC Traces and BotsV1 Traces sets. To e-liminate bias, the investigations were conducted by analysts without any external guidance. One hundred random matrices were also constructed for comparison purposes.

The distance to the reference matrix was computed for each transition matrix in the SUPSEC Traces and BotsV1 Traces sets as well as for the 100 random matrices. The distance $d(A, B)$ between two $n \times n$ matrices A and B is given by:

$$d(A, B) = \sum_{i=1}^{n} \sum_{j=1}^{n} |a_{ij} - b_{ij}|$$

Figure 6 shows the distributions of the distances of multiple sets of investigation traces to the reference matrix. The distribution of the distances between the randomly-constructed matrices to the reference matrix has a mean around 7.2. On the other hand, the distributions of the SUPSEC Traces and BotsV1 Traces sets to the reference matrix have means of around 6 and 6.4, respectively. These results demonstrate that the Markov chain recommendations are better than the recommendations based on randomly-generated matrices.

Markov Chain Relevance. A second experiment was conducted to confirm that the subjects were not biased when the reference matrix was constructed.

Table 2. Mean log-likelihood values of sequences generated by the Markov chain.

Matrices/Sequences	Reference Traces	SUPSEC Traces	BotsV1 Traces
Reference Matrix	**21.556**	19.573	26.951
SUPSEC Matrix	20.317	**20.378**	26.736
BotsV1 Matrix	19.076	18.445	**27.956**
Av. Random Matrix	10.131	9.676	14.414

Therefore, it was decided to compare the transition matrices against a set of traces and check if the analyst investigations could have been generated by them. The log-likelihood method was used in this evaluation of Markov chain relevance.

Specifically, log-likelihood was used to determine if a sequence of intentions I was likely to have been generated by a matrix M representing the Markov chain. The log-likelihood L is computed by summing the natural logarithms of transition probabilities (I_i, I_{i+1}) between consecutive intentions in the Markov chain:

$$L = |\sum_{i=o}^{n-1} \ln(Transition_M(I_i, I_{i+1}))|$$

Table 2 presents the results. For each investigation present in a trace of investigations (column in the table), the log-likelihood values were computed for the matrices extracted from the three sets of investigations as well as for a matrix constructed from the average of 100 randomly-generated matrices. The results should be considered separately for each column because the number of investigations differed for the three sets, rendering the log-likelihood values non-comparable.

The diagonal (boldface) values in Table 2 are local maximums because the matrices built from the set of investigations were compared against the same sets of investigations. The interesting result is that the mean log-likelihood values of the other matrices are close to the maximum value, except for the 100 random matrices that have significantly lower mean log-likelihood values. This result demonstrates that the intentions of the analysts were framed successfully during investigations.

7.2 Prototype and Recommendation Evaluation

A third experiment involving red team and blue team capture the flag exercises was conducted during a larger security event. Due to space constraints, the experiment is described briefly and the focus is on the datasets that were obtained.

Datasets. The red team exercise involved variations of the same attack scenario, which yielded 13 datasets. Five of the most complete datasets were selected to be investigated. Each investigated dataset contained various attacks; their network and system logs contained 1,000 to 8,000 events. The sources of data were Auditd services on machines in the infrastructure and Suricata intrusion detection systems in the network.

The blue team exercise involved nine analysts (subjects). During their investigations, the subjects employed a version of the log investigation platform that integrated the recommender system. In the experiment, the recommender system employed a slightly less refined matrix than the reference matrix in Section 7.1 in the recommendation engine due to time and implementation constraints.

Recommendation Evaluation. A fourth experiment was conducted to evaluate whether or not the recommendations were followed by the analysts. The triggered recommendations corresponded to the most probable transitions, i.e., highest probabilities of the rows in Figure 5. Over the seven possible transitions, five were triggered during the experiment. This is not abnormal because the remaining two transitions corresponded to rare cases.

Every recommendation was recorded during the experiment. A recommendation was deemed to be followed by an analyst if at least one of its actions was performed within the next one to three actions following the recommendation. Deeming recommendations with actions outside this range as being followed would have yielded too much imprecision.

Figure 7 shows that, for every transition considered, recommendations were followed much more often than the theoretical value anticipated by the transition matrix. In fact, in some instances, the recommendations were always followed by the analysts. Only one instance was observed, in the case of the next action after a report findings to report findings (RR) transition, when an analyst did not follow the recommendation directly. This is because framing the report findings intention in an investigation can mean any number of things – from saving a simple reminder during the investigation to completing the investigation and leaving the investigation platform. This is makes it more complex to predict the next intention of an analyst.

Nevertheless, the experimental results are promising. They demonstrate that analyst behaviors are effectively captured by the recommender system and its recommendations are followed by analysts.

8   Conclusions

The recommender system described in this chapter recommends exploration paths to analysts during incident response. The underlying recommendation engine detects relevant analyst actions and employs a Markov chain to recommend the associated analyst actions based on the predicted analyst intentions. The recommender system was evaluated extensively via four experiments involving five datasets. The experimental results demonstrate that the system effectively captures analyst intentions during investigations and recommends actions that analysts tend to follow.

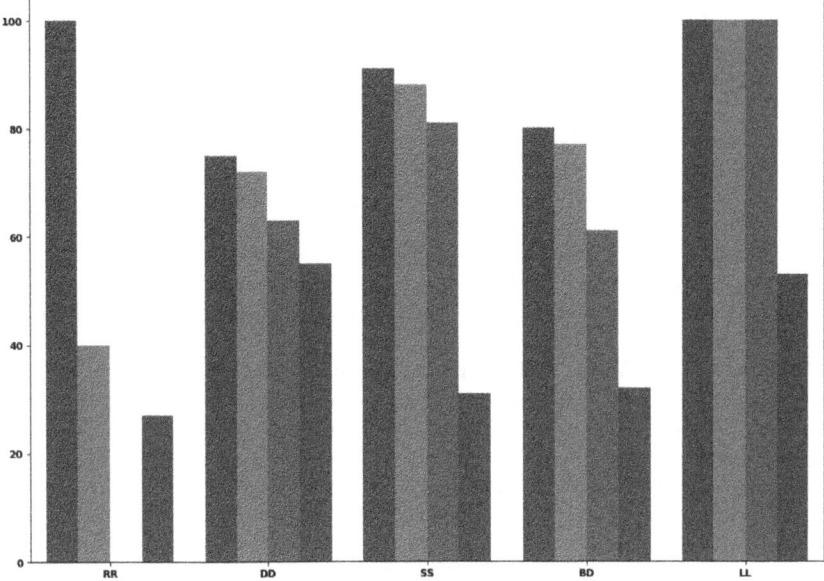

Fig. 7. Extent of recommendations followed and transition matrix probabilities.

Current research is attempting to make it easier for analysts to interact with recommendations. Future research will focus on further substantiating the recommendations by hybridizing the recommender system [2] and implementing a learning component that self-actualizes the Markov chain as investigations are conducted using the log investigation platform.

References

1. J. Bennett and S. Lanning, The Netflix Prize, *Proceedings of the KDD Cup and Workshop*, pp. 3–6, 2007.
2. R. Brisse, S. Boche, F. Majorczyk and J. Lalande, Kraken: A knowledge-based recommender system for analysts to kick exploration up a notch, *Proceedings of the Fourteenth International Conference on Innovative Security Solutions for Information Technology and Communications Security*, pp. 1–17, 2021.
3. R. Burke, Knowledge-based recommender systems, *Encyclopedia of Library and Information Systems*, vol. 69(32), pp. 175–186, 2000.
4. R. Burke, Hybrid recommender systems: Survey and experiments, *User Modeling and User-Adapted Interaction*, vol. 12(4), pp. 331–370, 2002.
5. A. de Moura Del Esposte, R. Campiolo, F. Kon and D. Batista, A collaboration model to recommend network security alerts based on the mixed hybrid approach,

presented at the *Brazilian Symposium on Computer Networks and Distributed Systems*, 2016.

6. European Network and Information Security Agency, Good Practice Guide for Incident Management, Heraklion, Greece, 2010.

7. L. Ferreira, D. Castro Silva and M. Uriarte, Recommender systems in cybersecurity, *Knowledge and Information Systems*, vol. 65(12), pp. 5523–5559, 2023.

8. M. Franco, B. Rodrigues and B. Stiller, MENTOR: The design and evaluation of a protection services recommender system, *Proceedings of the Fifteenth International Conference on Network and Service Management*, 2019.

9. G. Grillenmeier, Protecting Active Directory against modern threats, *Network Security*, vol. 2021(11), pp. 15–17, 2021.

10. M. Husak and M. Cermak, SoK: Applications and challenges of using recommender systems in cybersecurity incident handling and response, *Proceedings of the Seventeenth International Conference on Availability, Reliability and Security*, article no. 25, 2022.

11. D. Jannach, M. Zanker, A. Felfernig and G. Friedrich, *Recommender Systems: An Introduction*, Cambridge University Press, Cambridge, United Kingdom, 2010.

12. S. Moskal and S. Yang, Translating intrusion alerts to cyberattack stages using pseudo-active transfer learning (PATRL), *Proceedings of the IEEE Conference on Communications and Network Security*, pp. 110–118, 2021.

13. A. Pawlicka, M. Choras and M. Pawlicki, The stray sheep of cyberspace a.k.a. the actors who claim they break the law for the greater good, *Personal and Ubiquitous Computing*, vol. 25(5), pp. 843–852, 2021.

14. A. Pawlicka, M. Pawlicki, R. Kozik and R. Choras, A systematic review of recommender systems and their applications in cybersecurity, *Sensors*, vol. 21(15), article no. 5248, 2021.

15. N. Polatidis, E. Pimenidis, M. Pavlidis, S. Papastergiou and H. Mouratidis, From product recommendation to cyber-attack prediction: Generating attack graphs and predicting future attacks, *Evolving Systems*, vol. 11(3), pp. 479–490, 2020.

16. N. Privault, *Understanding Markov Chains: Examples and Applications*, Springer, Singapore, 2018.

17. F. Ricci, L. Rokach and B. Shapira, Introduction to Recommender Systems Handbook, in *Recommender Systems Handbook*, F. Ricci, L. Rokach, B. Shapira and P. Kantor (Eds.), pp. 1–35, Springer, Boston, Massachusetts, 2011.

18. F. Soldo, A. Le and A. Markopoulou, Predictive blacklisting as an implicit recommendation system, *Proceedings of the Twenty-Ninth IEEE Conference on Information Communications*, 2010.

19. Z. Sworna, C. Islam and M. Babar, APIRO, A framework for automated security tool API recommendation, *ACM Transactions on Software Engineering and Methodology*, vol. 32(1), article no. 24, 2023.

20. C. Zhong, T. Lin, P. Liu, J. Yen and K. Chen, A cyber security data triage operation retrieval system, *Computers and Security*, vol 76(7), pp. 12–31, 2018.

21. C. Zimmerman, Ten Strategies of a World-Class Cybersecurity Operations Center, The MITRE Corporation, Bedford, Massachusetts, 2014.

Correction to: Text File Recovery Using an N-Gram Model

Kaparthi Srinivas, Chalicheemala Gireesh, Eswara Sai Prasad Chunduru, and Venugopal Temberveni

Correction to:
Chapter 11 in: E. Kurkowski and S. Shenoi (Eds.): *Advances in Digital Forensics XX*, IFIP AICT 724,
https://doi.org/10.1007/978-3-031-71025-4_11

In the original version of this chapter, the affiliation for the second author was wrong. This has been corrected.

The updated version of this chapter can be found at
https://doi.org/10.1007/978-3-031-71025-4_11

The manufacturer's authorised representative in the EU is Springer
Nature Customer Service Centre GmbH, Europaplatz 3, 69115 Heidelberg,
Germany. If you have any concerns regarding our products, please
contact ProductSafety@springernature.com

Printed and bound by CPI Group (UK) Ltd, Croydon, CR0 4YY

24/04/2026

02096315-0019